MOROCCO

MOROCCO

The Traveller's Companion

Margaret Bidwell
and
Robin Bidwell

I.B.Tauris & Co Ltd
Publishers
London · New York

Published in 1992 by
I.B.Tauris & Co Ltd
45 Bloomsbury Square
London WC1A 2HY

175 Fifth Avenue
New York
NY 10010

In the United States of America
and Canada distributed by
St Martin's Press
175 Fifth Avenue
New York
NY 10010

A full CIP record for this book is available from the British Library

Library of Congress cataloging-in-publication card number: available
A full CIP record is available from the Library of Congress

ISBN 1-85043-556-1

Printed and bound by WBC, Bridgend, Mid Glam.

For Leila with love

Contents

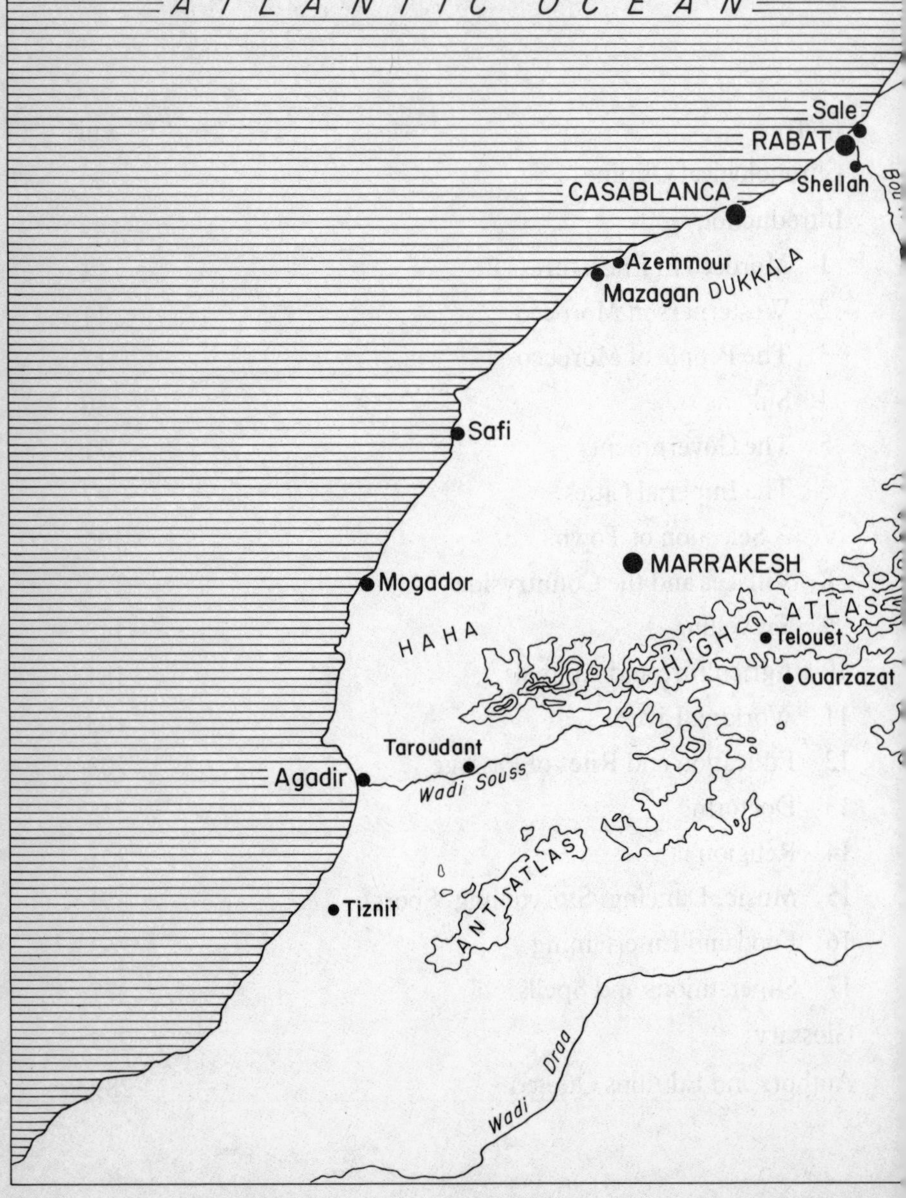

ATLANTIC OCEAN
Sale
RABAT
Shellah
CASABLANCA
Azemmour
Mazagan
DUKKALA
Safi
MARRAKESH
Mogador
HAHA
HIGH ATLAS
Telouet
Ouarzazat
Taroudant
Agadir
Wadi Souss
ANTI ATLAS
Tiznit
Wadi Draa

STRAITS OF GIBRALTAR
angier
Ceuta
Tetuan
Arzila
Larache
Jebala
XAUN
Alcassar
R I F F
Wazan
Melilla
Oudjda
River Sebou
olub'lis
Taza
FEZ
ALGERIA
Sefrou
MEKNES
MIDDLE ATLAS
H ATLAS
TAFILALET
SIJILMASSA
SAGHO

MOROCCO

Chronological Outline*

42	Morocco annexed to the Roman Empire as Mauritania Tingitana
430	Vandals invade from Spain
650	First appearance of Muslim Arab raiders
700	Much of the country Islamicized
710	Arabs and Berbers start to conquer Spain
788	Idris, a descendant of the Prophet Muhammad, arrives in Morocco
791–829	Reign of Idris II – creation of the Makhzan and foundation of Fez
1062	Yusuf bin Tashfin, a Berber from the Sahara, establishes the Almoravid dynasty, founds Marrakesh and conquers Spain, Algeria and Tunisia
1130	Almohad dynasty, Berbers from the Atlas, succeed Almoravids
1170	Almohad capital transferred to Seville
1213	Start of Almohad decadence – end of a single North African empire
1270	The Merinids, a Berber dynasty from the Algerian Sahara, establish their rule and found New Fez
1400	Merinids in decay and losing much of Spain
1465	Berber dynasty of the Beni Ouattas establishing itself
1492	Spaniards capture Granada, finally driving the Moors from Spain and then start to capture ports in Morocco itself
1511	The Saadiens, a family descended from the Prophet Muhammad, call for holy war to resist the Christian invasion and establish themselves as rulers

* Many of the dates, particularly the early ones, are approximate

1526	Publication of the book of Leo Africanus, the first work on Morocco in a European language
1551	First English trading voyage to Morocco
1577	First English Ambassador appointed
1578	Battle of Al Qasr in which three kings were killed
1578	Ahmad al-Mansur, 'the Golden' becomes sultan, embellishes Marrakesh and conquers the Sahara
1603	Death of Ahmad followed by period of civil war so terrible that 'the hair of babies turned white at their mother's breasts'
1659	Rashid, the founder of the present dynasty, became sultan
1662	Tangier given to Charles II by the King of Portugal as part of the dowry of Catherine of Braganza
1672	Accession of Mulai Ismail who made Meknes his capital and kept the country submissive by terror. He is said to have sired 700 sons and an unknown number of daughters
1684	English evacuate Tangier
1727	Death of Mulai Ismail followed by thirty years of anarchy
1757	Muhammad III restores order in a period of much building in Rabat
1768	Portuguese driven from Mazagan
1790	Accession of blood-thirsty Sultan Yazid who was killed in battle two years later
1795	Sultan Sulaiman provides period of quiet
1822	Sultan Abderrahman II during whose reign contacts with Europe increase
1844	The French defeat the Moroccans at the battle of the Isly, showing them for the first time the overwhelming superiority of European technology
1859	Accession of Muhammad IV
1859	Spanish force a war on Morocco, capturing Tetuan
1873	Accession of Hassan I whose military and diplomatic skills held the country together despite western encroachments
1880	Madrid Convention gives foreigners and their Moroccan associates virtual immunity from the jurisdiction of the sultan
1893	Accession of Abdel Aziz – an irresponsible youth

1901	Major revolt of 'the man on the she-ass' in eastern Morocco
1904	The *Entente Cordiale* meant that the British would no longer protect Morocco from a French takeover
1907	After the murder of a French doctor in Marrakesh, the French occupied Oudjda. Five months later they occupy Casablanca. This leads to a revolt by the sultan's brother, Mulai Hafid, who seizes the throne
1911	Profiting from the general anarchy the Spanish occupy Larache and Alcazar el-Kabir while the French go to Fez. This leads the Germans to send a gunboat to Agadir which nearly precipitates a European war
1912	Mulai Hafid signs the Treaty of Fez which makes Morocco a French Protectorate administered from Rabat. Mulai Yusuf is appointed sultan and the first resident-general is General Lyautey. The Riff and the rest of the north become a Spanish Protectorate administered from Tetuan
1914	French troops pacifying the tribes capture Taza, linking western Morocco with Algeria
1921	Abdel Karim launches the Riff Revolt by defeating the Spanish at Anual. He goes on to set up an independent republic
1925	Abdel Karim attacks the French zone but is forced to surrender the following year
1927	Mulai Yusuf is succeeded by his son Muhammad V
1934	The pacification of the tribes is completed after 23 years of sporadic fighting. A few months later young nationalists present demands for reform
1936	Moroccan troops return to Spain as part of the army of General Franco
1943	The sultan meets President Roosevelt and is encouraged to think of independence. The Istiqlal (Independence) Party is founded
1944	First major riots for independence
1947	In a speech at Tangier, his first without previous French approval, the sultan stressed the affiliation of Morocco with the Arab world and called for independence

1953	(August) The French deport Muhammad V and his son Hassan to Madagascar. They install a puppet sultan, Muhammad ben Arafa
1955	(November) Return of Muhammad V who takes the title of king
1956	(March 2) Morocco regains its independence
1961	(February 28) Sudden death of Muhammad V while undergoing an operation – accession of Hassan II
1972	(August) The king survives an attempt on his life

Note on Titles

'Mulai' (often transcribed in earlier centuries as 'Muley') is an Arabic title meaning 'My Lord', and was and is used interchangeably with 'King', 'Sultan' and 'Sharif'. Thus Mulai Hafid, Sidi Hafid, and Sultan Hafid, for example, are all the same person.

Introduction

When we started this anthology we asked ourselves the question 'What is Morocco and how can we portray it?' In the course of our reading we came across the following passage by a French Academician who, although he was writing in the 1920s, said, we thought, very much what we wanted to convey:

Without doubt Morocco, with one or two of the kingdoms of Asia, represents the last surviving example of a civilization of the ancient world. A civilization rich in types and models unchanged for centuries, similar in some of its essential features to types of culture that used to exist in Europe, in many features older even than Islam or Christianity. One finds there ideas and customs, moral and physical aspects of mankind that are eternal simply because they have never changed. Constantly, watching a gesture of prayer or a salutation, a dance, a semi-naked beggar, the way a tailor prepares his cloth, a pilgrim following his donkey across the vast expanse of the bled, or looking into the smoky shade of a mill where occasional shafts of light pierce the tangle of beams, we feel that we have seen it all before. Of course, just because these people are naïve and simple, because they have remained in the old state of human civilization that the West, buttressed by all its growing power has left behind, because they have preserved the old community with nature, because they can show themselves both grave and spontaneous, they seem to us almost symbolic figures, embodying something essential and permanent in mankind. In the shades of the souk or of ancient dwellings, in the glare of the plains, they take on the universal significance of figures by Rembrandt, Poussin or Virgil. For all the differences of appearance they recall to us the essential identity of mankind. If such a world, which shares so deeply the spirit of the past, had disappeared two thousand years ago, we would have lost a certain understanding of the past and of ourselves for we could never have recreated it. How many learned tomes would have been written on the subject! But that it has survived until our own times, that we can see it, we can touch it, we can mix with its people, is a miracle that never ceases to astonish. (André Chevrillon, *Marrakech dans les palmes*, Paris, 1920, pp. 203–4).

There have of course been many changes since this piece was written but most of these developments are not included in our anthology because we wish to stress what is unique in Morocco. We have not chosen passages which illustrate what can be found everywhere in the world today – there is little difference between a secondary school in Fez and one in Canterbury, or between a modern hospital in Casablanca and one in Washington. Travelling in Morocco today is not as adventurous as it was for the writers we have chosen for Chapter 9, nor is the system of government archaic like that described in Chapter 5 nor the rulers blood-thirsty like those in Chapter 4. Yet many of the impressions of some of the famous visitors we quote in Chapter 1 and the less famous ones that occur throughout the book may not be very different from our own.

As we show, many of the important aspects, the personal aspects, the unofficial aspects, of Moroccan life are unchanged. This can be seen in the chapters on superstitions, rites of passage, food, music and dancing. Snake charmers and story-tellers carry on as they have done for centuries. We can see how the cores of the Imperial cities still resemble the descriptions given of them centuries ago because they embodied a way of life which suited the genius of their citizens. In these chapters we see a civilization which in many respects is timeless – it might have begun thousands of years ago but unlike the modern western world it retains the knowledge and ways of life of the past in the present.

The choice of passages for an anthology is, of course, a subjective one. We have chosen pieces that we liked and hoped that other people would too. We hope most sincerely that none of them will offend our readers, particularly Moroccans, who, we feel, will have the self-confidence to enjoy these accounts of what many foreign travellers saw as the eccentricities and short-comings of their ancestors just as we enjoy reading anthologies of travel writings about England. This anthology was fun to compile and in the course of it we became very fond of some of our authors, such as the Shareefa of Wazan whose descriptions of life in an upper-class household are often delightful; one cannot but enjoy the condescension of Lady Grove or the bigotry of Robert Kerr.

We have not tried to present either an encyclopaedia of the past nor a guide-book for the present but pictures of Morocco that will both inform and entertain the visitor to Morocco who, relaxing on a beach after a splendid meal, wishes to know more about the country and at the same time be entertained. We hope also that it will appeal to people who have not visited the country and will persuade them to do so – this particularly applies to our daughter Leila.

Coney Weston, Suffolk
August 1992

1

Morocco in Literature

Writers on Morocco have included some famous people and our first piece is by Shakespeare. Although Francis Fletcher, who chronicled Drake's voyage around the world, may not qualify as a famous writer, his account of sailing along its coast is certainly interesting. John Smith, the founder of Virginia, who again may not count as a literary figure, relates interesting anecdotes about English craftsmen in Marrakesh. Samuel Pepys' account of Tangier shows that the British garrison led lives not dissimilar to those of their later compatriots, while Robinson Crusoe was lucky not to have been as long in captivity as was the woebegone prisoner whose letter appears in the next chapter. Mark Twain and George Orwell were brief visitors whose impressions may still be those of contemporary visitors. It is unfortunate that St Francis cannot be counted amongst travellers to Morocco: he set out to convert the country but lost his voice in Spain and so could not proceed on a missionary voyage. Some of his followers were more successful but were put to death, while other Franciscans established a bishopric and a convent in Marrakesh that survived for centuries. Marrakesh was also a favourite resort – according to his physician he called it 'the most lovely spot in the whole world' – of Winston Churchill who seems to have painted rather than written his impressions. He visited it with Roosevelt and chose it for his convalescence after a serious illness.

Among Shakespeare's patrons were members of the Barbary Company which traded with Morocco, buying sugar (before that honey had been the only available sweetener) and saltpetre in return for cloth. There are sixty references to Morocco in the works of Shakespeare, though he seems to have thought that its people were black. Marshal Lyautey, among others, has considered Othello, with his claim 'I fetch my life and being from men of royal siege', to be a portrait of a chief not dissimilar from one of the contemporary Great Caids of the Atlas. The Prince of Morocco in The Merchant of Venice *who came to woo Portia could have been based on the reports of English traders and envoys who had seen the Saadian rulers in Marrakesh.*

The Merchant of Venice, Act 2, Scenes 1 and 7.

Mislike me not for my complexion
The shadow'd livery of the burnished sun,
To whom I am neighbour and near bred.
Bring me the fairest creature northward born,
Where Phoebus' fire scarce thaws the icicles,
And let us make incision for your love,
To prove whose blood is reddest, his or mine.
I tell thee, lady, this aspect of mine,
Hath fear'd the valiant; by my love, I swear
The best regarded virgins of our clime
Have lov'd it too: I would not change this hue,
Except to steal your thoughts, my gentle queen.

Therefore, I pray you, lead me to the caskets
To try my fortune. By this scimitar, —
That slew the Sophy, and a Persian prince
That won three fields of Sultan Solyman, —
I would outstare the sternest eyes that look,
Outbrave the heart most daring on the earth,
Pluck the young sucking cubs from the she-bear,
Yea, mock the lion when he roars for prey,
To win thee lady, But alas the while!
If Hercules and Lichas play at dice
Which is the better man, the greater throw
May turn by fortune from the weaker hand:
So is Alcides beaten by his page;
And so may I, blind fortune leading me,
Miss that which one unworthier may attain,
And die with grieving.

When the Prince opened the wrong casket, Portia, rather ungraciously, remarked:

A gentle riddance. Draw the curtains: go.
Let all of his complexion choose me so.

Sir Francis Drake set off from Plymouth in December 1577 to circumnavigate the globe 'withe 5 shipps, 150 men, and some boyes'. An account of the voyage was written by his chaplain, Francis Fletcher.

From Henry de Castries, *Sources de l'Histoire du Maroc*, 1905–, Series 1, vol. I, pp. 281, 284.

wee sayled neere the citty of Lions, which sometime is said to have been a citty of great fame, being frequented with marchants out of many nations and kingdoms; but the inhabitants being proud and exceeding in all other wickednesses, the Lord sent an army of lyons upon them, whoe sparing neither man, woman nor child, but consumeing all from the face of the earth, took the city in possession to themselves and their posterity to this day, whereof it is named Civitas Leonum ever since; from whence, being night, the lyons with great fierceness came foarth rageing along the shoare with fearfull roreings and cryes, making many offers to enter the sea and to make a prey of our boate rowing along, but as their nature is not to abide the light of the sonn or of fyre, so it seemeth that they cannot endure to come in water . . .

Saileing from Magador to this place [Cap Blanc], upp in the country did appeare a high and mighty spire, covered at topp with aboundance of snow as white as salmon, which notwithstanding the country be exceeding hott, yet it seemeth never to be dissolved, because it reacheth so high into the colde or frozen region that the reflection of the sonn can never com to it from the face of the earth; whereby, as it is reputed, the inhabitants of Moroccho have singular benefitt, for from thence they ever continually fetch snow and bring it into the citty and other places to sell in the marketts, which they use for many things, but chiefly to mix with wines and other drinks, which otherwise would (for the extreame heat of the country) be unnaturall and contagious to their bodyes. Neither may this seeme a thing strange to be used in Barbary, seeing it is ordinary in Civill and many other places of Spaine, and that which is more, Russia, which is one of the coldest countryes of the world in their winter, yet in their summer, which is exceeding hott, they are inforced to temper their drinks with ice and snow, which they keep and preserve of purpose to that use, lest it might breed in their bodyes a general contagion throughout their whole land. These things I write of my owne knowledg in my former travailes, not by report or by conjecture.

From *The Adventures and Discourses of Captain John Smith*, 1883 edn, pp. 59–61.

Hearing of the wars in Barbary, I went from Gibraltar to Tangiers and thence to Saffee and, although the country was much disturbed by civil war, I went about and saw many curious things, as, being an Englishman, I was unharmed; for Mulai Hamet,[1] a former Emperor, had a great liking for Englishmen, and, having no good artificers of his own, he welcomed handicraftmen from England, such as goldsmiths, watchmakers, plumbers, carvers, and polishers of stone. He allowed all these a standing fee of ten shillings a day,[2] a sufficient quantity of linen, woollen, silk, or what not for their apparel, and stinted them not in diet, besides which, they could transport, or import, what they would, customs free. One of them, Mr Henry Archer, afterwards came over to England, and set up in business as a watchmaker.

Concerning this Archer, there is one thing more worth noting. Not far from Mount Atlas, a great lioness, in the heat of the day, did use to bathe herself and teach her puppies to swim in the river. This was a good breadth, yet she would carry them over the river, one after the other; which some Moors perceiving, watched their opportunity, and, when the river was between her and them, stole four of her whelps; which perceiving, she passed the river with all the speed she could, and, coming near them, they let fall a whelp (and fled with the rest), which she took in her mouth and swam the river back again.

They gave a male and a female to Mr Archer, who kept them in the King's garden, till the male killed the female, when he brought him up like a puppy-dog, having it to lie on his bed, until he grew as great as a mastiff, and no dog could be more tame and gentle to those he knew, than he was. Being about to return to England, Mr Archer gave him to a merchant of Marseilles, who presented it to the French King, who, in his turn, sent it to King James as a gift.

It had been in the Tower seven years, when one John Bull, who had been servant to Mr Archer, went with divers of his friends to see the lions, not knowing his old friend was there; yet this rare beast smelt him before he saw him, whining, groaning, and trembling with such an expression of acquaintance, that, being informed by the keepers how he came there, Bull so prevailed, that the keeper opened the grate, and Bull went in. But no dog could fawn more on his master than the lion on him, licking his feet, hands, and face, skipping and tumbling to and fro, to the wonder of all beholders. Bull was quite satisfied with this recognition, and managed to get out of the grate; but when the lion saw his friend gone, no beast by bellowing, roaring, scratching, and howling, could express more rage and sorrow, nor would he either eat, or drink, for four whole days afterwards.

1. This is Ahmed el-Mansur
2. This figure, if correct, seems enormous when the English Representative of the Barbary Company in Marrakesh was only paid £70 a year.

From *The Tangier Papers of Samuel Pepys*, 1683 (1935 edn), pp. 78–9, 89–90.

1. That as the strength and security of it as a garrison, what by its original misplacing and irregularity of its fortifications, and the present decayed condition thereof (notwithstanding all that has been thus spent toward their repair) it remains at this day in a state wholly untenable, the Governor having represented its main wall in many places to be ready to fall, and the same therefore necessary to be new built, and that at the excessive charge of bringing all materials from England or Spain, and with extraordinary wages to be allowed to all workmen, to which is to be added the necessity there will be (from its situation) of taking in and regularly fortifying an extraordinary space of ground from hill to hill, before it can be rendered secure against an enemy, especially when it is considered that the Moors are no more the ignorant and unskilful neighbours they were to the Portuguese.
2. That whatever has been the reason of it (which must be best known to its inhabitants) his Majesty do not find any fruits of the provisions he so long since, and with so much care and indulgence, made by his letters of incorporation and other grants, for the inviting and encouraging of trade and drawing of foreigners to the place, they not appearing to have met with any suitable success, but on the contrary, the trade of the place is said to be at this day greatly sunk from what it has heretofore sometimes been.
3. That instead of the effects expected from so many years' labour and expense towards rendering the harbour of Tangier a place of reception and security to ships of his subjects, and cleaning and refitting of his own men-at-war by virtue of the Mole, it is most apparent that from the backwardness of the work his Majesty has been driven in this late war with the Algerines to remove all his naval stores from thence to Gibraltar, at the courtesy and within the command of another prince, to the great increase of his charge and obstruction of his service . . .

This memorandum was written by Samuel Pepys, former Secretary to the Commissioners of the Admiralty, who was sent by the King as an adviser to Lord Dartmouth. Some words were omitted by the original editor, presumably because of their bawdy or obscene nature.

Nothing but vice in the whole place of all sorts, for swearing, cursing, drinking and whoring.

Dr Balam, their Recorder heretofore, left his servant his estate with the caution that if ever he married a woman of Tangier, or that had ever been there, he should lose it all. I have a copy of his will. Kirke [the Governor] himself told publicly at table how there was one wench, her name (as I remember) Joyce, that (*10 words omitted*) was banished the town for her lewdness, and all this by the time she was 16 years old, a mighty pretty creature; and of another wench called Dover (*38 words omitted*).

No going by a door almost but you hear people swearing and damning, and the women as much as the men. The Governor is said to have got his wife's sister with child and that she has gone over to Spain to be brought to bed. And that while he is with his whores at his little bathing house which he has furnished with a jade a-purpose for that use there, his wife whom he keeps in by awe, sends for her gallants, and plays the jade by herself at home.

The greater part, if not the whole use of the hospital (saving now that many are fallen down by the unseasonableness of the weather as to water of the flux) is for rogues and jades that have the pox.

The Governor told us publicly at table of a foot jade, a bawd here in town that he went to (*16 words omitted*) and the beastly discourse about it, between her and him.

[Admiral Herbert] had a settled house on shore where he constantly lay (*28 words omitted*).

From Daniel Defoe, *The Life and Surprising Adventures of Robinson Crusoe*, 1869 edn, pp. 14–15.

I fell into terrible Misfortunes on this Voyage; and the first was this, *viz*, Our Ship making her Course towards the *Canary* Islands, or rather between those Islands and the African shore, was surprised in the Grey of the Morning, by a Turkish Rover of *Sallee*, who gave Chase to us with all the Sail she could make. We crowded also as much Canvas as our Yards would spread, or our Masts carry, to have got clear; but finding the Pirate gained upon us, and would certainly come up with us in a few Hours, we prepared to fight; our Ship having 12 guns, and the Rogue 18. About three in the Afternoon he came up with us, and bringing by Mistake, just athwart our Quarter, instead of athwart our Stern, as he intended, we brought 8 of our Guns to bear on that Side, and poured in a Broadside upon him, which made him sheer off again, after returning our Fire, and pouring in also his small Shot from near 200 men which he had on Board. However, we had not a man touched, all our men keeping close. He prepar'd to attack us again, and we to defend ourselves; but laying us on Board the next time upon our other Quarter, he entered 60 men upon our Decks, who immediately fell to cutting and hacking the Decks and Rigging. We plied them with Small-shot, Half-Pikes, Powder-Chests, and such like, and cleared our Deck of them twice. However, to cut short this melancholy Part of our Story, our Ship being disabled, and three of our men killed, and eight wounded, we were obliged to yield, and were carried all Prisoners into *Sallee*, a Port belonging to the Moors.

From Mark Twain, *The Innocents Abroad*, n.d., pp. 52–3.

Tangier has been mentioned in history for three thousand years. And it was a town, although a queer one, when Hercules, clad in his lion-skin landed here four thousand years ago. In the streets he met Anitus, the king of the country, and brained him with his club, which was the fashion among gentlemen in those days. The people of Tangier (called Tingis, then), lived in the rudest possible huts, and dressed in skins and carried clubs, and were as savage as the wild beasts they were constantly obliged to war with. But they were a gentlemanly race, and did no work. They lived on the natural products of the land. Their king's country residence was at the famous Gardens of the Hesperides, seventy miles down the coast from here. The garden with its golden apples (oranges), is gone now – no vestige of it remains. Antiquarians concede that such a personage as Hercules did exist in ancient times, and agree that he was an enterprising and energetic man, but decline to believe him a good, bona fide god, because that would be unconstitutional.

The general size of a store in Tangier is about that of an ordinary shower-bath in a civilised land. The Mohammedan merchant, tinman, shoemaker, or vendor of trifles, sits cross-legged on the floor, and reaches after any article you may want to buy. You can rent a whole block of these pigeon-holes for fifty dollars a month. The market people crowd the market-place with their baskets of figs, dates, melons, apricots etc., and among them file trains of asses, not much larger, if any, than a Newfoundland dog. The scene is lively, is picturesque and smells like a police court. The Jewish money-changers have their dens close at hand; and all day long are counting bronze coins and transferring them from one bushel basket to another. They don't coin much money nowadays, I think. I saw none but was dated four or five hundred years back, and was badly worn and battered. These coins are not very valuable. Jack went out to get a Napoleon changed, so as to have money suited to the general cheapness of things, and came back and said he had 'swamped the bank; had bought eleven quarts of coin, and the head of the firm had gone on the street to negotiate for the balance of the change'. I bought nearly half a pint of their money for a shilling myself. I am not proud of having so much money though. I care nothing for wealth.

The Moors have some small silver coins, and also some silver slugs worth a dollar each. The latter are exceedingly scarce – so much so that when poor ragged Arabs see one they beg to be allowed to kiss it.

From George Orwell, *Collected Essays, Journalism and Letters*, 1968 edn, vol. I, pp. 388–91.

As the corpse went past the flies left the restaurant table in a cloud and rushed after it, but they came back a few minutes later. The little crowd of mourners – all men and boys, no women – threaded their way across the market place between the piles of pomegranates and the taxis and the camels, wailing a short chant over and over again. What really appeals to the flies is that the corpses here are never put into coffins, they are merely wrapped in a piece of rag and carried on a rough wooden bier on the shoulder of four friends. When the friends get to the burying-ground they hack an oblong hole a foot or two deep, dump the body in it and fling over it a little of the dried-up lumpy earth, which is like broken brick. No grave-stone, no name, no identifying mark of any kind. The burying-ground is merely a huge waste of hummocky earth, like a derelict building lot. After a month or so no one can even be certain where his own relatives are buried.

When you walk through a town like this [Marrakesh] – two hundred thousand inhabitants, of whom at least twenty thousand own literally nothing except the rags they stand up in – when you see how the people live, and still more easily how they die, it is always difficult to believe that you are walking among human beings. All colonial empires are in reality founded upon that fact. The people have brown faces – besides there are so many of them! Are they the same flesh as yourself? Do they even have names? Or are they merely a kind of undifferentiated brown stuff, about as individual as bees or coral insects? They rise out of the earth, they sweat and starve for a few years, and then they sink back into the nameless mounds of the graveyard and nobody notices they are gone. And even the graves themselves soon fade back into the soil. Sometimes out for a walk, as you break your way through the prickly pear, you notice that it is rather bumpy underfoot, and only a certain regularity in the bumps tells you that you are walking over skeletons . . .

All people who work with their hands are partly invisible, and the more important the work they do, the less visible they are. Still, a white skin is always fairly conspicuous. In northern Europe, when you see a labourer ploughing a field, you probably give him a second glance. In a hot country, anywhere south of Gibraltar or east of Suez, the chances are that you don't even see him. I have noticed this again and again. In a tropical landscape one's eye takes in everything except the human beings. It takes in the dried-up soil, the prickly pear, the palm-tree and the distant mountain, but it always misses the peasant hoeing at his patch. He is the same colour as the earth, and a great deal less interesting to look at.

It is only because of this that the starved countries of Asia and Africa are accepted as tourist resorts. No one thinks of running cheap trips to the Distressed Areas. But where the human beings have brown skins their poverty is simply not noticed. What does Morocco mean to a Frenchman? An orange-grove or a job in government service. Or to an Englishman? Camels, castles, palm-trees, Foreign Legionnaires, brass trays and bandits. One could probably live here for years without noticing that for nine-tenths of the people the reality of life is an endless, back-breaking struggle to wring a little food out of an eroded soil . . .

Every afternoon a file of very old women passes down the road outside my house, each carrying a load of firewood. All of them are mummified by age and the sun, and all of them are tiny. It seems to be generally the case in primitive communities that the women when they get beyond a certain age, shrink to the size of children. One day a poor old creature who could not have been more than four feet tall crept past me under a vast load of wood. I stopped her and put a five-sou piece (a little more than a farthing) into her hand. She answered with a shrill wail, almost a scream which was partly gratitude but mainly surprise. I suppose that from her point of view, by taking any notice of her, I seemed almost to be violating a law of nature. She accepted her status as an old woman, that is to say as a beast of burden. When a family is travelling, it is quite usual to see a father and grown up son riding ahead on donkeys, and an old woman following on foot, carrying the baggage.

2

Westerners in Morocco

Before the middle of the nineteenth century the tourist was unknown in Morocco – only Lithgow and perhaps Leblanc (if he did indeed make the journey that he recounts) would qualify as such. On the other hand, there were as early as the sixteenth century communities of resident merchants, such as that described by Willan. From about the same time there were the victims of the corsairs, one of whom wrote the pathetic letter found by de Castries. To ransom these prisoners came the numerous envoys whose accounts, or those of other members of their missions such as Windhus and Braithwaite, provide most of the earlier part of Chapter 4. The visits of embassies gave way in the nineteenth century to the presence of regular consuls and we include the stories of a rather unsound American and of a dubious Patagonian. Later residents were the missionaries, one of whom, the splendid Robert Kerr, is quoted in several chapters and finally the very unmissionary-like expatriates of Tangier whose activities are mentioned in Chapter 7.

An account of the salary and expenses of three Englishmen in Marrakesh.
From Thomas Willan, *Studies in Elizabethan Foreign Trade*, 1959, pp. 246–50.

The Barbary Company relied on the service of six factors, three of them centred on Marrakesh and three on Agadir. The three at Marrakesh were Robert Lion, Miles Dickinson, and Edmond Manstidge. They occupied a house there at a rent of £14 8s. p.a. The accommodation included two counting houses, one for Lion and one for Dickinson, two warehouses, and a 'stody'. Its furnishing cost £20 3s. 6d, and included boards and trestles for beds, stools, and tables, candlesticks and snuffers, mats and water pots, and two pairs of scales with weights for gold and silver. Repairs had to be done to the houses; a 'newe windowe' was put into Lion's counting house and shelves were put into the 'lower counting house'. Water had to be bought, at 12s. p.a., and candles which cost £3 1s. 10d in 1587–8. This house in Marrakesh formed the headquarters of the partnership in Morocco, where Robert Lion was in charge.

Lion arrived in Marrakesh as factor on 19 September 1585: it had cost £5 6s. to get him there. He was paid not a commission but a salary which was £70 a year, out of which he had to provide for his wife, who remained behind in London. On one occasion the partners lent her £40 which Lion repaid. He received a good salary, but unfortunately it was not paid with regularity. At the end of his first year of service Lion had received only £40; the remaining £30 was subsequently paid, but by midsummer 1589 the salary was two years in arrears.

In addition to his salary Lion received his board and lodging in Morocco. He lived at the house at Marrakesh rented by the partnership and was allowed his 'diet', which amounted to about £41 p.a., or 2s. 3d a day. Laundry and doctoring were also provided. The washing of Lion's linen cost £1 4s p.a., and the healing of his 'legge bytten by a dogge' cost £1 5s. 3d in 1585–6. The following year £1 2s. was paid for 'our parte of a surgeon which was kept in the Alfandica this yeare, generally, of all men' which suggests that the English factors in Marrakesh maintained a club doctor. Finally the partners had to provide their factors with the means of transport. Two horses and a mule were bought for use at Marrakesh at a total cost of £34 16s. 10d. Their upkeep for nine months, from September 1585 to June 1586 came to £30 9s. 7d and this did not include the Moorish groom's wages of £4 10s for the same period.

Edmond Manstidge, the third of the factors based on Marrakesh, received his diet and his apparel but no salary. He arrived in Marrakesh in November 1585 after a journey which had cost £3 3s. 2d, though this included the cost of a pair of shoes in London, a pair of stockings in Gravesend and the mending of his shirts, doublet and breeches. In addition Manstidge was provided with a quite elaborate outfit for his first year's service in Morocco. This comprised a 'white fustyan dublite, with lyninge, buttons and makeinge', 32s; a 'payre of durance breeches, with lyninge, makeinge and all charges', 24s etc. The total cost which included 12s. 6d. for a year's mending was £10 10s. 5d.

On his way home Manstidge fell ill at Agadir where 'the charges layd out in his sicknes before he came a shipborede' amounted to £5 14. 3d. This included 6s. 'to the surgeon of the Flemishe shipp, for letinge him blude'; 16s. for a sugarloaf given to the surgeon of the *Amity* 'for makinge many drinkes for him, and his paynes otherwise'; 12s. 3d for 7 bottles of milk and 7s. for 'rosed veniger, acquavitye, egges, and other things to make meate for him in his sicknes'.

On his recovery Manstidge laid in provisions for his return voyage. These he shared with a fellow passenger, and together the two men provided themselves with raisin wine, aquavitae, 4 barrells of wine, 16 lb. rice, a quarter of beef, 3oz. pepper, 200 eggs, 'a barrell of staneche being fishe', 2 pots of oil and olives, 3/4 cwt 'byskett', 97 hens, 23 cocks, and 2 sheep (and barley 'for our hennes and shepe at sea'). Manstidge's share of all this came to £6 16s.

A letter written by a captive to his parents. From Henry de Castries, *Sources de l'Histoire du Maroc*, 1905–, Series II, vol. II, pp. 591–2.

From Salley, this 4th of November, anno 1625

Lovinge and kind Father and Mother, my humble duty remembered to you, both prayinge to God continually for your health as me owne. You may please to understand that I am hear in Salley, in most miserable captivitye, under the hands of most cruel tyrants. For, after I was sould, my patroone made mee worke at a mill like a horse, from morninge untill night, with chains uppon my leggs, of 36 pounds waigths a peece, my meat nothinge but a litell course bread and water, my lodginge in a dungion under ground, wher some 150 or 200 of us lay altogether, havinge no comfort of the light but a litell hole, and beeinge soe full of vermine for want of shift and not beeing alowed tyme for to pick myselfe, that I am allmost eaten up with them, and every day beaten to make me either turne Turke, or come to my ransome. For our master's boy had tould my patroons that I was the owner's sonn of the shipp and you were able to ransome home 40 such as I was; which was no sooner knowne, but they forced me to come to my ransome and agree to them, though I alwayes pleaded povertye. For then they made me grind moor then I did formerly, and continually beat me, and almost starved me. Soe, though unwillinge, I agreed at 730 duckats of Barbery; for I was forced to it, beeinge brought so low for want of sustenance that I could not goe without a staff.

Soe I have 6 months tyme for my ransome to come, whereof 3 months are gone; and if it come not then I must arm myselfe to indure the most miserye of any creature in the world. Therefore I humbly desire you on my bended knees, and with sighs from the bottam of my hart, to commiserat at my poor destressed estate, and seek some meanes for my delivery out of this miserable slavery. For hear are some 1500 Englishmen hear in as bad case as myselfe, though somthing better used; for they misuse none but such as are able to pay their ransome. And, dear father, I humbly beseech you, for Christ Jesus sake, to take some course for my deliverance; for, if neither the Kinge take course, nor my ransome come, I am out of all hope ever to behould my cuntry again.

Thus ceasing to trouble you, I rest
Your most dutifull and obdient sonn till death
Robert Adams

I have sent 3 or 4 letters before this by severall men and never heard from you

From Robert Cunninghame Graham, *Mogreb-el-Acksa*, 1898, pp. 34–6.

It seemed that about eighteen months ago, one Abdul Kerim Bey, an Austrian subject, had arrived in Mogador and hoisted his flag as Paragonian consul. Brazil and Portugal, Andorra, San Marino, Guatemala, Hayti, and San Domingo, Siam, the Sandwich Islands, Kotei, Acheen, the Transvaal, Orange Free State, and almost every place where there was revenue sufficient to buy a flag and issue postage stamps for philatelists, had long ago sent consuls to Mogador. Their flag-staffs reared aloft looked like a mighty canebrake from the sea; their banners shaded the streets after the fashion of the covering which the Romans drew over their amphitheatres, and half the population were consuls of some semi-bankrupt state. Yet Patagonia, even in Mogador, excited some surprise. Jews who had been in Buenos Aires (and a considerable quantity emigrate thence from Mogador) argued that Patagonia was under the authority of the Argentine Republic. Those who had been in Valparaiso said that it belonged to Chile. Few knew where Patagonia really was. The Arabs, whose geography is fragmentary, thought that 'Batagonia' was situated somewhere in Franguestan, and that contented them. What struck their fancy most was the colour and design of the new oriflamme.

Barred white and blue, a rising sun grinning across three mountain tops, a cap of liberty, and a huanaco ruminant in one corner, and here and there stars, daggers, scales and other democratic trade-marks, made up a banner the like of which had seldom been seen in all the much be-bannered town of Mogador. The owner of this standard and the defender in Morocco of the lives and liberties of Patagonian subjects, dressed like a Turk (long single-breasted frock coat and fez) and spoke a little Turkish but no Arabic. His age was that of all the world, that is, somewhere between twenty-eight and fifty, and his appearance insignificant, all but his eyes, which some declared to have the power of seeing through a brick, and others of piercing through cloth and leather, and discerning gold from silver in the recesses of a purse. Be that all as it may, a travelled man, a doctor but although Dr el Haj Abdul Kerim apparently enjoyed this designation by the grace of God, his consulate he held by virtue of a mandate of an extraordinary potentate.

Some two-and-twenty years ago, a Frenchman, one Aureille de Tounens, a man of family and an advocate of Bordeaux, succeeded in persuading the Indians of Arauco that he was their king. For a brief space de Tounens flourished under the style of 'Aurelio Primero, rey de los Araucanos', and then diplomacy or treachery, or both, ousted him and he died 'i' the spital' in his own town of Bordeaux. During his efflorescence he coined money, designed a flag, gave titles of nobility and appointed consuls; and it appears that one of them was this Kerim Bey, the Turco-Austrian, who swooped upon Mogador, out-consulling all the consuls hitherto known by the size and pattern of his flag. It is not likely that Aurelio Primero ever heard of Mogador, still less that from Arauco he sent a special envoy to the place. Most probably he sent out consuls generally, after the fashion of bishops *in partibus*, with a roving consulship, and with instructions to set up their flags wherever they found three or four dozen fools assembled and a sufficient roof to bear the pole.

From Luella Hall, *The United States and Morocco, 1776–1956*, 1971, 113–14.

When Thomas N. Carr arrived as American Consul in Tangier in August 1838, he found that his predecessor, James R. Leib, had left for Cadiz as a drunken maniac, threatening the life of his successor. Several later dispatches described the deplorable conditions in the consulate. The archives were scattered about from Tangier to Cadiz, no records had been kept by Leib, the storeroom keys were missing, and claims were being made daily by Leib's creditors. Reports were that Leib had been really insane for the last two years. Presents promised to the Sultan, many of them damaged, were still in the storerooms of the consulate. Roofs of several rooms were tumbling down.

More serious than material damages were those to the prestige of the United States which once had been ranked with France and Great Britain. Leib's conduct had lowered the reputation of the United States, for he had been offensive and disagreeable to both Moors and his fellow consuls. During the preceding winter Leib's madness had manifested in scenes such as this:

Wrapped up in the American flag, he would spend whole nights upon the terrace, making signals by running lanterns up and down the flagstaff to the fleet which he had ordered from the Mediterranean for the purpose of battering the town; at the same time uttering the most discordant sounds, and alarming all the inhabitants. The Moors, like other Mahometans, have a great respect for an insane person, but the immediate causes of the insanity in this case are too well known, and, even by an insane person, it was not very agreeable to the Moorish authorities to have it demonstrated that there was an American line of battle ship, the *Pennsylvania*, which could knock down all the walls and batteries of Tangier in fifteen minutes, and to be assured that she was coming in a short time to do so.

3

The People of Morocco

The people whom the European travellers, from whose writings this anthology has been selected, called 'Moors' were inhabitants of the cities. They were usually of Arab descent, many of them the descendants of those expelled from Spain after the fall of Granada in 1492. They included, however, descendants of Berbers who had moved to the cities and become Arabized. Their dress was regarded as picturesque (for example by Delacroix) and their way of life totally different from that of Europe. Also in the cities lived the Jews who had a separate area called the Mellah – the place of salt, for it was their task to salt the heads of executed criminals so that they could be exhibited on spikes. They were not officially persecuted but they were frequently treated with contempt and were the victims of unofficial violence. They were the main point of contact with visiting Euopeans for, unlike the Moors, many of them knew a western language and also, as non-Muslims, they were able to supply some tolerable spirits. In the mountains lived the Berbers, descendants of the original inhabitants of North Africa before the Arab invasions of the seventh century. Their intolerance of any authority but their own elected leaders fascinated travellers and accounts of them vary little between those of Leo in the sixteenth century and those of modern social anthropologists such as Eickelman. They were said to regard fighting with their neighbours as the natural state of things and so declared peace rather than war. Their particular institutions were the *jemaa*, the tribal council, explained by Surdon, and the fortified village store-house, the *agadir* described in Chapter 8. The other main types were the nomadic Arabs of the Sahara, amongst whom as prisoners lived Paddock and Riley. We include an extract, dealing with yet another group, the dwarfs, unsure whether it is fact or fiction. Many travellers wrote about women: those of the city who greeted Loti from the rooftops or allowed Mrs Murray to watch them at their toilette, or the Berber who had tortured French prisoners and whom West found charming. The system of the harem fascinated western travellers, many of whom wrote about it with or without inside knowledge. We have chosen an extract from Lempriere who visited the royal harem at the end of the eighteenth century.

The first three extracts are about the Arabs of the towns, referred to as Moors.

From G. A. Jackson, *Algiers: A Picture of the Barbary Coast*, 1817, pp. 133–4.

The Moors are naturally of a grave and pensive disposition, fervid in professions of friendship, but very insincere in their attachments. They have no curiosity, no ambition of knowledge; an indolent habit, united to the want of mental cultivation, renders them perhaps more callous than other unenlightened people to every delicate sensation, and they require more than ordinary excitement to render them sensible of pleasure or of pain. It is to this circumstance, and to their religion, which teaches them to impute everything to a blind predestination, that we may attribute that passive obedience which the Moors discover under all their misfortunes and oppressions. This languor of sentiment is, however, unaccompanied with the smallest spark of courage or fortitude. When in adversity they manifest the most abject submission to their superiors, and in prosperity their tyranny and pride is unsupportable. They frequently *smile*, but are seldom heard to laugh aloud. The most infallible mark of internal tranquillity is when they amuse themselves by stroking or playing with the beard. When roused by resentment their disputes rarely proceed further than violently to abuse each other in the most opprobious language. They never fight or box with their fists, like our peasantry, but when a quarrel proceeds to great extremities, they collar each other, and sometimes terminate a dispute by assassination.

The Moors speak very loud, and generally two or three at a time, as they are not very exact in waiting for a reply.

From Eugène Delacroix, *Selected Letters 1813–1863*, 1971, pp. 184, 186, 191.

You will be glad to learn of all the enjoyment I am finding here amidst a people so different in many respects from other Mahometan peoples. I was above all surprised at the extreme simplicity of their dress, and at the same time by the variety of ways in which they arrange the articles that compose it. . . . I am really sorry, now, for those artists, endowed with any degree of imagination, who are fated never to get a glimpse of the marvellous grace of these unspoilt, sublime children of nature. . . . This place is made for painters. . . . Economists and Saint-Simonians might find much to criticise as regards to human rights and equality before the law, but beauty abounds here; not the over-praised beauty of fashionable paintings. The heroes of David and Co. with their rose-pink limbs would cut a sorry figure beside these children of the sun, who moreover wear the dress of classical antiquity with a noble air. . . . Imagine what it is like to see lying in the sun, walking about the streets, cobbling shoes, figures like Roman consuls, like Cato or Brutus, not even lacking the disdainful look which those rulers of the world must have worn; these people possess only a single blanket, in which they walk about, sleep or are buried, and they look as satisfied as Cicero must have been in his curule chair.

From Arthur Leared, *Marocco and the Moors*, 1891, pp. 225–7.

In the matter of dress, the national colour of Marocco is white. Men as well as women appear in flowing robes of this colour. The dress of the men consists of a finely worked shirt (kumja) fastened down the breast by numerous small buttons and loops, and of very loose drawers. Over this is sometimes worn a coat with large sleeves (caftan), buttoned closely in front. For outdoor wear the haik is indispensable. This garment is a wide piece of thin cotton, woollen, or occasionally silk material, wound round the body and also the head in a series of artistic folds, which, in our own case, rendered dressing without assistance an utterly hopeless process. Stockings are not used, and the feet are thrust into a pair of loose-fitting yellow slippers, to walk in which without fatigue, the wearer must be to the manner born. A red fez cap is worn on the head, and round this a turban made of a many-folded length of thin muslin.

In cold or rainy weather a cloak of thick woollen material (jalabiyah) is worn instead of the haik. This has a pointed hood, which, placed over the head, gives the wearer a cone-like appearance. When not in use this hood hangs down the back. The jalabiyah has holes for the arms to pass through, and descends low enough to cover the knees. Many of the poorer classes always wear the jalabiyah. Sometimes, and especially in the north of Marocco, the jalabiyah is of a dark colour. The dress of the women is much the same as that of the men; but the haik is arranged differently, and is employed in concealing the features when any of the opposite sex are present. The hair is carefully covered by a handkerchief of black silk, over which another of gay colours is coquettishly arranged. The women wear red slippers, and these are often handsomely embroidered in gold.

Before the French Protectorate Morocco was divided into two areas – the Bled el-Makhzen *where the government performed some administrative functions and the* Bled es-Siba, *literally the land of wild beasts, where the sultan, while venerated as a religious leader, had little or no effective power. The towns and the coastal plains constituted the former and the mountains the latter but the extent of each area fluctuated according to the prestige and determination of the sultan. The first description of the Jews of the* Bled es-Siba *has unique authority because the writer travelled amongst them accompanied by a respected rabbi and was himself disguised and accepted as a Jew.*

From Charles de Foucauld, *Reconnaissance au Maroc en 1883–1884*, 1888, pp. 398–400.

Every Jew of the *Bled es-Siba* belongs with his person and all his goods to his lord, his *Sid*. If his family has been long established in the area, he has passed to him by inheritance, like any other piece of property, according to Muslim or tribal law. If he is a newcomer to a place he has immediately to find a master and his homage once paid, he is bound to him for ever and his children after him. The Sid protects his Jew against outsiders as he defends anything else that belongs to him. He exploits him, as he does his other possessions, according to his character. If he is wise, he manages him as he would a farm; he only seeks income on his capital – a small annual payment, calculated on the year's gain is all that he takes and he is careful not to ask too much and impoverish his man – on the contrary he helps him to make money because the richer the Jew becomes, the more he will pay. He does not make demands upon the Jew's wife or daughter in case he wants to escape. But if the lord is foolish he 'eats' his Jew as one wastes an inheritance; he demands excessive sums; the Jew says that he cannot pay, the lord takes his wife as a hostage, keeping her until the money is forthcoming. Soon there is a fresh demand and new threats; the Jew leads the poorest and most miserable of lives, he can earn nothing that is not snatched from him, his children are taken away. Finally the Jew may himself be sold, although this only happens in some parts of the Sahara, or his house may be pillaged and destroyed while he and his family are chased out naked. The traveller is astonished to come across villages which have one quarter totally deserted and to learn that one day the Sids, *en masse*, decided to expel their Jews.

There is no protection for a Jew against his master. If he wants to travel, he has to seek permission, but this is rarely refused because it is necessary for business; but under no circumstances may he take his wife or his children for they must remain with his lord to guarantee his return. Should a Jew wish to marry his daughter to an outsider who will take her away from the area, the young man must 'buy' her from the Sid at whatever price the latter chooses to ask. I saw at Tikirt a pretty Jewess from Ouarzazat for whom her husband had to pay 400 francs, a fortune in a Mellah where the richest inhabitant has no more than 1500 francs.

The Jew, restricted as he is, can buy his freedom and permission to leave if his master agrees, but usually this request is refused; if the owner agrees it is probably because he knows that the Jew has money beyond his reach. If the Sid consents, he fixes the price, either for the family as a whole or for each individual member and the sum demanded usually represents all the money that he thinks his vassal may have secreted away. A bargain struck, the Jew is free to leave with his family.

If the Sid does not consent to his leaving and the Jew is still determined, he can have recourse only to flight; carefully prepared, and carried out in the greatest secrecy. On a dark night, when the village is asleep, he creeps from his house, followed by his family. Reaching the gate he finds there pack-animals and an escort of Muslims from another village; he mounts and rides off at full speed. Travelling by night and hiding by day, avoiding inhabited places, choosing by-roads or desert tracks he heads for the *Bled el-Makhzen*; there, at last he can breathe, but he is not really safe until he reaches a large town. The Jew who escapes is in mortal danger. His Sid, finding him gone, will hurry in pursuit; if he catches him he will kill him as a thief making off with his property.

When he has succeeded in escaping, the Jew, and his descendants for several generations, will never go near his old home; he will stay at least three or four days' journey away and even then he is uneasy. I have met Jews, fifty years old and more, whose fathers had fled from Mhamid el Rozlan before they were born, who still regarded it as dangerous to pass Tanzida or Mrimima, where they might, they say, meet members of the Beraber tride and be caught by them. Wherever a Sid comes across his Jew, or even one of his descendants, he will seize him. There have been cases of Jews whose grand-fathers had escaped eighty years before, being carried off in chains by descendants of their Sids. Strange things can happen as a result of this law. One day two travelling Rabbis from Jerusalem arrived in the Dads and, as they passed through a market, a Muslim grabbed them by the throat; 'these are my Jews', he cried, 'I recognise them. Forty years ago, as youths, they fled with their father. God has returned them to me. May He be praised!' The poor Rabbis protested that for ten generations their families had lived in Jerusalem; it was the first time that they had ever left the city, cursed be the day that they had! 'Cursed be your thief of a father. I swear that I recognise you and that you are my Jews' and he carried them off, only releasing them upon the receipt of 800 francs which was subscribed for them by the village of Tiilit. If a Muslim murders a Jew, he settles the matter by paying 30 francs to the Sid.

Treated like animals, misfortune makes them savage; they fight, wound and even kill each other. At Ait ou Akeddir I saw, one morning, a man entering the synagogue who had just cut the throat of his nephew and boasted of the deed: it was such a common occurrence that no one blamed him. I myself was nearly murdered on two occasions in a fortnight by Jews in the Ouaouizert area. On the first occasion I was travelling with a Muslim *zitat* [guide and guarantor] and a caravan of local Jews when the guide showed signs of disquiet; he took me aside and whispered that two of the Jews seemed to be plotting together but nevertheless he continued to lead us along a route that could only lead to an ambush. Suddenly he saw ahead a group of horsemen – 'they are Ait Seri, enemies of my tribe; the Jews have betrayed us'. I turned back; the Jews tried to stop me but did not dare to use force in the presence of my Muslim. The two of us returned at full speed and in the village I learned from relatives of my *zitat* that the Jews in my caravan had plotted with the Ait Seri to kill us both to steal my luggage. I left quickly with an escort of Muslims and no local Jews.

From Edith Wharton, *In Morocco*, 1927 edn, pp. 99–100.

It was a Jewish feast-day. The Hebrew stalls in the souks were closed, and the whole population of the Mellah thronged its tunnels in holiday dress. Hurrying past us were young women with plump white faces and lovely eyes, turbaned in brilliant gauzes, with draperies of dirty curtain muslin over tawdry brocaded caftans. Their paler children swarmed about them, little long-earringed girls like wax dolls dressed in scraps of old finery, little boys in tattered caftans with long-lashed eyes and wily smiles; and, waddling in the rear, their unwieldy grandmothers, huge lumps of tallowy flesh who were probably still in their thirties.

With them were the men of the family, in black gabardines and skull-caps: sallow striplings, incalculably aged ancestors, round-bellied husbands and fathers bumping along like black balloons; all hastening to the low doorways dressed with lamps and paper garlands behind which the feast was spread.

The following extracts concern the Berbers and Arabs of the south.

From Leo Africanus, *Description of Africa*, 1550 (1896 edn), vol. I, p. 129.

OF THE HABITATIONS OF AFRICA AND OF THE SIGNIFICANCE OF THIS WORD *BARBAR*

Our cosmographers and historiographers affirme, that in times past Africa was altogether disinhabited, except that parte which is now called the land of Negros: and most certain it is, that Barbarie and Numidia were for many ages destitute of inhabitants. The tawnie people of the same region were called by the name of *Barbar* being derived of the verbe *Barbara*, which in their toong signifieth to murmur: because the African toong soundeth in the eares of the Arabians, no otherwise than the voice of beasts, which utter their sounds without any accents. Others will have *Barbar* to be one word twise repeated forsomuch as *Barb* in the Arabian toong signifieth a desert. For (say they) when King *Iphricus* being by the Assyrians or Aethiopians driven out of his owne kingdome, travelled towards Aegypt, and seing himselfe so oppressed with his enimies, that he knew not what should become of him and his followers, he asked of his people how or which way it was possible to escape, who answered him *Bar-Bar*, that is, to the desert: giving him to understand by this speech that he could have no safer refuge, than to crosse over Nilus, and to flee into the desert of Africa. And this reason seemeth to agree with them, which affirme the Africans to be descended from the people of Arabia foelix.

From Patrick Turnbull, *Black Barbary*, 1938, pp. 17–18.

The word 'Berber' is not employed by the tribes to describe themselves, but 'Shloh', meaning noble. The Berber language is generally known as Shleuh, although there are an enormous number of dialects. It is a language absolutely distinct from Arabic, and in the cities, except Marrakesh, it is very rare to find anyone who understands a word of it.

In Morocco it is divided into four main branches: (a) Shleuh proper as spoken in the Glaoua, Ouazazat, Dades region and Souss, (b) the Riff branch spoken in the Riff and Djebala, (c) Dra dialect in the regions centred on that river, and (d) Tamazirt spoken in the Middle Atlas. These dialects are each so varied that a man from one district would have great difficulty in understanding his neighbour, while men from so widely separated zones as the Riff and Sous would be totally incomprehensible to each other. Most of the Berbers today, however, are bilingual, employing Moghrebi Arabic as a *lingua franca*.

From Dale Eickelman, *Moroccan Islam*, 1976, pp. 117–18.

Prior to the French Protectorate, local communities and sections could formally symbolise mutual support through a contractual ritual alliance (*tata*). The contracting parties agreed to refrain from fighting and raiding each other and, in general, to aid each other against external threats. Informants explained that such alliances were like the existence of milk brotherhoods except that intermarriage was permitted. In principle, one was supposed to treat a *tata* ally as a brother.

Tata was contracted in formal rituals. For instance, the Flalha local community of the Bni Isa section, concluded an alliance with the Abasa section of the same tribe. The councils of the two groups met in Boujad at the shrine of a marabout, clasped hands over his cenotaph, and swore their alliance.

In another instance, *tata* was concluded by a communal meal or the councils of the two sections. Afterward, each man present removed one of his slippers and placed it in a pile along with those of other men of his section. These were then matched at random. All members of the two groups were henceforth in a *tata* relation, and those whose slippers were paired generally approached the other group through their counterpart. In another case, lactating women of the two sections nursed each other's children after the communal meal of the two councils. In the final case, a *cous-cous* eaten by the councils had in it milk from the women of both groups. Once *tata* was contracted, any violation of it such as theft, was thought to incur supernatural retribution.

From Georges Surdon, *Institutions et coutumes des Berbères du Maghreb*, 1938, pp. 178–86.

Every Berber group has a *jemaa*, an assembly, and its executive agent, an *amrhar*. There are no rules laying down who belongs to the *jemaa* but there are two qualifications. One is to have enough wealth to entertain the other members periodically and the other is to be regarded as having moral influence, resulting from a sound view of the needs of the community. They are not selected but join by co-option of those who are thought fit, and who think themselves fit, to be members. If a member becomes unsuitable, he is no longer invited to meetings. This can arise from becoming too old or too ill, from being a nuisance to the other members, or from some dishonourable deed or breach of customary law. Membership is not hereditary but often a man deputises for and then replaces his aged father, but essentially it depends upon merit. A newcomer to a tribe cannot be a member but his son, born into the group, is eligible.

The members are unpaid because, in a community of shepherds and peasant farmers, the idea of payment is itself practically unknown. Membership, however, does have advantages, apart from the moral satisfaction of being regarded as an important person, for the members are frequently invited to ceremonial feasts to celebrate marriages, the arrival of guests from another community, settlement of murder cases, conclusion of alliances, punishments etc. The members share with the *amrhar* any fines that may be levied.

A member should be able to fight for the tribe. This excludes the old and infirm, except those who have been wounded in battle. It also, of course, excludes women but they can usually put forward their point of view through someone else. It is not at all infrequent that a woman can have a dominant influence on the *jemaa*.

The *jemaa* does not have regular meetings but convenes when there is something to discuss, a crime, a breach of a truce, the negotiation or conclusion of a treaty. Decisions are unanimous and are communicated to those concerned by the *amrhar*, or any member of the *jemaa* who happens to meet him, or, if necessary, by announcement in the suq. A meeting usually takes place informally, sitting around a tea-urn in the house of the member who has asked for it.

More formal sessions are held in the house of the *amrhar* and are preceded by a meal paid for by the members if it is to discuss general policy or by individuals if it is to discuss their affairs or their crimes. Custom demands that there be no discussion of business during the meal. When the last glass of tea has been drunk, the *amrhar* rises and says 'Praise the Prophet' and then amidst silence he outlines the agenda. Each member gives his view and may do so passionately for the Berber peasant is convinced that the louder he shouts, the more important his view will appear; he can, however, be silenced by someone saying 'Praise the Prophet'. When agreement has been reached, the meeting disperses, leaving the execution of any decision to the *amrhar*.

If a minority does not agree, the majority makes no effort to force it to do so for that might make it ally with outsiders to the detriment of the group. The meeting is simply adjourned until another day and during the interval members of the majority work on the others in the hope of changing their minds. If no agreement can be reached, the matter is abandoned.

The decisions of the *jemaa* are not recorded in writing, even if one of the members can write. The only things that may be written are a change in customary law or an alliance with a neighbouring tribe.

It is not easy to define the functions of a *jemaa* because there is nothing like it in European law. Its functions cannot be divided into administrative, political or judicial because it is quite simply the government of the group. It works to arbitrate conflicts that rise within the tribe, to conciliate differing interests, to decide where to camp, to regulate the move from the mountains to the plains and back, to share out pasture land, to manage the common property of the tribe. In brief, it decides and acts for the group for which it is the sole authority.

From Judah Paddock, *Narrative of the Shipwreck of the Oswego . . .*, 1818, pp. 117–19, 215.

Among the tribe we were in there was a variety of colours from a light copper colour to a complexion very dark, almost black; but their features were still the same, sharp nosed and raw boned. The average weight of these Arabs would very little exceed a hundred pounds, and their average height was about five feet nine or ten inches. They were so much in the habit of sitting or squatting upon the calf of the leg, that that part was particularly large in proportion to the rest of their bodies. The women, however, showed a much better leg, as well as an arm, than the men. They were generally little more than four feet high. Their breasts were monstrously large, and their immodest exposure of them to us was the more disgusting on account of the continual abusiveness we experienced from them. Their inhumanity to us may be partly accounted for, however, from the degraded condition in which they were held by their husbands.

The barley which we found growing was such as had sprung up spontaneously; and in some places were seen patches of wild oats. The grass thereabouts was very scarce. On account of the scarcity of feed, the boys expected that we should soon remove further eastward, for the sake of finding pasture for their flocks which were very large. To this tribe belonged thirty camels, fifty fine horses, and a thousand sheep and goats. At night, when the flocks are brought in, it is singular to see how entirely tamed they all are. The women milk the camels first, and then come forward the sheep and lambs. Each parcel of sheep stop at the tent they belong to, before which is a long rope, drawn tight, each end of it being fastened to a stake in the ground; and in the rope, at suitable distances, are placed beckets with small lines. The lambs come of their own accord to the rope, when the woman of the tent separately fastens each lamb to its becket, and drives away to a little distance the sheep, which all lie down. The lambs also lie down, and remain so till morning; when the woman milks the sheep, and releases the lambs, and all are driven off together. In the course of the day the lambs suck all the milk which their dams give. As to the camels, they are milked night and morning; the young camel, if there is a young one, being, to the utmost of the keeper's power, prevented from sucking . . .

When this bowl [of meal] was finished, the two brothers came to our tent, and asked us if we had had enough? The boys answered, 'We have had but one potful, and that is not half enough'. Our host then turned from us, went to his tent which was not ten paces off, and in a very moderate tone of voice spoke to his wife thus: 'Did I not tell you to boil for these Christians both pots?' She replied, 'You did, but I thought one was as much as they deserved'. Without uttering another word, he took up a heavy club, and struck her over the breast, when she fell, and he continued to beat her until we could no longer hear her groans. Ahmed stood motionless; and when we besought him to intercede with his brother for her he shook his head and said nothing. When the old man ceased beating his wife, he called a woman in the next tent, and ordered her to boil a pot of meal for us; adding 'I will see if my orders can't be obeyed'. Upon this he walked back to the place where the men of his tribe were sitting on the ground; and he seemed as little discomposed as if he had been beating a dog.

From Robert George Haliburton, *The Dwarfs of Mount Atlas*, 1891 (pamphlet).

The late Mr Aissa Farar, a Colporteur, was visited at Beni Miskeen by a dwarf not over four feet high, who wished to buy an Arabic copy of the Gospels, and who, on being told the price, went away and returned with poultry etc equal in value to the price named, and on receiving the book, kissed it reverently and hid it away in a fold in his dress. He was much more cordial and friendly than any of the Moors had been, a circumstance that lends some colour to the statements often made as to these dwarfs, that some of them are Christians. The dwarf said he came from a very wild and inaccessible country to the eastward, where *his tribe lived* secluded from other people, and he told a curious story as to the creation of '*a dwarf race*' and why the Creator allowed them to be so small, and so many other races so tall.

Another person who made enquiries as to whether there was really a race of dwarfs was Miss Herdman, at that time residing in Fez in connection with the Mission to the Berbers. Her letter says '*There is a tribe of dwarfs* inhabiting a part of Sus, called Sidi Hamed ou Moussa. Some of them are acrobats and come occasionally to Fez. They are expected in the spring. There is a man living at Fez of the tribe. I know persons who know him. Unfortunately he is too ill to leave his bed at present, I am told, and likely to die. They are about four feet high. *Various persons from Sus have described them to me* and say that a woman is the size of an ordinary little girl, and a man with a beard is like a little boy. *You may rely upon the information I have given you, as I have it from various sources*. The dwarfs are said to be rather expert thieves, for they climb on each other's shoulders and so scale high walls. Others say they can climb like cats without any foothold'.

[In November 1890 the writer met a dwarf in Tangier.] 'I got him to let me mark his height on the wall, but he was in a tremor, evidently fearing the "evil-eye". He would not remove his fez but allowing for it we can make his height about four feet six inches. He is thirty years of age and a native of Wadnoon. His father is a native of Akka, and one of *the small race there*, and is, he says much smaller than himself. The dwarfs, he says, are very brave and active, and great hunters of ostriches, having small swift horses that are called by a name meaning 'those that drink the wind', and that are fed on dates and camels' milk, and are very lean. The dwarfs, he says, are so active that one of them can jump over three camels standing side by side. They wear a blue shirt embroidered on the breast and back, and have leggings that come nearly to the knee and wear a haik with a large yellow eye on its back. Their knife is different from that used by the Moors. They put camels' flesh into a bag when they travel. They weave cloth and make spinning wheels and spindles, which they sell. They go into the Sahara to a fair, and buy slaves and ostrich feathers, and bring them to the fair at Tazzawalt (a town near the sea, where the tomb of Sidi Hamed ou Moussa is, and where the chief of the acrobats reigns as king). They are called Sahara people, and live about eight days to the east of Wadnoon. They are about four feet high and are different from the Moors, negroes, and mulattoes, as they have a peculiar reddish complexion. They use firearms and sometimes bows and poisoned arrows.

'A Jew said "I have often heard of these dwarfs but the Moors would not talk about them. 'God has sent them to us. We must not talk about them', they have said to me when I wished to find out something about this race. The Moors worship the dwarfs, and are very superstitious about them." '

Women and the harem are the subject of the last group of extracts.

From Pierre Loti, 1889, *Morocco* (1929 edn), pp. 174–6.

Grey, all these terraces, colourless rather, of a dead, grey, neutral, indifferent shade, which changes with the weather and the light. Whitewashed once upon a time, and rewhitened again and again until they lost shape and sharpness under the superimposed layers; then baked by the sun, calcined by the burning heat, guttered by the rains, until they have become almost blackish. A little mournful, indeed, the high promenades of these women. And everywhere, on my own terrace as well as on those of my fair neighbours, the old walls on which we lean, and which serve as a parapet to prevent us from falling into the void, are crowned with lichen, with saxifrage and tiny yellow flowers.

They walk about in groups, these women, or sit down to talk on the ledges of the walls, their legs hanging over the courtyards and streets, or lie down, nonchalantly reclining, their upraised arms under their heads. They climb from one house to another, with the help sometimes of a ladder, or of planks forming an improvised bridge. The negresses, sculpturesque creatures, wear in their ears large silver rings; their robes are white or pink; scarves frame the blackness of their faces; their laughing voices sound like rattles, in droll, monkey-like merriment. The Arab women, their mistresses, wear tunics figured with gold and veiled by embroidered net; the long, wide sleeves disclose their shapely bare arms encircled with bracelets; high waistbands of silk laminated with gold, as stiff as cardboard, support their breasts; on all their foreheads there are headbands, formed of a double row of gold sequins, or of pearls or precious stones, and above all is placed the *hantouze*, the tall mitre, swathed always in scarves of golden gauze, the ends of which hang down loose, mingling with the mass of unbound hair; they walk with the head thrown back, the lips open, showing the white teeth; they sway their hips with a little exaggeration and with a voluptuous slowness.

And there are no veils on these faces, which in the streets are so carefully hidden, for men are not supposed ever to mount to the terraces of Fez.

I indeed am doing a very improper thing in remaining seated on mine. But I am a foreigner: and I am able to pretend that I do not know.

From Elizabeth Murray, *Sixteen years of an Artist's Life in Morocco . . .*, 1859, pp. 13–14, 42–6.

What appeared great balls of dirty clothes now came tumbling about me, and had it not been for the red slippers which terminated the mass, I should have never imagined the possibility of their being human creatures. The first idea suggested to my mind was that, on being disencumbered of the garments in which they were invested, the objects must be disclosed in the form of porpoises, barrels of flesh, or any hideous thing, difficult to recognise as really women. Such, however, they were, for out of each bundle peered an eye upon me, twinkling with all the curiosity with which the sex in every land is charged. While gazing at these monsters – at these women, if I must call them so – I suddenly felt something wet on my face. I had undergone one of those acts of humiliation to which these people think it proper to subject those of the Christian faith. On looking up, I met the grin of a shiny, frizzly black slave, her mouth, which was on the full stretch, disclosing a matchless set of teeth. My appearance was too much for her. 'A Nazarene woman, covered with little rags', she said. Nor was she altogether wrong in her description, for my gloves, collar, hat, shoes, stockings, ribbons &c, were certainly all little rags compared with the one great garment that covers the Moorish women, or the scanty cloth that served in her almost nude state . . .

I was fortunate enough to have an opportunity of witnessing the process of a lady's toilet, and of closely watching the various means by which the Moorish beauty endeavours by art to heighten the charms which nature may have given her. As great rejoicings were going on in a neighbouring house, on account of the birth of a son to a rich official, and my hostess had been invited to take part in them; and as it was now nearly time for her to set off for the house of joy, she proceeded to prepare her toilet, not at all abashed by my presence in her chamber, or by the curiosity with which I regarded the process. The first thing she did was to paint her face with a white creamy mixture, then to connect the eyebrows by a thick black daub of about half an inch in width, the thickest part coming over the nose. The eyes, also, had an extra tint of *al cohol*, and the cheeks were painted with two triangular patches of pure scarlet, which, from its coarse colour, and the extreme abruptness of its edges, communicated to them the appearance of a badly-painted mask. An artificial mole or two having been added to complete the adornment of the visage, the face was considered perfect, and regarded with considerable satisfaction. Happening to hold up a rose which I held in my hand, its hue absolutely appeared pale beside the highly-coloured cheek of the lady.

Her headdress was costly and magnificent beyond all description. It consisted, in the first place, of the richest jewels, the favourite emeralds and pearls predominating among them. They arose in glittering succession, one above another, until, in consequence of the manner in which they were arranged, they assumed the appearance of a magnificent bishop's mitre. The adornment of the head was completed by a knotted silk handkerchief, with which it was surmounted. But with all the richness and splendour of the ornaments, there was an utter absence of taste in the manner in which they were disposed, that the head and face formed altogether a most grotesque and barbarous spectacle. The remainder of her person was no less profusely covered with sparkling gems. Strings of gorgeous pearls, and antique chains of massive gold, were suspended from her neck. A pale blue caftan, or dress, much the shape of an English gentleman's dressing gown, was selected. Having found a way for her ample proportions into the selected garment, a somewhat shorter one, of crape-like material, which spangled all over, was thrown over it. Her bodice, which was worn open, was richly embroidered with gold; and one of those superb striped scarfs, which are generally worn in this country, was tied round her not very slender waist. The sleeves of her dress were wide and flowing, leaving the arms, except where they were covered with the peculiar bracelets worn here, quite exposed and bare. These bracelets, which are extremely heavy and massive, consist of a solid gold band, with silver and gold projections. Her fingers were painted with little sprigs in bright orange henna, as were her feet, which to match her hands, were stained with ornaments of the same colour. The latter, considering the immense proportions of the other parts of her body, were unnaturally diminutive and must have been very much impeded, in the process of locomotion, by the ponderous anklets of chased silver, with the burden of which Moorish women are oppressed. The red slippers were made to match in richness of material and ornament the other parts of her dress, being elaborately adorned with embroidery of silver thread and silks of varied colour. All these portions of her toilet having been carefully adjusted, a large clear muslin scarf was thrown over her shoulders; and as it retained all its crispness, it produced a remarkably angular effect in the appearance of her immense proportions.

From Gordon West, *By Bus to the Sahara*, n.d., pp. 136–7.

A young Berber woman approaches, offering a small bunch of flowers for sale. Heaven knows where she finds them in this barren wilderness; perhaps down on the banks of the Ziz not far away. She is a fine-looking girl, and there is an attractive shyness in her manner and her smile. Our sergeant knows her well, and greets her with some jest in her own tongue.

When we remark on her good looks and gentle manner, he laughs. There was a time, he says, when we would have held a different opinion as to her gentleness. She comes from the region of Mount Baddou, and she took part in the fighting not so long ago. Her business, like that of all the Berber women in battle, was to urge on their men from the rear and look after the captives and wounded. Her attentions consisted either of slitting their throats or torturing them. One method of finishing off a wounded prisoner was to cut open his stomach and fill it with glowing charcoal; and it had been this young woman's claim after the war that she had served eight Legionaires in this way.

From William Lempriere, *A Tour from Gibraltar to Tangier, Sallee . . .*, 1791, printed in Pinkerton, vol. XV, pp. 782–93.

The public and usual entrance to the harem is through a very large arched doorway, guarded on the outside by ten bodyguards, which leads to a lofty hall, where the captain or alcaide, with a guard of seventeen eunuchs, are posted. No person is admitted to this hall, but those who are known to have business in the harem.

The Emperor's order being delivered on the outside of the door to the alcaide, I was immediately, with my interpreter, conducted into the harem, by one of the negro eunuchs. Upon entering the court into which the womens' apartments open, I discovered a motley group of concubines, domestics, and negro slaves, who were variously employed. Those of the first description had formed themselves into circles, seated on the ground in the open court, and were apparently engaged in conversation. The domestics and slaves were partly employed in needle-work, and partly in preparing their cuscusoo. My appearance in the court, however, soon attracted their attention, and a considerable number of them, upon observing me, unacquainted with the means by which I had been admitted into the harem, retreated with the utmost precipitancy into their apartments, while others more courageous approached, and enquired of my black attendant who I was, and by whose orders he had brought me thither.

The moment it was known that I was of the medical profession, parties of them were detached to inform those who had fled that I was sent in by order of the Emperor, to attend Lalla Zara and requesting of them to come back and look at the Christian. Seranio tibib! Christian doctor! resounded from one end of the harem to the other; and in the course of a few minutes I was so completely surrounded by women and children, that I was unable to move a single step.

Every one of them appeared solicitous to find out some complaint on which she might consult me, and those who had not the ingenuity enough to invent one, obliged me to feel their pulse; and were highly displeased if I did not evince my excellence in my profession by the discovery of some ailment or other. All of them seemed so urgent to be attended at the same time, that while I was feeling the pulse of one, others were behind, pulling my coat and intreating me to examine their complaints, while a third party were upbraiding me for not paying them the same attention. Their ideas of delicacy did not at all correspond with those of our European ladies, for they exhibited the beauties of their limbs and form with a degree of freedom that in any other country would have been thought indecent; and their conversation was equally unrestrained . . .

From the first court into which I had been introduced I passed through two or three similar, till I at length arrived at the chamber of my intended patient. I found the lady sitting cross-legged on a mattress placed upon the floor, and covered with fine linen, with twelve white and negro attendants, seated on the floor also, in different parts of the chamber. A round cushion was placed for me next to the lady, on which I was desired to be seated. I should have remarked that, contrary to my expectations, I found none of the Emperor's women disguised their faces in the manner which I had experienced in the prince's harem, but I saw them with the same familiarity as if I had been introduced into the house of a European.

Lalla Zara, who was of Moorish parents, was about eight years ago remarkable for her beauty and accomplishments; on which account she was then in every respect the favourite wife of the Emperor. So dangerous a pre-eminence could not be enjoyed without exciting the jealousy of those females whose charms were less conspicuous; and who, besides, the mortification of having a less share of beauty, experienced also the disgrace of being deserted by their lord.

Determined to effect her ruin, they contrived to mix some poison (most probably arsenic) in her food, and conducted the detestable plot with so much art and address, that it was not perceived till the deleterious drug had began its baneful operations. She was seized with most violent spasms and a continual vomiting; and had she not been possessed of an uncommonly strong constitution, she must immediately have fallen a victim to the machinations of her rivals. After a severe struggle, however, between life and death, the effects of the poison in some degree abated; but it left the unhappy lady in a state of dreadful debility and irritation, and particularly in the stomach, from which it was not perhaps in the power of medecine to extricate her. Her beauty too, the fatal cause of her misfortune, was completely destroyed, and her enemies, though disappointed in their aim of destroying her life, yet enjoyed the malignant triumph of seeing those charms which had excited their uneasiness reduced below the standard of ordinary women . . .

Lalla Zara was at this time about six-and-thirty years of age, and though in so weak a state, had two beautiful young children; the first was in its sixth year, and the youngest, which was then under the care of a wet-nurse, was very little more than a twelvemonth old. I was quite astonished to observe such strong and apparently healthy children, the offspring of a mother whose constitution was so dreadfully impaired. It was certainly, however, a very fortunate circumstance for Lalla Zara that she had these children; since by the Mahometaman law a man cannot divorce his wife provided she bear him children; so that though the Emperor took very little notice of this poor lady, yet he was, for the above reason, obliged to maintain both herself and her offspring . . .

I was next conducted to Lalla Douyaw, the favourite wife of the Emperor, whom I found to be what would be termed in Europe a very fine and beautiful woman. She is a native of Genoa, and was, with her mother, ship-wrecked on the coast of Barbary, whence they became the Emperor's captives. At that period, though but eight years of age, her personal charms were so very promising and attractive, that they induced the Emperor to order her to be taken forcibly from her mother, and placed in his harem, where, though at so early a period of life, every means were in vain employed to entice her to change her religion, till at length the Emperor threatened to pull up every hair of her head by the roots if she desisted any longer; and she then found herself obliged to submit to his inclinations.

After remaining some time in the character of a concubine, the Emperor married her; and from her great beauty, address, and superior mental accomplishments, she soon gained his best affections, which she ever after possessed. She had, indeed, so much influence over him, that though he was naturally of a very stubborn disposition, she was never known to fail in any favour she solicited, provided she persevered in her request . . .

Each female had a separate daily allowance from the Emperor, proportioned to the estimation in which they were held by him. Out of this they were expected to furnish themselves with every article of which they might be in want; the harem is therefore to be considered as a place where so many distinct lodgers have apartments without paying for them, and the principal Sultana is the mistress of the whole.

The daily allowance which each lady received from the Emperor for her subsistence was very trifling indeed. Lalla Douyaw, the favourite Sultana, had very little more than half-a-crown English a day and the others less in proportion. It must be allowed that the Emperor made them occasional presents of money, dress, and trinkets; but this could never be sufficient to support the number of domestics and other expenses they must incur. Their greatest dependence, therefore, was on the presents they received from those Europeans and Moors who visited the court, and who employed their influence in obtaining some particular favour from the Emperor. Nor had the Monarch sufficient delicacy to discourage this mode of negotiation. He well knew that if his women had not obtained supplies by other means, they must have had recourse to his purse; and as he had taken too good precautions to allow any mischief to arise from this custom, he was always well pleased to have the business transacted through that channel. Ambassadors, consuls, and merchants indeed, perfectly knew that this was always the most successful mode that could be adopted. As an illustration of this assertion, when I was at Morocco, a Jew, desirous of obtaining a very advantageous favour from the Emperor, for which he had been for a long time unsuccessfully soliciting, sent to all the principal ladies of the harem presents of pearls to a very considerable amount; the consequence was that they all went in a body to the Emperor, and immediately obtained the wished-for concession . . .

The Emperor's harem consisted of between sixty and a hundred females, besides their domestics and slaves, which were very numerous. Many of the concubines were Moorish women, who had been presented to the Emperor, as the Moors consider it an honour to have their daughters in the harem; several were European slaves, who had either been made captives or purchased by the Emperor, and some were negresses . . .

From the idea which is so prevalent with this people, that corpulency is the most infallible mark of beauty, the women use a grain which they name Elhouba, for the purpose of acquiring that degree of personal excellence at which they aspire: this they powder and eat with their cuscusoo. They likewise take with the same intention, large quantities of paste, heated by the steam of boiling water, which they swallow in the form of boluses. It is certainly true that the number of corpulent women in this country is very considerable, but it is probable that this circumstance arises as much from their very confined and inactive mode of life, as from any of the particular means which they employ to produce that effect.

The dress of the ladies consists of a shirt, with remarkably full and loose sleeves, hanging almost to the ground, the neck and breast of which are left open, and their edges are neatly embroidered with gold. They wear linen drawers, and over the shirt a caftan, which is a dress something similar in form to a loose great coat without sleeves, hanging nearly to the feet, and is made either of silk and cotton or gold tissue. A sash of fine linen or cotton folded is tied gracefully round the waist, and its extremities fall below the knees. To this sash two broad straps are annexed, and passing under each arm over the shoulders form a cross on the breast, and to that part of which passes between the breast and shoulder of each arm is fixed a gold tortoise, carelessly suspending in front a gold chain. Over the whole dress extended a broad silk band of Fez manufacture, which surrounds the waist, and completes the dress, except when they go abroad, and then they invest themselves in a careless manner with the haick.

The hair is plaited from the front of the head backwards in different folds, which hang loose behind, and at the bottom are all fixed together with twisted silk. Over their heads they wear a long piece of silk about half a yard wide, which they tie close to the head, and suffer the long ends, which are edged with twisted silk, to hang in an easy manner nearly to the ground. The remainder of the headdress is completed by a common silk handkerchief, which surrounds the head like a woman's closecap, differing from it only by being fixed in a full bow behind instead of in front. At the upper part of each ear hangs a small gold ring, half open, which has at one end a cluster of precious stones. At the tip, or lower part of the ear, is likewise suspended a broad and solid gold ring, which is so large that it reaches as low as the neck, and which, as well as the other, has a cluster of precious stones, in proportion to the size of the ring. The ladies wear on their fingers several small gold rings, set with diamonds or other precious stones, and on the wrists broad and solid gold bracelets, sometimes set also with precious stones. Their necks are ornamented with a great variety of bead and pearl necklaces. Below these a gold chain surrounds the neck and suspends in front a gold ornament.

Like the men, the Moorish women wear no stockings, but use red slippers, curiously embroidered with gold, which they take off when they enter their rooms. Immediately above the ankle each leg is surrounded with a large solid gold ring, which is narrow in front but very broad behind.

The ladies paint their cheeks a deep red and stain their eyelids and eyebrows with a black powder, which I apprehend to be antimony. It is a branch of artificial beauty in this country to produce a long black mark on the forehead, another on the tip of the nose, and several others on each cheek. The chin is stained a deep red, and thence down to the throat runs a long black stripe. The insides of the hands and the nails are stained of a deep red, so deep indeed that in most lights it borders on black; and the backs of the hands have several fancy marks of the same colour. The feet are painted in a similar manner with the hands.

I seldom observed in the harem the women at any employment but that of forming themselves into different circles for the purpose of conversation, sometimes in the open courts, at others in the different apartments.

4

Sultans

Since the sixteenth century Morocco has been ruled by two dynasties of Sharifs, descendants of the Prophet Muhammad. Therefore they have *Barakah*, the ability to channel Grace from God to their subjects. This means that they have not merely temporal sovereignty but spiritual primacy and often in the past there have been areas – the *Bled es-Siba* – where tribes refused to obey the sultan in political matters but paid tribute to him as a religious leader. One of his functions has always been to lead the noon-day prayer on Fridays on behalf of his people, and the ceremony of his setting out to do this has remained practically unchanged except that a car is sometimes used instead of a horse. This chapter gives contemporary pictures of rulers of Morocco arranged in chronological order – the dates of their reigns may be found on pp. xi–xiv. We have chosen extracts which show them as individuals, and it will be seen what a remarkable group of men they have been, from kindly, mild gentlemen to cruel tyrants. The buildings of Mulai Ismail, conceived on a scale that almost equals the pyramids, may be found in Meknes and it takes little imagination to see the personage described by Windhus moving around the vast walls and gates. So great was his prestige in Europe that it became the custom to refer to him and his successors as 'emperors'. His death, like that of other strong rulers, was followed by a period of anarchy, and the eighteenth century saw two of the most insane men ever to occupy a throne, Sultans Ahmad and Yazid. During the seventeenth and eighteenth centuries there were infrequent visits by European ambassadors, mainly to negotiate the release of captives but in the nineteenth century there were often several embassies a year, and a piece by Pierre Loti describes the reception of one of them. Hassan I was the last of the traditional sultans who could claim that his throne was the saddle of his horse and who spent much of his time riding around the country personally administering justice and chastising rebels. In 1912 Mulai Hafid, of whose court we give a vivid description, acquiesced in a French Protectorate during which the role of the sultan was so diminished that we found nothing of interest about his successor, Mulai Yusuf, the first sultan to go abroad for any reason other than to subjugate infidels in Spain. His successor, Muhammad V, who later changed his title to king, led the campaign for independence and was exiled by the French with his son, the present king; the popular indignation was so great that the French were compelled to bring him back and end the protectorate. He then set himself the task of national reconciliation and the principles on which he set out to rule are taken from one of his speeches.

Anecdotes about Mulai Rashid, the founder of the present dynasty.
From Sieur Mouette, *Entertaining Travels* . . ., 1710, pp. 17 and 21.

The King one Day suspecting a young Spaniard was guilty of a very slight Fault, notwithstanding all the Captive could say to clear himself, he caus'd him to be walk'd in a shameful manner through all the Streets of Fez, to make sport for the Boys, who strove to out-do one another in pricking him with sharp-pointed Reeds, which he endur'd with a true Christian Fortitude. He was carried back half Dead to the Palace Gate, where the King order'd the Butchers to Murder him, and bring him his Head to see, his Body being cut into Fourteen pieces and thrown to the Dogs . . .

Muley Archy went to see his Town of Sale, and pass the Month of Ramadan or Lent there. Having seen several young Christians about the Streets, he ordered the Governor of the Town to bring them before him; There being Nineteen of them, and good likely Men, he sent them some Days after to Fez with orders that they should be shut up until his Return. They were carefully kept at the Palace, and the King's Commands punctually obey'd, that none of the Captives should ever come to talk to them. About the end of Ramadan, the King returned to Fez, to Celebrate their great Festival, like our Easter; and causing them all to be brought before him on that Day, Preach'd to them the excellency of his Religion, telling them They would infallibly be damn'd, if they did not follow the Law of Mahomet; Then he promis'd, That as soon as they were sufficiently instructed in the Alcoran and Arabick Tongue, he would make them all Governors of Towns, and Commanders of his Troops; That he would Marry them advantageously, give them Rich Garments, fine Horses, Gold, Silver, and all they could desire; and in short, that they should be treated as his own children, that he had begotten to Salvation. Those Young Men, being most of them Servants and Cabbin Boys, and consequently ill instructed in Religion, gave Ear to that Barbarous Prince's promises, and all turn'd Mahometans, except Two. He caus'd them to be immediately Richly Clad; gave each of them a Cymiter and a Horse, and thus sent them to all the Mosques; whither they were attended by the Great Men of the Kingdom, and follow'd by all the King' Musick, and Cavalry, Marching with their Standards display'd: All the people that stood in the Streets to see those new Mahometans, gave them a Thousand Blessings. The King having prepare'd a Sumptuous Entertainment made them eat at his own Table, attended by the Prime Nobility. Then he gave them a Summ of Money, and after being heal'd of their Circumcision, he Married such as were of Age to Rich Wives. Their prosperity was not lasting as we saw most of those Renegadoes die miserably in the next Reign.

A description of Mulai Ismail.
From John Windus, *A Journey to Mequinez* . . ., 1725, printed in Pinkerton, vol. XV, pp. 466–77.

The Emperor is about eighty-seven years old, and very active for such a age. He is a middle-sized man, and has the remains of a good face, with nothing of a negro's features, though his mother was a black; he has a high nose, which is pretty long from the eyebrows downward and thin. He has lost all his teeth, and breathes short as if his lungs were bad, coughs and spits pretty often, which never falls to the ground, men being always ready with handkerchiefs to receive it. His beard is thin and very white; his eyes seem to have been sparkling, but their vigour decayed through age, and his cheeks very much sunk in. He was mounted on a black horse, not so remarkable for his beauty as for being taught to please him. His negroes continually fan and beat the flies from his horse with cloths, and the umbrella is kept constantly twirling over his head, the man that carries it taking great care to move as his horse does, that no sun may come upon the Emperor. His dress was not much different from what his bashas wear, consisting of a fine alhague; his turban made with rolls of muslin, that came very low upon his forehead. The end of his scimiter hung out, it was covered with gold and handsomely set with large emeralds. His saddle was covered with scarlet cloth embroidered with gold, with one pistol in a cloth case, on the left side.

He is an early riser, whether from his natural disposition, or the horror of the many murders, exactions, and cruelties he has committed on his poor subjects and slaves, I cannot determine; but those who have been close to him in camps, (for in his palace he is waited upon by women, young wenches, boys and eunuchs, who dare not tell tales) report that his sleep is very much disturbed, and full of horror; when starting on a sudden, he has been heard to call upon those he had murdered; and sometimes awake, he asks for them whom he has killed but the day before; and if any of the standers by answer, He is dead, he presently replies, Who killed him? To which they must answer, They do not know, but suppose God killed him, unless they have a mind to follow.

As soon as his first prayer is over, which is before the morning star disappears, he goes to his works, which are of a vast extent within the walls of his palace; there his poor people all taste of his anger in their turns, beating, killing, or giving good words, according to the humour he is in. This is one of his top pleasures; in some of these places, and never within his palace, he gives audience to ambassadors, converses, sometimes sitting on the corner of a wall, walks often, and sometimes works.

About eight or nine his trembling court assemble, which consists of his great officers, and alcaydes, blacks, whites, tawnies and his favourite Jews, all barefooted; and there is bowing and whispering to this and the other eunuch, to know if the Emperor has been abroad (for if he keeps within doors there is no seeing him unless sent for), if he is in a good humour, which is well known by his very looks and motions; and sometimes by the colour of the habit he wears, yellow being observed to be his killing colour; from all of which they calculate whether they may hope to live twenty-four hours longer.

If he comes out, the necks are all held out, their eyes fixed on the ground, and after this manner the crouching creatures pay their homage. If he speaks, some swear by their God, what he says is true, others at every pause he makes, cry out, God lengthen thy days, my lord; which once occasioned an accidental jest, for he was saying, May I be called the greatest of liars if I have not always conceived a great esteem for the English, and making a little stop at the word liars, his officious court cried out, Yes, by G—d, it is true my lord.

Those days that he comes not abroad, the courtiers remain in an alley of his palace till dinner-time, when he sends them a great vessel of cuscusu, which they fall upon without ceremony, and having filled their bellies, return to their private affairs; but if he goes any distance from the town, those that have the privilege to go with him, call for their horses, which are held by their servants at some distance, none ever presuming to go unless bidden. Sometimes when he goes out of town, which is not above once in two or three months, he will be attended by fifteen or twenty thousand blacks on horseback, with whom he now and then diverts himself at the lance.

While he is abroad, there are carried after him a stool, a kettle of water, and a skin (which is his table-cloth) this belongs to his eating; and if he is out at dinner-time, his dinner is carried after him on the head of a negro, in a great wooden or copper vessel, which he does not take from his head until the Emperor asks for it. His other travelling utensils are two or three guns, a sword or two, and two lances, because one broke once when he was murdering; his boys carry short Brazil sticks, knotted cords for whipping, a change of cloaths to shift when bloody, and a hatchet, two of which he took in a Portuguese ship, and the first time they were brought to him, killed a negro without any provocation, to try if they were good.

Although the natives of his dominions are whites, yet they are not so esteemed by him as the blacks and copper-coloured, to whom he commits the guard of his person, and is so fond of their breed, that he takes care to mix them himself, by often ordering great numbers of people before him, whom he marries without any more ceremony than pointing to the man and women, and saying *Hadi y houd Hadi*, i.e. That take that, upon which the loving pair join together, and march off as firmly noosed as if they had been married by a Pope. He always yokes his best complexioned subjects to a black help-mate; and the fair lady must take up with a negro.

Thus he takes care to lay the foundation of his tawny nurseries, to supply his palace as he wants, into which they are admitted very young, are taught to worship and obey the successor of their Prophet, and being nursed in blood from their infancy, become the executioners and ministers of his wrath, whose terrible commands they put into execution with as much zeal and fury as if they had received them immediately from heaven. They are so ready to murder and destroy, even while young, that the alcaydes tremble at the very sight of them, and the Emperor seems to take a great deal of pleasure, and place much of his safety in them, for they surround him almost wherever he is. If they are well-looking and strong, they need no other quality; some who have relations that are able, are fed, cloathed and lodged by them; others who have not, are lodged in the outskirts of the palace, in great rooms, where they pig an hundred or two together. They wear only a short and small coat without any sleeves, which does not reach to their knees; their heads are shaved, and always exposed to the sun, for he affects to breed them hard. Most, sometimes all, of them are employed in his buildings, where they take off their cloaths, and laying them all in a heap, every one takes a basket, and removes earth, stones or wood; when they have done, he orders them to go to his Jew and receive so much soup.

He beats them in the cruellest manner imaginable, to try if they are hard; sometimes you shall see forty or fifty of them sprawling in their blood, none of them daring to rise till he leaves the palace. I never heard that he killed but three of them, one for sodomy, and two for hiding a piece of bread in the hole of a wall, for they are great reverencers of bread, and take up the least crumb wherever they find it and kiss it. When they want cloaths, the Emperor thinks of somebody that has too much money and bids them to go to him, and receive each a coat or shirt.

The Emperor never beats a man soundly, but the man is in the high way of preferment, and it is ten to one but His Majesty passing by him in chains a few days later, and finding him in a sad pickle, he calls him his dear friend, uncle or brother and enquires how he came in that condition, as if he knew nothing of the matter, sends for a suit of his own cloaths (which is a great compliment) makes him as fine as a prince and sends him to govern some of his great towns. This is the treatment of grandees, today hugged, kissed, and preferred, tomorrow stript, robbed and beaten. Many of the people about him bear the marks of his sword, lance or short sticks. If he chances to kill any body when he has not determined their death (as it frequently happens) he civilly begs their pardon, and says, he did not design to kill that poor man, and lays the fault on God, saying, his time was come, the powers above would have it so. His wrath is terrible, which Christians have sometimes felt; for one day passing by a high wall, on which they were at work, and being affronted that they did not keep time in their stroke, as he expects they should, he made his guards go up and throw them all off the wall, breaking their legs and arms, and knocking them on the head in a miserable manner; another time he ordered them to bury a man alive, and beat him down along with the mortar in the wall.

An account of a mission to the court of Ismail's successor, Mulai Ahmad.
From John Braithwaite, *History of the Revolutions . . .*, 1729, pp. 174–6.

We were kept waiting in an Anti-Apartment of the King's, when some were fighting, others quarrelling, some were smoaking, and all in such an Uproar, one would have thought himself rather on the commonside of a Jail, than in the Palace of a great Emperor. Behold at length two great wooden Gates were flung open, and we discovered his Impèrial Beastliness sitting under a wooden Canopy in an open Gallery; below his Majesty, at his Feet, his favourite Brother and his first Minister: Mr Russell was led up to the Throne, and making three Bows, pulled off his Hat, and delivered into the Emperor's own Hand his Majesty's Letter, ty'd up in a fine silk Handkerchief, and a Gold Watch ty'd up in another; he then covered, and made a Speech to the Emperor, importing the great Esteem and Regard the King of Great Britain had for his Majesty; condoled, and congratulated the Emperor upon his Father's Death, and his own Advancement; all which was interpreted but it might as well have been left alone, for his Imperial Majesty was so drunk he could scarce hold his Head up, but cried *Buono*, *Buono*; and then charged the Alcaide of the Christians to see we did not want for Wine, and roasted Pigs every Day. Then his Courtiers prostrated themselves upon their Faces, and crawled upon their Hands and Knees to kiss his Feet: After this his Court retired, and the Emperor's Eunuchs took him up and carried him away. The Emperor, as to his Person, is very tall, about 48 or 50; of a very fierce Countenance, and very much pitted with the Small-Pox; he seemed very much bloated in the Face, wanted his Fore-Teeth, and being a Mulatto, made altogether a very ugly Figure. His Dress was a long black Cloke, it being Winter, over a white Alhague; his Turbant was a green Silk Sash, but hung loose like a drunken Man's; his Cimetar was very rich, and the only thing about him worth taking notice of. It had been the Cimetar of old Muley Ismael; the Scabbard was of Gold, very richly set on both sides with Diamonds and precious Stones. The Audience being over, and the Emperor carried away, the whole Palace was in an Uproar, neither was there any manner of Care taken to see us back; they shoved us about in a strange Manner, demanding extravagant Sums of Money at every Gate to let us out, shutting all the Gates upon us wherever we came; and were so insolent, that taking my Buttons for Gold, which were Bath-metal gilt, they cut several of them off, in spite of all the Resistance I could make; and were so very expeditious, they cut the Cloth and all in several Places. We expected every Minute to be stripped, and it was by the Force of a good deal of Money, and promising much more to all the Porters, we were able to get through the Palace. It is impossible to convey an Idea to any Person who was not there, what a rascally Crew we met with, nor can any one conceive that what is called a Court should be worse than a Bear-Garden.

A meeting with Sidi Muhammad III.
From William Lempriere, *A Tour from Gibraltar to Tangier, Sallee . . .*, 1791, printed in Pinkerton, vol. XV, pp. 740–2.

On the day appointed for my reception at court, about twelve at noon, three negro soldiers, with large clubs in their hands, came to my apartments to escort me to the palace, telling me that they had directions to return with me instantaneously, and that they must answer for it with their heads, if they delayed a moment in the execution of their orders. I requested them to wait a few moments, till I could enable myself to appear in a decent dress before the Emperor. Far, however, from acceding to my request, the soldiers became quite impatient, and acquainted me that I must either proceed with them immediately, or they would return and inform the Sultan, that I had refused to comply with his orders. I now found myself under the necessity of setting off, and we all actually *ran* to the palace with the utmost expedition. When we arrived there, I was introduced to one of the masters of the audience, who desired me to wait on the outside of the palace till I was called for. From the abrupt and sudden manner in which I was forced away by the soldiers, I expected to be ushered immediately into the imperial presence; but so far was I still from the consummation of this expectation, that I remained on the spot where they first placed me, from twelve o'clock at noon till five in the evening.

The Moor, who introduced me, upon appearing in sight of the Emperor, prostrated himself on the earth, kissed it, and in a very humble manner exclaimed in Arabic, 'May God preserve the King!' The Emperor then ordered him to approach, and deliver what he had to say. He informed His Majesty, that in compliance with his order, he had brought before him the English doctor; after which, having made a very low bow, he retired, and the Emperor immediately desired me and my interpreter to advance towards him; but as soon as we got within ten yards of the Emperor, two soldiers came up, pulled us by the coat and acquainted us that we must not presume to approach any further . . .

His Majesty asked, in a very austere manner, 'What was the reason I had forbidden Muley Absulem the use of tea?' My reply was 'Muley Absulem has very weak nerves, and tea is injurious to the nervous system'. 'If tea is so unwholesome', replied His Majesty, 'why do the English drink so much?' I answered 'it is true, they drink it twice a day; but they do not make it so strong as the Moors, and they generally use milk with it, which lessens its pernicious effects. But the Moors, when they begin to use it, make it very strong, drink a great deal, and very frequently without milk'. 'You are right', said the Emperor 'and I know it sometimes makes their hands shake'. After this conversation about a dozen distilled waters, prepared from distilled herbs, were brought for me to taste, and inform the Emperor what they were, which were hot and which were cold etc.

These tales about Mulai Yazid are based on hearsay.
From James Richardson, *Travels in Morocco*, 1860, vol. II, pp. 41–2.

Mulai Yazeed was half-Irish, born of the renegade widow of an Irish sergeant of the corps of Sappers and Miners, who was placed at the disposition of this government by England and who died in Morocco. On his death, the facile buxom widow was admitted, 'nothing loath', into the harem of Sidi Mohammed, who boasted of having within its sacred enclosure of love and bliss, a woman from every clime.

Here the daughter of Erin brought forth this ferocious tyrant, whose maxim of carnage, and of inflicting suffering on humanity was 'My empire can never be well governed, unless a stream of blood flows from the gate of the palace to the gate of the city'. To do Yazeed justice, he followed out the instincts of his birth and made war on all the world except the English (or Irish). Tully's letters on Tripoli give a graphic account of the exploits of Yazeed, who, to his inherent cruelty, added a fondness for practical (Hibernian) jokes.

His father sent him several times to Mecca to expiate his crimes, when he amused, or alarmed, all the people whose country he passed through, by his terrific vagaries. One day he would cut off the heads of a couple of his domestics and play at bowls with them; another day he would ride across the path of an European, or a consul, and singe his whiskers with the discharge of a pistol-shot; another day he would collect all the poor of a district, and gorge them with a razzia he had made on the effects of some rich over-fed Bashaw. The multitude sometimes implored heaven's blessing on the head of Yazeed, at other times trembled for their own heads. Meanwhile our European consuls made profound obeisance to this son of the Shereef, enthroned in the west. So the tyrant passed the innocent days of his pilgrimage. So the godless herd of mankind acquiesced in the divine rights of royalty.

Ali Bey had many meetings with Mulai Sulaiman.
From Ali Bey, *The Travels of Ali Bey*, 1816, vol. I, pp. 64–9, 203, 293.

The Sultan, Mulai Sulaiman, appeared to be about forty years old; he is tall and lusty; his countenance has the expression of kindness; it was rather handsome, and not too brown; it was distinguished by large and lively eyes. He spoke fast, and comprehended quickly. His dress was very simple, not to say plain, for he was always wrapt up in a coarse Haik. He is Fakih or Doctor in Law, and his education is entirely Mussulman. His court has no splendour. During all the time of his stay at Tangier he was always encamped to the west of the town in tents, placed without any order . . .

The Sultan asked me in what countries I had travelled, what languages I spoke, and if I could write them; what were the sciences which I had studied in the christian schools, and how long I had resided in Europe? He praised God for having caused me to leave the country of the infidels, and regretted that a man like me had deferred so long his visit to Morocco, much satisfied that I had preferred his country to Algier, Tunis, or Tripoli. He repeated me the assurances of his protection and friendship. He then asked me whether I had any instruments to make observations, and having answered him in the affirmative, he told me that he wished to see them, and that I might bring them to him . . .

The next day I went to the castle at the appointed hour. The Sultan was waiting for me on the same place with his principal Fakih or Mufti, and another favourite. He was served with tea.

When I came into his presence, he bid me ascend the small stairs and sit down at his side. He took the tea-pot and poured some tea into a cup and having filled it up with milk, he himself presented it to me. He then called for pen and ink; they brought him a scrap of indifferent paper, a small horn ink-stand, and a pen made from a reed. He wrote a sort of prayer in four or five lines, which he gave to his Fakih to read, who observed to him that a word was wanting. The Sultan took the paper back and added the word. Having finished his tea, his Moorish Majesty presented me the writing to read, and accompanied me as I read, with his finger pointing word by word. He corrected my pronunciation when I made a mistake, as a master would do to his scholar. When I had finished reading he desired me to keep the writing, and I have it still in my possession . . .

The next day I attended the Sultan, and went into his chamber; he was laying on a small mattress and cushion; his high Fakih and two of his favourites sitting before him on a small carpet. The moment he saw me he raised himself upright, and ordered another small blue velvet cushion, like his own, to be brought for me; he had it placed at his side, and made me sit down.

After some compliments on both sides, I ordered my electrical machine and a camera obscura to be brought in. I presented these to him as objects of mere amusement, which had no scientifical application. Having prepared these two machines, I placed the camera obscura near the window. The Sultan got up and went twice into the camera; I covered him with baize all the while that he amused himself in contemplating the objects transmitted by it. He afterwards amused himself with seeing the electric jar discharged, and had it often repeated; but what surprised him most was the experiment of the electric shock, which I was obliged to repeat a great many times: all of us holding ourselves by the hands in order to form the chain. He asked me many and various explications of these machines, as also of the influence of electricity.

In the evening being at home, and in company with some of my friends, a servant arrived from the Sultan and brought me a present from him. In delivering it to me he fell on his knees, and laid before me something covered with a cloth wrought with gold and silver. The curiosity of seeing the Emperor of Morocco's present made me uncover it eagerly, and I found *two black loaves*. As I was by no means prepared for such a present, I could not, at the moment, make any conjecture of its meaning, and was for a time so much staggered, that I knew not what to answer; but those who were about me began eagerly to wish me joy; saying 'How happy you are: what good fortune! You are now the brother of the Sultan; the Sultan is your brother'. I then began to recollect that amongst the Arabians the most sacred sign of fraternity consists in presenting each other with a piece of bread; and both eating of it; and therefore these two loaves sent by the Sultan were his token of fraternity with me. They were black, because the bread made for the Sultan is baked in portable ovens of iron, which gives this black colour to their outside, but they are very white and very good within . . .

Though Mulai Sulaiman leads but a retired life and without any luxury, yet his household occasions him considerable expense, on account of the great number of his women and children. The law allows him but four wives, besides his concubines, but he repudiates them often in order to take new ones. The repudiated women are sent to Taffilet, where he grants them a pension. I have often seen inhabitants present him with their daughters. At first they were admitted into the Harem as servants, and if they pleased him, were raised to the rank of his women, to be repudiated in their turn.

Mulai Sulaiman is sober. He eats with his fingers like the other Arabs; but when I was invited to his table, he always ordered a wooden spoon to be given to me, as the law forbids the use of any table utensils made of rich metals. His plates were therefore not different from those of his subjects. He eats no other dishes but those which are prepared by his negro women in the harem; when he dined at my house he ate without difficulty of the dishes which had been dressed by my cooks . . .

I was strangely surprised when I heard *that the Sultan had sent me two women*. As I had fixed my resolution in this respect, and determined not to give way till my return from the Pilgrimage, I refused the present. But as the women had once been dismissed from the Sultan's Harem, and could not be admitted into it again, the good-natured Mulai Abdsulem took them to his house.

Captain Beauclerk stayed in the palace of Mulai Abderrahman. From Captain Beauclerk, *A Journey to Marocco*, 1828, pp. 159–62.

The Sultan is, from appearance, about forty-two years old, his figure rather inclined to be corpulent and squat, and his height five feet nine inches. The expression of a naturally good-humoured countenance is much destroyed by a white spot on his left eye, which gives him the appearance of squinting; his beard is short, black and bushy, and he is the only man in his dominions who grows the hair between the neck and lower joint of his chin, it being considered dangerous to allow of the too near approach of a razor to the royal throat. He remained sitting on a red cloth cushion placed on a projecting edge of the garden-wall built for this purpose. In this manner he receives all missions; no one sits in his presence or is offered refreshments, and yet there is no ostentation or pride in his dress or manners, which are both perfectly simple.

The arrangements of the royal hours are as follows. The Sultan rises at day-light, and having said prayers, walks in his garden unattended, giving orders to the workmen around him. At eight he mounts his horse, and rides for two or three hours, attended by all his great Caids, who continue to gallop past him, and discharge their long guns, loaded with blank cartridge, at his royal person, so that his ride is an unceasing Laib el Baroud. On returning from this exercise he retires to his women's appartments until four o'clock in the evening, enjoying the bath, and such other *et ceteras* as his harem can offer with all its numbered charms and charmers. At four he goes to the mosque for evening prayers, and afterwards either rides or transacts business, during the remainder of the evening.

Sultan Mulai Abderrahman appears to deserve the opinion formed of him by his uncle Mulai Soliman, who left him, by will, the sole heir of his crown and kingdom, to the prejudice of eighteen sons, because he looked upon him as a sensible man; and so he has proved himself to be, by his wise behaviour in establishing himself on his throne, not by the eastern mode – the extermination of the late Sultan's family – but by relying upon his people's affections, which he wins by his humanity and kindness to those very sons to whose prejudice he has mounted the throne. From the expression of Mulai Abderrahman's countenance, he seems possessed of much good-nature, and a degree of sly fun or humour, which is seldom found in a man of a bad disposition. Stories are told of his having performed the office of his own executioner, for the pleasure of gratifying his revenge; but these we heard from our Jew interpreter, and therefore gave no credit to them.

A description of the reception of a French ambassador by Mulai Hassan.

From Pierre Loti, *Morocco*, 1889 (1929 edn), pp. 148–57.

And at last we arrive before the outer wall of the palace, and, through a large ogival gateway, enter into the Courtyard of Ambassadors . . .

We are asked to dismount – for none is privileged to remain on horseback in the presence of the Chief of the Faithful – and our horses are led away. On foot now, all of us, on the wet grass, in the mud.

There is a movement amongst the troops; red soldiers and multi-coloured musicians advance in a double line, and form a wide avenue, from the centre of the courtyard where we stand to the bastion beyond, through which the Sultan is to come, and all eyes are now turned towards the arabesque-framed gateway awaiting the saintly apparition.

It is a full two hundred yards from us, this gateway, so immense is the courtyard, and through it, first of all, come viziers and other grand dignitaries; dark faces and long, grizzled beards; on foot, all of them, to-day, like us, and walking slowly in the whiteness of their veils and flowing burnouses. Almost all these personages are known to us already, for we saw them the day before yesterday, on our arrival; but they seemed more imposing then, mounted on their superb horses. Comes also the Kaid Belail, the black jester of the Court, his head still crowned with its fantastic, dome-shaped turban; he advances alone, swaying and swaggering, his gait strangely disquieting, leaning on an enormous loaded bludgeon; and there is something indescribably sinister and mocking in his whole person; he seems to glory in the consciousness of the extreme favour he enjoys . . .

And here now, come to a stop quite near us, is the last authentic descendant of Mohammed, bastardised with Nubian blood. His costume, like a cloud of fine woollen muslin, is of immaculate whiteness. His horse, too, is pure white; his large stirrups are of gold; his silken saddle and harness are of very pale water-green, delicately broidered with golden-green paler still. The slaves who lead his horse, the one who bears the huge red parasol, and the two – the pink and the blue – who wave the white napkins to drive from about the sovereign imaginary flies, are Herculean negroes, fiercely smiling; all of them are old, and their white and grey beards stand out sharply against the black of their cheeks. And this ceremonial of another age harmonises with this music of lamentation, is framed with perfect fitness by these immense surrounding walls, which upraise in the air their dilapidated battlements.

This man, who has been brought before us with such pomp and circumstance, is the last true representative of a religion, of a civilisation, in way of dying. He is the very personification of old Islam; for, as is well known, pure Mussulmans consider the Sultan of Stamboul an almost sacrilegious usurper and turn their eyes and their prayers towards Al Moghreb, where dwells, for them, the true successor of the Prophet . . .

Assuredly he is not cruel; with those kind, melancholy eyes of his he could not be so; in the just exercise of his divine power he sometimes punishes severely, but, it is said, he likes much better to pardon. He is priest and warrior, and he is both to excess; penetrated, as might be a prophet, with his celestial mission, chaste in the midst of his seraglio, faithful to the most rigorous religious observances and fanatical by heredity, he seeks to model himself as far as possible on Mohammed. One may read all this, indeed, in his eyes, in his handsome countenance, in his majestically upright carriage. Such as he is, we cannot hope, in our epoch, either to understand or judge him; but, such as he is, he is beyond all question grand and imposing.

And there, before us, people of another world brought near him for a few minutes, he betrays an indefinable shyness, almost timidity, which gives his personality a singular and altogether unexpected charm.

It was the custom that each ambassador visiting the sultan took with him presents to show the artefacts of his country. The first French mission, that of 1533 took 44 large decorated mirrors, 24 combs some made of ivory, 5 gold watches, 2 striking clocks, baskets made of silver wire and equipment for falconry. The Moroccans gave presents in return and the ambassador, whose comments have not been preserved, found himself in charge of a female jackal, a lion, three ostriches and four greyhounds destined for the royal menagerie. Sometimes things went wrong: during the Napoleonic Wars the Governor of Gibraltar intercepted a French ambassador on his way to Fez bearing six gold and five silver watches, clocks, rings, a diamond plume, a tent with a bed and cases of porcelain, impounded the presents and forwarded them as a gift from London. Unfortunately Mulai Sulaiman discovered the deception and sent them to the French consul for him to re-present in the name of Paris. One French mission to Muhammad III unluckily dropped in the Sebou the cannon it was to present but another was more successful with a stethoscope and a pistol 'for use in a drawing room'. This extract describes some presents to Mulai Hassan.

From H. M. P. de la Martinière, *Souvenirs . . .*, 1919, pp. 44, 112, 132.

Unfortunately the presents were hardly chosen with discernment. The most striking of them, carried on a litter slung between camels, was an electric canoe. There were great expectations of the effect that the manoeuvres of this little craft would produce, but unfortunately, the palace at Fez, unlike that of Marrakesh, did not contain a pond big enough for it. After a hopeless attempt to sail it along the stream of Wadi Fez, it was moved to a distant shed where some time later we saw it providing a comfortable home for the royal pigeons . . .

One of the first German missions was that of Colonel von Conring to Marrakesh in about 1878 to present to Mulai Hassan some artillery pieces, telephones and various shoddy articles. The Sultan, with a bad grace, consented to watch a trial of the guns, but astonishingly for something put on by Germans, it was so badly organised that he left in the middle, refusing to watch any more. Probably they remembered the previous time that the Germans had brought a present. This was a machine for making ice which had exploded killing several bystanders and after that there was little faith in German products. The Colonel took his revenge by publishing a scandalous collection of anecdotes about Tangier and about the diplomatic corps. He had this miserable pamphlet translated into Spanish but it had little success . . .

A Belgian mission, with a team of engineers and mechanics, took with it a light railway which, it was hoped, would lead to an order for a whole network, or at least a line connecting the royal residence of Fez and Meknes. However the little train was not a success – it worked only once and that badly in the presence of His Majesty. Running on rails hastily laid across uneven ground in a courtyard of the palace, it stopped at every difficult place and there was much shouting for negro slaves to get it going again with vigorous pushing. The effect was decisive for the Sultan firmly refused to enter the so-called Imperial Coach, even though it was decorated with green satin – the sharifian colour. The train ended its days in one of the dustiest sheds in the palace.

A description of the death march of Mulai Hassan when his death had to be concealed from an undisciplined army and hostile tribes.

From Gavin Maxwell, *Lords of the Atlas*, 1966, pp. 50–52.

While camping in enemy country he died. Now the death of a Sultan under such circumstances was fraught with danger to the state. He was an absolute monarch, and with his disappearance all authority and government lapsed until his successor should have taken up the reins. Again, the expedition was in hostile country, and any inkling of the Sultan's death would have brought the tribes down to loot and pillage the Imperial camp. As long as the Sultan lived, and was present with his expedition, his prestige was sufficient to prevent an attack of the tribes and to hold his forces together. But his death, if known, would have meant speedy disorganisation, nor could the troops themselves be trusted not to seize the opportunity to murder and loot.

It was therefore necessary that the Sultan's demise should be kept an absolute secret. He had died in the recesses of his tents, themselves enclosed in a great canvas wall, inside which, except on very special occasions, no one was permitted to penetrate. The knowledge of his death was therefore limited to the personal slaves and to his Chamberlain, Bou Ahmed.

Orders were given that the Sultan would start on his journey at dawn, and before daylight the State palanquin was carried into the Imperial enclosure, the corpse laid within it, and its doors closed and the curtains drawn. At the first pale break of dawn the palanquin was brought out, supported by sturdy mules. Bugles were blown, the band played, and the bowing courtiers and officials poured forth their stentorian cry, 'My God preserves the life of our Lord!' The procession formed up, and, led by flying banners, the dead Sultan set out on his march.

A great distance was covered that day. Only once did the procession stop, when the palanquin was carried into a tent by the roadside that the Sultan might breakfast. Food was borne in and out; tea, with all the paraphernalia of its brewing was served; but no one but the slaves who knew the secret were permitted to enter. The Chamberlain remained with the corpse, and when a certain time had passed, he emerged to state that His Majesty has rested and had breakfasted, and would proceed on his journey – and once more the procession moved on. Another long march was made to where the great camp was pitched for the night.

The Sultan was tired, the Chamberlain said, he would not come out of his enclosure to transact business as usual in the *Siwan* tent, where he granted audiences. Documents were taken into the royal quarters by the Chamberlain himself, and when necessary, they emerged bearing the seal of State, and verbal replies were given to a host of questions.

Then another day of forced marches, for the expedition was still in dangerous country; but Mulai Hassan's death could no longer be concealed. It was summer, and the state of the Sultan's body told its own secret.

Bou Ahmed announced that His Majesty had died two days before, and that by this time his young son Moulay Abd El Aziz, chosen and nominated by his father, had been proclaimed in Rabat, whither the fleetest of runners had been sent with the news immediately after the death had occurred. It was a *fait accompli*. The army was now free of the danger of being attacked by the tribes; and the knowledge that the new Sultan was already reigning, and that tranquillity existed elsewhere, deterred the troops from any excesses.

Two days later the body of the dead Sultan, now in a terrible state of decomposition, arrived at Rabat. It must have been a gruesome procession, the hurried arrival of the palanquin bearing its terrible burden, five days dead in the great heat of summer; the escort, who had bound scarves over their faces – but even this precaution could not keep them from constant sickness – and even the mules that bore the palanquin seemed affected by the horrible atmosphere, and tried from time to time to break loose.

No corpse is, by tradition, allowed to enter through the gates into a Moorish city, and even in the case of the Sovereign no exception was made. A hole was excavated in the town hall, through which the procession passed directly into the precincts of the palace, where the burial took place. Immediately after, the wall was restored.

Edouard Michaux-Bellaire in the August 1908 number of the *Revue du Monde Musulmane* describes life in the palace of Mulai Hafid in an article which is here translated and abridged by the editors.

The palace of the Sultan, the *Dar al-Makhzan* consists of three distinct areas. The first, the outside courts which contain the offices of the Ministers, the stables, the stores for tents, the armoury and guard-rooms are accessible to their staff and even to members of the public who wish to see the Minister for Complaints.

The second part contains the quarters of the Sultan and is under the control of the *Hajib*, an officer usually called by Europeans the Grand Chamberlain although literally it means Curtain, for he is the Curtain through which one must approach the Sultan. He arrives at the Palace at dawn and stays until ten at night and the two men perform the five daily prayers together. The Hajib is responsible for the domestic staff, the corporations of the people of the washing water, the people of the bed, of the slippers, the tea, the pages who are the sons of provincial governors, the keepers of clothes and jewels, who number about twenty and are almost all negroes. The Hajib shares with the Kaid of the Courtyard command of the people of the guns, of the swords, of the lances, the camp equipment and the stables. He shares with the Chief of the Negroes, a eunuch, responsibility for those employed on domestic duties and for the eunuchs who alone can go into the private appartments of the Sultan. There are numerous eunuchs who have been brought from Mecca. The Hajib also looks after the personal stables of the Sultan which once contained more than 500 horses and as many mules but is now reduced to less than 100 of each. Personal presents to the Sultan, gold, jewels and valuable fabrics, are taken by the Hajib, checked by him and then handed over to a eunuch who carries them to a private treasury of which the Sultan alone has the key.

The costs of feeding the palace are met by a special government office after being passed on by the Provost of the Merchants. Other expenses, clothes, perfumes etc, are met by a different office on the instructions of the Hajib.

The third, the innermost part of the palace, in addition to the private apartments of the Sultan contains those of the numerous Sharifas, aunts, sisters or cousins of the Sultan who live there with their slaves. Mulai Hassan was survived by 26 sisters and 70 daughters. A large number of them have married members of the royal family, for a Sharifa can only marry another Alawite. These married ladies often have numerous children so that estimates of the number living in the inner palace vary from 3000 to 6000. These figures are for the palace of Fez, for in addition that at Meknes contains another 2000 and that of Marrakesh another 1200. On the death of a Sultan his successor leaves the wives and children of his father in possession of his house and builds himself a new one within the precincts of the palace. The descendants of a Sultan can continue to live in his house but if they prefer to move outside, government lodgings are found for them and they receive maintenance in cash according to their importance.

The Hajib exercises authority within this part of the palace through the Chief Eunuch in matters which concern these descendants and through two *Arifas* over the women. The women are organised into corporations like the men in the second part of the palace but the Sultan does not call upon their services unless he is ill, for otherwise he goes into the part served by men. The Senior Arifa is in charge of the elderly women while the Junior is responsible for those that are young. The Senior Arifa is often a widow of the previous Sultan and can wield considerable political influence. These two ladies are assisted by subordinate Arifas in the maintenance of discipline, enforced if necessary by a whip of leather thongs. At night the two Arifas sleep in a room next to that of the Sultan. They ensure that the women detailed to share his bed have been properly washed, dressed and perfumed.

The Sultan always eats alone but after his evening meal he drinks tea before retiring to bed. One of his women, sitting in front of him but some distance away, prepares the beverage which is handed to him by a slave who had been standing by the door. When the Sultan has finished his tea, if he decides to retain the girl sitting opposite him, he gives orders for the doors of the chamber to be closed: if not he calls the Senior Arifa and names the one whose presence he requires. Inside the door in a recess sit cross-legged two negresses who are relieved every hour by the Arifa. If the Sultan requires anything during the night he gives an order to the negresses. It happens sometimes that the Sultan decides to have a different woman whereupon the Arifa is awoken, brings in the new one and takes away the previous one.

The marriage ceremonies of a Sultan take place within the palace and are attended only by women. Outside there is powder-play for several days and a grand banquet in the courtyard attended by government officials and religious leaders. The divorces of the Sultan take place privately within the palace.

If a woman who has been repudiated by the Sultan has children she and her children are given a house within the palace precincts. If she is childless she is free either to stay or leave. If she prefers the former she is given lodging, food and clothing. If she decides to return to her family she is given numerous presents and is free to marry again, although it is considered respectful to seek the permission of the Sultan who sends a wedding present. It happens that the Sultan often gives one of his childless former wives to a member of his family. If a former wife who has gone back to her parents finds, within three months, that she is pregnant, the Sultan is immediately informed. He then immediately sends a Court Midwife and two Arifas who do not leave her side until the baby is born. This seldom happens, however, as most repudiated wives prefer to stay on in the palace.

Women, such as the daughters of provincial governors, presented to the Sultan by their families, are not considered concubines but await their turn to become one of his four legitimate wives. It can happen that their turn never comes and they sadly grow old in the palace. It can happen that the Sultan decides not himself to marry a young girl presented to him but passes her on to one of his relations or officials but this is rare as it is considered wounding to her family.

The only man in a city of women, mostly his relatives, including possibly his mother and even his grandmother, the Sultan finds himself confronted with endless problems and the victim of numerous conflicting pressures. The caprices of the reigning favourite can cause continual expenses and the Sultan can rarely refuse her requests. To please her he notes her desires and sends a note to the Hajib who sends an order to the Payment Office to buy what she has asked for. By the time the gifts arrive often either the lady has changed her mind or the Sultan has changed his favourite so the objects are consigned to a storeroom and forgotten. It is said that one favourite craved for apples and after none could be found in Fez, a messenger was sent hotfoot to Tangier. Despite his best efforts he returned too late, for the new object of the Sultan's affections did not care for apples.

So the Sultan, faced in his public capacity by the intrigues of courtiers, the claims of the *ulama*, the demands of the Sharifs and of the tribes, to say nothing of the ultimatums of European powers, has from the nagging of the old sharifas and the demands of his wives, little more peace in his private life.

A description of Muhammad V fulfilling one of the most important of the duties of a Moroccan ruler – leading his people in prayer.

From Admiral Usborne, *First Moroccan Journey*, 1938, pp. 31–4.

The mosque where the Sultan worships stands isolated in a field, half a mile from the palace, and when we arrived a broad route connecting the two was already lined by the Sultan's black cavalry, magnificent men in red tunics with bulging green and white turbans, mounted on grey horses, their faces black as coal. They carried tall lances and on each the green penon of Islam fluttered in the breeze. They were not men to play tricks with. When I tried to cross their line, one wheeled round at me at once, and with a threatening gesture, ordered me sharply to go back! I thought it better to obey.

It was almost time for the ceremony. Troops had assembled outside the palace, while near the Mosque stood a crowd of religious officials, and a band in pink djellabas, carrying long brass trumpets of the kind one supposes Joshua used to blow down the walls of Jericho. The Mosque itself was crammed, there were crowds outside each door, and crowds lining the route behind the guards.

At last came a burst of music from the palace and a cavalry guard, riding shoulder to shoulder forty abreast, moved slowly forward. A mounted band followed, playing as they rode. Behind them came a horse-drawn coach, not unlike an old-fashioned London four-wheeler but decorated in white, green and gold and drawn by white horses. In it, dressed in pure white, sat the Sultan. More guards followed and the whole cortege moved steadily forward to the Mosque. It was very impressive. Perhaps it was the broad front of the cavalry, impossible in a street procession, which made the effect unique.

The crowd bowed to the ground as their Sultan passed and a few veiled women, grouped in the background, started to chant in a high-pitched tremolo. Others took it up. This was the first time we had heard this weird scream. They call it the *You-you*. It is hideous, penetrating, stunning to the ears. They You-you at weddings, and they You-you'd, so we were told, when Fez revolted and massacred the French. When you hear the cry you know something unusual is happening, but whether good or bad you cannot tell.

The white flag fluttered above the minaret of the Mosque; the sun beat down on its walls, which shone with a blinding white light; the pink-robed musicians raised their trumpets. As the Sultan's carriage drew up, they blared a greeting so loud that all Rabat must have heard it. Then he entered the Mosque and everything was hushed, while the great Moslem crowd, both inside and out, knelt in prayer. Presently the Muezzin appearing to the gallery of the minaret, gave forth the old cry 'There is no god but God, and Mohammed is His Prophet'.

Through one of the open doors, over the backs of the prostrate Moors outside, I could see the mass of humanity within, their foreheads pressed to the ground in passionate devotion.

The prayer was over. The guards formed up again, the trumpets sounded a fanfare. The Sultan came out on foot, mounted a white Arab while an attendant on a black horse opened the red umbrella of state, and riding behind him, held it over his head. Then the cortege moved forward at a canter, the cavalry closed round and the Sultan returned to his palace.

King Muhammad V made frequent addresses to his people. His speeches were published as *Le Maroc à l'heure de l'indépendence*, in about 1957. These extracts, translated by the editors, are from pages 6 to 18.

My Faithful People,
Twenty-five years have passed since We mounted the Throne, following Our Noble Ancestors who have given our Country an immortal glory and an unperishable renown.

Thanks to the help of God, the period has been fruitful since was assumed our delicate mission. We have not ceased to make every effort and consecrate every activity to the public interest, striving to link the present with our glorious past and to build the future of our country on these solid bases.

We have not recoiled from any obstacle to defend the rights of the Nation; and, to win for it every advantage while preserving it from every danger, We have used every method at Our disposal to reduce, as far as possible, its difficulties. All this has strengthened the links of solidarity and love between the People and its Sovereign. Our people have not failed to value Our efforts at their true worth and to assist Us in Our task.

Thanks be to God Who has created this ideal link between Our people and Ourselves. As the People sustain Us with their loyalty so the Throne, for Its part, watches over the essential rights and vital interests of the people. Indeed, by word and by action We have defended the rights and interests of Our people and have let slip no opportunity to recommend what will improve their lot and preserve them from false steps. We have never ceased to urge Our people to remain attached to the true religion and the principles of Islamic morality, to follow the example of the Prophet and to make a model of his actions. No nation can flourish if it does not understand its religion and abandons its virtues for the sake of superstition and vanities.

We have been particularly concerned with the education of women, who, formerly were held prisoners of traditions that were foreign to the spirit of Islamic law, which proclaims the equality of men and women in the face of its commandments, and imposes upon both sexes the duty of seeking instruction. This education has developed and already is bearing fruit. Thus the Moroccan woman will become conscious of her duties and her obligations before God, her home and her country.

In every country, the economy forms the base of all improvement and progress. It is therefore necessary to pay particular attention to economic problems, in their various aspects and in all their different branches. A nation which lacks a sound economic policy finds itself inevitably exposed to instability and sometimes collapse. That is why We had advised you on many occasions to widen the field of your economic activities, in agriculture, in industry and in commerce and to modernise them by adopting new methods; also to take an active part in developing the mineral resources of the country. The lot of the peasant has always been one of our main concerns: we have always had the aspiration that he should keep the source of his livelihood, his land, and that he should benefit from the building of dams and irrigation canals and from new methods of production.

As justice is the basis of every civilisation, We have never ceased to repeat that all those who hold public office should scrupulously observe the principles of fairness and honesty. We have aimed to put an end to all arbitrary action and Our subjects, Muslim and Jew alike, should be guaranteed in their personal rights and in their property, and that rich and poor, strong and weak, should be equal before the law.

In the field of social policy, We have always declared it was necessary to ensure that the working class should receive the same sympathy and esteem as the salaried employees of commerce and industry. It is to the efforts of the workers that we owe all the material benefits that we enjoy today. It is therefore just that they should be allowed to defend their interests by forming trade unions with complete freedom of association. Thus it will be possible for the labourers to lead a life compatible with human dignity, free of the nightmares of ignorance, fear and poverty.

A country such as Morocco, where water and minerals abound and where the inhabitants are distinguished by their natural gifts and their dynamism, is destined to possess a vast modern industrial system. But industrial progress, the development of modern means of production and the adoption of modern techniques is bound to produce a new phenomenon, the appearance of a new class of workers, more and more numerous, and with new needs created by new conditions. From this will arise new and varied problems. The working class is acquiring rights and obligations to participate in the evolution and the development of the economy. Misunderstanding the needs of the workers and failure to satisfy their just claims has led western capitalism to the verge of revolution and a struggle between the classes. This struggle has accentuated because of the materialistic nature of western society. Spirituality has given place to materialism. Greed has triumphed. Faith has grown weak and spiritual values declined. It is necessary for us to make use of the enlightenment of Islam in facing these problems, to profit from the experience of our ancestors, and to choose a wise way to face the social problems inherent in progress.

We pray that God will spare the world the horrors of war and of persecution, that He will purify hearts of hatred and resentment, infusing in them love and the spirit of conciliation, and will extend upon humanity the reign of harmony and peace.

In 1902, as dissatisfaction mounted at the follies of Mulai Abdel Aziz, a former disgraced Makhzen clerk declared himself to be Prince Mohammed, the elder brother of the sultan. He was variously referred to as the Rogui or Bou Hamara, the Man on the She-Ass. He attracted much support amongst the tribes of the North East which he buttressed by reported miracles – it was said that his curse could set a house on fire at long range and that his face was green in the morning, yellow after lunch and black at night. The Makhzen sent an army which checked him in a skirmish near Taza. This extract shows his methods of gaining support.

From A. J. Dawson, *Things Seen in Morocco*, 1904, pp. 308–10.

One of the Rogui's thick-and-thin supporters warned him afterwards that much dissatisfaction existed in the camp, owing to the fact that men who had been promised immunity from bullet wounds and the like had been wounded, and even slain, by the Sultan's men. The Rogui pondered, took his informant into his confidence, dug a grave in his tent and therein buried the informant with a hollow bamboo so placed in the man's mouth as to communicate with the surface air. Then the Pretender summoned a delegation of the disaffected.

'My sons', says he, 'I hear there are some among ye foolish and doubting ones who repine because some of your comrades appear to have suffered at the hands of our enemies. This is foolish of you, but yet I would have you reassured. Therefore shall ye speak with one who, slain in my service, serves me still in another world, and that without repining. Let us speak with Abd er-Rahman, say, whom the infidel-lovers shot yesterday. Ho Abd er-Rahman! Ho, there in Paradise! Speak to these my faint-hearted disciples, I pray thee.'

The juggler waved his arm, in stately fashion to be sure, and from out the bowels of the earth apparently the simple tribesmen heard the voice of a departed associate rally them on their lack of faith and courage. The voice described a sumptuous pavilion in Paradise, under which ran a crystal-clear river, about which luscious fruits, ever of perfect ripeness awaited the hand that would pluck them, in which a thousand big-eyed houris of dazzling beauty tended him, the thrice-blessed Abd er-Rahman, who, having by good luck died fighting for the Rogui, now enjoyed a felicity to attain which, could they but realise a tenth of it, every mother's son in the Pretender's horde would straightaway rush to seek death while fighting the Shareefian troops.

The malcontents drew back in satisfied awe and happy reverence. From that moment they vowed they were the Rogui's, soul and body. 'It is well, my sons', quoth the Rogui, stepping backwards and placing one foot over the orifice through which his unfortunate accomplice spoke and breathed.

The rebellion of Bu Hamara, the Rogui, continued until the summer of 1909 when it was repressed by the forces of the new Sultan, Mulai Hafid. J. M. MacLeod, the British Consul in Fez, sent two dispatches, extracts of which are given here, to the Foreign Secretary, Sir Edward Grey describing the victory celebrations and the punishment of the rank and file of the rebels. In a third dispatch, not given here, he reported that Bu Hamara himself, after being exhibited in a cage for three days, was shot and stabbed either by the Sultan himself or in his presence by a slave. His body was thrown to the lions, who, it was said, merely scratched at it; it was then burned.

(No. 30.)

Sir, *Fez, August* 16, 1909.

ON Wednesday, the 11th instant, I went to the palace and asked an audience of the Sultan to congratulate him on the successes his men had begun to achieve against the Pretender and to urge afresh that Dr. Verdon's services be used to tend the wounded and sick amongst the troops, as no doctor had been sent with the Mehalla . . .

By Friday afternoon, the 13th instant, the total of prisoners who had arrived from the Mehalla was about 232.

These were paraded before the Sultan, who was seated in his open kiosk in state, accompanied by the Grand Vizier, Glawi, Sid Aissa-ben-Omar, Vizier of Foreign Affairs, Kaïd Mtougi, and a leading highly respected Shereef of Fez, Mulai Dris-ben-Abdelhadi.

Some twenty-four of the prisoners were then selected for special punishment. Of these, twenty were old infantry soldiers, or palace slaves, who had deserted from Oudjah or Fez to Buhamara, and one an infantry drummer – a lad of 16 or 17 years old – who had deserted long ago from Oudjah. The remaining three were Buhamara's master of ceremonies, his master of horse, and a trumpeter, formerly a member of the Sultan's band.

The trumpeter had, then and there, his back teeth pulled out by way of preventing him ever blowing a trumpet again, and was sent to prison.

The remaining twenty-three were thrashed from the palace to Bab Mahrok in charge of the Sultan's master of ceremonies and the Acting Governor Zerowti.

There the Pretender's master of horse and master of ceremonies had their right hands and left feet taken off by a barber, and the rest (including the lad of 16) had their right hands taken off. The stumps were thrust into hot tar to stop the bleeding, two of them succumbing almost immediately. The survivors were taken to prison.

This was all carried out within an hour or so. None of these men were heard in their defence, nor was any but the very briefest enquiry made into their cases . . .

Returning to my house I heard that another batch of prisoners had arrived. I then went to Sid Aissa-ben-Omar (Vizier of Foreign Affairs), found him asleep, but had him awakened. I explained carefully that I made no claim to speak officially, as of course this was a purely Moorish affair, but from motives both of humanity and against these execrable punishments. He answered that the Sultan had desired to shoot all these twenty-four prisoners, but the viziers had induced him to commute the punishment to loss of a hand, or a hand and foot, so as to give the men a chance of their lives. However, he would tell the Sultan all I had said, should any further prisoners be likely to be similarly dealt with.

At 4 o'clock I called on the Grand Vizier. He held similar language to Sid Aissa's, said it was all less than the rigour of Moslem law, and expatiated on the necessity for severity in view of the state to which Buhamara and his people had brought Morocco, their burning of villages in sight of Fez itself, and the deaths and wounds suffered by the Sultan's troops.

He dissented wholly from my contention that it would have been more humane to shoot or decapitate these prisoners, and ended by saying that when he was in Oran the governor chanced to be run over by a carriage and his arm had to be amputated. Everybody congratulated him on his life being saved and on his escaping with the loss of his arm! Moslems were not like Christians as regards death. They believed they died at a time decreed by God, and so death merely was not held in great fear. However, he would at once tell the Sultan all I had said.

He then proceeded to the palace and sat with the Sultan for the rest of the afternoon, in public, in His Majesty's open kiosk.

I followed him to the palace and entered Sid Aissa-ben-Omar's office. Sid Aissa sent a message at once to the Sultan saying I had come for an audience as requested on the 11th instant.

The sight was indeed strange and barbaric for the twentieth century, and for a place within 200 miles of Europe. In the high-walled quadrangle of Bab Bujat, opposite to the Sultan's kiosk and the viziers' offices, the Sultan's infantry guard were drawn up with bugles and drums. Beyond them groups of gaily dressed cavalrymen galloped about firing *feux de joie*. Crowds of people filled the eastern side, and the roofs there were covered with women uttering shrill cries of joy and beating tom-toms. In front of us moved parties of white robed ushers and palace slaves, while facing us stood some ninety-three prisoners roped together in parties of about twenty. At their left, on horseback, sat a black soldier with the head of the Pretender's lieutenant held aloft on a pole. The prisoners had been standing in the sun for over two hours (itself a torture with the temperature then at about 105 degrees in the shade), and they sang in unison a plaintive chant to the words 'God give you the Victory, Oh! Mulai Hafid!'

Presently two of them were selected and brought to within 20 yards of where the Sultan was seated, and in a minute or two were sent off with the acting governor of Fez. One was a former slave of the palace, and the other a former colonel of infantry. It was whispered around that the Sultan had ordered them to be decapitated, but I learned later that one had had his right hand taken off, and the other his right hand and left foot. A third man, a leading slave of Buhamara, was selected and was sent off to be flogged only. This happened while I was yet waiting to see the Sultan, but after His Majesty had been joined by Glawi, with whom I had been remonstrating only a little while previously, and it seemed to be the end of the day's business. I was then sent for by the Sultan. The situation was that I felt I must speak strongly to him, but in such wise as (1) not to give him a chance to cut me short by saying it all was none of my business, and next to secure his consent to Dr. Verdon's assisting the sick and wounded soldiers.

The Sultan was seated on a sofa in the portico of his kiosk in full public view.

I said I had come on Wednesday to congratulate him on the course of events about Buhamara, because for many years I had looked forward impatiently to see him defeated . . .

I said that, while nobody rejoiced more sincerely than I over the victory, I was more sorry, indeed sick, than I could well express about these punishments. These people and Buhamara's followers, and Moorish tribes generally, had, I knew, to be treated with severity.

We English had had to put down the Indian mutiny with great severity. But to dismember prisoners was another matter. People in Europe had been hoping the Sultan would inaugurate a new and more civilised era in Morocco. Such methods, not used by the Makhzen in living memory, would show surely that it was backwards and downwards the Sultan wished to go, and so forth.

The Sultan answered in quite a calm judicial manner that he had, indeed, reflected beforehand on all that. He knew what Europe would think, but this disadvantage was far outweighed by the absolute necessity of bringing these tribes back to a salutary fear of the Makhzen. This was a first necessity even for the safety and prosperity of Europeans in Morocco. Rebels were by Moslem law liable to death by crucifixion. He was trying lesser punishment, and had given these people a chance of their lives. Only some twenty-six – specially bad cases – out of more than 300 prisoners had been so punished. Were not rebels in Russia put to death in great numbers? I interjected 'God forbid that your Majesty should take Russia for a model!' And I reminded him of the feeling even yet in England and France towards the Czar, even though the Czar was trying to get rid of these old practices.

The Sultan concluded by saying that we Europeans had no idea of the stubbornness of the Moorish tribes. Ordinary punishments such as ours were no use. Buhamara and his people had brought Morocco into ruin, and only the other day were busy burning villages in sight of Fez itself. They had killed the other day 113 of his soldiers and wounded many more, and yet the punishments they had suffered were less than those Buhamara employed, such (which is quite true) as burning prisoners alive. When all was said, these punishments were well within the law, and the Moorish public would rejoice to see the law once more enforced.

I replied that these penalties were possibly allowed by law – in the last resort, but no humane ruler ever adopted them until ordinary ones had been tried and failed. Nobody had tried ordinary means yet. Mulai Abdel Aziz had tried little more than bribery and palavers with the tribes. A few prompt executions and the enforcement of discipline in his army would have stopped Buhamara at once, or even now. But these recent punishments would perpetuate hatred of himself and the Makhzen, to which the Sultan replied, with a cynical smile, 'But who ever heard of anybody liking the Makhzen!' I replied I had hoped he would have had that aim.

The Makhzen's plea that they were trying to be 'merciful' is the bitterest of mockeries.

The prisoners, mutilated ones included, were left without food or water during the whole of the day and night of their arrival, and not until the following evening was food (one small loaf each) issued to them.

Fifteen of the twenty-six mutilated prisoners have now died in prison, and the rest are in a dying state. The sufferings of these people – untended, starving, thirsty, over crowded into filthy prisons, and in the present great heat – can be more readily imagined than described.

Except amongst the very lowest classes, the impression produced by all this has been of disgust. The inhabitants in general, of Arab descent, say that justice would have been amply satisfied by the shooting or decapitation of the prisoners, and mutter jealously 'This is Berber government; Mulai Al Hassan did not do such things!'

But as the victims are not Fez people there is no disposition to resent the Sultan's action.

In the event Dr. Verdon has been enabled to treat some fifty-eight soldier patients a-day, who would probably have been untended had the Sultan, in pique at too strong language from me (for such are Moorish Sultan's ways), avoided the use of this English doctor's services, or had His Majesty's attention, amid his many other preoccupations, not been called to their necessities.

(No. 33.)

Sir, *Fez, August* 30, 1909.

ACCORDING to the more exact information now available it appears that Buhamara met with some resistance by that tribe on reaching Beni Messara, but managed to instal himself in the sanctuary of Bu Amuran, about 8 miles south-east of Wazzan, and opened negotiations for their support. He was, however, unable to proceed any further, and meanwhile the Beni Messara, moved by the Shereef Mulai Ali of Wazzan, deserted him when the Sultan's troops arrived, as did also his remaining followers. He then hid himself in the sanctuary itself. The sanctuary was surrounded by troops, who then set fire to it, whereupon the Pretender came out and surrendered. When he was seen outside, unarmed, he was approached by several of the chief officers of the Sultan, the Basha Abdelkrim Eshirgui, Bu Owdah, Ben Jellali, Najjim Mahabub, Mohamed and Seyd Bagdadi, and others, amongst whom a furious struggle began for possession of him, each officer being frantic to pose as his captor. They even knocked off each other's turbans, tore each other's clothes, and threatened each other with their rifles. This lasted for about two hours while the whole party were proceeding to the soldiers' camp, the prisoner indulging in all manner of sarcasms both upon this and upon their bad generalship and cowardice, especially 'of that our Abdelkrim Eshirgui,' and so forth, remarking that for weeks the Mehalla had outnumbered them by ten to one, he should have been caught long before; had any of his men behaved so badly he should have shaved off their beards, and so forth.

At Fez most extraordinary preparations were made for his reception. Public holidays to last seven days were proclaimed. From dawn on the 24th, when he arrived, salvoes of cannon began to be fired, together with powder play by all the cavalry and Palace slaves. Enormous crowds poured out on the roads and into the old Meshwar of the Palace to meet the prisoner.

In an entirely private way I was amongst the crowd in the Old Meshwar, and so was myself a witness of nearly all that happened there. To have a chance of getting in privately one had to be there before 7 in the morning.

I have seen many spectacles in that Meshwar – reception of foreign missions and the like – but this one far transcended them all, and showed what the Moorish Government really can do when they have a visitor whom they are in the most sincere and highest degree delighted to receive! The reception of the German Emperor at Tangier may have equalled it, but I am sure, even it did not, in enthusiasm and gaudy splendour excel the entry of Buhamara. Gaily coloured new clothes were issued to all the troops on duty.

From 6 in the morning infantry were drawn up opposite the Sultan's kiosk in the Meshwar. The Sultan's brass bands, alternately with bugle bands and Moorish pipe and drum bands, discoursed music. The Kaïd-al-Meshwar, the Minister of War (Glawi, junior), and scores of other high functionaries played powder in front of the Sultan's kiosk in view of the thousands of spectators. The Sultan seated himself with his vizirs inside the Palace gateway at the inside of the Meshwar about 8 o'clock.

Guns boomed from time to time, and the streets and roofs to the east of the Meshwar were filled with men, women, and children of the populace all in their gayest attire, keeping up a din with tom-toms, Moorish pipes, and drums, parties of women even dancing in the streets.

About 10 o'clock a party of horsemen sent off with a camel carrying a square-shaped cage about 4 feet high by 3 feet wide and 3 feet deep in which the prisoner was to arrive.

About 11 o'clock the prisoner's party, surrounded by a huge crowd, reached the top of the hill above the Meshwar, and was saluted with a salvo of cannons, and half-an-hour later, amid more cannon firing, entered the north-west gate of the Meshwar, which it crossed, and finally the camel with the prisoner was halted in front of the Sultan just inside the Palace gateway.

I had a good view of the prisoner as he crossed the Meshwar, but as regards what passed subsequently I have the details from Europeans in the Sultan's service who were inside the gateway.

The prisoner was seated cross-legged in the cage. He seemed fatigued, but every one was struck with the undaunted composure – indeed, almost the dignity – of his demeanour.

When the prisoner was brought forward and the cage taken off the camel, the Sultan asked 'What is the meaning of you disturbing the country all these years? Who told you to do it?' To this the prisoner answered with quiet composure, 'This is not the place for conversation. First of all I ask for "Aman" (i.e. security and safety)'. The Sultan answered, 'You shall have "aman" for your own person'.

Buhamara said 'Good,' and then at once remarked that he was tired and very hungry – moreover his clothes had been taken by his captors, who had given him the common dirty things he was wearing, and with which he was unaccustomed. He would like some refreshment and clean clothes.

The Sultan seemed much struck with the prisoner's composure, granted these requests, and then retired, whereupon the assemblage began to disperse. The prisoner was then taken to a room close at hand, was given clean clothes and an excellent meal – to which he did full justice.

In that afternoon and during several hours on the three succeeding days, he has been publicly exhibited in a still smaller cage, placed on a pedestal in the centre of the 'Meshwar,' and under a canopy made of his own 'State' tent and amid continued rejoicings, music, crowds, and 'Powder Play.' The Sultan himself and the Viziers Glawi and Aissa Ben Omar and Kaid Mtugi took part in the Powder Play there next day.

5

The Government

The government of Morocco has had a longer continuous existence than that of any other state in the western world apart from that of the Vatican, for it was founded at the beginning of the ninth century by Mulai Idris. It is easy to see from the first extract, written by a French diplomat early this century, how little it must have changed over the centuries. The extent of the area that it controlled depended upon the weight of the Sultan's fist, for whereas the writ of a strong ruler like Mulai Ismail or Hassan I ran throughout most of the country, that of a weak one like Abdul Aziz hardly extended beyond his own palace. In the administered area, the *Bled el-Makhzen*, the Sultan was represented at local levels by officials that Europeans tended to call pashas if they were in the towns and caids if they were in rural areas. They were often, from the accounts of travellers, extremely picturesque characters and not infrequently corrupt. We give accounts of punishments inflicted by the Makhzen and its officials. In the rural areas, the *Bled es-Siba*, the mountain-dwellers controlled their own affairs by means of the *Jemaas* described in Chapter 3 although they respected the religious authority of the Sultan. There were frequent attempts by the Sultans to discipline them and collect taxes, and some of these are described in our extracts. We conclude with the principles on which the first French Resident-General attempted to reform the administration. His successors were less sensitive to Moroccan opinion and were very much under the thumb of their civil servants and of the *colons* and provoked the nationalist sentiments that led to the regaining of independence.

How the system of government worked.
From Eugène Aubin, *Morocco of To-Day*, 1904, pp. 163–9.

The Viziers or Secretaries meet every morning in that part of the Dar el-Makhzen which is specially reserved for them. At Fez it is a series of courts and passages, crowned by the minaret of the Djemaa el-Khadra, which is set apart for the official devotions. One enters it from the old *mechouar*, by a gate flanked by two battlemented towers, and guarded by soldiers of the Makhzen. Their mounts draw up in the old *mechouar*, whilst the riders, passing through the principal gate and the entrance passages, reach a large court. Its arrangement is uniform, for the Government of the Empire must always meet in the same sort of premises, that is, in an oblong court with, first a colonnade, and then a series of chambers, the *beniqas* of the ministers, opening onto it. Right at the foot, opening on a balcony, is the Koubbet en-Nasr, the pavilion of victory, in which the Sovereign's study is enclosed, with a direct access from his palace by an interior corridor. In this single court meet together all the ministerial departments, which deal with the affairs of the entire kingdom.

Up to a recent date, a Vizier and several secretaries were sufficient to handle all this political mechanism. Under the reign of Mulai Abderrahman, they were seven in all. But in these later times, questions have become more complicated, and the *makhzeniya* has developed enormously. It now comprises a veritable Ministry consisting of some eighty secretaries. The chief Ministers are now called Viziers by courtesy – for, in reality, the only one of them who has a right to the title is the Grand Vizier, the Ouzir, Minister of the Interior. Theoretically, this functionary is the real head of the Government, the statesman on whom devolves the formidable duty of fomenting the tribal jealousies in order to secure the supremacy of the Makhzen. The Ouzir becomes, in this way, the Prime Minister of the Moroccan Government. On him depend both the Kaïds and the Kadis – that is, the organisation of the tribes, and the services arising from the religious law. Correspondence with the Sultan is made through him, and, thanks to his position as negotiator with the tribes, he is qualified to unite in his hands the whole internal policy of Morocco.

By the side of the Ouzir's immense powers, other Ministers could only be, in the past, unimportant functionaries. External policy is in the hands of the Ouzir el-Bahr (the Minister of the Sea), so named because he deals with affairs from without, that is to say – except on the Algerian frontier – from beyond the sea. It is he who secures the relations of Morocco with the powers, and corresponds with the Kaïds on questions relative to interests abroad. As the diplomatic corps resides at Tangier, far from the Makhzen, contact is established through the medium of a Naïb es-Sultan, resident in that city, who becomes, for the occasion, the Khalifa of the Minister of Foreign Affairs. The Allef (the payer) fulfils the duties of Minister of War. Originally he was only the agent, charged with the pay and upkeep of the troops. He had gradually taken the Sultan's place as real head of the army.

The Amin el-Oumana is the head of the body of the Oumana, who are chosen from the families of wealthy merchants and entrusted throughout the country with the regulation of economic conditions, for it is thought that they would have both more experience in the fulfilment of their duties, and sufficient means to guarantee the purity of their administration. The Amin el-Oumana has the whole financial service in his hands, and is thus the Minister of Finance. Formerly he lived permanently at Fez, despite the wanderings of the Makhzen. But when the house of the Amin el-Oumana, then in office, was pillaged by the populace at Fez, after the accession of Moulay el-Hassan, that Sovereign realised the necessity of assuring, at all times, the immediate protection of the Makhzen to his Minister of Finance, and, since then, this official has been requested to follow the movements of the Court. At the side of the Amin el-Oumana figure three high officials whose *beniqas* are offices that are, in a way, connected with the Department of Finance. One, the Amin ed-Dekhel (Amin of the Income), collects the revenue, and deposits it in the Treasury; the second, the Amin ech-Chkara (Amin of the Expenditure), draws from the same Treasury to settle the debts of the Makhzen; the last, the Amin el-Hsab (Amin of the Accounts), checks the accounts transmitted to the Makhzen and the Oumana in office throughout the Empire, and fulfils the function of Audit Office.

The Ouzir, the Ouzir el-Bahr, the Allef, and the Amin el-Oumana, are the four chief Viziers whose authority dominates the counsels of the Government. There exists, however, another functionary, dowered with a special *beniqa*, who may be looked upon as the Minister of Justice – the Ouzir ech-Shikayat, the Minister of Claims. All claims addressed to the Makhzen by the Kaïds or the tribes reach this official, who distributes them among the departments competent to deal with them, submitting them, it may be to the Chraa, it may be to the

Sultan, it may be to the *beniqa* of the Minister concerned. The plaintiffs, who throng the Dar el-Makhzen at the hours of *makhzeniya*, have access to this Minister, who has been created for the express purpose of hearing their grievances.

Although the function of the Hagib, who is head of the household services of the palace, is a Court rather than a State office, the Chamberlain is none the less possessed of a *beniqa*, in which he regulates the expenses of the Court. He is, under this head, the Minister of the Imperial Household, and, as his duties bring him into constant contact with the Sultan, he often takes upon himself to intervene officiously with the Sovereign, and bring requests before him. The Kaïd el-Mechouar, head of the External Services of the palace, possesses no *beniqa* of his own, but is nevertheless regarded as one of the great Makhzen officials. On solemn occasions he performs the duties of Master of Ceremonies. It is he who puts the correspondence addressed to the Sovereign into the proper hands, and introduces the Kaïds who have obtained the favour of an audience. He, too, has the task of arresting them when they have incurred the Shereefian displeasure.

Each of the nine *beniqas* that open on the inner Court of the Dar el-Makhzen represents a Ministerial Department. They are great apartments, completely bare, with mats and carpets spread on the ground. Viziers and secretaries enter them with their felt hats folded beneath their arm, and squat down at the accustomed spot. On the ground, in front of the Minister, is a little desk, containing an inkstand, pens, and paper. The secretaries, less favoured, have to take all the necessary articles from their own chkara. There is no table, and every one uses his hand instead. The only large piece of furniture in the *beniqa* is a set of drawers, sacred to the archives, where the secretary of the archives piles up the documents to be used for the copy of the minutes and the letters received, which are arranged in little bundles, enveloped in white flowered material. The Vizier has his seat in the centre of the farther end of the chamber. The secretaries sit in lines on his right and his left in accordance with a strict hierarchy, in obedience to which they move up from left to right, as vacancies arise. The two first secretaries, on the left and right, are the most important officials of the Department. In the *beniqa* of the Grand Vizier, they are the directors of the South and of the North, the one on the right dealing with the affairs of the Haouz, the one on the left with those of the Gharb. The work of the other secretaries is not determinate. They are employed, according to their aptitudes, in this or that department of the clerical work of the Administration. One is charged with calling out the *harkas*, whilst another is better at announcing victories and publishing the number of heads cut off. A third finds it easy to write 'thank you', whilst a fourth has a keen pen for abuse. And so each is commissioned to draw up the documents which are best suited to his manner. In this way the official correspondence of the *beniqa* is carried on. If it contains orders to be executed, it must receive the imperial signature. The special correspondence, in which the Minister furnishes the Kaïds with instructions or information, is entrusted to three or four secretaries, who squat in front of the great man. They are termed the 'secretaries who sit opposite,' and are, in reality, the Cabinet of the Vizier.

Each *beniqa* is continually visited by people who have business with it. It is customary for the Kaïds of the tribes to frequent the Dar el-Makhzen, when they are present at Court. They take advantage of it to settle the affairs of their district with the Department competent to deal with them, or else they establish themselves in the *beniqa* of a Vizier who is their friend. If not, they wait, humbly seated near the door, on one of these straw sacks in use in Moroccan houses, and called *fertalas*. Petitioners come and lay siege to the Minister of Claims. The Kaïds er-Raha visit the Allef to settle with him all that concerns their troops. So there is always, at the hours of the *makhzeniya*, an immense amount of movement in the special court which is devoted to the Government of Morocco.

Each *beniqa* employs a greater or less number of secretaries, according to its importance. It is naturally the Grand Vizier who has the largest number, for his correspondence is voluminous, and he has to be constantly despatching confidental agents on missions to settle all delicate matters in the provinces. His staff contains not less than thirty individuals. The *beniqa* of the Amin el-Oumana is also well staffed. The Allef has some ten secretaries, and the Minister for Foreign Affairs a slightly smaller staff. Each Minister has the right to make suggestions in his own *beniqa*, and chooses his men, subject to the Sultan's approval. He is free to take what he wishes, where he can get it, from the best known *tolba* of Karaouiyin (the University students of Fez), or from the youths who have distinguished themselves as secretaries in the employ of some Governor. As a matter of fact, the Viziers show a very marked tendency to prefer those candidates whose fathers were in the service before them. Further, the great proportion of the secretaries are people of Fez, more rarely of Marrakech, Rabat, or Tetouan. The tribes supply only a favoured individual here and there, such as the present second secretary of the Grand Vizier, Si el-Arbi el-Hasnaoui, who is one of the Beni-Hasen. Among the Fasis, who overrun the different *beniqas* at the present time, one can find two secretaries who are of Algerian origin – from Mascara – one with the Grand Vizier, the other with the Minister for Foreign Affairs.

Tradition demands that the Hagib shall be the first to arrive at the Dar el-Makhzen to engage with the Sovereign in the morning prayer. As soon as the Sultan has taken his place in the Koubbet en-Nasr to attend to State business, the *moualin el-oudhou* (men of the bath) line up in front of him ready to obey their master's requests, and a *fraigui* (bodyguard) goes off to announce the Shereef's presence in every *beniqa*; for the Viziers are not allowed to solicit an audience, but must await the Imperial summons. If the Sultan wishes to talk with one of his Ministers, he confines himself to pronouncing the baptismal name of the man he wants to see, and a *moul el-oudhou* hastens off to fetch him. The Vizier discusses his affairs with the Sultan, answers his questions, and entrusts to him the letters drawn up in his *beniqa*. The Sultan reads the correspondence carefully, and to indicate his assent makes a round pencil mark at the end of the last line. After that, the missive may be stamped by the Hagib with the Imperial Seal and despatched to its destination.

Formerly the *makhzeniya* was under very strict regulations. Moulay el-Hassan had an instinct for authority. He took an active interest in the business, and aimed at directing it himself, and controlling the actions of his Viziers. Each of them had to stay in his place without the power to encroach on his neighbour's domain. The Grand Vizier was the actual Prime Minister, and it was but rarely that the position was not occupied by one whose voice was predominant in the Councils of the State. Moulay el-Hassan had friends, but no favourites. He was content with the society of his Hagibs, who are a Sultan's natural confidants, and if the ties of affection which bound him to Si Ali el-Mesfioui, his Vizier of Claims, were notorious, yet the wisdom and the rectitude of the latter were such that the severest censors found nothing to say against so legitimate an influence.

The hours of work were clearly defined at the Dar el-Makhzen. Viziers and secretaries had to be there from six to ten o'clock in the morning, and from three to sunset. They were free only on Thursday, on Friday morning, and during the three great religious festivals. Each day, without exception, all the Ministers were summoned by the Sultan, in a regular rotation, beginning with the Hagib and the Grand

Vizier. The Minister of War and the Amin of the Expenditure were received last, in the afternoon.

Stories of bribery in the government.
From Isabel Savory, *In the Tail of the Peacock*, 1903, pp. 149–51.

The Government of Morocco has but one hinge – a golden one. Thirty thousand pounds was paid by the late governor of Marocco City for his billet, and a capable man would still make his fortune before he retired by means of bribes and presents from every one in connection with him, and a little undue pressure and taxation here and there. But no governor is exempt from that war-cry in Morocco, 'Pay! Pay! Pay!'. And if he or a basha wish for the sultan's favour, which in order to remain in office is most desirable, he will forward a present regularly to the court, though at every feast he is obliged to send another in addition.

Tetuan had a favourite tale of bribery. A man wanted to make sure of a case he was bringing before the basha. He knew that the basha had a weakness for mirrors. He was a poor man, but he bought the best looking-glass he could afford, and dispatched it. The case came on; the basha gave against him.

'What!', cried the poor, discomfited loser; 'did you not receive the mirror?'

'Yes', replied the basha coolly; 'but immediately afterwards a very fine mule came along, and *he kicked the looking-glass into a thousand fragments*'.

So when a man is disappointed of his due, they say, 'The mule has kicked the glass'.

Another man had a brother in prison whom he wished to buy out: he took the basha a mule, and presented himself with his present.

'You shall not bribe me', said the basha. 'Soldier! put this man into prison with his brother, and put the mule into my stable'.

A meeting with the Glaoui.
Gordon West, *By Bus to the Sahara*, n.d., pp. 211–15.

Today we are invited to meet Haj Thami El Glaoui, paramount Pasha of Marrakesh, and one of the Grand Caids of the Atlas. He is a man of whom the people in the south speak almost with bated breath, so fabulous are his riches, so great his power. Men who delight in political machinations envy him his skill in such matters, for it has raised him to a position which gives him an influence greater than that of the Sultan. Those who delight in the pleasures of love, envy him his harem, in which it is said there are two hundred women or more. One of his wives, now dead, came to him through a game of cards. He was playing with a Turkish pasha, and the stakes ran so high and his opponent lost so heavily that at last he put up his latest and loveliest Circassian bride in a final effort to retrieve his lost fortune. The Glaoui won her; but with a fine gesture he waived his claim, to the gratification of his rival. He had not reckoned with the lady who had been the trophy. She was a woman of high principles, and insisted that the debt be honoured.

El Glaoui owns five great palaces in Marrakesh. His domains extend far beyond the Atlas mountains into the south. He owns a gold mine, but has not bothered to develop it. The great pass through which we travelled belongs to him, and by the skilful use of a few hundred men of his private army of ten thousand he can cut off the Sahara from the north and disorganise the whole of Morocco. In this pass, dominated by the great *kasbah* of Telouet, with its dungeons where men can live and die forgotten, rules his son, to whom the Glaoui has delegated many of his privileges and powers.

The French, who call this Pasha the Black Panther, pay great respect for his power and much money into his coffers, for he keeps the peace among the tribes of the south and so liberates many troops who would otherwise be needed for the task. A word from the Glaoui, and the tribes would be in revolt. It was chiefly with his aid that France was able to hold Morocco during the war. His father before him was of little account; he is said to have been a mere trader in salt. His mother was a black slave. Today the son is a feudal chief who lives like Haroun al Rashid, yet has brokers to do his business on the Stock Exchanges of Paris, London and New York.

The Glaoui advances to meet us and takes our hands. He is a tall man, six feet or more and slim. He is perhaps fifty years of age. He wears the graceful robes of his race, with a transparent muslin slip over a pale blue undergarment. He has a dark skin, a tuft of beard, full lips, and heavy-lidded eyes that shine brilliantly as he talks in a quiet restrained voice. His manner is courtly and strangely gentle for a man who has been a savage fighter and bears the scars of sixteen wounds on his seemingly frail body.

Though he is so pleasant a host, he is unfathomable. He is knowledgeable, he talks with quiet fluency on many subjects in that soft musical voice of his; he tells a story, laughs restrainedly with a genuine humour that shines in his deep-set eyes; yet there is an air of aloofness about him. He gives the impression that his thoughts do not coincide with his words. When his face is in repose it has a passive, almost sorrowful expression, as though he were brooding on the tragedies of the world. It is hard to realise that this man with the delicate movements and gestures is a great warrior; but it is easy to see in him a subtle diplomat, a dangerous enemy and a merciless overlord.

Every year now he pays a visit to London. He likes to play golf at Coombe Hill, and has his own golf course outside Marrakesh, where he would be happy to see us. He likes to go shopping in Oxford Street and thinks Hyde Park and Kensington Gardens pleasant places worthy of a great capital. He may also revisit Brighton, which he thinks one of the most graceful towns in the world.

The Glaoui had a genius for creating legends about himself, which convinced even Winston Churchill and were swallowed whole by visiting writers, who, however obscure, were lavishly entertained. Much of his power after the First World War came from the total support of the French which was maintained by exploiting the myth of his indispensability and by wholesale corruption of politicians and even senior officials. Much of his wealth came from monopolies of hashish and prostitution (there were said to be 27,000 public women in Marrakesh who paid him a percentage), misappropriation of mining rights, forced labour and forgery. Acting as the agent of the French, in 1953 he organized tribal unrest which gave them the pretext for exiling the Sultan Muhammad V (whom they were bound by treaty to support). This caused such opposition that even the ruthless henchmen that he had placed over the tribes told the Glaoui that they could not control it. He therefore was reduced to crawling on his hands and knees to Muhammad who granted him forgiveness.

The next few extracts detail punishments formerly imposed for various crimes.

From the Rev. Lancelot Addison, *An Account of West Barbary*, 1671, printed in Pinkerton, vol. XV, pp. 426–7.

In the Moresco catalogue of crimes, adultery and fornication are found in the first comma, whose difference in the Moors' opinion may be collected from their penalties. For adultery, it is always capital, insomuch that without regard of any eminence or quality, the convict thereof is certainly stoned to death, which is done with most notorious circumstances. For first the day of execution is published, then the criminal is brought to the Calvary, where buried up to the navel in a pit digged for that purpose, every one present casts one stone, and no more at him, saying, this is for thy filthy transgression of the law; but if the adulterous be persons of condition, their friends have licence to dispatch them privily, to prevent the open reproach to their family.

In the punishing of fornication they are less rigorous, as finding the mischief thereof not to be of so large a derivation, as that of adultery. And if the persons convicted of this unchastity are in the state of celibate, they are only chastised with scourges; but if either be married, or under matrimonial contract, death is the certain penance. But the Moors are no less solemn in whipping the fornicator, than in stoning the adulterer. For on Friday, after the arch priest has ended his lecture, the offender, if a man, is placed at the great door of the giamma gueber, or cathedral church, naked down the back, and in the presence of the congregation receives an hundred stripes on his back from an officer appointed for that purpose, who has a certain number of blankeles (or Moresco twopences) for his service; the Moors as they pass by the chastised, use these deprecatory words, *Allah Iffecni min had El ham* i.e. God deliver me from this wicked fellow. The woman who has been partner in the filthiness, suffers the punishment in the night, when she is whipt through the streets, but with more severity than the man, because the Moors suppose the female to be of a predominant allurement in such unclean commixtures.

The Moors who live in a roving condition are much addicted to thievery, against which the alcaddee proceeds by these steps of punishment: for the first theft the convict is publicly whipt in the alsouck or market; for the second, he loseth his hand; for the third theft he may truly be said to die without mercy. For the Moors observe Caligula's severity in making the offender exquisitely sensible of his death, which they inflict. Against the day of the thief's execution, the youth of the place are advertised to prepare their instruments of blood, which are little dry canes, made in the fashion of darts, accurately sharp pointed, these they hurl at the naked body of the malefactor, till his whole skin be struck therewith full of holes, and when they find him sinking under the torture, they drag and hang him up by the heels upon a gate, or the like, where he breathes out his last in torments, and being dead he is loathsomely exposed to the birds of prey.

This extract has been translated and abridged by the editors. From Dr Mauran, *La Société marocaine*, 1912, pp. 229–33.

Some women who were washing wool happened to spot, stuck on the rocks, a shapeless bundle. They went to have a look but, having pulled off some old rags, they recoiled, white with fear, as they saw chunks of still bleeding flesh. They ran to the Pasha and a few moments later a crowd of soldiers and townsfolk were able to identify the body of a fourteen-year-old boy. He was a young Sharif, known to have been the friend of a shoemaker of the town, who, dragged before the Pasha, admitted that, while drunk the previous evening, he had strangled the victim. Then, terrified of the consequences and not knowing what to do with the body, he had cut it up, bundled it into a sack, hid it in a corner of his shop until early the following morning when he had thrown it into the sea.

The Pasha condemned him to be handed over to the crowd.

This is the story that my servant told me while I was dressing, woken early by a strange and growing murmur. I hesitated to go and watch 'the process of justice' when I heard a howling storm outside my windows. I ran down the stairs, four at a time, pushed by I do not know what unhealthy curiosity, in time to see a human swell come surging down my street.

At first I could see nothing but a forest of arms, each hand grasping a slipper. Slowly I could see more details: all the shaven heads, running with sweat in the hot sun, all the faces, black, bronzed and white, the cruel eyes, the mouths distorted by the cries of wild beasts or savage laughter showing the sharp teeth of a jackal after its prey: this crowd crazed and roaring around the miserable, impassive shoemaker, already half-dead and walking at a slow, automatic pace, dragged along by two soldiers. It seemed like a terrible nightmare. What added to the horror of the spectacle was the evident refinement of cruelty as the crowd struck, not to kill, but to prolong the agony, for every morning, as long as he had breath in his body, the wretch had to re-emerge from prison and endure for another two hours this march towards his death.

But a large red spot, always growing, appeared on his head and drops of blood snaked down his neck and shoulders despite the efforts of the soldiers to discourage a killing blow.

I have to admit that the following day I had not the courage to attend the 'repeat performance' but I was told, with graphic detail, how, when he could walk no further, he was hoisted on to a donkey and the grizzly promenade continued. Half way along the route he fell to the ground, and the mob, implacable and unwearied, continued to beat this human rag, showing no pity until he breathed his last.

From Arthur Leared, *Marocco and the Moors*, 1891, pp. 244–5.

Certain laws are well defined and vigourously enforced. One of these is the *lex talionis*, that which extracts an eye for an eye, a tooth for a tooth, a life for a life, unless the bodily injury to the person, or his death, is expiated by the payment of a fine to the nearest of kin. Instances have occurred in which Europeans have become involved in the action of this law. Many years ago, Mr. Leyton, an English merchant residing in Mogador, was accused by an old mendicant of having knocked out two of her teeth by striking her with his whip while out riding. Although she was known to be toothless, her complaint made so much noise in the town that the governor before whom it was brought was obliged to report it to the reigning Sultan, for Mr. Leyton steadily refused to pay any compensation. In consequence of this, the Sultan, by the hand of one of his ministers, wrote and requested him to yield; but not succeeding, the merchant was summoned to Marrakesh. Mr. Leyton obeyed, but on arriving there he still obstinately refused to pay any fine. Thereupon popular clamour increased to such a degree that, as a matter of state policy, a penalty had to be enforced, and Mr. Leyton submitted to the extraction of two of his teeth. But the injustice of his case was tacitly acknowledged, for on his return to Mogador he was, by order of the Sultan, presented with two shiploads of grain.

The administration of justice in a tribal area.
From Robert Kerr, *Morocco . . .*, 1912, pp. 64–6.

Annually several tribes meet and join hands, when they elect a representative called the Sheikh Er-Rabea (Captain of the Grass Season), who is given absolute power in the control of the affairs in the various districts, which often cover an area of from thirty to forty square miles.

He informs himself of all who are able to purchase a horse and repeating rifle for the safety of the tribe, and issues orders accordingly; and all who fail to comply must either flee the tribe or submit to their animals being impounded and sold.

Whenever the sheikh is informed of someone guilty of a

misdemeanour he will suddenly appear the following morning and ask the shepherd to point out the cattle belonging to so-and-so, and according to the offence one or more animals will be hamstrung. The sheikh and his officers will take what they desire, and leave the rest to the villagers, who enjoy the fun immensely. The victim has to grin and bear it with as good grace as possible, as there is no redress or court of appeal. The sheikh, as a rule, keeps admirable order, much more respect being shown to him than to the Sultan.

Some years ago, in the tribe of Amar, a poor widowed Arab woman went to the Sheikh Er-Rabea accusing some young men in another village of stealing her cows and thereafter selling them in Zimoor, and implored his help. 'Go home, my daughter', said the sheikh; 'God will restore you better cows than those stolen'. Calling on one of his officers, he ordered him to saddle his horse and proceed with all haste to the village in question and order the thieves to return the cows in three days, which he knew was impossible. On the morning of the fourth day the sheikh started off for the village with his officers, who are never more than three or four mounted men. On his arrival he hamstrung two of the fattest of the offenders' cattle, and then ordered the sheikh of the village to procure him at once two of the finest milk cows with their calves from the village herd, at the same time calling out, 'Do you wish the widow and orphans to cry for vengeance against you at the judgement day?' to make the scene more dramatic.

The animals were immediately forthcoming, and the sheikh marched off with them to gladden the poor widow's heart. Instead of being displeased at the arbitrary manner in which he administered the law, he was applauded by the whole village.

Tribal responsibility is one of the surest safe-guards in a semi-civilised country like Morocco for the preservation of order. Its adoption at home in some districts, I believe would have beneficial results. In fact, the County Councils in Ireland have had to resort to similar measures in levying payment in cases of *cattle raiding*. So, after all, the Moors are not so far behind as is frequently represented.

From Dr John Buffa, *Travels . . .*, 1810, p. 178.

I was called upon to attend a man who had had his arm and leg amputated; he soon recovered, and, to my great surprise, instead of sorrowing for his loss, he skipped about as nimbly as possible, and afterwards enlisted in the police. After the fellow was turned away yesterday, a peasant, who had walked nearly two hundred miles, presented himself before the Emperor, to complain of the Governor of his province, for not having done him justice in assisting him to recover a debt of about six shillings. The Emperor listened to his grievance, issued an order to enforce the payment of the debt, and gave the poor man a sum of money to enable him to return home.

Collecting taxes.
From Lord Edward Gleichen, *A Guardsman's Memories*, 1932, pp. 127–8.

A few months before we arrived at Larache the then Basha had set out to chastise a certain hill tribe, the Helserif, who had refused to pay the outrageous and impossible taxes demanded from them. By the simple expedient of retreating into their hills in front of the Basha's troops and then cutting off their retreat, the rebels had succeeded in killing half the enemy and capturing the Basha, and him they roasted alive in a pit lined with white-hot stones. This sort of thing was not at all uncommon throughout the country; indeed, under the Sherifian system of government something of the sort was inevitable. For the immemorial system of raising money wherewith to pay the Sultan's troops and administer the country was put up to auction the Governorships of the various provinces. The Bashas used to give sometimes colossal sums – say, thirty to fifty thousand pounds apiece for this privilege; and then they proceeded to recoup themselves – with something over – from their unhappy subjects. No man was safe from spoliation – nor was there any incentive to progress. For directly a man made a little money – by hard work, agriculture or other means – he was denounced and his money taken from him; and bribery, corruption and crime were consequently rampant.

Here Marshal Hubert Lyautey set out his principles for ruling Morocco in a speech of February 1916 which has been translated and abridged by the editors.
From Marshal Hubert Lyautey, *Paroles d'action*, 1927, pp. 172–4.

If Algeria is a 'colony', Morocco is a 'protectorate' and this is not merely a question of a label. When France arrived in Algeria there was only a dust-heap, chaos, in which the only power, held by a Turkish Dey, had crumbled at our approach whereas in Morocco, on the other hand, we were confronted by an historic and independent Empire, rightly jealous of its independence, resistance to subjugation, which until the last few years had the organisation of a state, with a hierarchy of officials, representation abroad, and a society which, despite the recent weakness of central authority, still exists. Remember that there are still in Morocco men who, only six years ago, were the Ambassadors of an independent Morocco in Petersburg, in London, in Berlin, in Madrid, in Paris, men of a wide culture who were treated as equals with European statesmen, men with a gift and a feeling for political life: there is nothing like that in Algeria or Tunisia.

Alongside this political cadre, there existed also a religious establishment, by no means negligible. The Present Minister of Justice has been a Professor of Muslim Law in Cairo, in Stamboul and in Damascus; he is a man who corresponds with scholars as far away as India and he is not the only Moroccan who has links with the élite of the Islamic world.

There are businessmen of the first rank, great merchants with interests in Hamburg, in Manchester and Marseilles – cities they themselves know well.

We found ourselves, therefore, in the presence of an élite, political, religious and economic, which it would have been foolish to ignore, to despise and not to use – associating it closely with the work that we are trying to do because it can do much to help. Add – and all of you who know Morocco know this well – there is a people industrious, hard-working, intelligent, looking for progress provided that it sees the things that it respects, scrupulously respected by us. This country fulfils all the conditions for the greatest, the best of all tasks, that of co-operation with the local people for their progress. It is absolutely necessary to set aside all prejudice and insensitive behaviour, symbolised by the expression 'sale bicot' [*dirty wog*], applied wholesale to all Moroccans, an expression so profoundly shocking and dangerous because those to whom it is addressed realise only too well that it implies a contempt and a menace which leaves a bitterness that nothing will efface.

There is no land more suited for the regime of a protectorate, not a temporary but a long-lasting regime, of which the essential is the association and close co-operation of the protected and protector peoples in mutual respect, in the scrupulous safeguard of the best of local traditions. No regime better enables us to use native talents and to develop them. To decree annexation, to turn the country into a colony, would mean the immediate and automatic application of French laws and that French administration with its immutable strait-jacket, its heavy fetters would land with all its weight on this unfortunate country. It would be French laws, so unsuitable for habits, customs and institutions such as ours that would apply here. I can assure you that there is nothing less like the *arrondissements* of Guingamp or Trevoux than Fez or Marrakesh. Oh, let us congratulate ourselves that it is the concept of a protectorate that has prevailed in Morocco, and let us guard it jealously.

6
The Imperial Cities

The four cities, Fez, Marrakesh, Meknes and Rabat, which have served as the capitals of the country, are known as the Imperial Cities. At a time when almost all visitors to Morocco were there on official missions to its rulers they were naturally the ones that most people saw, for they often had to remain many weeks conducting their business. There are therefore many more descriptions of them than of other places, with the possible exception of Tangier. They all bear the marks of the French policy of leaving the old cities mainly intact within their walls while building new cities alongside them. Parts of the centres of the Imperial Cities have therefore changed little since their foundation. Fez, the oldest, dating from the ninth century, still has many of the features described by Leo in the sixteenth century, particularly in the area of the suqs. It is still remarkable for the storks described by Ali Bey at the beginning of the nineteenth. Fez is the site of the Karaouiyin, the oldest university in the world after that of Al Azhar in Cairo and one in which a mediaeval pope once studied. Scholars from the Karaouiyin founded the University of Salamanca from which learning passed to Bologna, to Paris and then to Oxford. Like Oxford and Cambridge it consists of individual colleges, the *medersas*, like the one described by Horne. Marrakesh for most people means the unchanging Kutubia tower, similar to those in Rabat and Seville, and the equally unchanging Jamaa al Fnaa, of both of which we have accounts. In the past it was often referred to as Marocco City or even simply as Marocco which can cause some confusion for readers today. Meknes evokes Mulai Ismail and his mighty buildings, some crumbling now they are three centuries old. Rabat, once the capital of an independent republic of corsairs and since the start of the French Protectorate the capital of the country, provides an astonishing example of an old city and a new city divided by a wall. Sale, across the River Bu Ragrag, was mainly known for its pirates but is a fine city in its own right. Nearby Shellah is evocatively described by Tranchant de Lunel who, under Marshal Lyautey, was the main executive in preserving the best ancient Moroccan buildings.

A seventeenth-century account of the city and people of Fez. From William Lithgow, *Rare Adventures and Painful Peregrinations* . . ., 1614, pp. 322–5.

The streetes being covered above, twixt these plaine-set Fabrickes, have large Lights cut through the tectur'd tops every where; in whose lower shoppes or Roomes are infinite Merchandize, and Ware of all sorts to bee sold.

The people of both kindes are cloathed in long breeches and bare Ancles, with red or yellow shooes shod with Iron on the Heeles, and on the Toes with white Horne; and weare on their bodies long Robes of Linning or Dimmety, and silken Wast-coates of diverse Colours: The behaviour of the Vulgars being far more civill toward Strangers than at Constantinople; or else where in all Turkey.

The Women here go unmasked abroad, wearing on their heads, broad, and round Capes, made of Straw or small Reedes, to shade their faces from the Sunne; and damnable Libidinous, beeing prepared both wayes to satisfie the lust of their Luxurious Villaines; neyther are they so strictly kept as the Turkish Women, marching where they please.

There are some twelve thousand allowed Brothell-houses in this Towne, the Courtezans being neatly kept, and weekely well looked to by Physitians; but worst of all, in the Summer time, they openly Lycentiat three thousand common Stewes of Sodomiticall boyes: Nay I have seene at mid-day, in the very Market places, the Moores buggering these filthy Carrions, and without shame or punishment go freely away.

There are severall Seates of Justice heere (though none to vindicate beastlinesse) occupied by Cadeis and Sanzackes, which twice a Weeke heare all differences and complaints: their chiefe Seriff, or Vicegerent, being sent from Morocco, is returned hither agayne every third yeare.

The two Hills on both sides the planur'd Citty, East, and West, are over-cled with streetes and Houses of two stories high, beeing beautified also with delicate Gardens, and on their extreame devalling parts, with numbers of Mosquees and Watch-towers: On which heights, and round about the Towne, there stand some three hundred Wind-mils; most part whereof pertayne to the Mosques, and the two magnifick Colledges erected for education of Children, in the Mahometanicall Law,

One of which Accademies, cost the King Habahennor in building of it, foure hundred and three score thousand Duckets. Jacob sonne to Abdulach the first King of the Families of Meennons, divided Fez in three parts, and with three severall Walles, though now invironed with onely one, and that broken downe in sundry parts.

The chiefest Mosque in it, is called Mammo-Currarad, signifying the glory of Mahomet, being an Italian mile in Compasse, and beautified with seventeene high ground Steeples, besides Turrets and Towers: having thirty foure entring Doores; beeing supported within, and by the length, with forty eight pillars, and some twenty three Ranges of pillars in breadth, besides many Iles, Quires, and circulary Rotundoes: Every Pillar having a Lampe of Oyle burning thereat; where there, and through the whole Mosque, there are every night nine hundred Lamps lighted; and to maintaine them, and a hundred Totsecks and preaching Talsumans, the rent of it extendeth to two hundred Duccats a day: Neverthelesse there are in the City besides it, more then foure hundred and threescore Mosquees; fifty whereof are well benefited and superbiously decored within and without, with glorious and extraordinary workmanship, whose rooffes within are all Mosaick worke, and curiously indented with Gold, and the walles and pillars being of grey Marble, interlarded with white Alabaster, and so is the chiefe Mosque too in which Monsieur Chatteline and I had three sundry recourses accompanied with our Moorish hoste, who from their Priests had procured that licence for us. This City aboundeth in all manner of provision fit for man or beast, & is the goodliest place of all North Affrick, contayning a hundred and twenty thousand fire-houses, and in them a million of soules: Truely this is a world for a City, and may rather second Grand Caire, than subjoyne it selfe to Constantinople, being farre superior in greatnesse with Aleppo: For these are the foure greatest Cities, that ever I saw in the world, either at home or abroad.

The Cittizens here are very modest and zealous at their divine services, but great dauncers and revellers on their solemne festivall dayes, wherein they have Bull-beating, Maskerats, singing of rimes, and processions of Priests. The Moores in times past of Fez and Morocco, had divers excellent personages, well learned, and very civill; for amongst the Kings Mahometan one can not praise too much the Kings Almansor, Maunon, and Hucceph, being most excellent men in their superstition.

In whose times flourished the most famous medicines, and Philosophers that were among the Pagans, as A Vicenne, Rasis, Albumazar, Averroes, &c. with other great numbers maintained by the Kings of Morocco, that then were Masters of all Barbary and Spaine: As in Spaine may be seene yet, (though now fallen in decay) a great number of their Colledges, shewing they were great lovers of their Religion and Doctrine, and are so to this day, save onely in their drinking of Wine forbidden by their Alcoran. They were great devisers too of gallant sportings, exercises, turnaments, and Bull-beating, which Spayne retaineth to this time; yea, and the Romanes did learne, and follow many of them.

Here in Fez there be a great number of Poets, that make Songs on divers subjects, especially of Love, and Lovers, whom they openly name in their rimes, without rebuke or shame: All which Poets once every yeare, agane Mahomets birth-day, make rimes to his praise; meanewhile in the after noone of that festivall day, the whole Poets assembling in the market place, there is a Dasked chayre prepared for them, whereon they mount one after another to recite their verses in audience of all the people; and who by them is judged to be best, is esteemed all that yeare above the rest, having this Epithite the Prince of Poets, and is by the Vicegerent and Towne rewarded; But in the time of the Maennon Kings, the Prince on that day in his owne Pallace did conveine the whole Cittizens, in whose presence he made a solemne feast to all the best Poets; causing every one of them to recite the praise of Mahomet before his face, standing on a high scaffold: And to him that was thought to excell the rest, the King gave him 100. Sultans of gold, an horse, a woman slave, & the long Robe that was about him for the time: And to each one of the rest he caused give fifty Sultans, so that every one should have some recompense for their paines: Indeed a worthy observance; and would to God it were now the custome of our Europian Princes to doe the like, and especially of this Ile, then would bravest wits, and quickest braines, studdy and strive to show the exquisit ingeniosity of their best styles, and pregnant invention, which now is ecclipsed, and smotherd downe, because now a dayes, there is neither regard nor reward for such excellent Pen-men.

Leblanc was quite the most unreliable of travellers but should not be left out of any anthology. There were festivities in Fez for mid-summer and for the *Mawlud* (the Birthday of the Prophet) which must have led to his references to St John and Christmas.

From Vincent Leblanc, *Famous Voyages and Travailes . . .*, 1660, p. 290.

The houses for the great part are of brick, with Towres and Tarrasses, where the women prune themselves in the evening, for they seldom stirr abroad. There are *Mosquees* of fine building with *Marabouts* for their service; the Principall called *Cairimen* is of as large circumference as the Town of *Arles*, with 31 principall gates, sustained by 38 large Arches in length, and 20 in breadth, every night 900 lamps are lighted, and on festivall days, as in their *Romadan*, the feast of St John, the Nativity of our Lord, more Lamps without number upon brasse candlesticks, where after Mid-night they sing Mattens.

Some scenes from Fez.
From Ali Bey, *Travels*, 1816, vol. I, pp. 92–3.

The baths are all the day open to the public. The men go there in the morning, and the women in the evening. I went there generally at night and took the whole house to myself, in order to prevent interruption from strangers; some friend and two of my servants usually accompanied me. The first time I went there, I observed that pails full of hot water were placed with symmetry in the corners of every room and cabinet. I asked the reason of this. 'Do not touch them, sir', answered all the people belonging to the bath; 'do not touch them.' 'Why not?' 'These pails are for the people below'. 'Who are they?' 'The demons who come here to bathe themselves at night'. On this topic they told me many ridiculous stories. As I have this long while declared war against the devil and all his earthly vice-regents, I had the satisfaction of employing in my bath some of these pails of water, and of thus depriving these poor devils of their entertainment.

Fez has an hospital which is very richly endowed, and used only for the treatment of lunatics. It is very strange, that a great part of the funds to maintain this establishment has been bequeathed by the wills of various charitable testators for the express purpose of assisting and nursing sick cranes and storks, and of burying them when dead.

They believe that the storks are men from some distant islands, who at certain seasons of the year take the shape of birds to come here; that they return again at a certain time to their country, where they resume their human shape till the next season.

For this reason it would be considered as a crime to kill one of these birds. They tell thousands of ridiculous stories upon this occasion. Undoubtedly it is the utility of these animals, who are continually making war with the reptiles which abound so much in hot climates, which has occasioned the general respect and anxiety for their preservation. But the love of the marvellous here as elsewhere has substituted absurd fables for the actual truth.

The timeless character of Fez.
From Jerôme and Jean Tharaud, *Fes*, 1930, p. 22.

Much luxury, no innovation. In architecture, as in everything else, the Fassi follows tradition. Too lazy to conserve, too little gifted to invent, what he does today is exactly the same as what he did yesterday. In the cities of Europe, the variations of style bring constantly to our eyes the contrast of the past and the present, and remind us all the time of a way of life and of tastes that have ceased to exist. Nothing like that in Fez. Ideas that never change, indeed something resembling an instinct, mean that in Fez there is only one age and one style: that of yesterday. It is the site of a miracle – that of suppressing the passage of time. That has given this city a unique character – unique perhaps in the universe, certainly in the Mediterranean world.

John Horne was mainly interested in the architecture of Fez which he illustrated with superb photographs. This is his description of a *Medersa*, a place of residence for students at the University of the Karaouiyin.
From John Horne, *Many Days in Morocco*, 1932, pp. 60–62.

Through a small doorway leading from the *souk* one enters an irregularly shaped courtyard about thirty feet square, surrounded on three sides by buildings whose doors and windows pierce the walls in the most unexpected places, while, higher up, parts of the original cornice and green-tiled roof protrude from under a house which has been planted upon them. Mosaic of green and yellow and black covers the floor of the courtyard and the rim of its rectangular basin of clear water; and from a little patch of earth in a corner, a vine, perhaps as ancient as the medersa itself, has spread its branches over a rough wooden pergola, forming a crown of green and yellow that repeats the mosaic of the pavement and turns the water of the pool into a dancing mirror of colour. The archway of the chapel of the medersa occupies the fourth side of the courtyard. It is very simple, with only slight stucco decoration on the upper part; but above it are the remains of a projecting wooden roof, once covered with tiles, and very likely an early attempt at the superposed arcades to be found above many of the later gateways. A plain wooden screen with an opening in the centre fills the lower part of the archway, remnant perhaps of something more ornate, though it would seem that Es Seffarin never received much decoration. It had the simplicity and dignity of very early buildings. Completed about 1270 by Abou Youssef Yakoub El Mansour, it was not only the first medersa, but for a time possessed the only library in the capital. In the peace treaty concluded in 1274 with Don Sancho, King of Castille, the Emir stipulated that a large number of manuscripts which had fallen into the hands of the Christians at Seville and Cordova – exactly thirteen mule loads according to the *Roud El Qartas* – should be returned to the Moslems. The manuscripts duly reached Es Seffarin, but were eventually removed to the great mosque of El Karouiyin, and no medersa has since possessed a library.

If Es Seffarin is lacking in ornate decoration the same cannot be said of the next medersa I visited. The way to it lay through dark and narrow streets, filled with crowds of pale-faced Fasis whose glances grew more and more hostile as we approached our destination. But though the way was unpleasant the goal was worth it, for it was here that I stepped from the cold world of history into that fairyland of Moorish art where I was to pass so many interesting hours. The step was not taken without opposition on the part of the scent-makers of Fez, for as its name implies, El Attarin stands in the *souk* of perfumes and spices, whose people showed such open hostility that I was hard put to it to preserve a dignified or at least an indifferent attitude while Ibrahim explained my intentions to the authorities of the medersa. The enforced wait had one advantage. It gave me ample time to watch the crowd, and to remark upon the countenances of these Fasis the very combination of dignity and indifference which I was trying so hard to attain, with the addition – for my special benefit I suppose – of the most infinite scorn. I came to the conclusion that we Europeans have no idea how to look scornful: in fact, by over-cultivating a tolerance which kills expression, we are rapidly losing the power of *looking* anything in particular. The proof of this was all around me, and I was just beginning to enjoy an interesting lesson in physiognomy when Ibrahim returned triumphant. 'Come at once,' he said, and disappeared through a wonderful bronze-covered door on the opposite side of the street. I followed as quickly as possible, with, I fear, but little dignity and no scorn at all, and found myself in total darkness as the door closed behind me and was carefully barred and bolted. A moment later, with the scraping of ancient hinges, another door opened, and then I understood why I had been encouraged to photograph the medersas.

This description of Marrakesh was first published in 1573. From Luis de Marmol, *Descripcion general de Áffrica . . .*, (1667 edn), pp. 50–52.

It is a great city, the best situated in all Africa, in a fine plain, five or six leagues from the Atlas Mountains, surrounded by the richest countryside of all Mauritania. It was built by Abu Teshfin, the first king of the Almoravids, about the year 1050 according to Abdulmalic, the historian of Morocco. Some make it much older and attribute it to Abe Dramon, son of Moavia, who wanted it to outshine Buchafar, the Caliph of Arabia, who was in the course of building the city of Babylon. But Abdulmalic attributs it to the king that I have mentioned and its completion to his son Joseph, who gained great victories over the christians of Spain. He used for the task 30,000 slaves and made it his capital and one can still see, written in Arabic letters on alabaster tablets, on certain old buildings, that they were built in the reign of Joseph. The city of Marrakesh is enclosed in fine walls, made of lime and sand, mixed with earth which makes them so hard that if they are struck by a pick, they give forth a spark as does a flint. Though the town has been taken several times, its walls have never been breached which is a remarkable fact given their height. It is clear that this city is the work of great masters because the design is as good as is its execution. It has 24 gates and can contain 100,000 inhabitants.

I have seen a piece of alabaster, as tall as a man, on an ancient sepulchre outside the gate of Bibletobul which has these words in Arabic *Here lies Ali, son of Atia, who commanded a hundred thousand men, had 10,000 horses and had dug for them one hundred and one wells in a single day. I married three hundred women. I was faithful and victorious and one of twenty-four generals of Yakub Almansor. I ended my days at the age of forty. He who reads this epitaph, pray to God that He will pardon me.*

On the southern side there is a great and beautiful fortress, holding 4000 houses, and enclosed by fine walls with a ditch and a ravelin. There are only two gates, one on the south side facing open country and the other on the north side opening on to the city and is usually guarded to see that Christian slaves go out only with their escorts. The first entrance of the ravelin leads on to a little square where there are several shops and granaries where former kings stored their grain. The second gate leads to a straight road at the end of which is a great square where stands the Mosque of Abdulmumen, a building equally fine within and without.

Hugh Stutfield was one of many nineteenth-century writers who were struck by the differences between the capitals of northern and southern Morocco.
From Hugh Stutfield, *El Maghreb*, 1886, pp. 244–5.

The city [Marrakesh] is a great contrast to Fez, and though covering a greater extent of ground, it has little more than half the population. This in ordinary times is probably about 60,000, but when, as at present, the Sultan is there his court causes a considerable increase. There is an air of desolation about the place, as of a city of the past, which is very different from the bustle and stir of Fez, where trade is brisker and the citizens are richer and work harder. It is a more rambling place, dirtier and meaner in appearance. The streets are mostly narrow lanes, often half choked with muck-heaps and rotting carcases lying about; the houses are chiefly of one storey, with miserable entrances, and devoid of external ornamentation. There are no picturesque corners of remains of arabesque work such as are to be seen here and there in the northern city – all is bare, uncouth and unlovely. Dirt and decay are undoubtedly important articles in the picturesque – were they the sole ones Marrakesh would be the most picturesque city in the world – but after a while one wearies of the fearful squalor and wretchedness, the endless rags and dirt and poverty, the disease, deformity and delapidation that everywhere meets the eye. Many of the buildings are in ruins, and much of the space within the walls is taken up with waste ground, rubbish, and extensive gardens. Manuel told us we could get some shooting in the heart of the city if we liked.

Like all visitors, Edith Wharton was impressed by the bustle of the suqs of Marrakesh.
From Edith Wharton, *In Morocco*, 1927, pp. 110–14.

Passing out of the enchanted circle of the Bahia it is startling to plunge into the native life about its gates.

Marrakech is the great market of the south; and the south means not only the Atlas with its feudal chiefs and their wild clansmen, but all that lies beyond of heat and savagery: the Sahara of the veiled Touaregs, Dakka, Timbuctoo, Senegal and the Soudan. Here come the camel caravans from Demnat and Tameslout, from the Moulouya and the Souss, and those from the Atlantic ports and the confines of Algeria. The population of this old city of the southern march has always been even more mixed than that of the northerly Moroccan towns. It is made up of the descendants of all the peoples conquered by a long line of Sultans who brought their trains of captives across the sea from Moorish Spain and across the Sahara from Timbuctoo. Even in the highly cultivated region on the lower slopes of the Atlas there are groups of varied ethnic origin, the descendants of tribes transplanted by long-gone rulers and still preserving many of their original characteristics.

In the bazaars all these peoples meet and mingle: cattle-dealers, olive-growers, peasants from the Atlas, the Souss and the Draa, Blue Men of the Sahara, blacks from Senegal and the Soudan, coming in to trade with the wool-merchants, tanners, leather-merchants, silk-weavers, armourers, and makers of agricultural implements.

Dark, fierce and fanatical are these narrow *souks* of Marrakech. They are mere mud lanes roofed with rushes, as in South Tunisia and Timbuctoo, and the crowds swarming in them are so dense that it is hardly possible, at certain hours, to approach the tiny raised kennels where the merchants sit like idols among their wares. One feels at once that something more than the thought of bargaining – dear as this is to the African heart – animates these incessantly moving throngs. The *souks* of Marrakech seem, more than any others, the central organ of a native life that extends far beyond the city walls into secret clefts of the mountains and far-off oases where plots are hatched and holy wars fomented – farther still, to yellow deserts whence negroes are secretly brought across the Atlas to that inmost recess of the bazaar where the ancient traffic in flesh and blood still surreptitiously goes on.

All these many threads of the native life, woven of greed and lust, of fetishism and fear and blind hate of the stranger, form, in the *souks*, a thick network in which at times one's feet seem literally to stumble. Fanatics in sheepskins glowering from the guarded thresholds of the mosques, fierce tribesmen with inlaid arms in their belts and the fighters' tufts of wiry hair escaping from camel's-hair turbans, mad negroes standing stark naked in niches of the walls and pouring down Soudanese incantations upon the fascinated crowd, consumptive Jews with pathos and cunning in their large eyes and smiling lips, lusty slave-girls with earthen oil-jars resting against swaying hips, almond-eyed boys leading fat merchants by the hand, and bare-legged Berber women, tattooed and insolently gay, trading their striped blankets, or bags of dried roses and irises, for sugar, tea, or Manchester cottons – from all these hundreds of unknown and unknowable people, bound together by secret affinities, or intriguing against each other with secret hate, there emanated an atmosphere of mystery and menace more stifling than the smell of camels and spices and black bodies and smoking fry which hangs like a fog under the close roofing of the *souks*.

And suddenly one leaves the crowd and the turbid air for one of those quiet corners that are like the back-waters of the bazaars: a small square where a vine stretches across a shop-front and hangs ripe clusters of grapes through the reeds. In the patterning of grape-shadows a very old donkey, tethered to a stone-post, dozes under a pack-saddle that is never taken off; and near by, in a matted niche, sits a very old man in white. This is the chief of the Guild of 'morocco' Workers of Marrakech, the most accomplished craftsman in Morocco in the preparing and using of the skins to which the city gives its name. Of these sleek moroccos, cream-white or dyed with cochineal or pomegranate skins, are made the rich bags of the Chleuh dancing-boys, the embroidered slippers for the harem, the belts and harnesses that figure so largely in Moroccan trade – and of the finest, in old days, were made the pomegranate-red morocco bindings of European bibliophiles.

From this peaceful corner one passes into the barbaric splendour of a *souk* hung with innumerable plumy bunches of floss silk – skeins of citron yellow, crimson, grasshopper green and pure purple. This is the silk-spinners' quarter, and next to it comes that of the dyers, with great seething vats into which the raw silk is plunged, and ropes overhead where the rainbow masses are hung out to dry.

Another turn leads into the street of the metal-workers and armourers, where the sunlight through the thatch flames on round flanks of beaten copper or picks out the silver bosses of ornate powder-flasks and pistols; and near by is the *souk* of the ploughshares, crowded with peasants in rough Chleuh cloaks who are waiting to have their archaic ploughs repaired, and that of the smiths, in an outer lane of mud huts where negroes squat in the dust and sinewy naked figures in tattered loin cloths bend over blazing coals. And here ends the maze of the bazaars.

This is the first description for Europeans of the great tower of the Kutubia in Marrakesh with its four golden balls. In about 1700 Thomas Pellow tried to steal them.

From Leo Africanus, *Description of Africa*, 1550 (1896 edn), vol. II, pp. 263–4.

The staires of the said turret or steeple are each of them nine handfuls in bredth. The said turret hath seaven lofts, unto which the staires ascending are very lightsome: for there are great store of windowes, which to the end that they may give more light, are made broader within than without. Upon the top of this turret is built a certaine spire or pinnacle rising sharpe in forme of a sugar-loafe, and containing five and twentie elles in compasse, but in height being not much more than two speares length: the said spire hath three lofts one above another, unto every of which they ascend with woodden ladders. Likewise on the top of this spire standeth a golden halfe moone, upon a barre of iron, with three spheares of golde under it; which golden spheares are so fastened unto the saide iron barre; that the greatest is lowest, and the least highest. It woulde make a man giddie to looke downe from the top of the turret; for men walking on the grounde, be they never so tall, seeme no bigger then a childe of one yeere old. From thence likewise may you plainly escrie the promontorie of Azaphi, which notwithstanding is an hundred and thirtie miles distant. But the mountaines (you will say) by reason of their huge bignes may easily be seene a farre off: howbeit from this turret a man may in cleere weather most easily see fiftie miles into the plaine countries.

From Thomas Pellow, *The Adventures of . . .*, 1890 edn, p. 99.

The four globes are, by computation, seven hundred pounds, Barbary weight, each pound consisting of 24 ounces, which make in all 1,050 pounds English; and frequent attempts had been made to take them away, but without success; for, as the notion ran, any attempting it were soon to desist from it, they being affrightened, and especially at their near approach to them, in a very strange and surprising manner, and seized with an extraordinary faintness and trembling, hearing at the same time a great rumbling noise, like as if the whole fabric was tumbling down about their ears, so that, in great confusion, they all returned faster than they advanced.

This did I often hear, yet had I a very strong itching to try the truth of it; and to gratify my curiosity, I one night (having communicated my intentions to two of my men, and persuaded them to go with me, and provided myself with candles, flint, steel and tinder) entered the foot of the tower, lighted my candles, and advanced with my comrades close at my heels till I had gained at least two-thirds of the height, I still going on. Then really, to my seeming, I both felt and heard such a dismal rumbling noise and shaking of the tower (my lights at that instant quite going out), as I thought far surpassed that of common fame. Yet was I resolved to proceed, and called to my comrades to be of good courage, but having no answer from them, I soon found that they had left me in the lurch; upon which, falling into a very great sweat, I went back also, and found them at the bottom in a terrible condition. And so ended my mad project, and which was, I think, a very mad one indeed, for had I obtained the globes, in what could it have bettered my deplorable condition, being always obliged to follow my Emperor's pleasure, and with whom it was a most sufficient crime to be rich. And so much for my foolish attempt on the golden globes.

Dr Robert Brown, editor of the 1890 edition adds a note that 'the globes (three in number and not four) though often an object of cupidity to kings in want of coin, remained in situ *to early in this century, mainly owing to the difficulty which their mode of fixation offered the plunderer, these failures giving rise to the story that they were protected by "djinns". But they were finally taken down, and replaced by others, or, when their true value was discovered, replaced by gilded facsimiles.' One story is that their origin was due to the desire of the Queen of Muley Abd al-Mumin (1128–1162) to ornament the mosque built by her husband, and that the gold they were made of was derived from the jewels presented to her by the king. Captain John Smith, visiting Morocco in 1604, saw them on what he called the 'Christian Church'. Against 'these golden Bals of Affrica', he tells us, 'hath shot many a shot' though none ever hit them. He repeats the tale that he heard of their origin, which was to the effect that the Prince of Morocco betrothed himself to the 'King's*

Daughter of Etheopea'. *But he dying before their marriage*, '*she caused those three golden Balls to be set up for his Monument*', *while she herself remained single all her life*.

All travellers were fascinated by the vitality of the Jamaa al Fnaa in Marrakesh.
From C. E. Andrews, *Old Morocco* . . ., 1922, p. 32.

The square itself is a great space paved only with the sun-baked earth of the brown plain in which the city was built. At one end are a few European shops, a cafe, a post-office, and the sign of a garage – jarring elements of western progress that has begun to thrust in its ugliness and disturb the mediaeval peace of old Marrakesh, mournful among its crumbling monuments. From another angle, one catches glimpses of the old walls, with here and there a twisted palm tree reaching over them, black against the gold of the sun. The farther end of the square shows only the low roofs of the city, and the openings of one or two streets, that plunge into a dark, covered labyrinth lined with a thousand shops. From these mysterious streets that in the daytime conceal so many hushed mysteries, now pour forth streams of strange humanity. Swirls of dust rise from the feet of asses and camels, and the crimson sunset light, diffused through the yellow haze hovering above the square, casts over the innumerable strange faces the glamour of eastern romance that glimmers in old tales and in poets' dreams. The magnificent minaret of the Koutoubia, severe with the puritanism of ancient Islam, stretches its long shadow over the frivolities of the square and the passionate sins of the dark streets and close-shut gardens.

Being a missionary, Robert Kerr expected to be shocked by Meknes, and he was.
From Robert Kerr, *Pioneering* . . ., 1894, pp. 174–5.

As one looks at the massive concrete walls, built by fellow-Christians enslaved, groaning under the yoke of a heathen potentate – a servitude tenfold more severe than that of Egyptian bondage – one is constrained to say 'How long, O Lord, does thou not judge and avenge the blood of them who were slain for the Word of God?' Many of the Christian slaves were thrown from the top of these walls to gratify that bloodthirsty monarch.

The population, I should say, is between 40,000 and 50,000 of which 5,000 or 6,000 are Jews. The inhabitants are poor, and mostly of the Arab class. The streets, as a rule, are wide, but the mud is plentiful as in other towns, the Jewish Quarter, for filth, surpassing anything I have seen in Morocco; and the great wonder is that the people flourish as they do.

The manufactures of Mequinez are few – principally guns, ploughs, swords, saddles and pack-saddles. The Jews are the artisans – brassworkers, making trays, tinsmiths, silversmiths and goldsmiths.

The Jews have not the same liberty as in Fez or any of the coast towns. Here, also, when in the Moorish Quarter, they have to take off their slippers and carry them in their hands.

The climate of Mequinez is very good, as it stands high, and has always a cool breeze. In winter it is piercingly cold, and in summer considerably hotter than on the coast.

'The reputation Mequinez has earned for morals is one of the worst possible to be obtained, rivalling Sodom and Gomorrah in the tale of its wickedness'. The wickedness of the place is accounted for by the large number of shereefs who live in the city; and yet these shereefs are supposed to be holy men, descended in direct line from their Prophet!

Much good work might yet be done here. At present Mequinez is without a missionary.

A picture of Rabat and the twin city of Sale. From Reginald Rankin, *In Morocco . . .*, 1908, pp. 241–2.

They call Rabat the Pearl of Morocco. It stands high on the steep southern bank of the Bouragrag where the green river lashes the blue sea, above cactus-grown ochre rocks, a long rambling line of white and yellow, everywhere dominated by the huge grey Tower of Hassan.

Across the river, on a flat sandy shore, lies Sallee, a compact town protected by a mighty bastioned wall, and treeless, save for a solitary palm. No two places, so close together, could be more unlike. Sallee, grim, dusty, arid, crouches in the sand like a beast of prey; Rabat, aloft amidst her orange groves, deck with emeralds and gold, looks out smiling on the world like a queen.

The winding river fades into rolling, grassy hills; not far away the sea thunders; a great wall joining the guardian waters, and the raging surf of her bar, keep Rabat inviolate. The crossing of the bar, always an experience, is sometimes a peril, and often an impossibility. Vessels have lain for twenty days outside the port, waiting in vain for the opportunity to land their cargo.

The cities are linked by the long white lines of foam cresting the Atlantic rollers; and the descendants of the Rovers are hardy, skilful mariners, always ready to urge their great barcasses into the maelstrom, singing antiphonally as they wield the long sweeps, and utterly untinged by the 'sadness of farewell'.

This description of the royal necropolis of Shellah near Rabat has been translated and abridged by the editors.
From Tranchant de Lunel, *Au pays du paradoxe*, 1924, pp. 37–40.

Shellah stands on a plateau which dominates the Bou-Regreg. The crenellated walls, which follow in their winding, the steep slope of the hill which stands over the river, are now no more than the shroud which faithfully pick out the shape of a corpse crumbling into dust. Of the city that flourished in the eleventh century, nothing remains but the walls and the main gate. The walls and the gate have, in the rays of the setting sun, the red tint of glowing coals. The cold tones which, at the same moment in the same fading light enwrap Sale on the opposite side of the river, serve to make a striking contrast.

The golden gate, of which the carving and the stalactites show at their best in the late afternoon when the sun plays upon their contours, opens as if onto a wide jewel-box. There is no trace of a house, no remnant of a fallen wall. No stone remains to which the imagination could anchor a vision of the past. A pebbly path leads steeply down into the hollow of the valley.

On both sides of the stony footpath, scrappy cultivation, arid land, too much trampled in the past, where grass can grow only with an effort. Hedges of prickly pears guard the illusory promise of their fruit against passers-by. Lower down rises abruptly a forest of great trees speckled by the white domes of massive kubbahs.

A ruined wall, where the stones are gradually being defeated by the unrelenting efforts of vegetation to push in its roots, grips the ancient mosque of which there remains, almost intact, a minaret delightfully covered with enamel of a pale blue which mingles beautifully with the golden network carved on the mellow granite.

A stork's nest crowns it with its prickly thatch.

To push oneself through a gap in this abandoned enclosure, is suddenly to see a most romantic sight of which men dreamed long ago. Amidst the rubble of grandiose arches, lean huge fig trees, exhausted by a struggle for existence that has lasted three centuries. In the battle with the works of man, the forces of nature have gradually proved the masters. Squeezed by the bloated roots of high nettle-trees, of which the leaves hang down like locks of hair, widespread and always moving, push up some high, broad sculptured tombstones, three-quarters eaten away with red moss.

Beyond, in a field of nettles, stretched out like the dead they represent, more tombstones – marble but with the appearance of old ivory and with inscriptions that no one bothers to read.

A little further still, in an almost abandoned garden of orange trees, a lofty ruin of which the massive silhouette blocks out a whole area of sky.

More marble tombstones – always more marble tombstones.

On the Southern face of the ruin, inscriptions in Kufic characters surround an impressive carving. It is the necropolis of a dynasty that disappeared long ago.

I could not then spend long in this wonderful setting. Night was falling and I had to return to Rabat. In the great silence that had fallen on the city and the camp, one could hear distant explosions marking, like a threat to all this peace and beauty, the steady advance of our troops who had already reached Bou-Znika. Passionately though I longed for their success, I could not help trembling for the artistic treasures of old Morocco: cannon are the enemies of the treasures of the past.

An account of the pirates of Sale who captured 'Robinson Crusoe' and carried off women from Ireland and even Iceland in the seventeenth and eighteenth centuries. They were so powerful that for many years they ignored the sultan and had a republic of their own which was once presided over by an Englishman, who later returned home to become a Member of Parliament.

From Stanley Lane-Poole, *The Barbary Corsairs*, 1890, pp. 190–1.

Sale was, after the middle of the seventeenth century, the only port in Morocco that sent forth buccaneers. Reefs of rock and drifts of sand render the west coast unsuitable for anchorage, and the roads are unsafe when the wind is in the south-west. Consequently the piracy of Sale, though notorious and dreaded by merchantman, was on a small scale; large vessels could not enter the harbour, and 200-ton ships had to be lightened before they could pass the bar. The cruisers of Sale were therefore built very light and small, with which they did not dare to attack considerable and well-armed ships. There was not a single full-sized galley at Sale in 1634, and accounts a hundred years later agree that the Sale rovers had but insignificant vessels, and very few of them, while their docks were practically disused, in spite of an abundance of timber. In the latter part of the eighteenth century there seems to have been an increase in the depredations of the Sale pirates, which probably earned them their exaggerated reputation. At that time they had vessels of 30 and 36 guns, but unwieldy and badly built, with which they captured Provençal ships and did considerable mischief, till the Chevalier Acton in 1773, with a single Tuscan frigate, destroyed three out of their five ships. The rovers of Sale formed at one time a sort of republic of pirates, paying the emperor a tithe of prize-money and slaves, in return for non-interference; but gradually the Government absorbed most of the profits, and the trade declined, till the emperors, in return for rich presents, concluded treaties with the chief maritime Powers, and to a large extent suppressed piracy.

7

A Selection of Towns

This chapter gives descriptions of towns likely to be on the itinerary of the traveller in Morocco. Some of them will have changed out of recognition: the Agadir of Cowan and Johnston was totally destroyed in the earthquake of 1960 and Casablanca has something new every time one visits it. Incidentally, there is no Café Americain where Humphrey Bogart ordered Sam to 'play it' at the end of the runway of the airfield, although there is one in the centre of the town. We have chosen several accounts of Tangier from its earlier days as the home of martyrs, to more recent times when its expatriates were more colourful than respectable. It was often the first and sometimes the only place in Morocco seen by visitors who gaped at its exotic ways. Tetuan still has the charm noticed by our writers. Visitors to Meknes should try to see Volubilis, the only Roman site in the country, which is well described by Miège.

A description of Old Agadir.
From George Cowan and R. L. N. Johnston, *Moorish Lotos Leaves*, 1883, pp. 207–9.

The venerable Amin commissioned by His Majesty to rule the port of Agadir reclines on a heap of empty sacks under the shade of a tiny reed hut; repairing, when wearied with official state, to the roof of a neighbouring cistern, there to enjoy *otium cum dignitate* in the shape of green tea and biscuits. The Amin, without actually inviting us to visit the town, gave us to understand that no objection would be made to our entering it. To scale the steep sides of Agadir hill, however, animals of some kind were indispensable, and we obtained from the village of Fonte the required number of pack mules, saddles being a luxury beyond purchase. That procession, straining up the rocky winding path under a midday sun, was possibly picturesque; it was certainly calculated, from the bold eccentricity of costume adopted by the British abroad, to astonish the natives, who, startled out of their habitual repose, awaited us in a small crowd outside the massive archway which, with its studded gates and cool alcove, forms the sole entrance to the town.

Once inside, the narrow streets, abounding in blank, whitewashed walls, seemed almost deserted, save where in miniature smithies, about the size of an ordinary bathing machine, grimy Vulcans were shaping the square horse-shoe with which the Moorish trooper disfigures his barb's hoof, and where, in the Jews' quarter, adjoining the residence of the governor and tax-gatherers, every doorway had its group of women – most of them old, all of them ugly – who showered blessings upon the Christians bringing employment for their men folk. As a fortress, except that it is commanded by a hill of equal height to the south-east, and that water has to be carried up by an acclivitous path from Fonte, Agadir might be made a place of considerable strength, commanding every approach by sea, and efficiently protecting any town built on the side of Fonte. As a commercial centre, its limited area and difficulty of access would seem to render it almost valueless, a remark which does not apply to the undulating plain below.

On the origin and appearance of Alcassar.
From Arthur Leared, *A visit . . .*, 1879, pp. 6–7.

From the point of view where we encamped, Alcassar el Kebir was imposing enough. About a dozen mosque towers, with here and there a few tall palms, and a crowd of flat-roofed houses enclosed within high walls, gave it an air of importance. Outside the walls there were also some fine gardens.

We entered and all illusion was dispelled. It was market day, and the crowds gathered round our party in the hot, filthy, and dusty streets in a way that was almost unbearable. The shops had no attractions; nothing was to be seen in them except articles of food and clothing. And yet the size and appearance of some of the houses showed that there were citizens of substance in the midst of this squalor. But a general decay was only too plain. Here was to be seen an open space covered with mouldering ruins. There, a minaret, the mosque of which no longer existed. An extraordinary number of storks' nests, perched on towers, on housetops, on old walls and trees, was a feature of the place. Look almost where one would, and one of these big untidy structures met the eye. And sitting in each were two or three ungainly-looking juveniles, over which papa and mamma storks stood gazing at the hopeful but hungry family below.

I judged the town to contain between five and six thousand souls.

Every town in Morocco seems to have a legend of its own concerning its origin. The story about the foundation of this town is that Sultan Mansor, having lost his way on a hunting expedition, was entertained *incognito* by a poor fisherman, in whose hut he passed the night. The Sultan was so well pleased, that he bestowed upon the fisherman some royal buildings, situated not far off. These buildings having been enclosed within a wall, soon took the form of a town, to which the name of Alcassar el Kebir, or, the Great Palace, was given.

An ill-tempered account of Arzila.
From George Montbard, *Among the Moors*, 1894, pp. 55–7.

Surrounded by the still imposing zone of its old, ruinous grey ramparts covered with lichen that preys upon them, the ancient town, so often captured and recaptured, is quietly dying away in the proud sepulchre of its lofty decaying walls, corroded at the base, its embattled summits crowned with plants and bushes, perforated with wide gaps, split with deep fissures, the haunt of vipers and the abode of beasts of prey. About fifteen hundred Moors and Jews give a semblance of animation to the place, and carry on some slight traffic, which decreases every day. The time is not very far distant when the vultures will hover about the crumbled towers, when the yelping of the jackals will fill the silence of its ruins, when the dwarf palms will strike root where its white terraces were standing, and the herdsman will drive his goats to browse where the high walls raised their menacing fronts. And he will crush beneath his bare feet the stalks of wild flowers, unconscious of the fact that a dead town is lying there, under the soil which he is treading, that his ancestors lived there, and Nature, in her slow and ceaseless toil, will have retaken from man what man has wrested from her.

What pestilent streets! a black sewer full of foul things emitting abominable smells, running along dilapidated walls, hideous shops, with pendant, dislocated weather-boards. We tack along the walls, clinging to the fastenings of the shops, to every projection and cavity, wherever we can get any support, in order to avoid coming into contact with this horrible filth. As we thus proceed, in single file, along the goats' track, we have now and then to make some trying dead halts when coming face to face with a pedestrian from the opposite direction. We glare at him and he at us, with suppressed rage, and obstinately cling to the wall, anxiously waiting till the one who is in the greatest hurry, shall take the outer side, and, with the utmost precaution, skirt round the other, running the risk of being stretched his full length in this putrefaction. It generally happened that we were the most eager to get on, and we thought ourselves lucky if at such critical junctures a passing mule or prancing horse didn't splash us from head to foot in this black and fetid mud.

Women, coming out of kennel-like hovels, draw back at once, terrified at the sight of us, and disappear indoors, shouting and shaking their fists at us.

A crowd of funny little bronzed urchins follow us at a distance with malicious curiosity. As good little Mussulmans, they treat us like dogs of Christians, and some throw stones at us, which fall short of their mark.

Some lean cats with bristling russet coats jump into the plashes, pursued by half-naked lads, and disappear into some wide-mouthed holes.

Dirty Jews with smooth, glossy hair, black skull-caps fastened on by a check handkerchief, brush by us with squinting eyes, clad in their ragged, patched robes of faded blue, and a musty smell escapes from under these sordid tatters.

A donkey bars our way. It is all skin and bone, and is gazing sadly into space, his head resting on the parapet of the wall with an expression of suffering and indelible melancholy. At every spot where the bones bulge the skin is cut, and swarms of flies settle on the naked flesh. Long wheals, destitute of hair, mark the place of old closed sores, and the body is furrowed with them.

Casablanca changed more than any other place in Morocco in the early years of the French Protectorate. Two separate worlds developed, one prosperous and one poor. The description of the first is from Eleanor Elsner, and that of the second from Jacques Borély, in a passage which has been translated and abridged by the editors.

From Eleanor Elsner, *The Present State of Morocco*, 1928, pp. 21–3; and from Jacques Borély, *Le Maroc au pinceau*, 1950, pp. 241–5.

The French are so proud of Casablanca, and so well indeed they may be, and yet – and yet, there is to me something almost terrifying about it. Twenty years ago Casablanca was not. A tiny Moslem town stood where it now stands: a town of no importance, without a bay, without even a river to break its low rocky coasts, the most unpropitious site one might imagine could have been chosen for the great seaport of Morocco.

That tiny Moslem town, little more than a village, lay on a flat and rocky coast without a beach, without the vestige of a harbour, and the Atlantic waves beat unmercifully on its front, while the west wind, a bad wind on that coast, shrieked and screamed through the streets. Why exactly this spot was selected no-one actually knew, but year by year it grew, millions of pounds have been spent on it, a hundred thousand emigrants came to it, it grew like the proverbial mushroom: 'We pushed the sea out on that side and we pushed the natives out on the other, and here is the great city of Casablanca!' one of its great men told me.

As a stupendous human effort, a triumph of engineering and building over Nature's measures it stands supreme, and it is no wonder it is a beautiful modern town. But, all the same, there is something terrifying about it. One cannot forget that Nature objects to being set at nought and defied, and a strange menace broods over Casablanca in spite of its white palaces, its broad boulevards, its magnificent offices, theatres, factories, and its most remarkable harbour.

A new native town has been built for the original inhabitants it is true, but they do not really like having been pushed out at the back, even into a more commodious native town; and certainly the sea does not like being pushed out in front, even for such a magnificent harbour as is now being constructed at Casablanca.

While it was being built the Moroccans looked at it askance. The men of Tangier, Mazagan, Safi and even Agadir, all fine natural harbours on the same coast, watched the port of Casablanca being constructed with interest and even with awe. 'It will never be finished', they said, 'the Atlantic will destroy it – the ocean will claim its own again'.

The first part of the prophecy seems likely to come true, for the harbour will probably never be really finished: the larger it grows the greater become the exports – those famous exports of phosphates – which multiply themselves by leaps and bounds each year, and more room is needed, more quays, more piers, more ship room. Not five years ago the great ocean liners had to anchor far outside, for the harbour would not hold enough water for them to enter. But today all that is changed: when I was there the huge ship *Ile de France* came right up to the quay and disembarked her passengers direct.

Huge cranes are always at work laying the foundations of new piers, docks, and warehouses. What matter that the mark of the flood tide is registered high on the wall of the old Custom House, well on the town side of the harbour? The harbour itself extends far out beyond the shore – 'We have pushed the sea out on that side'. What revenge will the sea take some day in the near or distant future?

There are, in a suburb of Casablanca, several dozen square houses – perhaps a hundred – grouped into a regular village, divided down the centre by a main road which has smaller ones coming off it at right-angles. The whole village is made of petrol-cans, or rather, of squares of tin cut from petrol-cans.

What distinguishes this area from certain quarters of New York where nameless streets are identified only with numbers, lies not in differences of height or luxury of furnishings – great though these are – but in the material in which they are built. The geometrical spirit which presides over the lay-out of the houses and the streets is the same.

The builder counts his tins, carefully measures their length and breadth and works out how many he will need to make the required number of squares for the size of the house that he is constructing. A builder in bricks or in blocks of stone does his calculations no differently. Then he carefully cuts out his squares and nails them to a wooden frame, leaving a space for his door. Does he need windows? He would not have them in the outside wall of a house in the old city. He makes the roof as he has done the walls, again with squares of tin, held up on the inside by cheap planks or branches. The shape of the house is not disguised by plaster or decoration: it is quite simply a cube, the walls and the roof white-washed with lime, and it looks as if it is made of paper. The builder then takes up residence with his family and to guard his privacy from inquisitive neighbours he hangs a curtain of coarse cloth over the door.

At a distance, in bright sunshine under a blue sky, the glimmering whiteness of the village is breath-taking. It is true that some of these little houses appear crooked or hunchbacked but that does not detract from the charm.

This little masterpiece of an Arab village, so modern in its appearance, is so situated that no other building could clash with it. It stands isolated on a waste land, in a shallow basin rimmed with piles of garbage that the sweepers have brought from the streets of Casablanca.

I discovered Bidonville, of which I had often heard, by chance, driving along a fine asphalt road that looks down upon it. I stopped, reversed the car and remained for perhaps a quarter of an hour just looking at it. I can say in all truth that I saw there nothing ugly, nothing vulgar, which is more than I can say for any other part of the city. All the houses were equal, all were white and all were more or less crooked. I thought that there was nothing as perfect in the whole of Casa. One could see in it a spirit devoid of all pretentiousness.

Around Bidonville the land stretched empty, destined for the expansion of the city. Only on the horizon a few clumps of trees, some shacks, horses grazing freely in the fields and a few little human figures moving in an immense plain.

These tin boxes, proudly inhabited by working people were usually well spaced out but some stood grouped together, like a family, supporting one another. I noticed that some of the owners had erected sheds, of the same squares of tin, or a little courtyard in which they kept an ass.

I could see, through some open doors, a few of the interiors. Here there were two men drinking tea; there, a woman sitting cross-legged, propped up by a cushion. Even out of the dip in which the village was built, I, on the road above, could see the brilliance of her eyes. She wore silver bangles on her arms for there is no Moroccan women, however poor, who does not wear some jewellery.

Above Bidonville, sitting in the car as if in the box of a theatre, I could hear coming up from somewhere in the village the crackle of iron castanets and the sounds of a *darbouka*. Was it a baptism? Was it a marriage?

Urchins ran and played in the streets, hens pecked at the gravel: there were also two donkeys, standing in the sunshine, plunged, I imagine, into the dreams that resignation brings.

I am not one of those who think it better to keep people in ignorance of the advantages that money can bring, but who could doubt, seeing the charm of this village, that one could be as happy there as in a palace.

I kept a soft spot for the Bidonville and one day, driving nearby with the former Resident Lucien Saint, I praised it and asked him to stop and look at it. He refused 'Be quiet', he said, 'the Americans are always criticising me for tolerating Bidonville'. I did not insist. I thought then that all Americans were millionaire philanthropists. Then some time later I read a book by Martha Gellhorn and learned that they have Bidonvilles in the States. I felt a bit aggrieved that they should reproach us for having a village of petrol-cans near Casablanca while they had exactly the same at home.

An incident in the history of the town of Mazagan.

From Jerôme and Jean Tharaud, *La chaîne d'or*, 1950, pp. 219–20.

Some leagues beyond Mogador lies Mazagan, so many times besieged but always saved by a miracle, 'the door and the seal of the Infidels' on Moroccan soil. The idea of closing this door and wiping out this stain haunted Sultan Muhammad III even in his sleep. One day in 1768 he camped in front of the city with a mighty army of infantry, sappers and gunners. He surrounded it with ditches and towers, and 35 cannon of all calibres poured upon it a rain of two thousand shells and bombs. The defenders of Mazagan wrote to Lisbon to beg for help: time passed, nothing happened. At last they saw a ship approaching under full sail. No one doubted that help was at hand. Alas! No one in Lisbon could be bothered about Morocco! The ship only carried a letter from the King ordering that the population should be embarked as soon as possible and the city surrendered to the Muslims.

One saw then at Mazagan the opposite of what had happened at Larache in the days of Mulai Ismail. At Larache, then, the soldiers had mutinied, begging the governor to open the gates to the enemy. At Mazagan the furious population hooted the King's messenger and only one cry could be heard 'This is our land, left to us by our ancestors. It has been watered with their blood. Our leaders and our citizens gave their lives for it. We shall not go. We shall fight to the last man'.

The Governor, though, was no hero: he thought only of obeying the order that he had received. The clergy who at Larache had led the party of courage and resistance here intervened to persuade the people to surrender. Little by little enthusiasm waned. The Governor asked the Sultan for a ceasefire of three days before he opened the gates. Muhammad agreed on condition that the inhabitants took away only what they could carry. Immediately they began to break or burn everything they possessed, furniture, goods, pots and pans. They crippled their horses. They laid mines, timed to explode when the enemy entered. Then they embarked.

On their arrival in Portugal the miserable refugees were grouped in the little town of Baylen. Many of them died there of misery and boredom. Others left for Brasil where they founded a new town that they named Mazagan, in memory of a history so long so heroic but which had ended in misery.

Among the many descriptions that have been given of Mogador, we have selected this one.
From James Richardson, *Travels* . . ., 1860, pp. 253–7.

The site is a sandy beach with a rocky foundation or a base on the sea, forming a peninsula, and is supposed to be the ancient Erythraea. The houses are regularly built, with streets in direct lines, extremely convenient though somewhat narrow. The residences of the consuls and the European merchants are elegant and spacious. There is a large market-place, which, on days when the market is not held, furnishes a splendid parade, or 'corso' for exercising cavalry.

The city is divided into two parts; one division contains the citadel, the public offices, the residence of the governor, and several houses occupied by European consuls and merchants, which are all the property of the Sultan; and the other is the space occupied by the houses of the Moors and Jews.

The Jews have a quarter to themselves which is locked up during the night, the key being kept by the police. Nevertheless, several Jews, especially Imperial traders, are allowed to occupy houses in the Moorish quarter or citadel portion of Mogador, with the Christian merchants.

Both quarters are surrounded by walls, not very thick or high, but which are a sufficient protection against the depredations of the mountaineers or Arabs of the plain. The port is formed by a curve in the land and the isle of Mogador, which is about two miles from the mainland.

This isle, on the verge of the ocean, contains some little forts and a mosque, and its marabout sparkles in the sun. It is a place of exile for political offenders. When the French landed, at the bombardment of Mogador, they released fifty or sixty state prisoners, some of whom had been Bashaws, or ministers of this and previous reigns. The isle, however, is finely situate off the Atlantic, fanned and swept by healthy gales, and the prisoners suffer only exclusion from the Continent. The exiles never attempt to escape, but quietly submit to their destiny.

The population is between thirteen and fifteen thousand souls, including four thousand Jews, and fifty Christians, who carry on an important commerce, principally with London and Marseilles. Excepting Tangier, it is now the only port which carries on uninterrupted commercial relations with Europe.

Mogador is situated in the midst of shifting sand-hills, that separate it from the cultivated parts of the country, which are distant from four to twelve miles. These sands have an extraordinary appearance on returning from the interior; they look, like huge pyramidal batteries raised round the suburbs of the city for its defences. The inhabitants are supplied with water by means of an aqueduct, fed by the little river, or rill of Wal Elghored, two miles distant to the south. The climate hereabouts is extremely salubrious, the rocky sandy site of the city being removed from all marshes or low lands, which produce pestiferous miasma or fever-exhaling vegetation. Rarely does it rain, but the whole tract of the adjoining country, between the Atlas and the sea, is tempered on one side by the loftiest ranges of the mountain, and on the other, by the north-east trade winds, blowing continually.

Rebellion in the town of Saffi.
From Frances MacNab, *A Ride in Morocco . . .*, 1902, pp. 310–11.

Saffi was the scene of some severe fighting at the time of the rebellion after the death of the late Sultan. The Abda tribe rose, but first some of the headmen came into Saffi and appealed to the leading merchants to do something to help them. They said: ‘It is not a case of paying taxes, nor even of paying what we can pay, but even our children’s food is taken from us.’ The merchants could not interfere, knowing that the Kaids who squeezed the people were in their turn squeezed by the authorities. Then the tribe rebelled.

The Kaid of the district fought a battle with them outside Saffi, and they took refuge in the saint's house on the hill. Their strength was considerable, and the Europeans in the town were in great fear, knowing that at any moment the feeling might turn against the Christians.

The attack upon the town was planned to take place on a public holiday. There was feasting going on, and all the town was given over to pleasure with that zest of enjoyment which is so marked a feature in the Moorish character. The extravagance of the harem is in all they do. They are feminine in their sensitiveness, in their fancy, in their intuition. They are childish in their thoughtlessness and abandonment. Just about an hour before sunset a man within the city was to give the signal to those outside by waving a flag. He was detected in the act and killed on the spot. Immediately the firing commenced. The people in the town ran hither and thither, talking and shouting in consternation and alarm. The rebels within the gates fought with the soldiers, and for some days the struggle went on. In some places the dead bodies lay in heaps; on one spot over 200 men were killed in one day. The Europeans remained passive, and probably saved their lives by so doing. One English merchant insisted upon going to his office as usual, as though nothing was happening, while his wife entertained the ladies to a champagne luncheon. But the town was in the direst jeopardy.

The Kaid of the district, Aissa Ben Omar, had massed all his troops, but the rebels came on in a greater force and fought with the courage of despair. Then Aissa offered terms of peace, and four of the rebel leaders were to come to him to sign the terms. He had four men in readiness with swords, and at a given signal the heads of the four rebel leaders were struck off simultaneously.

That it was an act of supreme treachery no one will deny, and act which no civilized people could readily excuse. Yet, in general opinion at Saffi, Aissa's conduct is condoned as having saved the town from massacre. The certainty that the wholesale massacre of men, women, and children was the alternative is clearly established in the mind of all who knew the situation.

The fighting in the town itself must have been very general. There was fighting at the gates, in the main street, at the sanctuary called Rabat, and on the kasbah hill. On the spot where my tent was pitched a great hole was made, and no one knows how many men were buried there. The order given was, 'Roll them in their haiks and bury them at once.'

This description of Qasbah Tadla has been translated and abridged by the editors.
From Charles de Foucauld, *Reconnaissance au Maroc*, 1888, pp. 57–8.

Before Mulai Ismail it was, people assured me, just a desert and not even a village stood there; certainly the present town dates from his time. It was he who founded the Qasba and the mosque; he was responsible also for the bridge of ten arches – the biggest in the world according to the locals. It stands on the right bank of the river Umm al-Rabia which flows rapidly past its walls, thirty to forty metres wide and very deep. You can only cross it at a few fords but otherwise one has to swim even in summer.

The Qasba itself is by far the finest fortress that I have seen in Morocco. It has an outer wall of *pise*, (earth or clay bricks baked in the sun), 1 metre 20 thick and 10 or 12 metres high, crenellated with huge towers. The inner wall is separated from the outer by a road six to eight metres wide and is also of *pise*, nearly as high as the first but not crenellated. The walls are still in a good state with no breach in the outer and in the second only one, a wide one it is true. A square divides the Qasba itself in two: to the east is the mosque and the Dar al-Makhzan and to the west the dwellings of the citizens. Both are falling into ruins and look deserted. I only saw one human being in all the vast fortress – a poor old man, sitting sadly outside the door of the Dar al-Makhzan; his rosary was in his hands and he told his beads with an air of such melancholy that I felt quite affected. Who was this old hermit, living in solitude and prayer? Why did he look so grief-stricken? Was he perhaps a converted sinner, doing penance for unknown crimes? Was he perhaps a holy marabout, weeping over the sins of mankind? No – it was the Caid – the poor devil did not dare to go out. He would be hooted at and insulted if he did.

Although the Qasba is not inhabited there are a few streets which are: one on the right bank consists of houses of pise and another on the left, the poor quarter, is only tents and brushwood. Qasba Tadla has 1,200 to 1,400 inhabitants of whom 100 or 150 are Israelites. It has no water other than the river – clear and good but rather salty. The neighbourhood is rich in salt – I saw fine blocks a metre long, 60cm wide and 15–20cm thick that had been extracted not far away. Qasba Tadla has no greenery, no gardens, no trees, not even a blade of grass. It is the only place in Morocco, town or village, without gardens however small.

Few visitors to Tangier would have expected it to have been the home of early Christian saints. The description of the martyrdom of one of them is given here.
From *Butler's Lives of the Saints* (1956 edn), vol. IV, pp. 220–1.

In the city of Tingis during the administration of the President Fortunatus, when all were feasting on the birthday of the Emperors Diocletian and Maximian, a certain Marcellus, one of the centurions, condemning the banquets as heathen, cast away his soldier's belt in front of the standards of the legion which were there. And he testified in a loud voice saying 'I serve Jesus Christ, the eternal King. I will no longer serve your Emperors, and I scorn to worship your gods of wood and stone which are deaf and dumb idols'.

The soldiers were dumbfounded at hearing such things, they laid hold on him and reported the matter to the President Fortunatus, who ordered him to be thrown into prison. When the feasting was over, he gave orders sitting in council, that the man should be brought in. When this was done Astasius Fortunatus, the President said to Marcellus 'What did you mean by ungirding yourself contrary to military discipline, and in casting away your belt and vine-switch? (the distinctive badge of the centurion)'.

Marcellus: 'On July 21 in the presence of the standards of your legion, when you celebrated the festival of the Emperors, I made answer openly and clearly that I was a Christian, and that I could not accept this allegiance but could serve only Jesus Christ, the Son of God the Almighty Father'.

Fortunatus: 'I cannot pass over your rash conduct and therefore I shall report this matter to the Emperors and Caesar. You shall be sent to my lord Aurelius Agricolan, deputy for the praetorian prefects'.

On October 30 at Tingis the centurion Marcellus having been brought to the court, it was officially reported 'Fortunatus the President has referred Marcellus, a centurion, to your authority. There is a letter from him, which at your command I will read'. Agricolan said 'Let it be read'. The official report was read 'From Fortunatus to you my lord' and so on. Then Agricolan asked 'Did you say these things, as set out in the President's official report?'

Marcellus: 'I did'.

Agricolan: 'Were you serving as a regular centurion?'

Marcellus: 'I was'.

Agricolan: 'What madness possessed you to throw away the badge of your allegiance and speak as you did?'

Marcellus: 'There is no madness in those who fear God'.

Agricolan: 'Did you say each of the things contained in the President's report?'

Marcellus: 'I did'.

Agricolan: 'Did you cast away your arms?'

Marcellus: 'I did. For it was not right for a Christian man, who serves the Lord Christ to serve in the armies of the world'.

'The doings of Marcellus are such as must be visited with disciplinary punishment', said Agricolan and he pronounced sentence. 'Marcellus, who held the rank of a regular centurion, and having admitted that he degraded himself by openly throwing off his allegiance, and having used insane speech, as appears in the official report, it is our pleasure that he be put to death by the sword'.

When he was being led away, Marcellus said, 'May God be good to you, Agricolan'. In so seemly a way did the glorious martyr Marcellus pass out of this world.

We have already seen how Samuel Pepys was involved in the withdrawal of British forces from Tangier. The most remarkable feature of the British occupation had been the building of a mole.

From Enid Routh, *Tangier . . .*, 1912, pp. 344–6.

The Mole was the greatest engineering work till then attempted by Englishmen. It was seen that without two essentials, a good harbour, and an effective seaward line of defence, Tangier was practically useless; its value as a naval station and as the starting point of a colony was nothing, unless ships could ride in the bay without fear of storm or enemy.

The site chosen was on the north side of the bay, where a ledge of rocks afforded a natural though inadequate protection from the Atlantic. The work was put in hand under the immediate supervision of Mr [later Sir Hugh] Cholmley who acted as resident-engineer from 1663 to 1674. He had made a special study of the subject and had gained practical experience in the construction of a pier at Whitby. The price agreed upon was 13 shillings per cubic yard.

Cholmley came out in June 1663, bringing with him 'about 40 masons, miners, and other proper artists and workmen', whom he had with difficulty persuaded to come to 'a place where, in the beginning, so many men had died'. The main work of the Mole was eventually done by soldiers of the garrison.

The foundations were begun in August 1663, but for some time progress was retarded by the want of materials. In February 1664 Cholmley was called home by the death of his elder brother and did not return till 18 January 1665 when he found that more delay had been caused owing to his workmen 'being forced to the duty of soldiers' while 'crosse weather' also hindered the work. A survey made immediately after his return shows that 10,558 cubic yards had been thrown into the sea to form the base of the work.

The engineers soon found that the cost of the work had been considerably under-estimated. It was the first great pier ever undertaken in deep tidal water. The price was increased to 17 shillings per cubic yard by an Order in Council of 31 March 1665. After Cholmley's return, rapid progress was made on the Mole. He soon had about two hundred soldiers at work under his energetic supervision, and would have liked a hundred or two more if they could have been spared from the fortifications. The winter was very stormy and Cholmley said he found it hard to keep the men to their work, as they and he also were daily wet to the skin both by sea and rain.

Fortunately plenty of stone was found close at hand, which, though soft at first, soon gathered 'a mossy coat' and hardened in the water. The stone quarries, named 'Whitby' by some Yorkshire miners, lay close to the shore just west of Tangier. The stone was blasted, says Cholmley, by means of mines both large and small, i.e. small drill mines, blasting about 200 or 300 tons of stone, and large ones with 30 barrels of powder, which brought down as much as 10,000 tons.

The stone was at first carried to the Mole by boat, but stormy weather made this so difficult that Cholmley had carts built, and brought it along the shore. He also built 'a little town' at Whitby, with quarters for the workmen and their families, stabling for ninety horses and storehouses for provisions and materials of all sorts. Oak for piles, and 'deales' were usually sent out from home, though Cholmley sometimes obtained very good wood from Spain.

Though many complaints were made of neglect and delay in the work, the harbour being still very unsafe, the Mole was so far advanced in 1665 that a battery of guns was placed on it in time to be of incalculable value during the Dutch war, when the town would otherwise have lain open to an attack from the sea.

There were disputes over payment and over methods of construction. Some favoured a method recently used in Genoa of sinking great wooden chests, filled with stones and cement, weighing from 500 to

2,000 tons on to a base of loose stones and rubble but Cholmley argued that although this had worked in the smooth waters of the Mediterranean, it would not withstand Atlantic storms. He preferred to build the Mole the usual way by casting loose stones into the sea up to the low water mark, as a foundation, and building on them with great stones cemented with lime and mortar and cramped with iron and lead. The main work would be protected by an outer breakwater consisting of three rows of piles 'shod with iron and well steeled at the points', set four feet apart, arranged like a series of fives on a dice. A survey made in April 1670 showed that the Mole was then 400 yards long, and Cholmley thought that only another 80 to 100 yards (built at a rate of 20 a year) would be necessary with a 'return' of 60 yards to break the Eastern seas. Storms in the winter of 1674/5 damaged both the Mole and Cholmley's reputation but he recommended that it should be extended a further 100 yards over the next six years. When this was rejected he proposed that, for £30,000 a year for four years he would complete it to 500 yards and later keep it in repair for £2000 a year. Mr (later Sir Henry) Shere or Sheeres contracted to do the work for £10,000 less with the chest method and he replaced Cholmley in 1676. From 1678 Tangier came under attack from the troops of Mulai Ismail who harassed the quarries and in the great siege of 1680 work had to stop as every man was needed to defend the walls. In 1683 (see Pepys extract) the British government decided to evacuate Tangier and destroy the Mole which had cost between £300,000 and £400,000. It had not been finished but its final length was 1,436 feet, its average breadth 110 feet and its average height from its top to the low water mark 18 feet. According to Shere it was 'by cubical computation 2,843, 280 solid feet, which being cast into tons are 167,251' and he estimated that it would take 1,000 men 290 days to destroy. Over 2,000 soldiers and seamen worked even on moonlit nights, throwing the debris into the sea to choke up the harbour, and in January 1684 the sea was able to pass over it. Remnants of the Mole could still be seen at low tide at the beginning of the twentieth century.

Two odd incidents in the history of nineteenth-century Tangier. **From John Drummond Hay, *Western Barbary*, 1861 edn, pp. 122 and 103–5.**

With much ostentation our guide pointed out to us on the road-side a wretched wheeled vehicle, ruder even in construction and form than a very ancient Egyptian cart which I saw shortly after its discovery on the banks of the Nile. This was the only wheeled carriage I have met with in all Morocco. It was drawn by oxen and was employed for transporting cannon-shot from the shore.

When Prince Federick of Hesse-Darmstadt arrived in 1839 at Tangier, whither he had exiled himself for some months, his Highness brought with him two carriages, which looked like those of the time of our great-great-grandsires. Finding that the local authorities objected to his making use of a wheeled vehicle in the town, he wrote to the Sultan, offering to pave the main street of Tangier, if he were permitted to use his carriages. The Shereefian monarch graciously consented, on condition that the Prince's vehicles were deprived of their wheels, as without that precaution, the Protector of the Faithful feared that the lives of his loyal subjects would be exposed to imminent danger.

Strange to say, the Prince followed this injunction to the very letter, and one of his carriages, deprived of its wheels, was borne as a litter between two stout mules.

The clock of the *Jamaa Kebeer*, the great mosque of Tangier, being much out of order, needed some skilful craftsman to repair it. None, however, of the Faithful were competent for the task, nor could they discover what part of the machinery was deranged, though many put forth their opinions with great pomp and authority; among the rest one man gravely declared that a *Jinn* had, in all probability, taken up its abode in the clock. Various exorcisms were accordingly essayed, sufficient, as every true believer supposed, to have expelled a legion of devils – yet all in vain: the clock continued dumb.

A Christian clockmaker was now their sole resource; and such a one fortunately was sojourning in Tangier. He was from Genoa, and of course a pious Christian; how then were they to manage to employ him? The clock was fixed to the wall of the tower, and it was, of course, a thing impossible to allow the Kaffer to defile God's house of prayer by his sacrilegious steps.

The Caid entered feelingly into all the difficulty of the case, and forthwith summoned the other authorities to his porch, where various propositions were put forward by the learned members of the council.

One proposed to abandon the clock altogether; another would lay down boards over which the infidel might pass without touching the sacred floor; but this was held not to be a sufficient safeguard; and it was finally decided to pull up that part of the pavement upon which the Unbeliever trod, and whitewash the walls near which he passed.

The Christian was now sent for, and told what was required of him;

and he was expressly commanded to take off his shoes and stockings on entering the Jemaa. 'That I won't' said the stout little watchmaker; 'I never took them off when I entered the chapel of the Most Holy Virgin and I won't take them off in the house of your Prophet'.

They cursed in their hearts the watchmaker and all his race, and were in a state of vast perplexity. The respected scholars had met early in the morning; it was already noon, and yet, so far from having got over their difficulty, they were in fact exactly where they had been before breakfast; when a grey-bearded Muezzin, who had hitherto been silent, craved permission to speak. The Caid and the Qadi nodded their assent.

'If', said the venerable gentleman, 'the mosque be out of repair, and lime and bricks have to be conveyed into the interior for the use of the masons, do not asses carry those loads, and do they not enter with their shoes on?'

'You speak truly', was the general reply.

'And does the donkey', resumed the Muezzin, 'believe in the One God, or in Mahomed, the Prophet of God?'

'No, in truth', all replied.

'Then', said the Muezzin, 'let the Christian go in shod as a donkey would do, and come out like a donkey'.

The argument of the Muezzin was unanimously applauded. In the character of a donkey, therefore, did the Christian enter the mosque, mended the clock – not indeed at all like a donkey – but as such, in the opinion of the Faithful, came out again; and the great mosque of Tangier has never since needed another visit of the donkey to its clock.

Later in the twentieth century Tangier had many inhabitants who had left their own countries. Descriptions of its cosmopolitan society abound and we have chosen two.
From Lawdom Vaidon, *Tangier: A Different Way*, 1977, pp. 301–14; and from Aleko Lilius, *Turbulent Tangier*, 1956, p. 73.

The Soco Chico of the 1950s brimmed with bona fide characters of a hundred different origins and convictions, the brilliant and the dull, the fey and the psychopathic. The Café Central, whose tea, coffee and wine were good and cheap at any hour (for it never closed) played headquarters for a special group whom journalist David Woodman dubbed 'the Soco Foreign Legion'. Of enormously disparate backgrounds, education, philosophy, life style and usefulness, the single quality these 'legionnaires' shared in common was their devotion to the Soco Chico and its environs, and to the ineffably memorable personalities, of whom they themselves made so picturesque a part, to be seen and met there. What brought them all to this extraordinary plaza in this most extraordinary of cities from such diverse origins was each legionnaire's own story which he might or might not reveal. An accurate roster of the Soco Foreign Legion would be impossible to resurrect, but descriptions of some of the legionnaires follow.

Bill Burroughs, a tall saturnine American originally from St Louis whose grandfather had been the adding machine tycoon. Burroughs had lived an exceedingly full life to date, having graduated from Harvard, taken post-graduate medical studies in the University of Vienna, done a stint in the US Army where in order to prove that he was unworthy of that organisation, he cut off the joint of a finger, entered a common-law marriage that ended when he accidentally shot and killed his wife in Mexico during a drunken or kif-inspired game of William Tell. Since 1941 he had carried on a running battle with heroin addiction which he was still fighting and still losing in Tangier. He could produce an excellent curry when he felt like it, and though his quarters usually resembled a sea of books, typing paper, temporarily discarded clothes, syringes, needles and the remains of yesterday's spaghetti, he remained a popular host. The 'different' novel that he was writing was published in 1959 as *The Naked Lunch*.

Everybody in the Soco was respectful to Paul Lund, a self-styled and proved criminal – he had spent three years in Dartmoor – who was on the run from the English Midlands. He had served as a private in the British Army along India's North West frontier and in China. He joined a smuggler's crew at Tangier, but subsequently got caught, wounded in a shoot-out and imprisoned in Livorno. Somehow he got freed, made his way back to Tangier, and managed a bar near the Soco Chico for a while.

Wearing a huge, floppy, chocolate brown hat, shoulder length hair, a white beard and moustache, having merry brown eyes and ruddy cheeks (a combination of props that made him look like a cross between Franz Hals' *Laughing Cavalier* and Santa Claus), Dr Deodar Brondgeest sat in the same rickety chair at the Café Central most of the day and until 8 o'clock each evening like a pontiff awarding dispensations.

Madame Lycia Heikka, one-time wife of Tangier's Swedish Consul, was a thin, intense woman with brassy blonde hair and bursting enthusiasm, particularly for handsome young men. Her parties were indicative of the fey gaiety to be experienced in the medina. She seldom had enough money to pay for heat or light, and since the house held an absolute minimum of furniture, all her parties depended upon the contribution of guests.

Among the legionnaires was Rupert Croft-Cooke, who wrote a book about his being implicated in a homosexual scandal in England and the prison sentence he had served in Wormwood Scrubs. On one bizarre occasion he won a degree of admiration by continuing to sit at the Café Central smoking his inevitable cigar although he had just been hit over the head so hard by an irate Tanjawi newspaper boy that the heavy glass ashtray used as the weapon had broken, and blood coursed down Croft-Cooke's face and on to his suit.

Dowell Jones, a robust Welshman of 70, admired very young Spanish and Moroccan boys, entertained them constantly in wholesale lots, and enjoyed himself immensely. Owning a fine voice and a resounding laugh, Jones competed with a large number of other men in his favourite avocation, but he certainly ranked as their uncrowned king. Handy at distributing Moroccan francs, of which he had a large surplus emanating from a very healthy auction business in Putney, Jones had fled London a single hurdle ahead of Scotland Yard agents, the British taking less kindly to his preoccupation with small lads than did Tanjawis.

Franz Brody, tall, slender, with a Lincolnesque craggy face, was a middle-aged gentleman of polite, courtly manners, an Hungarian refugee and an interesting enigma. In Tangier he worked publicly as a caricaturist and quick-sketch artist at fairs and other gala events, and privately, rumour had it, as a fence for smugglers.

Sir Cyril Hampson was a Briton who had inherited property at Tangier along with a penchant for black girls. To see the tiny Hampson squiring round a hefty, buxom Nigerian girl dressed like a black Carmen Miranda, that Latin exponent of racy songs and wild head-dresses, was a sight not easily forgotten.

While Soco Chico during Tangier's international spree undoubtedly attracted a marvellous pot-pourri of off-beats, many of them possessed intelligence, talent and integrity. If Paul Bowles' interesting observation that 'Tangier doesn't make a man disintegrate, but it does attract people who are going to disintegrate anyway' seemed to be true, it would be just as fair to say that more than one Westerner came to Tangier and the Soco Chico feeling lost, despairing and deeply troubled, and actually found in this maelstrom of tragi-comedy the strength to forge disciplined, successful and useful lives.

For once I was not accosted in the Soco Chico by guides who wanted to 'show you all, sar, very beautiful girls or, if you like, a sweet young boy, sar'.

What had happened to all the city's pimps? Had the Tangier world of hetaerae gone on strike and had their salesmen, always an unsympathetic lot, consequently lost their jobs? I felt like cheering. But suddenly I saw one of the most important of them all, a prosperous-looking Dutchman. He specializes in homosexuals. He was stalking a likely customer in the milling crowds of the Soco.

Tony Horstenkuck doesn't look like a 'male pimp', but more like a well-to-do European man of affairs. Now and then he is seen with his two pretty poodles on a leash, supping his coffee at one of the pavement cafés, usually in the company of a beautiful woman – or a handsome male sample of his wares.

As to the lady, I understand, she performs a similar service for the 'queer' members of her own sex. In short, she pimps for followers of the cult of ancient Lesbos.

A little later I saw Tony in the company of an ex-White Russian officer, now a successful motor-car salesman. Obviously, the Dutchman had caught his prey. They talked for a short while, then the Russian nodded and walked off in the direction I expected him to take – towards the Rue des Arcs, No 1, where Tony Horstenkuck maintains his four-room male brothel. There a 'partner' would be awaiting his client.

Henri Basset in the journal *Hespéris* in 1925 wrote an article on a community of troglodytes to be found in Taza which has been translated and abridged by the editors. In some cities in Morocco, and in other parts of North Africa, such communities may still be found.

Many people in the east and north-east of the Taza area live in grottos, natural or artificial, dug entirely, or almost entirely, below the level of the ground. There is generally a standard pattern of a few steps down and then one comes into a hall which divides two chambers of equal size, either a living-room and a cattle-shed or two living-rooms.

The fortress city of Taza is a fine example of troglodytism. It stands on a peak at the end of a spur with sheer drops on three sides. The summit itself is a honey-comb of caves, natural and artificial, of which the inhabitants, when danger threatened, could take refuge in the fortress. Some live in caverns or ancient graves and wherever possible they flatten a little court-yard up to the edge of the cliff. Sometimes they surround it with a thorn hedge and pass much of the day there in fine weather. Often this courtyard gives access to other caves on the same level and serves as a primitive street.

The entrance to the dwelling, unless it is naturally very narrow, is made smaller with dry stone walls in order to keep out the cold: this makes the place very dark and smoky but the inhabitants are prepared to put up with this for the sake of added warmth. The rectangular entrances of tombs have been made smaller with wooden frames behind which stones are packed. Sometimes curtains of thick branches are used instead of stones. The entrance is covered with old sacks. Inside, the soil has been flattened and a bed of packed earth softens the hardness of the rock floor. Niches have been dug in the walls to serve as cupboards and sticks have been stuck into small holes so that kitchen-ware can be hung up.

Generally each grotto consists of a single room, inhabited by a family. Sometimes it is divided in two by a rough curtain. If an entrance leads into two caves, separated by a wall, two families may live there.

By the side of the cave, a smaller grotto, or a hut made of branches is called the *Kuzina* (kitchen: sometimes it is part of the cave at a higher level). Despite its name this is really a sort of store for provisions of all kinds, particularly the firewood. There is hardly any furniture and what there is is mainly for the preparation of food. The essential item is a flour-mill and there are a few simple locally-made pots and pans. In a corner stands a great round jar for water which the women take to the wells. There are a few old tins and pots that have been found on rubbish-dumps. There are no carpets but occasionally one sees mats made of esparto-grass.

The men are out during the daytime, working in Taza as muleteers, gardeners, labourers etc and their earnings maintain the family. Sometimes they are able to buy a few goats or to grow a few beans or sow a tiny patch of grain. These little plots are the responsibility of the women – as are the poultry.

The principal work of the women is, of course, the running of the household. The preparation of flour is tedious work and this is cooked not in an oven but in a pot as a sort of couscous, in which meat rarely appears beside the vegetables. In addition to this the women fetch the firewood. The more active of them find time to spin wool and in the grottos of Taza one can see spindles and distaffs. The wool, often of very fine quality, is sold to tailors in Taza.

The housework finished, the lady often goes and sits outside the cave on a rock that long use has made comfortable: the troglodytes spend little of the day inside their home and prefer to look out on wide spaces. When caves are close together, neighbours can chat and watch innumerable children, covered in the strangest rags, play nearby or look after the flocks, helped by the dogs, the fierce defenders of troglodyte villages as they are of tented camps.

Such is life during the daylight hours: as evening approaches, the scene becomes more animated. From all the invisible entrances to the caves, blue smoke is pouring. The men come back, carrying their tools or driving a donkey. The women, like all their Berber sisters at the same moment, go down to the river in groups of two or three and then climb back up the steep slopes, bent under the heavy jars tied with rope on their shoulders.

These troglodytes are to some extent a community apart: not that they are without links to the city – very much the opposite. The men work there and for their very homes they depend upon the citizens. Although cheap, their caves are not free for they have to pay a rent to the owner of the land on which the cave is found. This is often the administrators of the Taza mosques.

Throughout the centuries travellers have written descriptions of Tetuan. We have chosen two.

From Sieur Mouette, *Entertaining Travels . . .*, 1710, p. 51; and from Isabel Savory, *In the Tail of the Peacock*, 1903, pp. 50–52, 92–3.

Tetuan is built on a Rock along the Side of a Hill, the Walls are not very strong of themselves; but the Rocks they stand on render them more Defensible than they would otherwise be. The Town is in the Shape of a St Andrew's Cross, and the Castle seated in the midst of the Hill to the Westward, has full Command over it. The Inhabitants are Wealthy, both on Account of their following Piracy, and the Trade they drive with the Kingdom of Algier and the Towns of Tangier and Ceuta. Below the Town is a curious Plain, about 5 Leagues in compass, enclos'd with high rocky Mountains, fruitful at the bottom, as bearing all Sorts of Fruit, and in the Plain there are many Gardens and Vineyards. A considerable River runs through the midst of it, into which their Brigantines, Frigats and Galliots draw up. From this Town great Quantities of Wax, Leather and Raisins of the Sun are transported into Europe; and in the midst of it is a large Mazmorra or Dungeon, which serves to shut up the poor Christian Captives, and has always a considerable number of them. The Inhabitants are for the most part those they called Andaluzians, being the Moors expell'd Spain with many Jews who live towards the Sea Gate. Being 2 Leagues from the Sea, when any Ships appear on the Coast, the Inhabitants have notice given them by Beacons, or Fires made on Towers, that they may Arm and come down to the Shore.

A long dark tunnel opens into sunlight and shops on each side, with great vines trailed on trellis-work – like a pergola – overhead and sunlight in blotches on the cobbled paving below: there, just beyond, the Slipper Quarter, and we find ourselves in the thick of the tap-tap of mallets on the hard-hammered leather – dozens of busy little shops on each side, lined with yellow matting, and hung from top to floor with rows of lemon-yellow slippers for the men, rose-red slippers for women, embroidered slippers for the wealthy, crimson slippers for slaves, slippers with heel-pieces and slippers without. In each shop a man and boys at work: the white turbans and dark faces bending over the leather, the coloured jellabs which they wear, the busy hard-white-wood mallets in the deft brown hands, even the waxed thread, the red jelly which glues the soles together, the gimlets, the sharp scissors, have a passing fascination for the wandering Moor himself, who sits down lazily in front and talks to the workers. Still more for ourselves. Leather bags are being sewn next door and ornamented with work in coloured leather and silks. Within hearing of the 'tap-tap' lies the skin yard, and the skins are scraped and tanned and dyed and turned into slippers all in the same square acre or two, whence they depart many of them for Egypt and supply the Cairo bazaars.

A few steps farther, and there is a steady clanking of hammers on anvils, beating out hot iron – the Blacksmiths' Quarter. Not the old turbaned blacksmiths nor boys with shaved heads, in tunics grimed with age, and leather aprons sewn with red leather, nor the primitive bellows and quaint iron points, all being beaten out for the ploughs, are the features of the Blacksmiths' Quarter; but the sheep. Every forge has its sheep, every shop its pen like a rabbit-hutch, made out of the side of a box, where the sheep lives when it is not lying, just at the threshold of the shop in the sun, beside a half-finished meal of bran in a box. Sheep after sheep, tame and fat, take up half the room in the street; there are sometimes a few hens, often a tortoiseshell cat curled up on a sack, but to every shop there is always a sheep fattening, as no other animal in Morocco fattens, against the *Aid-el-Kebeer*, the Great feast, when every family kills and eats its mutton.

The shops in Tetuan group themselves together more or less. There is another quarter where sieves are made, a corner where baskets and the countrywomen's huge straw hats are plaited, another where carpenters congregate, and an open square where rugs, carpets and curios cram the shops. We left the warm heat from the glowing cinders and cascade of sparks and walked on into the *feddan*, the market-place, which was teeming with women from the hills and villages around, come in to sell provisions.

The Jews' Quarter lies on one side of the feddan, shut in by a gate at night and locked – a squalid, noisy, over-populated spot, where the worst-kept donkeys and most filth are to be met with. Tetuan is a clean city: on every animal killed the butchers have to pay a tax; the tax goes to the sweeping of the streets once a week, and towards their paving – that is, if the basha is conscientious: the last basha ate and drank the tax.

A gutter runs down the middle of the streets, where chickens are killed, and the heads and uneatable parts of flesh, fish and fowl thrown. Mules and donkeys walk along the gutter, while foot people flatten themselves against the walls. A well-laden mule fairly absorbs the width of the little streets.

Before the annexation of the Western Sahara, Tiznit was the most southerly town in Morocco. Here is a local account of its origins.

From Nina Epton, *Saints and Sorcerers*, 1958, p. 186.

Tiznit spreads clover-pink and green and lonely in an immense golden plain; clover walls, clover kasbahs, clover mosques, relieved by a few judiciously spaced date palms to keep the inhabitants from being scorched off the face of the blistering earth – the only vertical lines in an otherwise monotonously horizontal landscape.

The women of Tiznit are justly famed for their beauty – a light-skinned, hot-house type of beauty. Many of them are said to follow the profession once exercised by the lady who gave the town its name.

Tiznit, an ex-prostitute of great charm, was converted to a virtuous life by a holy man. Virtue does not necessarily mean the absence of love, especially in Islam. Indeed, why should it? So the holy man married Tiznit and together they wandered through the desert proclaiming the laws of the Prophet. When the holy man died, Tiznit lived alone in a tent. One day bandits rode up to molest her while she was at her prayers. Furious at being coldly repelled by an unarmed woman, the leader struck her with his lance. Blood flowed from the mortal wound and when it touched the sand, a fountain sprang miraculously between two palm trees. The town eventually built on this spot was named Tiznit in honour of the saint.

A description of Tiznit, its dancing girls, and the coastline beyond the town.
From Sacheverell Sitwell, *Mauretania*, 1940, pp. 110–15.

From Agadir the road leads south, for sixty miles, to Tiznit, a distance taken up, in their millions, by the asphodels, seen nowhere else in such number and size as here, so far removed from their classical associations. The Atlantic is not more than a dozen or fifteen miles away, tempering the climate and conditions in this first of the desert posts that we encountered. Yet Tiznit is a small town; though its red walls, reached at last, take quite a time to circumnavigate, even in a motor until you reach the gateway. The walls of Tiznit are as red as the walls of Agadir are white: that is to say, nothing could be more red or flaming. In fact at Tiznit, the illumination is that of a perpetual sunset, in those slant rays that, suddenly, can dramatize a moment. The history of the town is obscure. It is even said that it was only founded, by Mulai El Hassane, in 1882. But it might belong, except for the rather exceptional condition of its mud walls, to any century of the middle ages that is preferred . . .

There is the possibility, in Tiznit, of finding objects worth buying, silver jewellery, chiefly, which is made by Jewish artificers, but there is, also, a Berber leather worker who is noted, even in France, for his bookbindings. But it is, more especially, for its Sheikhat dancing girls that Tiznit is known. There are enough of them, in this small town, to form a college or corporation; and they are famed for their beauty and their musical skill all over Morocco . . . [They] perform in the quartier reserve, down a network of dark passages and alleys guarded at every corner by formidable elderly matrons, of a significance that would make them into models for an Epstein and who are, really, the older or superannuated dancers, aged, it may be, thirty-five or forty years. The houses are all one-storeyed, with courtyards and flat roofs; and it is in a low room, leading off a court, that the dances take place.

Eight or nine dark figures, nuns or priestesses, snake goddesses of ancient cult, with something Phoenician in their air, votaries of

Ashtaroth or Astarte, sacred prostitutes who would dance in the temple precincts, such are the Sheikhat dancers of Tiznit. Their costume is peculiar to them; a long stiff gown, as black as black, down to their feet, many ear-rings and silver bangles, with a white coif which has nothing of the Gothic to it. Instead, it must suggest, as we have said, Carthage or Tyre, an antiquity of twenty-five centuries. The dancers are standing as we come into the room and running forward on noiseless bare feet, come up and kiss the hand of each person in turn. Such is their invariable welcome. After which they perform in unison, as it were, a most extraordinary throwing back or turning of their coifs, so that their heads are revealed as wearing silken handkerchiefs or turbans, in the manner of those dancers of Marrakesh. Now they take their instruments and the music begins. Some of their songs, after Marrakesh, are already familiar. At least two of the girls were exceptionally pretty, with a fascination of eyes and nose and lips that was a delight to watch, more particularly for the solemnity of their expression during each interminable number and for their smiles during the intervals. The age of these dancers was between fourteen and nineteen years old. . . . The Sheikhat look most impressive, also, when sitting on the floor in a long line, round three sides of a little room. Such proximity to dancers who have the identical appearance to what we must conceive of as the priestesses of so long ago is outside ordinary experience and has, in this instance, nothing of the familiar Orient about it. It is the custom, on occasion, to make one or more of the girls dance naked, and this must increase our imagined parallel to the groves of Astarte . . .

The ruins of Volubilis.
From Jean-Louis Miège, *Morocco*, 1952, pp. 154–6.

Less than a mile and a half from Mulai Idris stretch the ruins of Volubilis. And this juxtaposition of the great Islamic sanctuary and the Roman city which implanted Christianity in the country for a certain length of time, is very moving indeed. From the tableland, the last headland of the Zerhoun where Volubilis stands, one can see the white spot formed by Mulai Idris in the hollow of the mountain mass. One cannot help thinking of the antagonism and the bonds linking the two civilisations which have directed the human mind into different ways.

Morocco has very few Roman ruins whereas Proconsular and Numidia had many cities. Tingitan Mauritania was only romanized to a lesser degree. Volubilis only became Roman on Ptolemy's death but

Juba II had already transformed it. It was undoubtedly a small city but it was rather complex; successive cities arose on the site of a former Berber colony. It began to decline as early as the third century. Abandoned by the governor, who settled on the coast at Tangier, it was soon on the fringe of the Roman world but it remained a centre of 'Romanity'. Christian Berbers continued to live there and the last Latin inscriptions date from the seventh century.

In the fourteenth century, it was still described as 'a city surrounded by magnificent walls with ancient buildings and situated in a beautiful countryside'. But time, the levies made by the sultans who came there looking for stone for their buildings, the earthquake in the eighteenth century, the indifference of the population finally caused the ruin of the buildings.

In the centre of the tableland, the forum was only of medium size. The triumphal arch erected in 217 in honour of Caracalla and his mother by the governor of the province has been restored and cleared of rubble and vegetation; and its vast bay surmounted by a dedicatory inscription stands out against the horizon, facing the plain. A few steps lead up to the great basilican church (46 yards by 25) which was composed of a big central hall prolonged by an apse. It served as 'a meeting place for the council of decurions'. But with the little square around the forum it was above all the favourite meeting place of the inhabitants of Volubilis.

The details of daily life are more moving than these buildings; the public baths and their pipe-work, a house adorned with mosaics, a fountain. In this oil mill the stones that crushed the olives are intact. They crushed them exactly in the same way as we saw them crushed in a low ceilinged room in Mulai Idris.

In this country where ruins seem to fall back into their primitive state, when they disappear into the ground imperceptibly and finally cannot be made out because of the poor quality of the materials used, the columns and stones although time worn have kept their characteristics and even today we can see that they are the work of mankind. In spite of everything, Volubilis remains distant, rather sad and haughty; the bare outlines of the hills, the blue sky and the olive groves do not succeed in banishing its air of being a disdainful foreigner.

8

Villages and the Countryside

This is a random selection of writings about places of interest. People visiting the deserted site of Sijilmassa will wonder at the description of al-Idrisi, while Telouet also has lost its grandeur. Agadirs, village fortress-storehouses, described by Wyndham Lewis in the first extract, were once a feature of almost every village in Berber areas. Bus travellers can still see people assembling for the country suq as described by Fogg, and although some of the charlatans have now disappeared, we have ourselves seen patients being 'treated' with sizzling hot irons.

From Percy Wyndham Lewis, *Filibusters in Barbary*, 1932, pp. 206–7.

From a sunken court which is very intricately built you enter the main court (which is a short street) of the *Agadir*. This is a mass of deep lock-up shops, three stories high. There are not above a hundred chambers all-told in the *Agadir* of Assads: some of the largest *Agadirs* or *Ighrems*, of the Anti-Atlas, contain as many as two or three hundred. But the Assads Shop is one of the best built and is in perfect preservation.

What is most striking, externally, about this strange shuttered street is the enormous rough-hewn wedges of stone which protrude everywhere, thrust into the face of the masonry beside the doors or above the lintels, to serve as steps, up and down the fronts of the buildings of this concentrated village-street. The chambers are narrow and deep, the entrance six foot high, but in width not above four feet, penetrating to a depth of perhaps as much as fifteen feet. In the doors a small hole is cut sometimes, large enough to admit a cat. Mice are attracted by the grain, and in all the *Magazins Collectifs* cats are used to keep the mice in check.

As regards the best position, from the standpoint of the tribesmen, the middle chambers are preferred: the lowest of all are apt to be damp, being next to the ground, the uppermost suffer from leaking roofs, and the occupant of a top chamber is compelled to keep the roof in repair. One of the forms of theft most carefully provided against is that effected by making a small hole in the ceiling of a chamber and so causing the grain in the room overhead to pour down into your own. On the other hand, should rodents make holes in the wall, it is the duty of the occupier to repair them. Lastly, any door can be pulled down that is proved to be not rat-proof.

Every possible misdemeanour is provided for, and in some cases the fines imposed are rather curious. Here, for instance, is one of many such provisions:

'He who fornicates with a she-ass inside the *Agadir*, in view of the porter, or in view of any other witness (in whose testimony reliance may be placed) will pay a fine of 2 *dirkem* to the Oumanas and 3 *sa'as* of corn to the She-Ass'.

Leading out of this main court, which is also a village-street, is a narrow passage, two flights of steps, and then a subterranean passage or tunnel with shops on either side. Passing along this burrow in a crouching position, you cannot stand upright, you issue out, at the further end, upon the top of the outer ramparts. Access to the roofs is gained by means of the trunks of trees, into which steps have been cut, to serve as ladders.

Changes in a country suq after the Spanish occupation. From Walter Fogg, 'A Country Market . . .', in *Man*, 1941.

The Monday market of Sidi al-Yamani is located on an undulated sandy plateau covered with dwarf-palm scrub, where centuries of weekly trampling had left a large patch of bare, sandy ground. The market is an important one and attracts hundreds of people every week.

Before the Spanish occupation there was nothing of permanence at the market site, nor any restriction on the amount of ground-space the market occupied but the market assumed a similar plan every week. The terms *dakhl as-suq* (inside the market), *tarf as-suq* (the border of the market) and *barra min as-suq* (outside the market) were in general use, without the parts to which they referred having any definite boundaries or being of the same extent or shape every week. With a few exceptions, traders and officials of one kind invariably sat together and occupied each week a customary place, sometimes marked with stones. Officials such as the Shaykh and the notaries were on one side of the *tarf as-suq*; the slaughtering place, butchers, blacksmiths, barber-bleeders, and sheep-roasting ovens, were in the *barra min as-suq* in order to avoid the dangers attendant on the congregation of *jinnis* wherever there is blood, or fire and ashes: the animal vendors were near the outer border of the *tarf as-suq* in order to minimize the dangers through kicking, butting, goring etc; and the charcoal-sellers occupied each week the same site in the *tarf as-suq*, because of the avoidance of the blackened ground by other traders, on account of the idea of ill-luck associated with the colour black and of the soiling of feet, garments, goods etc. through contact with the soiled ground.

Before the Spanish occupation it was considered shameful for any woman in her prime to be at the market. Yet there was sex-differentiation in some of the sections. Earthen-ware, olive oil and bread, each produced in the tribal lands solely by women, and fresh green fodder, collected for sale only by women, were usually sold at the market by women only. In addition, there might be a few women, generally old or widowed and without male support in some of the other sections, e.g. those of butter, eggs, and live cocks and hens, the production or rearing of which is exclusively the concern of women. In general, however, the majority of vendors were men, and as buyers also were almost exclusively men the market as a whole was essentially a man's market.

One of the most important of recent changes has been the great increase in the number of women at the market, and this applies not only to vendors but, and even more so, to buyers. As to the vendors, commodities the production of which is the sole or part concern of the women are now sold at the market, mainly, if not exclusively, by women. Thus live cocks and hens, eggs, cheese, fresh and salt butter are now sold almost exclusively by women. Charcoal is also sold largely by women; they help their husbands in the making of it. Also even palmetto-leaf ropes, baskets and wooden spoons, although still made by men, are now sold by women. In a number of other commodities, i.e. tanned sheep and goat skins, honey and beeswax, wool, vegetables and fruit, grain and pulses, it is now the tendency for men to sell when there is for disposal a quantity large enough to require pack-animals for its transport, but for women to sell when there is for sale only an amount small enough to be transported as a back-load. In Morocco, it is the custom for country women to do much transporting of quite large and heavy quantities of goods as back-loads; it is unusual for men to do this.

Finally, there are the new women vendors who are makers of men's and women's ready-made garments of imported European-manufactured fabrics. Even now women take no part in general commerce so all goods obtained from abroad (European-manufactured cotton, silk and wool fabrics; tea, sugar, candles, soap and matches) and from other parts of Morocco (dates, dried fruits, spices and condiments) are sold at the market solely by men.

Many of the vendors, including craftsmen, made a round of markets which usually lasted a week. A Muslim making such a round would leave his home on the Friday afternoon, stay the night with a friend who lived near enough to the Saturday market for him to arrive in good time on the Saturday, leave early enough to spend Saturday night with another friend who lived near enough to the Sunday market for him to arrive in good time on the Sunday, and so on each day until the Thursday, when he would return home to spend Thursday night and most of Friday with his family. The following made the rounds regularly every week: blacksmiths, shoeing smiths, barber-bleeders, footwear-repairers; vendors of reed mats, of home-spun wool garments, of new foot-wear, of smoking-hemp and tobacco, of Moorish sweets, of dried fruits, of kerosene, of tea, of sugar, candles, soap and spices; makers of sponge-fritters, of cooked meat, of hot tea and coffee; and in season vendors of salted sardines, and of ploughing materials. In addition some water-carriers, some entertainers and one or two folk-doctors appeared at the market frequently.

Finally there were always in the past, between five and ten charm-writers at the market; now these are no longer permitted, the Spaniards considering them an indirect cause of disturbances of the market peace. Likewise because of their open excitement of homosexual passions, with possible ensuing jealousies and disturbances, acrobats and dancing boys are no longer permitted.

An account of Sijilmassa in the twelfth century which was based on hearsay.

From Abu Abdullah Muhammad al-Idrisi, *Géographie* 1154 (Paris, 1840 edn), vol. I, p. 207.

Sijilmassa is a capital, visited by travellers from every country, adorned with many buildings, surrounded by gardens, orchards and fields. It has no citadel but contains numerous palaces, houses and buildings of all sorts standing together. It is situated on the banks of a river with a flow as great as that of the Nile coming out of the desert from the east. The local people use the water for agriculture in the same way as the Egyptians. Crops are abundant and never fail and often, after years of flooding, they grow spontaneously. Ibn Haukal recounts that it is necessary only to sow once to harvest for the next six years but eventually the grain deteriorates into a cross between barley and oats. There are all sorts of fruit in abundance – notably a kind of green date which is very small but surpasses in sweetness all other fruits. The inhabitants also cultivate cotton, cumin, parsnips and henna: these they export through the Maghrib and beyond. The buildings are very beautiful but were much damaged during the recent troubles. The inhabitants eat dogs and lizards and the women suppose that it is to this diet that they owe the characteristic stoutness of their figures.

A description of Telouet, the stronghold of the House of Glaoua.

From Gavin Maxwell, *Lords of the Atlas . . .*, 1966, pp. 23–7.

The castle stands at an altitude of more than 8,000 feet in the High Atlas mountains of Morocco. It and its scattered rookery of crumbling predecessors occupy the corner of a desert plateau, circled by the giant peaks of the Central Massif, all of them rising to more than 10,000 feet, and some, such as the great Jebel Ghat to the eastward, reaching 12,500. When in the spring the snows begin to thaw and the river below the castle, the Oued Mellah, becomes a torrent of ice-grey and white, the mountains reveal their fantastic colours, each distinct and contrasting with its neighbour. The hues are for the most part the range of colours to be found upon fan shells – reds, vivid pinks, violets, yellows, but among these are peaks of cold mineral green or of dull blue. Nearer at hand, where the Oued Mellah turns to flow through the valley of salt, a cluster of ghostly spires, hundreds of feet high and needle-pointed at their summits, cluster before the face of a precipice; vultures wheel and turn upon the air currents between them . . .

Even in this setting the castle does not seem insignificant. It is neither beautiful nor gracious, but its sheer size, as if in competition with the scale of the mountains, compels attention as much as the fact that its pretension somehow falls short of the ridiculous. The castle, or *kasbah*, of Telouet is a tower of tragedy that leaves no room for laughter.

The double doors to the forecourt are twenty feet high. A giant Negro slave opens the lock with a key a foot long and sets his shoulder to the iron-bossed wood; the door gives way reluctantly, inch by inch, creaking and rasping upon rusty hinges. A kestrel hawk, disturbed from its nest in the wall above, flies out scolding with sharp staccato cries. The surface of the courtyard is an uneven rubble, sloping sharply to the left, down to the curtain wall, where row upon row of dark doorways lead to the stable quarters. Above them are castellated look-out posts facing the Jebel Ghat. There is sheep-dung scattered among the rubble, and the reddish curling horn of a Moroccan ram. To the right rises the whole mass of the *kasbah*, tower and rooftop: ill-ordered, ill-planned, but majestic in its proliferation and complete absence of symmetry. There are three colours only – whitewash, red stone or clay, and brilliant green roof tiles. Above these the ever-present birds of prey, the vultures, ravens and kites, weave slow and intricate patterns upon the hard blue sky. There is no sound but their calling, and the clacking bills of the storks which nest on every tower.

The slave unlocks an intricately carved door in the white wall to the right of the forecourt. The number and weight of keys that he carries is so great that in order to support them he wears a heavy silk rope about his shoulders, concealed by his *djellabah*, an ankle-length white woollen garment with a hood, and further hidden by his *selham*, a black woollen cloak, also with a hood, which envelops all.

He carries sixty-seven keys. He has been in sole charge of Telouet for three years, but even now he does not know his way through the labyrinth that was constructed intentionally as such. He can find his way to the kitchens (I counted two hundred and thirty-eight paces and twenty-two doors unlocked), but he cannot find his way from these to the harem without going back to the main reception quarters and looking out of the windows to reorientate himself.

It was to these reception rooms that he wanted always to return; they were the outward and visible sign of ultimate physical ambition. They were all on one floor, but three hundred men had worked on them for three years, plasterworkers, carvers, and one painter, who covered inches rather than feet daily. This man had been paid, by Moroccan standards, an enormous wage – about £22 a week. The owner of the castle had intended that it should become the most fabulous palace in the world, a Château de Coucy, an Xanadu. It had already been called 'The Palace of a Thousand and One Nights'.

The décor was in the main based upon the stalagmite theme of the Saadien tombs (the Saadiens were an earlier dynasty of Moroccan

Sultans who reigned from 1554 to 1659), but it embraced, also, every style that was luxurious, however debased, and made use of every traditional motif. A (comparatively) small salon in which the occupant entertained intimate guests incorporated continuous three-foot-high panels of silks and brocades from Lyons, rugs from Rabat, Persia, Turkestan and the High Atlas, comparatively crude work and bastard design alternating with high craftsmanship of all nations.

The harem is paved and walled with painted tiles that seem, for the most part, to be of modern Italian origin, though some have the detailed beauty of the ancient Hispano-Mauresque. The carved and painted yew wood ceilings of the reception rooms are Moorish in concept, as is the Saadien plasterwork of the noble alcoves. But deep invading cracks cut crudely through the intricate elaboration of years of work, for Telouet is empty now; only the Negro slaves, almost destitute, linger on to tend the relics of a dead dynasty.

I have various images of Telouet. The last and most enduring is after a great snowfall when more than four thousand sheep and goats in the surrounding mountains were buried and killed by suffocation. When the snows thawed and the carcases were exposed every vulture, kite and raven congregated on Telouet. As the sun went down the air was dark with them as with a swarm of locusts; they homed for Telouet in their thousands, like starlings in Trafalgar Square, till the branches of the trees broke under them, till the battlements of the castle were foul with their excreta, and still, as the last of the light went, the black wings were thronging in to alight and jostle their neighbours. It was on that night that, listening to the jackals howling, I became lost in the castle, and found my torch shining upon white but manacled bones in a dungeon. With the turbulent history of Telouet they could have been either a hundred or less than five years old.

'In every governor's *Kasbah*, deep in damp dungeons – as often as not holes scooped in the earth for storing grain – there lay and pined those who had committed, or not committed, as the case might be, some crime; and still more often, those who were rich enough to be squeezed. In such suffering, and in darkness, receiving just sufficient nourishment to support life, men were known to have existed for years, to emerge again long after their relations had given up all hope of seeing them. But there was always a chance – a chance that the Governor might die or fall into disgrace; and then the dungeons in his castle would be opened and the wrecks of his prisoners be released. And what prisons! what horrors of prisons they were, even those above ground and reserved for the ordinary class of criminal. Chained neck to neck, with heavy shackles on their legs, they sat or lay in filth, and often the cruel iron collars were only undone to take away a corpse.' 'The whole life in those great Atlas fortified *Kasbahs* was one of warfare and of gloom. Every tribe had its enemies, every family had its blood-feuds, and every man his would-be murderer.'

Work on Telouet was still in progress when the régime fell ten years ago, the only event that could logically bring it to a halt. The plasterers and tilers and mosaic-workers had a programme lasting for years ahead. There are windows still unglazed, others awaiting the addition of the elaborate wrought iron work with which they were all to be embellished. Many walls carry the bold charcoal outlines for an ambitious mosaic that was never begun, for the whole vast palace and all its uncountable rooms were to have been decorated with the same disregard for time or money. Builders were at work on further extensions to the castle itself, here a new wing, here a lofty gallery from which guests might watch feats of horsemanship on the green sward below.

Telouet presented, in fact, a picture that was almost unique, for it was not a mediaeval survival, as are the few European castles still occupied by the descendants of feudal barons, but a deliberate re-creation of the Middle Ages, with all their blatant extremes of beauty and ugliness, good and evil, elegance and violence, power and fear – by those who had full access to the inventions of contemporary science. No part of the *kasbah* is more than a hundred years old; no part of its ruined predecessors goes back further than another fifty. Part of the castle is built of stone, distinguishing it sharply from the other *kasbahs* that are made of *pisé*, or sun-dried mud, for no matter to what heights of beauty or fantasy these may aspire they are all, in the final analysis, soluble in water.

From this desolate group of ruins in the High Atlas, so far from the seat of government at Fez, there arose by a strange chain of coincidence a generation of kingmakers. They were two brothers, chiefs of an insignificant mountain tribe, and they rose in that one generation to depose two Sultans, to become the true rulers of Morocco, to shake the whole French political structure; and, with their downfall, to add a new and uncomfortable word to the French language. The name of the tribe was *Glaoua*, and *glaouisé* now means, in French political jargon, betrayed. Neither France nor Morocco is over-anxious to recall the tale behind the word; and for this reason, if for no other, a true reconstruction presents the historian with formidable difficulties.

We include two accounts of the Tafilet in the south-east corner of Morocco. The first was based on the account of an unknown writer who may have visited the area. The author of the second extract definitely saw it for himself.

From Simon Ockley, *An Account of South West Barbary . . .*, 1713, pp. 24–5; and from René Caillié, *Travels through Central Africa . . .*, 1830 (1968 edn), vol. II, pp. 186–90.

Southwards of Tarudant lies the vast country of Tafilet, where the present King of Morocco was born; it is reckoned nearly as large as the former, and is fruitful and better peopled. Here the inhabitants, as well as those of Tarudant, are a wild, savage, and cruel people, and generally more ignorant than those of the Low Countries. Their sheep are monstrously large and fat, and have short hair instead of wool: and on the contrary, the people have wool on their heads instead of hair. This country is reckoned about three weeks' journey from Meknes though if they could go straight to it, it would not be so much; but because there are mountains in the way which they cannot pass, but are forced to go round, they seldom make less of it.

The Tafilet is a small district forming, like el-Drah, part of the dominions of the Emperor of Morocco. Its inhabitants pay some imposts to this monarch, who maintains a pasha or governor at Ressant, a town distinguished by a magnificent gateway, surrounded by various coloured Dutch tiles, symmetrically arranged in a diamond pattern. The soil is level, composed of sand of an ash grey, and is very productive; much corn, and all sorts of European fruits and vegetables, are cultivated here; lucern thrives well, and when dry is stored for winter provender. The numberless date trees surrounding each property furnish their owners with a plentiful subsistence and a considerable branch of commerce. They sell a quantity of dates in all the dependencies of Morocco, and especially in the towns situated on the sea-coast.

The natives have fine sheep, with remarkably white wool; they use it in making very handsome wrappers, which are woven by the women. They have also some horned cattle, though fewer than the roving tribes, excellent horses, some asses, and many good mules. The horses are for the most part the property of the Berbers, who are very numerously established in Tafilet, but less addicted to pillage than those of el-Drah, and indeed formidable to strangers alone.

This country is in general very agreeable: its inhabitants carry on a considerable commerce with the Soudan, whither they export tobacco in leaves of their own growing, together with European commodities; and receive in exchange gold, ivory, gum, ostrich-feathers, dried provisions, and slaves: for unhappily, the infamous traffic in the latter exists in full vigour in this part of Africa. The commodities which the merchants dispatch to Timbuctoo, through the medium of the roving Moors, are transported on camels to the confines of the desert by Berbers, who deliver them to the Moors engaged to convey them to their destination. The Berbers receive a tribute for this service, a species of indemnity given to them by agreement, since they do not, like the Arabs, extend their travels through all the negro countries. If the merchants were to neglect this prudent precaution, their caravans would be pillaged by these barbarians, as they sometimes are by the Touariks. I have already said that the most distinguished Moors of Tafilet usually settle in Timbuctoo, in the hope of making a fortune, as amongst us Europe is left for the new world; these Moors, after devoting five or six years to commerce, purchase gold and slaves, and return to live peaceably in their own country.

The inhabitants of Tafilet tan a great quantity of leather; they make excellent morocco, which is much esteemed in commerce, and finds at Fez a ready market. The people of this country are more industrious than I have any where remarked in the different parts of Africa which I have visited.

Each proprietor is accustomed to enclose his lands either with an earth wall or a ditch; all the villages are walled, and those I have seen have but one gate of entrance, which is shut every evening. The inhabitants rear much poultry, as large as ours, and eat the eggs boiled. They have pigeons, but these birds are scarce. Some individuals keep a dog and a cat, which live upon dates.

Throughout the districts of el-Drah and Tafilet are found Jews who inhabit the same villages with the Musulmans; they are in a pitiable condition, wandering about almost naked, and continually insulted by the Moors; these fanatics even beat them shamefully, and throw stones at them as at dogs; the smallest children may abuse them with impunity, since they dare not revenge themselves, and cannot expect protection from authority.

The Jews of Tafilet are excessively dirty, and always go barefoot, perhaps to avoid the inconvenience of frequently taking off their sandals, which they are compelled to do in passing before a mosque or the door of a sherif. They shave their heads after the example of the Moors, but leave a tuft of hair which falls over the forehead. Some are pedlars, others artizans; they manufacture shoes and mats from palm-leaves; some of them also are blacksmiths. They lend their money upon usury to merchants trading in the Soudan, whither they never go themselves.

The Jews live better than the Mahometans, couscous and gruel forming but a small portion of their food; their bread is of wheat, kneaded and baked by themselves and their principal beverage, beer of their own brewing, though in the season of the vintage they make a little wine.

We have accounts of other provinces by old writers, once again one is based on personal observation and the other on the information brought back by travellers. The first, that of the province of Haha, the hinterland of Mogador; the second concerns that of the Dukala, further north, inland from Mazagan.

From Leo Africanus, *Description of Africa*, 1550 (1896 edn), vol. II, pp. 227–9; and from John Ogilby, *Africa* . . ., 1670, p. 160.

The region of Hea is an uneeven and rough soile, full of rockie mountaines, shadie woods and chrystall-streames in all places; being woonderfully rich and wel stored with inhabitants. They have in the said region greate abundance of goates and asses, but not such plentie of sheepe, oxen and horses. All kinds of fruites are very scarce among them, not that the ground is uncapable of fruit, but that the people are so rude and ignorant in this behalfe, that very few of them are skilfull in planting, graffing, or pruning of trees. . . . They have great abundance of honie, which they use in stead of ordinary foode, but the waxe they cast away, little regarding it, because they know not the value thereof . . .

Manner of living and foode

The people for the most part eateth barlie-bread unlevened, which is like rather unto a cake, then to a loafe: this bread is baked in a kinde of earthen baking-pan, somewhat like unto that wherewith in Italie they use to cover iunkats and daintie dishes. They use also a certaine unsavourie and base kinde of meate which is made in the manner following: they cast barlie-meale into boiling water, continually tempering and stirring the same with a sticke, till they perceive it to be sufficiently sodden. Then setting this pap or hastie-pudding upon the table, and powring in some of their countrie-oile, all the whole familie stand round about the platter, and eate the said pap not with spoones, but with their hands and fingers. Howbeit in the spring and summer season they temper the said meale with milke, and cast in butter instead of oile: and this kind of meate is not usuall among them, but only at supper. For in winter time they breake their fast with bread and honie: and in summer with milke, butter and bread. Moreover sometimes they use to eat sodden flesh, whereunto some adde onions, others beanes, and some other a kinde of seasoning or sauce called by them *Cuscuscu*. With them tables and table-cloathes are quite out of use, in stead whereof they spread a certaine round mat upon the ground, which serveth among this rude people both for table, cloth and all.

Apparell and customs of the foresaid people

The greatest part of them are clad in kinde of cloath-garment made of wooll after the manner of a coverlet and not unlike unto those coverlets or blankets which Italians lay upon their beds. In these kinde of mantles they wrap themselves; and then are girt with a woollen girdle, not about their waste, but about their hippes. They have also a certaine piece of cloath of ten handfuls in length and two in bredth, wherewith they use to adorne their heads: these kind of ornaments or head-tires they dye with the iuice of walnut-tree-rootes, being so put upon their heads that their crownes are alwaies bare. None of them weare any cap, except it be an olde man, or a man of learning; albeit learned men are verie rare among them; which caps of theirs are double and rounde, not much unlike the caps of certain Phisitians in Italy. You shall seldom finde any linnen shirts or smockes among this people; and that (as I suppose) either because their soile will yeeld no flaxe nor hemp, or else that they have none skilfull in the art of weaving. Their seats whereupon they sit, are nought else but certaine mats made of hayre and rushes. For beds they use a certaine kinde of hairie flockbed or mattresse; some of which beds are ten elles in length, some more and some lesse, yea some you shall finde of twenty elles long, but none longer: one part of the mattresses they lye upon insteed of a couch, and with the residue they cover their bodies as it were with blankets and coverlets. In the Spring-time alwaies they lay the hairie side next unto their bodies, because it is somewhat warmer; but in Sommer-time they turn the smooth side upward and thereupon they rest themselves. The women goe commonly with their faces uncovered, using for their huswifery turned vessels and cups of wood: their platters, dishes, and other kitchin-vessels be for the most part of earth. You may easily discerne which of them is married, and who is not: for an unmarried man must always keepe his beard shaven, which, after hee be once married, hee suffereth to grow at length. The said region bringeth foorth no great plentie of horses, but those that it doth bring foorth, are so nimble and full of mettall, that they will climbe like cats over the steepe and craggie mountaines. These horses are always unshod: and the people of this region use to till their ground with no other cattell, but onely with horses and asses. You shall heere finde great store of deere, of wild goats, and of hares: Howbeit the people are not whit delighted in hunting. Which is the cause (as I thinke) why the said beasts do so multiply. And it is somewhat strange, that so many rivers runing through the countrey, they should have such scarcity of water-mils: but the reason is, because everie household almost have a woodden mill of their owne, whereat their women usually grinde with their hands. No good learning nor liberall artes are heere to be found; except it bee a little skill in the lawes, which some few chalenge unto themselves; otherwise you shall find not so much as any shadow of vertue among them. They have neither Phisition nor Surgeon of any learning or account. But if a disease or infirmitie befall any of them, they presently seare or cauterize the sicke partie with red hot yrons, even as the Italians use their horses. Howbeit some churugians there are among them, whose duty and occupation consisteth onely in circumcising of their male children. They make no sope in all the countrey, but instead thereof they use to wash with lee made of ashes. They are at continuall warre, but it is civill and among themselves, insomuch that they have no leisure to fight against other nations. Whosoever will travell into a forren countrey must take either a harlot, or a wife, or a religious man of the contrarie part, to bear him companie.

In Dukala breed a kind of wilde oxen, by the inhabitants call'd Guahix, and by the Spaniards *Vacas Bravas* or *Mad Bulls*; they run as swift as a Hart, and are smaller than an ox, with a dark brown leather. They generally range through the woods in great Herds. In the Rivers are found great pieces of Amber, abounding also with Shad, Pikes, Eels and other varieties of Fish.

We have also chosen an ancient and a modern account of life in the mountains of Morocco. Once again we have selected a passage from Leo Africanus who wrote about Jabal Zerhoun near Meknes. From Jim Ingram comes a description of a tramp across the Middle Atlas.

From Leo Africanus, *Description of Africa*, 1550 (1896 edn), vol. II, pp. 488–9; and from Jim Ingram, *Land of Mud Castles*, 1952, pp. 136–8.

This mountaine beginneth from the plaine of Essais lying ten miles distant from the citie of Fez; westward it extendeth thirtie miles, and is almost ten miles broad. This mountaine is all covered with waste and desert woods, being otherwise well stored with olives. In this mountaine there are of sheepe-foldes and castles to the number of fiftie, and the inhabitants are very wealthy, for it standeth betweene two flourishing cities, that is to say Fez to the east, and Mecnase on the west. The women weave woollen cloth, according to the custome of that place, and are adorned with many silver rings and bracelets. The men of this mountaine are most valiant, and are much given to pursue and take lions, whereof they send great store unto the king of Fez. And the king hunteth the said lions in manner following: in a large field there are certaine little cels made, being so high, that a man may stand upright in them: each of these cels is shut fast with a little doore: and containe within every of them an armed man, who opening the doore presents himself to the view of the lion: then the lion seeing the doores open, comes running towards them with great furie, but the doores being shut againe, he waxeth more furious than before: then bring they foorth a bull to combate with the lion, who enter a fierce and bloudie conflict, wherein if the bull kill the lion, that daies sport is at an end; but if the lion get the victorie, then all the armed men, being ordinarily twelve, leape foorth of their cels and invade the lion: each one having a iavelin with a pike of a cubite and an halfe long. And if these armed men seme to bee too hard for the lion, the king causeth their number to be diminished: but perceiving them too weake, the king with his companie from a certaine high place, where he standeth to behold the sport, kill the lion with their crossebowes. And oftentimes it falleth out, that before the lion be slaine, some one of the men dies for it, the residue being sore wounded. The reward of those who encounter the lion is ten duckats apeece, and a new garment: neither are any admitted unto this combat but men of redoubted valour, and such as come from mount Zelagi; but those that take the lion first are inhabitants of mount Zarhon.

Timhadit is an interesting, even exciting place, for it is perched beneath the rim of an extinct volcano and below it the Guigo River plunges seaward through a gorge walled in by cliffs of lava and black basalt. Crowning the crater's rim is a French military outpost, guarding the road below, an outpost often isolated by snow in the winter months when it can only be reached on skis.

A few miles further along the track, perched atop a nine-thousand-foot mountain peak, is the isolated fort of Bekrit, whose history is one of the stormiest and bloodiest in Morocco; several times it has been besieged, and relieving columns have had to fight their way through to rescue the garrison.

The extinct crater of Timhadit marks the beginning of a wierd and fascinating scenic area which has been described by some French writers as 'the landscape of the moon'. And Mountains of the Moon is certainly an apt description, for the similarity to photographs of lunar landscapes strikes one immediately, a landscape dominated by dead volcanoes and seamed with ancient lava flows. There is a peculiar atmosphere about this region which impressed itself upon me while tramping southwards, an atmosphere of utter lifelessness, as though man had no place in this bleak volcanic country, an atmosphere of complete timelessness, so that it might have been but the day before yesterday when the red lava broke through earth's crust and flowed in turgid streams over the land.

Hour after hour I tramped steadily southward, resting five minutes in every hour, glad to squat beneath my umbrella in the scanty shade of ditches and rocks. Though I did not know it till later, this sun-scorched pass over seven thousand feet high was the Col du Zad, and from thence onward there was a steady descent to the Moulouya Valley; my ambition of tramping over the Middle Atlas Mountains was achieved. But at the moment all I was conscious of was heat and thirst, and my main concern was whether there was a canteen between the pass and the settlement of Midelt, fifty-five miles away.

In the midst of this bleak volcanic country is a scene of beauty where the Lake of Sidi Ali lies blue and tranquil within its encircling mountain walls. I had heard of this big crater lake, occupying the interior of a six-thousand-foot volcanic cone, so the following morning found me tramping over the reddish, lava-scarred countryside to its shores. A little lakeside resort was coming into being, for a few tents were perched on a grassy bank above the water, and a canteen was being constructed near by. Several motor-cars were parked somewhat incongruously beside half a dozen supercilious-looking camels.

A blue-cloaked *Mokhazni*, or native policeman, carrying a rifle under his arm, came up for a chat, and under his watchful eye I undressed and had a bathe. The water was cold, so I did not stay in long: the lake is said to be several hundred feet deep. Some men were fishing from boats farther out in the lake, for the place was a resort of French officers with a penchant for fishing.

Another day of tramping across desolate lava-strewn country followed. Every so often forts could be seen crowning the hill tops, and men seemed to carry rifles as a matter of course. As the road descended to the six-thousand-foot level it passed through a belt of cedar forest corresponding to that on the northern side of the range. Once again it was a joy to see these big trees towering up into the sky; a forest of such trees is, I think, more impressive than anything made by man.

9

Travelling

This chapter shows what travelling was like in Morocco before the days of modern transport. Travellers had to assume that nothing could be bought locally and they should take the huge amount of necessities described by Lady Grove, Watson and Kerr. There was a traditional view that it was preferable to set out late in the day so as to leave time to go home to collect anything that had been forgotten. In the absence of a courier, an interpreter was needed and might be shanghaied from a synagogue, as Lempriere described. Sometimes travellers had to swim across rivers – as described by Thomson. In the absence of hotels the occupants of houses were expelled. In the wilder parts a guide was vital and it was just possible that on arrival the traveller would be attacked by the local people, as happened to Rohlfs. There were, however, compensations for all these hardships in *mona* – the obligation upon villagers to feed travellers, even tourists.

A picture of her life under a tent.
From Lady Grove, *Seventy-one Days Camping in Morocco*, 1902, pp. 7 and 18–19.

Our staff of servants consisted of fifteen Moors as far as Morocco City, and to these were added five of the Sultan's soldiers to protect us on our perilous mountain ascent. Thus making twenty-five strong, twenty-four of whom were armed. The four fully adult Christians carried pistols. My pistol never left my side . . .

I acquired a quite cat-like affection for my tent. And a very nice dear tent it is. A white tent 12 × 10, the floor covered with ground sheets and rugs; on the right-hand side my bed, on the left my table, which was dressing-table, wash-stand or writing-table 'at will'; my small box, two chairs, and last, but not least, my beloved hold-all. This hold-all was the comfort of my life, containing the various necessaries of life, combs, soap, brushes, nail-cleaners, eau-de-cologne, *vinaigre de toilette*, hair-wash, boracic acid, borax, powders, slippers etc. The contents of this hold-all were never misplaced – no one ever packed or unpacked it but I myself.

Like the good little girl who was never late for school, I 'did my washing over-night'. I hasten to add, lest I should be misunderstood, that the whole time – over two months – that we were under canvas, I never went one single day without my hot bath in the morning; not even when, as we were obliged to do latterly, we got up at five every morning.

I forgot to mention that in addition to the veil a white, green-lined umbrella was always used. I never rode a yard in the sun without holding it up, and I do not think the whole time I had a single headache.

R. S. Watson hired a guide to take him from Tangier to Al Kasar, Wazan, Tetuan and back to Tangier. His guide was to provide an approved riding mule with saddle and bridle, five good baggage mules, two approved tents, and good and sufficient bedding, washing utensils, cooking utensils and everything necessary for the journey. He would also provide a good cook, good and sufficient food, two soldiers as an escort, and a sufficient number of attendants. For this Watson was to pay ten douros a day. He also took the following supplies.

From R. S. Watson, *A Visit to Wazan*, 1880, p. 319.

One pound green tea, one pound black tea, two pounds of coffee, six pounds of loaf sugar, four pounds of wax candles, two pounds of salt, quarter pound of pepper, three pounds of rice, jar of Durham mustard, large packet of cake chocolate, three boxes of night-lights to burn eight hours, six large boxes of extra-sized wax matches, two pounds of tobacco, twelve boxes of vesuvians, eight cases of coloured fires, twenty yards of magnesium ribbon, tin case of filter papers, guttapercha funnel, three pots of jam, two pots of marmalade, two tins of sardines, three boxes of water biscuits, two tins of condensed milk, sixteen boxes of rhubarb pills, sixteen boxes of seidlitz powders; three revolvers, a double-barrelled pistol, two watches, and six boxes of percussion caps, and bullet moulds for each pistol, for presents; a case of Keating's insect powder, one bottle Florida water, one bottle Hollands, one bottle pale brandy.

Advice to travellers on what to wear and what not to eat. From Dr Robert Kerr, *Morocco* . . ., 1912, pp. 359–60.

Clothing should always be of good quality, but never too heavy. Much more attention should be paid to underclothing than is generally done. Flannel should be worn summer and winter, lighter and heavier according to season.

Cotton or linen suits for summer are very agreeable, and one should never have more clothing than is absolutely necessary as it is eaten by insects. Full dress suits are unnecessary, and only an encumbrance, except for those who may desire them for evening parties. Jacket suits are by far the most convenient.

Good pith helmets for summer, the lighter the more serviceable. Guard always the nape of the neck when travelling by wearing puggarees. Boots should never be heavy, yet they must have good firm soles. Never be without a waterproof coat, leggings, rain and sun umbrellas.

Cholera belts I have found most useful, and strongly recommend every one never to be without them.

Diet will always vary according to one's tastes. Food in summer should be light and nourishing. Not so much quantity as quality. Oatmeal, cheese and bacon should be avoided in summer, as they are far too heating.

Many people on coming to Morocco pride themselves on being able to eat every kind of Moorish dish, but this is most unwise.

Fish, fowls &c, cooked in oil and rancid butter almost invariably upset one's digestion.

Care must also be exercised as regards fruit, even though ripe, while I have seen the most alarming symptoms produced from eating pears, apricots, and dates, even among adults . . .

Bread from newly cut grain is very injurious.

Milk, unless one knows the source of the supply, should be boiled. All water used for drinking purposes should first be filtered and then boiled. This is of paramount importance and the best safeguard against sickness.

Finding an interpreter.
From William Lempriere, *A Tour from Gibraltar to Tangier, Sallee* . . ., 1791, printed in Pinkerton, vol. XV, pp. 634–5.

Two horsemen of the Black of Negro cavalry, armed with long muskets and sabres, were dispatched by the prince to escort me and had been waiting for that purpose for some time. The governor of the town had orders to supply me with a tent, mules, and an interpreter. But it was not without much difficulty that a person could be found in Tangier who could speak the English and Arabic languages sufficiently well to perform that office; and it was owing to an accident that I at length was enabled to obtain one.

After searching the whole town in vain, the governor ordered, during the Jewish hour of prayer, that enquiries should be made among all the synagogues for a person who understood both languages. An unfortunate Jew, whose occupation was that of selling fruit in the streets of Gibraltar, and who had come to Tangier merely to spend a few days with his wife and family during a Jewish festival, being unacquainted with the intent of the enquiry, unguardedly answered in the affirmative. Without further ceremony the poor man was dragged away from his friends and home, and constrained by force to accompany me.

Of the mode in this despotic government of seizing persons at the arbitrary pleasure of a governor, an Englishman can scarcely form an idea. Three or four lusty Moors with large clubs in their hands, grasp the wretched and defenceless victim with as much energy as if he was an Hercules, from whom they expected the most formidable resistance, and half shake him to death before they deliver him up to the superior power. Such exactly was the situation of my unfortunate interpreter.

From the sudden and abrupt manner in which he was hurried away, in the midst of his devotions, the women immediately took alarm, flew in a body to the house of the consul, and with shrieks and lamentations endeavoured to prevail upon him to get the man excused from his journey. Upon the consul's assuring them that the wife would be taken care of, and the husband sent back without any expence to him on our arrival at Mogadore, where I was to be furnished with another interpreter, and upon my promising to protect the Jew from insult, and, if he behaved well, to reward him for his trouble, the women immediately dispersed, and returned home apparently satisfied.

When this business was completed, the consul furnished me with a proper quantity of liquors, two days provisions, a bedstead formed by three folding stools, for the conveniency of packing it on the mules, with proper cooking utensils, and an oil-skin case to carry my bedding. The whole of my equipage, therefore, consisted of two Negro soldiers, a Jewish interpreter, one saddle-mule for myself, and another for him, two baggage-mules, and a Moorish muleteer on foot to take care of them.

How he forded a flooded river.
From Joseph Thomson, *Travels in the Atlas*, 1889, pp. 109–11.

I was the first to attempt the crossing [of a flooded ford on the Tensift]. Mounting the tall horse of one of the soldiers, and stripped to the shirt, I plunged into the swift stream, one naked Moor guiding the horse, and leaving me nothing to do but hold on, while another swam alongside in the event of accident. At the first plunge the horse quite disappeared, and the water nearly reached my waist. The crowd on the bank filled the air with cries of 'Allah' or directions to the swimming man. For a moment the situation looked nasty, the rushing water producing in me a momentary giddiness. After a second or two the horse's head reappeared with a snort, and we drifted rapidly down the stream. Soon, however, the horse struck ground, and then wildly plunged forward.

Shortly after C-B, bolder than I was, and desirous of showing the Moors how swimming ought to be done, dashed into the flood by himself. But alas for the pride and the arrogance of youth! He soon found out that he had altogether miscalculated the force of the current, and he drifted down the stream with alarming rapidity, while making almost no headway across. Fifty voices yelled directions in Arabic. The soldiers, who were responsible for our safety, danced about in despair, and having no hair on their heads, tore their beards. A score or more of swarthy natives dashed into the stream, while others ran along the bank gesticulating like madmen.

The most exciting incident was the passage of one of the soldiers. In some fashion or other the horse he bestrode was caught by the swift current and rolled over and over, he clinging desperately thereunto. Sometimes a man's head and shoulders would appear above water, sometimes four horse's legs striking madly out, or it might be the horse's head, with wild, terror-stricken eyeballs. He too reached the bank in safety. A mule was nearly drowned, and some of our things were wetted, but no worse damage happened. It took us three hours to complete the fording of the river.

Next morning, while quickly demolishing some breakfast before starting for Saffi, I had occasion to remonstrate sharply with our man, Abdul Kader, for allowing Selim the camel-driver, to wash some dishes in our drinking-water. He as sharply answered that it was not true. Whereupon, assuming paternal authority, I slapped him in the face, with all due deliberation, as one doing a painful duty for the welfare of the one castigated. His face became perfectly ashy in colour, and his hand sought his dagger. It was not by his side. All the men had seen the blow, and all alike started as if each himself had received it.

There was a moment of thunderstruck silence. Then Abdul Kader, finding vent to his choking passion, poured out an incoherent torrent of Arabic, English and Spanish phrases. I did not strike without thought or reason. I had waited for this opportunity to finally settle the exact conditions on which we were to travel together. My time had come, and I had acted.

Some further hazards of nineteenth-century travel. From Dr Robert Kerr, *Pioneering in Morocco*, 1894, pp. 25–6, 212–13, and 175.

February 2nd 1886. We arrived at Rabat about 7 a.m. Here we lay rolling the whole day. Owing to the heavy surf on the bar the lighters were unable to cross, although they made several attempts to do so. The bar is very treacherous, and we were informed that sometimes ships have to lie at anchor for several days before they are able to communicate.

February 3rd. We spent rather a restless night, thinking of the not very pleasing prospect of being carried sixty miles down the coast. At 7.30 a.m. to our great delight, the steward came to our cabin and informed us that a lighter had crossed the bar. After reading the 92nd Psalm we knelt and unitedly thanked God for his journeying mercies.

Breakfast over we bade farewell to the S.S. *Empusa*. It is rather a strange experience, for the first time, going down a rope ladder, on the side of a rolling ship. Safely into the lighter with ten other passengers, and some fifteen tons of cargo, we pulled for the shore, on the top of enormous waves. On approaching the bar, the scene was changed. We were now in the midst of the breakers, and at the same time were being carried towards the rocks by the undercurrent of the river. The boatmen shrieked, calling on God and all the patron saints; while the captain's voice was heard above the noise of all the surging waves, calling out 'Oh be men! God will help you'. The sailors, at great odds, held on manfully to their oars.

The scene ended in one great climax. An enormous wave overtook us, and, breaking over the lighter, thoroughly drenched us, and half filled the lighter with water. Mr Mackintosh was driven against a cross-bar and had one of his ribs fractured. Withal, he appeared to enjoy it, for he laughed, and called out to me 'Baptized into Rabat'. April 8th, 1891. We arrived at Mequinez about noon, but had to wait two hours before we got a house. There are no inns for travellers, so the people had to be turned out of their house to make room for us. We had just gathered all our belongings into the house, when one of the occupants, a woman, came. She screamed, yelled and shouted. 'Why have you brought Christians into my house?' The soldiers answered 'One word more and you are off to prison'. As two rooms were quite sufficient for us, we allowed the occupants to remain in the others. Highly appreciating our considerateness, they remarked that we were more kind-hearted than their brothers the Moslems.

An account of the system of protection for travellers in country areas.

From Walter Harris, *Tafilet*, 1895, pp. 97–9.

A few words must be said as to the manner in which native travellers proceed in safety through districts in which bloodshed and murder are of everyday occurrence. The system under which immunity from murder and robbery is accorded to the stranger is known by two names, *mzareg* or *zitat*. *Mzareg* originally means a spear, and the term was thus applied from the fact that in the old days a spear was given by one of the tribe to the traveller, which, having been recognised as the property of one of their number, accorded him safety in his journey. However, spears have long since disappeared from these districts, though the name *mzareg* still remains. Nowadays the common custom is for a member of the tribe, in consideration of a small fee, to conduct the traveller in person, both being sacred from attack while passing through the land over which the tribe in question holds jurisdiction. As soon as the limits are reached, a new *mzareg* or *zitat* has to be obtained. Sometimes, especially in the case of Jews living and trading in the Sahara, some mark or token is given, such as a turban or handkerchief; which is considered sufficient; but in cases of caravans and total strangers a man invariably is employed, who answers the double purpose of guide and protector. From Dads to Tafilet I was accompanied on my journey by a *zitat*, without whom I could never have reached my destination, as amongst the many Berber tribes we passed through his presence afforded me immunity from inquisition and annoyance. Here again I was fortunate, for I was not obliged to change my *zitat*, the fact being that members of the tribe of Dads can travel in safety amongst nearly all the other Berber tribes, by a reciprocal arrangement by which the caravans of the others are allowed to pass through their district without fear of plunder. Dads has gained this unique privilege from its situation, blocking as it does the entire road from east to west.

With regard to the Jews living amongst the Berbers a similar practice exists, only in their case it is known as *debeha*, or sacrifice. This name has been applied from the fact that the system first arose from Jews seeking the protection of the Berbers by sacrificing an ox or a sheep to them: nowadays native Jews no longer need to perform this, the patronage of the Berbers being hereditary, the vassalage descending in both families from father to son. Any injury suffered by the Jew is revenged by the Berber as though it had been committed to a member of his own family.

The experience described by Gerhard Rohlfs took place in an oasis of Draa, the area between the Atlantic and the Tafilet. From Gerhard Rohlfs, *Adventures in Morocco . . .*, 1874, pp. 361–2.

Thaleb Mohammed, the Sheikh of the Boanan Oasis, changed the money; but I am now certain that from the moment his eyes rested on my little hoard he had determined to murder me. There was no more talk of waiting for a caravan. He was suddenly of the opinion that with the help of his servant, who would serve quite well as guide, I could easily reach the Knetsa oasis, about two days' journey distant. He added, further, that I might place implicit confidence in his servant, and that the charge for conducting me would be eight francs, to be paid in advance.

We started in the evening, there being besides the guide and myself a pilgrim, who, in return for his food, had accompanied me as a servant. After a four hours' march, we camped near a small stream, and made a large fire of dry tamarisk boughs, which the guide kept piling on so as to give his master a mark where to find us. The pilgrim and I were soon stretched asleep near the fire, and had seen our guide apparently prepare to do the same. Excepting a pistol I carried, both the pilgrim and myself were unarmed: the guide carried a carbine. How long I had been asleep I cannot say, but when I awoke I found the Sheikh of the Oasis, my friendly host, standing over me, with the smoking mouth of his long gun still pointing to my breast. Luckily, he had not, as he intended, struck my heart, but had only broken my left arm above the elbow. I was seizing my pistol, when he slashed my hand nearly off with his sabre. From that moment, what with the pain and loss of blood, which was streaming from my arm, I became unconscious. The pilgrim saved himself by flight.

When I regained consciousness next morning, I found myself alone, with nine wounds; for, after I had fainted, those ruffians had shot and slashed me, to make sure of me as they thought. They had robbed me of everything but the bloody clothes I had on. Although the water was close to me, I could not get to it; I was too weak to get up. I tried to roll myself to it, but all in vain, and burning thirst added to my agony.

I remained in this helpless condition for two days and two nights. During this time I was in a half-conscious, half-wandering state of mind. I had the most terrible visions. Sometimes I thought I saw people, and strained every nerve to attract their attention; but it was always a delusion. I quite gave up all idea of living. I was tormented with the most terrible anxiety lest I should be attacked and eaten alive by hyenas or jackals: this part of the Sahara being crossed by a caravan track, abounds in these cowardly beasts of prey. I should have been quite helpless against them.

At last on the third day, two men came. Was it a reality, or a delusion again? No, they were men – Marabouts – and their joy at finding me alive was almost as great as mine at seeing them.

The Marabouts carried him to a small village on a donkey. He asked for a knife, requesting the village Sheikh to cut off his hanging arm. They said that this would be contrary to Islam and made a splint out of sticks, bound up in a goat's skin, covered with clay and dressed his other wounds with cotton wool soaked in butter. The villagers, although extremely poor, worked together to feed him, buying food from a neighbouring oasis and hunting ostriches so that he could have meat. Women poked food into his mouth as he could not use his hands.

John Buffa travelled in the company of a governor who had been summoned to the court.
From John Buffa, *Travels through the Empire of Morocco*, 1810, pp. 94–5.

We were received by a great concourse of men, women, and children, shouting, and making a noise exactly resembling the whoop of the North American savages. I was informed, that this was their usual mode of expressing their joy and mirth, on all great and solemn occasions. A venerable Moor, the chief of the surrounding villages, accompanied by the military and civil officers, and by the principal inhabitants, advanced to kiss the garment of His Excellency: this ceremony was closed by a train of women, preceded by an elderly matron, carrying a standard of colours, made of various fillets of silk; and by a young one of great beauty, supporting on her head a bowl of fresh milk, which she presented, first to the Governor (or, as he is otherwise called, the Sheikh), then to me, and afterwards to all the officers. This ceremony is always performed by the prettiest young woman of the village; and it not unfrequently happens, that her beauty captivates the affections of the great men (sometimes even the Emperor), and she becomes the legitimate and favourite wife.

When we arrived at any village, His Excellency halted to receive the report of the commanding officer; and to inquire if any murder, robbery, or other crimes, militating against the laws and constitution of the empire, had been perpetrated. This excellent man patiently listened to all the complaints made to him; and after hearing both parties with the greatest impartiality, he ordered such delinquents as stood fairly convicted to be punished by imprisonment, or fine, according to the nature of their offences. At one place where he held a court of justice, he received information of a band of assassins who had lately committed several murders and highway robberies, and had violated many young women, whom they afterwards destroyed. By this prompt and judicious arrangement, they were all secured, and brought before him. He ordered them to be dragged in the rear of his troops to Fez; there to receive whatever punishment the Emperor might think fit to award them.

Spending the night in a *Nzala*.
From Walter Harris, *Tafilet*, 1895, pp. 15–16.

It may be as well to explain the purpose of a *Nzala*. Owing to the lawlessness of the tribes, small villages have been planted by the government along all the tracks which in Morocco answer the purposes of roads. Usually the inhabitants of these wayside caravanserais are natives of some other tribe, brought there and given a small grant of land. The villages consist merely of thatch huts and the brown *ghiem* or tents of the Arabs: but there is always a large *zariba*, or open space enclosed with a high and thick thorn hedge, in which travellers and their pack-animals spend the night. The village community furnishes a guard at the only entrance to this *zariba*, and in case of robbery the inhabitants are held responsible by the Government. In return for this responsibility they collect a small tax from any who make use of their protection. The system is a good one, and theft is very uncommon, it being greatly to the villagers' benefit to carefully guard the traveller's property and exact the small fee, rather than by stealing call down upon themselves the wrath of the Government and the rapacity of the local officials.

So at the last *nzala* on the road from Safi to Marrakesh we spent the night, pitching our one little tent in the *zariba*, and hiring an elderly female, who possessed only one eye, to cook us some supper in her hut of thatch: and, considering that her fire consisted only of bunches of thistles, which had to be replaced almost as soon as they were lit, she performed her task with skill and success.

10

Agriculture and Animals

Morocco, as yet unpolluted by agricultural chemicals, still grows the beautiful and sweet-smelling wild flowers described in the first two extracts by Loti and Hooker and Ball; and the gardens are as fine as those seen by Cowan and Johnston. The argan-tree, found only in Morocco, still astonishes visitors who see the hair faces of goats peering out amongst its leaves. Agriculture, however, no longer relies on the picturesque magic noticed by Bel. We include a selection of writing on animals varying from the noble lion which is no longer to be found in the wild to the humble bug which is.

A vivid picture of carpets of flowers.
From Pierre Loti, *Morocco*, 1889 (1929 edn), pp. 70–5.

About midday, once more in wild solitary country, we pitch our dining tent in a delightful spot, of uttermost fragrance. It is in the hollow of a green valley that has no name, where springs spurt on all sides from between mossy stones, where small clear streams run amongst myosotis and watercress and anemones. The sky, now wholly blue, is of an infinite clearness; we are reminded of those glorious noontides of the month of June at the time of haymaking. No trees anywhere, nothing but these carpets of flowers; as far as the view extends, incomparable patterns on the plain; but the expression, a 'carpet of flowers,' has been so abused in application to ordinary meadows that it has lost the force needed for description here: zones absolutely pink with large mallows; marblings white as snow, which are masses of daisies; streaks of magnificent yellow, which are trails of buttercups. Never, in any garden, in any artificial English flower bed, have I seen such a luxuriance of flowers, such a packed grouping of the same kinds, giving together such vivid colours. The Arabs must have been inspired by their desert prairies in the weaving of those carpets of fine wool, diapered with bright and striking colours, that are made at Rabat and at Mogador. And the hillsides, where the earth is dryer, are draped with another and different kind of finery; there it is the kingdom of lavender; of lavender so closely growing, flowering so uniformly to the exclusion of every other plant, that the ground is absolutely violet, with an ashy violet, a powdered violet; it is as if the hillside were covered with some softly tinted plush; and the contrast with the frank brilliance of the prairie is striking. As we tread the lavender underfoot, a strong healthy perfume escapes from the bruised stalks, impregnates our clothing, impregnates the air. And butterflies in thousands, beetles, flies, and little winged creatures of divers sorts, circle about, buzzing, intoxicated with the fragrance and the light. In our paler countries of the north, or in the countries of the tropics enervated by continual heat, there is nothing to equal the splendour of such a spring.

Early in the afternoon's march we return to a boundless region of white daffodils, which continues till the evening.

At about two o'clock we quit the territory of El-Araish and enter that of the Sefiann. As always, on the boundary of the new tribe, two or three hundred horsemen await us, drawn up in line, their straightened guns glinting in the sun.

As soon as they are in sight, those who have been escorting us from Czar gallop ahead and range themselves in line, facing the others; we file then between these two columns; and, in proportion as we pass, there is a movement behind us on right and left, and the two lines close, mingle and follow us.

The place where this happens is a wilderness of flowers, as entrancing as the most marvellous of gardens; amongst the white distaffs of the daffodils, are scattered, here and there, tall red gladioli and large purple irises; our horses are breast-high in flowers; we could gather them in sheaves without dismounting, by merely stretching out a hand. And the whole plain is the same, with never a human vestige, bounded on the horizon by a girdle of wild mountains.

The long stalks of the flowers bending before our passage make a light noise, like the rustling of silk.

From Sir Joseph Hooker and John Ball, *Journal of a Tour in Marocco*, 1878, pp. 16–17.

We soon got clear of the enclosures around Tangier and descended through cultivated land into a little grassy valley that lies below the hilly range of the Djebel Kebir. Bright spring annuals – blue and yellow lupen, crimson Adonis, a deep orange marigold*, blue pimpernel, and other less conspicuous flowers – enlivened the tillage ground; but the northern botanist is more struck by the perennial species that hold their ground on the large portion of the soil that the plough has not touched. Predominant among these, as elsewhere throughout a large part of the Mediterranean region, is the palmetto or dwarf palm. Where unmolested by animals, and protected from the periodic fires that the native herdsmen renew for the sake of getting herbage for their cattle, it forms a thick trunk, ten or twelve feet in height, which probably takes a long time to attain its full size; but in the open spaces it is completely stemless, and covers the ground with its radiating tufts of stiff fan-shaped leaves. Many of the plants of the lily tribe abound; but in this mild climate most of them had flowered in winter, and few now showed more than their tufts of large root-leaves. Most conspicuous is the large maritime squill. The flowers are not large or showy, and do not correspond with the size of the bulb which often equals that of a man's head. The slender iris whose delicate flower lasts only a few hours – opening one at a time on successive days, appearing about midday and withering in the afternoon – is very abundant.

On reaching the hollow ground, where a slender stream runs through damp meadows, we were charmed by the delicate tint of a pale blue daisy that enamels the green turf. It is merely a slight variety of the little annual daisy, so common in many parts of Southern Europe; but the blue tint does not seem to have been noticed elsewhere. The large blue daisy, afterwards seen as one of the ornaments of the mountain region of the Great Atlas, was at first supposed to belong to the same species; but besides that this is perennial, it shows other less obvious differences.

* *The authors, as professional botanists, naturally give the scientific names of the plants mentioned here but, in the interests of the general reader, the editors have omitted them.*

The beauty and coolness of Moroccan gardens.

From George Cowan and R. L. N. Johnson, *Moorish Lotos Leaves*, 1883, pp. 89–92.

It may be well to remark, in the words of Sir Joseph Hooker, that 'a garden in Marocco means something very different from what we understand by it at home. So far as any idea of enjoyment is connected with it, the paramount object is shade and coolness. Trees and running water, without which in this climate few trees will grow, are the essential requisites. Beyond this the Moor, if he be rich and luxurious, may plant a few sweet-scented flowers; but otherwise no mere pleasure of the eye is dreamed of, and there seems to be among the natives a complete want of the sense of beauty. To the Moor the chief object of the garden is not pleasure, but profit'. Consequently, the gardens of Marrakesh, containing no trim array of terrace, no neat symmetrical parterres, no close-clipped foliage, no box borders, no velvet lawns, no pomp of statuary or rockery, are merely green and teeming wildernesses, wherein botany runs riot in defiance of symmetry. Intersected by broad grass-grown avenues, overarched here with interlacing boughs, there with trellised vines, these sylvan retreats, brimful of sweet sounds, delicious perfumes, and rich colouring, are the favourite resorts of the lotos-eating Moor. Each garden contains one or more summer-houses, gay with arabesqued walls, painted ceilings and tesselated floors, where merry-makers often wile away the afternoon with tea and music. But we choose to recline on the striped carpet in the fig tree's ample shade, while we feast our eyes on the bewildering colours worn by motley spring, and inhale the sunny breeze which reeks with scents of orange blossoms, roses, jessamine and lilac blooms.

Hark! the great tank is opened, and waters disbursed from Atlas's aerial treasury of snow babble through a score of tiny channels, adding their music to the wood-notes of blackbirds, doves, and finches, accompanied at intervals by the chatter of magpie, the caw of crow, the hoarse croak of frog, the scream of a hawk poised high above innumerable swifts threading airy mazes in the cloudless blue; and once from a myrtle thicket the *Om el Hassan*, or 'Mother of the Beautiful', as the Moors appropriately call the nightingale, trilled forth in airily exquisite cadences her welcome to the spring. White butterflies are paying afternoon calls on the flower fairies dwelling in rose, hollyhock, violet, scarlet poppy, yellow cornflower and white clover; the gauzy-winged dragon-fly skims sportively past in search of his afternoon blue-bottle, followed by a lustrous beetle humming as loud as any top. Wavering shafts of amber light quiver through foliage where the delicate grace of blue convolvulus entwines the fierce beauty of the pomegranate's blood-red flower. Lemon and lime blossoms here and there peep forth from amidst the leafage of white poplar, walnut, olive, mulberry, almond, apricot, willow, aspen, and the evergreen cypress and myrtle. Towering above all, the lordly date-palm waves its golden tassels.

A description of the appearance and uses of the argan tree. From Sir Joseph Hooker and John Ball, *Journal of a Tour in Morocco*, 1878, pp. 96–7.

The Argan tree is in many respects the most remarkable plant of South Morocco; and it attracts the more attention as it is the only tree that commonly attains a large size, and forms a conspicuous feature of the landscape in the low country near the coast. In structure and properties it is nearly allied to the tropical genus *Sideroxylon* (Ironwood); but there is enough of general resemblance, both in its mode of growth and its economic uses, to the familiar olive tree of the Mediterranean region to make it the local representative of that plant. Its home is the sub-littoral zone of South-western Morocco, where it is common between the rivers Tensift and Sous. A few scattered trees only are said to be found north of the Tensift; but it seems to be not infrequent in the hilly district between the Sous and the river of Oued Noun, making the total length of its area about 200 miles. Extending from near the coast for a distance of thirty or forty miles inland, it is absolutely unknown elsewhere in the world. The trunk always divides at a height of eight or ten feet from the ground, and sends out numerous spreading, nearly horizontal branches. The growth is apparently very slow, and the trees that attain a girth of twelve to fifteen feet are probably of great antiquity. The minor branches and the young shoots are beset with stiff thick spines, and the leaves are like those of the olive in shape, but of a fuller green, somewhat paler on the under side. Unlike the olive, the wood is of extreme hardness, and seemingly indestructible by insects, as we saw no examples of a hollow trunk. The fruit, much like a large olive in appearance, but varying much in size and shape, is greeedily devoured by goats, sheep, camels, and cows, but refused by horses and mules; its hard kernel furnishes the oil which replaces the olive in the cookery of South Morocco, and is so unpleasant to the unaccustomed palate of Europeans. On an average Argan, about twenty-five feet in height, and covering a space sixty or seventy feet in diameter goats can be seen feeding high in the branches, a scene which much amused us as we had not been accustomed to consider the goat as an arboreal quadruped. Owing to the spreading habit of the branches, which in the older trees approach very near the ground, no young seedlings are seen where the trees are close together, and but little vegetation excepting small annuals.

Further information is contained in a letter from the Vice-Consul at Mogador, printed as an appendix. I should imagine, from the appearance of some of the trees, that they are from one hundred to two hundred years old; and a remarkably large one in this neighbourhood is probably at least three hundred. This individual measures 26 feet round the trunk, at the height of three feet it branches off, the branches (one of which measures 11 feet in circumference near the trunk), rest on the ground, extending about 15 feet from the trunk and again ascend. The highest branch of this tree is not more than 16 to 18 feet from the ground, while the outer branches spread to give a circumference of 220 feet: this is the largest I am aware of.

The mode of propagation is mostly by seed. When sowing this, a little manure is placed with it, and it is well watered until it shoots; from which period it requires nothing further. In from three to five years after sowing it bears fruit, which ripens between May and August. When the fruit ripens, herds of goats, sheep, and cows are driven thither; a man beats the tree with a large pole, and the fruits fall and are devoured voraciously by the cattle. In the evening they are led home, and, when comfortably settled in their yards, they commence chewing the cud and throw out the nuts, which are collected each morning as soon as the animals have departed upon their daily excursion. I have heard it remarked that the nut passes through the stomach.

The next two extracts concern agriculture. The first is an account of the farming methods seen that had not changed for centuries.

From Arthur Leared, *Marocco* . . ., 1891, pp. 280–84.

Except in the neighbourhood of towns, land is of no value. In many of the best grain-growing areas, as in Abda, Duqalla, and Stooka, thousands of fertile acres lie waste and ownerless. Manure is never used, and when the soil is exhausted, the farmer moves to another locality. Almost the entire surface of the land, except that of the mountains, is covered with a rich soil, often of surprising depth. In some places, as in Bled al-Ahmar (the red country), this soil is of a reddish colour, the dust of which, in the dry season, gives the faces of the country and everything in it, the same appearance. The great requisite of the Moorish farmer is water. Unless in the district through which rivers flow, neither himself nor his cattle could exist through the long rainless summers except by the aid of wells. Some of these are of great depth, and the water is drawn from them after the most clumsy fashion. A bar is placed across the well's mouth, and to this bar a long rope is fastened, having a bucket, or rather bag, made of cow-skin, attached to it. The wells are not private property, but belong to the tribe; and it is the constant occupation of three or four men to draw up water for the use of the farmers. The stranger must get permission to get water for his animals, or even for his own use. The irrigating wheel, so common in the East, is sometimes seen.

The first thing to be done when the farmer settles on a plot of ground is to erect a hut. In the northern provinces this consists of low *tabia* walls covered with thatch; but in the south, where the population is more nomadic, the hut, or *novella*, is formed of reeds, in the shape of a bee-hive. Whatever its shape, it is generally surrounded with an impenetrable fence of cut thorn-bushes. Within this a sufficient space is enclosed to house his cattle at night, and for himself and his family protection is afforded against surprise and injury. As a further security, the huts are arranged in clusters so as to form villages; and the authority of one individual as headman is always acknowledged. An isolated hut is never seen throughout the country, and the migration of a whole village is not uncommon. But in the remote parts of the country, where the population is still more nomadic, the Arabs live in tents made of goats' hair. The black sloping roofs may be seen clustered in groups in the vicinity of water.

If the land selected for agricultural purposes is overgrown with brushwood, it is cleared by fire. At the commencement of the rainy season, which is generally October, the land is ploughed. The plough consists of a log of tough wood about three feet long, roughly squared and pointed at one end. A handle is inserted at the other end, while another shaft projects from the centre of the log. To this shaft a pair of bullocks is yoked by means of a rope. Sometimes a pair of mares, or a mare and a donkey, are employed. But the Moor is by no means particular as to his motive power. A camel and a donkey are occasionally used; and, as in Ireland, a woman may sometimes be seen joined to the fortunes of a donkey in this useful but lowly toil. It unfortunately too often happens that the oxen have been seized by the revenue officers of the Sultan, or rather of the governor who acts for the Sultan.

Adam, driven by necessity, could not have devised a more primitive or ruder implement than this Arab plough. The furrows it makes are most irregular, and consist of a mere scratching of the earth to a depth of a few inches. For heavy soils, such as the plains of Marrakesh and

Abda, the plough is sometimes tipped with iron. Another implement used is the hoe. This consists of a piece of flat iron, having an eye on one side, into which a short handle is inserted at a right angle. This serves the purpose of a spade. It is used in digging canals and wells, and is also the special tool of gardeners. The plough, thorn-bush, or hoe, *hadge*, or native sickle, and dagger, comprise the whole of the implements used by the Arab farmer. Yet, as already said, the results of his farming are often astonishing.

Barley and wheat are sown broadcast; but maize, beans, and peas are placed in the earth by means of the fingers, or in holes made with a pointed stick. A large thorn-bush, upon which a few stones are placed to give it weight, is then drawn over the surface to cover the seed, and the planting operations are complete. Yet, such are the advantages of climate and soil, that the crops are often splendid. Sufficient rain is the one thing requisite, and if this is forthcoming, the rapidity and luxuriance of growth are marvellous.

Corn is reaped with little sickles, which makes the work very tedious and imperfect. Not more than half the straw is cut, and one reason for this seems to be the interference of rank weeds. Maize and beans, having thick stems, are cut with the large curved daggers worn by the Moors.

The corn, when cut, is tied in small bundles, which are collected first into small heaps, and then afterwards into one large heap close to the threshing floor. This is made of clay, well beaten down, and enclosed by thorn bushes. Into this enclosure cattle are put, which are constantly driven round, while the corn is thrown under their feet by women and children. After the grain in this manner has been trodden out, it is cleaned by tossing in the air. When it is sufficiently dry it is stowed away in excavations made in the ground, and plastered with *tabia*. As the mouth of the cavity is hermetically sealed, grain will remain perfectly sound in these receptacles for many years.

The daily life of country people.
From Donald Mackenzie, *The Khalifate of the West*, 1911, pp. 58–9.

The Moorish agriculturalists form themselves into small communities for mutual protection. The nomadic portion have encampments or douars from which they look after their flocks. The more settled portion of the inhabitants live in villages, or hamlets in some convenient spot. Each douar and village has a chief who is invested with authority for governing and superintending these places. The Moors residing in these country districts live in the utmost simplicity, and present a faithful picture of the earth's inhabitants in the first ages. In the milk and wool of their flock they find everything necessary for their food and clothing. It is their custom to have several wives, who are employed in all domestic affairs. They milk the cows and make butter, they sort and sift the wheat and barley, gather vegetables, and grind flour. This is done in a mill composed of two round stones eighteen inches in diameter, in the upper one of which is fixed a handle by which it is made to turn on an axle. Bread is made daily between two earthen plates, which are heated by the fire. This is a fair outline of the simple life as practised by the country people of Morocco.

The farming methods described above by Leared had to be supplemented by magic. Westermarck showed the methods that might produce rain if all went well, while Bel suggested that even when the rain came further spells were necessary.

From Westermarck, *Ritual and Belief* . . ., 1926, pp. 271–5; and from Alfred Bel, *La Réligion musulmane* . . ., 1938, pp. 76–8.

Among the Ait Warain two or four naked women play a kind of hockey for the purpose of obtaining rain. Among the Igliwa of the Great Atlas a tug of war is resorted to; the men pull at one end of the rope and the women at the other, and while they are pulling one of the men suddenly cuts the rope so that the women tumble down and show their nakedness.

In Andjra, if rain is wanted at the time the durra is sown, the ploughmen turn their ploughs upside down so that the points are directed towards the sky, and leave them in that position until it begins to rain; or if this proves ineffective, they go to the shrine of the patron saint of the village and place their ploughs there as *ar* on the saint.

To stop rain at Fez a woman lies down on her stomach with the palms of her hands turned upwards, and another women pushes a plough without its point along her back; the expanded hands are said to represent sunshine, but it is obvious that a magical effect is attributed also to the 'ploughing'. A widespread method of stopping or preventing rain is to plough with two cats 'yoked' to a toy plough. In the spring of 1910 when I was staying at Fez, it was reported that a woman at Meknes had just been thrown into prison because she had ploughed with cats and sown salt. It was said that she had been bribed to do so for four dollars a day by a man who had a large quantity of corn and consequently wanted its value to rise. I was told that the ploughing with cats is an act of sorcery only done for wicked and selfish purposes.

At every stage of the agricultural year, which follows the solar and not the lunar calendar adopted by Islam, one finds ancient ceremonies devised to chase away from the dwelling-place, the field or the flock the demons which haunt and threaten them or at least to conciliate them through offerings. On the same occasions, ploughing, winter solstice, harvest time etc, as they perform rituals against malevolent spirits they perform others to ingratiate themselves with those that might be friendly. The ritual fires, for example, that burn at the summer solstice have the double purpose of destroying evil spirits and of strengthening by their flames, their smoke and their ashes protective influences which the Berber cannot define but which he believes can ensure success.

Alongside these rites of expulsion of evil and wooing of good are others of great age that have survived both Christianity and Islam and show how the Berber understands the mysteries of the germination and the growth of crops. For them, the Earth, mother of grain harvests, can only bring them forth when, like a woman, she has been rendered pregnant by a male. The husband of the Earth is the Rain, which if he does not arrive at the right time, leaves the land barren. It is the task of the farmer, and of the shepherd who needs grass for his flock, to help every year the mating of Earth and Rain at the appropriate moment.

So still in some parts of Barbary, there is a solemn procession with a doll dressed in the wedding garb of a bride. Sometimes there is also a second procession carrying the effigy of her husband. This is the old practice of sympathetic magic to provoke the similar results that are desired, to incite Earth to consummate her union with Rain. Sometimes, to make the message even clearer, there is a scattering of water.

These wedding processions with dolls are only the survivals of earlier times when the parts were played by human beings. Their physical union was supposed to ensure the subsequent mating of Earth and Rain. This ritual marriage, known around the Mediterranean in the most remote antiquity, is still practised and an instance has recently been reported amongst the Berbers of Southern Morocco. In the village of Douzrou the bringing together of a symbolic bride and bridegroom appears to be followed by similar action amongst the young men and girls of the village. This recalls the ceremonies of ritual prostitution which have been described by classical authors and have been recorded at various times and places amongst the Berbers, recently in Oudjda, Taza, Sefrou etc. Here and there, on a certain night in summer, called by some 'The Night of Error', by others 'The Night of Renewal', in a designated place perhaps in a cave, men, or perhaps only specially selected men, have intercourse with women as happened in the fertility rites of pagan Greece and Rome.

A description of the effects of smoking hashish.
From James Grey Jackson, *An Account of the Empire of Marocco . . .*, 1809, pp. 78–9.

The plant called Hashisha is the African hemp plant; it grows in all the gardens; and is reared in the plains of Marocco, for the manufacture of string; but in most parts of the country it is cultivated for the extraordinary and pleasing voluptuous vacuity of mind which it produces in those who smoke it; unlike the intoxication from wine, a fascinating stupour pervades the mind, and the dreams are agreeable. The Kief, which is the flower and seeds of the plant, is the strongest, and a pipe of it half the size of a common English tobacco-pipe, is sufficient to intoxicate. The infatuation of those who use it is such that they cannot exist without it. The Kief is usually pounded, and mixed with an invigorating confection which is sold at an enormous price; a piece of this as big as a walnut will for a time entirely deprive a man of all reason and intellect: they prefer it to opium from the voluptuous sensations which it never fails to produce. Wine or brandy, they say, does not stand in competition with it. The Habisha, or leaves of the plant, are dried and cut like tobacco, and are smoked in very small pipes; but when the person wishes to indulge in the sensual stupour it occasions, he smokes the Hashisha pure, and in less than half an hour it operates: the person under its influence is said to experience pleasing images: he fancies himself in company with beautiful women; he dreams that he is an emperor, or a bashaw, and that the world is at his nod. There are other plants which possess a similar exhilarating quality, amongst which is a species of the Palma Christi, the nuts of which, mixed with any kind of food, affect a person for three hours, and then pass off. These they often use when they wish to discover the mind of a person, or what occupies his thoughts.

Mouette, who was a prisoner for many years, wrote of lions and lion dens.

From Sieur Mouette, *Entertaining Travels . . .*, 1710, pp. 29 and 34–6.

There are Abundance of Lions on the Mountains, who in the Day Time withdraw into Caves, whence they Sally at Night to seek their Prey. The Barbarians being well acquainted with their ways, lay Snares to take them alive after this Manner.

They dig a deep Pit, over the Mouth whereof they place a Trap Door made fast to a Pin, equally poiz'd; and to that Pin or Plug, they tie a Dead Sheep: When the Lion comes down from the Mountain and smells the Flesh, he makes up to devour it, but as soon as he sets his forefeet on the Trap Door, he flips into the Pit, the head foremost. On the side of this Pit, is another, made like a Ditch, and as deep as the first, in which is a great Chest like a Mouse Trap, and in it a Quarter of Mutton: There being a Communication from one Pit to the other, by means of a Hole or Passage made on purpose, the open end of the Chest is set right before the Gap or Opening, to the end, that when the Lion is Hungry, he may go in, where he is taken as a Mouse is in a Trap. There are great Iron Rings at the Four Corners of the Chest, for the Cords it is to be drawn up with to run through, and then fasten it upon a Horse, so to carry the Lion to the next *Alcayde*, who takes the Pleasure of Killing him; or if they have a mind to destroy him upon the Spot, do it with their Spears in the first Pit he falls into.

The habits of camels.

From Rev. Lancelot Addison, *West Barbary*, 1671, printed in Pinkerton, vol. XV, p. 407.

The camel is a creature of strange bulk and humour, whose diet is mean and incredibly little; for they will travel great journies under heavy loads, without further allowance than the tops of thistles or any mean herbage. Nor are they less abstemious in their beverage than meat; being so patient of thirst, that they travel four days without touching water, and then at one drinking take in as much as will serve them as many days more.

There is a presumption that camels engender backward, but Ali Mulud, an ancient and inquisitive Moor, would often swear by the hairs of his chin (an oath that he had learned in the time of his being a slave in Spain) that he had much enquired after the manner of the camel's copulation, but could meet no certain information therein; for (said he) these creatures are strangely bashful in their embraces; which makes them very secret at the time of their amours; and to retire, if possible even from their keeper's eye. At the season of their coition, both sexes are very furious, and like their Morisco masters, they never forget to avenge injuries done them at that time. I was told by an Arab, who had no temptation to abuse my credulity in such an unconcerning story, that the macho or male camel, generated with the female when she is asleep, and that the female brings forth in a kind of negligent slumber. But I leave it to the curious inquisitors of nature to discover the frailties of this story, and pass on to remark the docile gentleness of the camel, which is evident in their submission, kneeling to be loaden and unloaden at their driver's pleasure. And we find it reported that camels have been taught to dance exact measures, which is no more strange than the Balletto di Cavalli that no long since graced the nuptials of a duke of Florence.

Attempts to keep scorpions out of the house. From Arthur Leared, *Marocco* . . ., 1891, pp. 172–4.

The belief of Jews in the 'evil eye' is very steadfast. They assure you that far more deaths take place from this than from natural causes. The sign of one harmless piece of superstition may be observed in almost every house. The city of Marrakesh is greatly infested by scorpions. In order to keep such venomous intruders out of the house, a paper on which is drawn a rude picture of one or two scorpions, is stuck on the door-post of every house. Above this, in Hebrew characters, is an array of mystical words and below it a solemn imprecation. The rabbi who prepares this precious document must, in order to make it effective, rightly observe certain circumstances. It must be written only on the first night of Sivan, near Pentecost, and previous to his labours he must immerse himself three times in a bath and also cut his nails.

The translation reads thus 'O scorpion, daughter, daughter of a scorpion, be thou accursed by the strength of every power that exists. From the mouth of the Prophet Joshua, the son of Nun; from the mouth of the High Priest Judah Bar Eli; and also from the mouth of the High Priest Judah Bar Ezekiel; so that you may not pass the threshold of this door, nor hurt any Israelite now and for ever-more. This is by command of the High Priest Simon Bar Yuli. Amen'. 'They shall not hurt nor destroy in all My holy mountain; for the earth shall be full of the knowledge of the Lord, as the waters cover the sea'.

A Jew told me that a short time previously he was the eye-witness to the efficacy of this imprecation. A large scorpion ran to the door of a room, and then stopped suddenly, as if stupified; it was, in fact, a case of no admittance. Several members of his family were summoned, and all agreed in the truth of this prodigy.

A description of an animal known locally as the *Sibsib*. From James Grey Jackson, *An Account of the Empire of Marocco* . . ., 1809, pp. 36–7.

This animal appears to be of an intermediate species between the rat and the squirrel; it is somewhat similar to the ichneumon in form, but not half his size; it inhabits the Atlas, and lives in holes amongst the stones and caverns of the mountains; it has brown hair and a beautiful tail (resembling that of the squirrel) about the length of its body. The Shelluhs and Arabs eat this animal and consider it a delicacy; and it is the only one the Mohammedans torment before death. This is done by taking hold of its fore and hind legs, and rubbing its back on a stone or a flat surface for a few minutes, which causes the animal to scream out; they then cut its throat according to the Mohammedan custom. Seeing some Shelluhs in the South Atlas performing this operation, and asking their motives for it, they informed that the rubbing made the flesh tender; that in taste it resembled a rabbit, but that without the friction it was not palatable. Being a subterraneous animal, it is prohibited food; but the eating of any forbidden thing becomes lawful to the Mohammedan by ascribing to it some medicinal property; it is then denominated medicine, and not food; by this evasion, wine is drunk by many who are not rigorous mooselmin. I never saw the *sibsib* north of the province of Suse, but it abounds in the mountains of that district. Its motions are so excessively quick that it is extremely difficult to shoot it.

Storks used to be held in high regard as described in this extract. From Budgett Meakin, *Land of the Moors*, 1905, pp. 70–71.

The stork (*bilarj*) holds a special place. On roofs of houses, on cottage thatch, on ruins, and mosque-towers, the storks collect the rude assemblage of sticks which form their nest, adding certainly a picturesque effect, though from their noisiness they are no pleasant neighbours. As a slayer of serpents the stork is held sacred, and if he fails to return any year to his accustomed haunt, some evil is feared. From his coign of vantage he can look down into the women's quarters, so the love-sick trust to him their messages and secrets. Thus an imaginative writer on Morocco hears a lad sing to the stately bird: 'O Stork, O thou of the tall figure; thou who dwellest on the top of the tower; go thou and salute for me the scornful coquette who wears anklets on her echoing feet, and who spurns my passion'. One story represents these birds as transformed Arabs who have ventured to plunder the Mecca caravans.

In Fez there once was money left to provide for the care of sick storks, of which I gleaned the following account in the city, where there is still a 'Stork Street' (*Zunkat Bilarj*) in memory of the affair. The story runs that several hundred years ago a stork came to the Qadi of Fez, and laid at his feet a pearl necklace. The Qadi sent for the muezzins to see if they, who got good views of the town, could say whence the bird came. One of them recognized it as the owner of a nest which a certain man had just cleared away from his roof. The Qadi sent for the man, who confessed to having done so, upon which the Qadi asked him what he would take for the whole house, selling the necklace and paying him out of the funds. The surplus and the rent of the house he handed to Sidi Farj, with instructions to always tend, doctor and feed any sick storks which might be brought to the place, while the dispossessed bird went and rebuilt its nest. The truth of the matter seems to be that a stork let drop a pearl necklace it had stolen, like the Jackdaw of Rheims, with the proceeds of which, as the owner could not be found, the Qadi purchased a house still in existence, since called Stork House, the rent of which is collected by the administrator of Sidi Farj, with the injunction to receive storks as if human beings, since the house came to them through the instrumentality of those birds. There is a similar 'Stork Hospital' in Marrakesh.

The remaining pieces in this chapter describe a variety of animals, insects and reptiles, starting with snakes.

From James Grey Jackson, *An Account of the Empire of Marocco . . .*, 1809, pp. 58–9.

The *Boah* or desert snake, is an enormous monster, from twenty to eighty feet long, as thick as a man's body, and of a dingy colour; this inhabitant of the Sahara is not venomous though it is not less destructive; the Arabs (speaking of it figuratively), affirm that as it passes along the desert it fires the ground with the velocity of its motion. It is impossible to escape it; it will twist itself around an ox, and after crushing its bones, will swallow it gradually, after which it lies supinely on the ground two or three days, unable to proceed till the animal be digested. Two of these monsters stationed themselves near the road from Marocco to Tarudant, near to the latter city, a few years since; one of them was killed, the other remained there several days, and prevented travellers from passing the road; they were both young ones, being about twenty feet long.

The Domestic serpents claim some attention. In the city of Marocco these animals abound; there is scarcely a house without its domestic serpent, which is sometimes seen moving along the roofs of the apartments; they are never molested by the family, who would not hurt them for any consideration, conceiving them a benediction of the household; they have been known to suck the breasts of women whilst asleep, and retire without offering any further injury. They are so susceptible as to be sensible of any enmity towards them, and it is though imprudent to incur their displeasure; for this reason the inhabitants of Marocco treat them kindly, and as members of the family, not wishing to disturb an animal that claims rights of hospitality in their house.

From James Grey Jackson, *An Account of the Empire of Marocco . . .*, 1809, pp. 60–63.

I have seen ostriches from Cape Bojador eight feet high from the foot to the beak when the neck was erect. The ostrich appears a stupid bird and indifferent to everything; taking no notice of persons except they have metal buttons on their clothes at which they will eagerly snap.

The ostrich lays several eggs of the size of an African citron or a six-and-thirty pound shot, white and weighing from eight to ten pounds; after laying these eggs the bird goes away, forgetting or forsaking them, and if some other ostrich discover them she hatches them, as if they were her own, forgetting probably whether they are or not; so deficient is the recollection of this bird. In addition to their usual food they swallow stones, gravel, sand and metals; it is not ascertained whether they drink or not.

Among the various animals which the Arabs hunt for sport or profit, that which most fully rewards their exertions is the ostrich: a party of about twenty Arabs set out together, riding gently against the wind, one after the other, at a distance of about half a mile asunder: they walk on, tracing the foot-marks until they discover those of the ostrich which they then follow; when they come within sight of their game, they rush towards it at full speed, always keeping nearly the same distance as at first; the bird, finding her wings an impediment to her progress against the wind, turns towards the horsemen, and after escaping the first and second, is perhaps brought down by the third or fourth, or some of those that follow: they are often however a whole day in the chase before they secure their bird. Were it not for this xstratagem, aided by the stupidity of the ostrich, it would be impossible to take it; thus we see that Providence, whenever it gives an extraordinary quality to an animal, gives it also another to neutralize that quality, and thereby bring it under the power of man. The Saharawans carry muskets, but in hunting the ostrich they rarely use them, trusting rather to their Zerwata, which is a stick about two feet long and three inches in circumference, taken from the Alk Soudan tree, or the tree that produces the Senegal gum, being a hard close-grained, heavy wood; this Zerwata they throw with an extraordinary dexterity at the legs of the birds, and by breaking or maiming them, impede their progress and by that means secure them. Having cut the throat according to the Mohammedan practice, they pluck off the feathers and divide them, as well as the carcase, into different xportions: on this occasion, as on all others, whether in hunting, pillaging or attacking caravans from the Soudan, they divide the booty into as many shares as there are persons to partake, caring but little about the equality of them: then each person taking something that he has about him (such as a key, a knife, or a piece of money), he puts it into the corner of a hayk or garment, and covers it over, waiting until some stranger or uninterested person appears, whom they engage to take out the garment before mentioned, the different articles deposited therein, and to place one on each of the parcels or lots of feathers and meat, when each person takes up that portion on which the article belonging to him is placed.

From James Grey Jackson, *An Account of the Empire of Marocco . . .*, 1809, pp. 27–8.

The Dubbah, a term which designates the hyaena amongst the Arabs, is an animal of a ferocious countenance; but in its disposition, more stupid than fierce; it is found in all the mountains of Barbary, and wherever rocks and caverns are seen. The flesh of this animal is not eaten, except in cases of extreme hunger; those, however, who have tasted it assert, that it causes stupefaction for a certain time; hence, when a person displays extraordinary stupidity, the Arabs say *kulu ras dubbah*, he has been eating the head of a hyaena.

The mode of hunting this animal is singular; a party of ten or twelve persons, accompanied with as many dogs of various kinds, go to the cavern which they have previously ascertained to be the haunt of the hyaena; one of the party then strips himself naked, and taking the end of a rope with a noose to it in one hand, he advances gradually into the cave, speaking gently and in an insinuating tone of voice, pretending to fascinate the hyaena by words; when he reaches the animal, he strokes him down the back which appears to soothe him; he then dexterously slips the noose round his neck, and instantly pulling the rope to indicate to those on the outside of the cave, who hold the other end, that it is fixed, he retires behind, throwing a handkerchief or cloth over the eyes of the hyaena; the men then pull the rope from without, whilst he who fixes the noose urges the animal forward, when the dogs attack him. Some of the Shelluh are very expert at securing the hyaena in this manner, and although there may be some danger in case the rope breaks, yet the man who enters the cave always carries a dagger, or a large knife with him, with which he has considerably the advantage, for this animal is by no means so ferocious as he appears to be.

From Lady Grove, *Seventy-one Days Camping in Morocco*, 1902, pp. 26–37.

Laraiche is a picturesque old Portuguese town, with a large open sok, flanked with white arches, giving it a more imposing appearance than most of these Moorish towns. But the other characteristics are the same – indescribable dirt and filth at every street corner, and swarms and swarms of flies rising in black clouds a few inches from their disgusting heaps as one passes, and then resettling to their impossible task of scavenging, and more often, I should imagine, spreading disease from their contaminating touch through food and skin. But flies are not the worst scourge in this country. It has always been quoted as a sign of excessive kindness of heart in a person that they would not hurt a fly. Why should hurting flies have particular attraction for evilly disposed persons? However, at the risk of incurring the censure of my colleagues on the Committee of the Anti-Vivisection Society, I hearby assert that I would gladly torture mosquitoes . . .

It was on the plain by the side of the lake between Laraiche and Rabat that the mosquitoes were most offensive. They came into my tent in swarms, dyeing the ceiling of my tent black with their unwelcome presence. But I had a mosquito net. Some others had not, consequently I was awoke in the middle of the night by a visitor who had 'taken up his bed and walked', so as to share my net. He was, of course, a most welcome guest, but he would have been more welcome if he had not let in a lively troupe of mosquitoes with him which we spent most of the rest of the night, at first with much good-humour, later on with less and finally, I regret to say, with some humour of a contrary sort, in trying to expel . . .

Never have I been in such a country for 'bugs' – bugs in the sense in which the American speaks of them – though I believe that South Africa is more prolific still of various and extraordinary species of insects. Of the domestic bug I came across one specimen only. This was at Glawi, in the Kaid's sumptuous apartment, where we were hospitably lodged. I saw him in broad daylight crawling up the wall just above the large square mattress in the middle of the room, and on which I did not sleep, preferring my own little bed. He was slain with a hammer which happened to be handy, and then impaled in the place where he died for verification and identification against the return of a connoisseur in these matters. He was pronounced to be genuine, and we felt we had done a good day's work. But if bugs did not bother us, fleas did, and on more than one occasion (three, I think) insects of another and even more loathsome kind were found crawling about and biting, whose name I will not offend polite and refined ears by mentioning.

We came across some beautiful green beetles sitting about in the bushes; their metallic scales flashed like emeralds in the sun. I was with difficulty restrained from collecting pocketsful of them for ornamental purposes. But we had no means of killing them quickly and painlessly, so the poor things were allowed to live.

Beetles there are, from the little bright gem-like green ones to huge black-winged beetles, that will come buzzing against your tent at night with the violence of an inconsequent cyclone, and by day roll with indefatigible perseverance huge round burdens, several sizes bigger than themselves, to their desired destination. Dragon-flies in their twenties and thirties flash before one's eyes; grasshoppers and crickets, the size of some of which their cotton-wool, Japanese counterparts by no means exaggerate.

Then there are tortoises, pursuing their proverbially slow but steady course, and which in spite of their traditional wisdom, run the risk of being crushed underfoot if one is not on the look-out.

From George Borrow, *The Bible in Spain*, 1843 (1893 edn), p. 542.

One thing was wanting, and its absence was strangely remarkable in a garden at this time of the year: scarcely a leaf was to be seen. The direst of all plagues which devastated Egypt was now busy in this part of Africa: the locust was at work, and in no place more fiercely than in the particular spot where I was now standing. All around looked blasted. The trees were brown and bald as in winter. Nothing green save the fruits, especially the grapes, huge clusters of which were depending from the 'parras'; for the locust touches not the fruit whilst a single leaf remains to be devoured. As we passed along the walks these horrible insects flew against us in every direction, and perished by hundreds beneath our feet. 'See the ayanas!' said the old Mahasni, 'and hear them eating! Powerful is the ayana, more powerful than the Sultan or the consul. Should the Sultan send all his Mahashniah against the ayana, should he send me with them, the ayana would say "Ha ha!" Powerful is the ayana. He fears not the consul. A few weeks ago the consul said "I am stronger than the ayana, and I will extirpate him from the land". So he shouted through the city "O Tangerines! speed forth to fight the ayana – destroy him in the egg; for know, that whosoever shall bring me one pound weight of the eggs of the ayana, unto him will I give five reals of Spain. There shall be no ayanas this year". So all Tangier rushed forth to fight the ayana, and to collect the eggs which the ayana had laid to hatch beneath the sand on the sides of the hills, and in the roads, and in the plains. And my own child, who is seven years old, went forth to fight the ayana, and he alone collected eggs to the weight of five pounds, eggs which the ayana had placed beneath the sand, and he carried them to the consul, and the consul paid the price. And hundreds carried eggs to the consul, more or less, and the consul paid them the price, and in less than three days the treasure-chest of the consul was exhausted. And then he cried "Desist, O Tangerines! perhaps we have destroyed the ayana, perhaps we have destroyed them all". Ha, ha! Look around you, and beneath you, and above you, and tell me whether the consul has destroyed the ayana. Oh, powerful is the ayana, more powerful than the consul, more powerful than the Sultan and all his armies'.

It will be as well to observe here that within a week from this time all the locusts had disappeared, no one knew how, only a few stragglers remained. But for this providential deliverance, the fields and gardens in the vicinity of Tangier would have been totally devastated. These insects were of an immense size and of a loathly aspect.

11

Working Lives

Moroccans have long been famous for their craftsmanship and a selection of their trades is given in this chapter. Leather-workers can still be seen in every suq and one need only look at a lady's 'best' *kaftan* to see that the art of embroidery still flourishes. Many travellers still bring home examples of jewellery and metalwork. We cannot fail to mention snake-charming, whether it be an art or a profession, which one can still see practised on the main squares of great cities along with the acrobats. The Moroccans were also known as traders and we have extracts showing their activities in places as diverse as Manchester and Timbuktu. Finally we show that slaves were not just servants but often valued friends of their masters.

An account of trading in the eighteenth century.
From Sieur Mouette, *Entertaining Travels* . . ., 1710, pp. 72–4.

The Arabs trading into the Kingdom of Sudan, Guinea and Tomboutou make use of Dromedaries, which are Creatures of an incredibly Swiftness, whom they load with white Salt to trade with those Blacks for Gold Dust. Their Way of Dealing is very odd, and it being forbid to speak a Word, I will here describe it, as told to me by divers Moors of Dras and Taffilet, who had been there several times.

When the Arabs have pass'd the Sandy Deserts that divide the Kingdoms abovemention'd, and are come to the Frontiers of the Blacks, they travel along them till they come to one of those Places, where the Meeting us'd to be for Trade. That Place is generally about a Cannon Shot from the Dwelling of the Alcair or Commanding Officer on those Frontiers: There they meet an Arab, who is kept by the Alcair, and who only has the Privilege of Speaking, to inform them what they are to do, and how they are to trade, without speaking to the Blacks. This Arab writes down the Names of all the new Comers, and what Quantities of Salt they bring, that those who come first may sell before the last. The Exchange is made twice a Day, Morning and Evening, the Sun being too hot in the Middle Part of the Day. At the appointed Hour the Alcair sends some of his Guards, who walk along some Mats that are laid on the Ground to put the Salt on. The Sellers make several Heaps, greater and smaller, on those Mats, and then draw back at a Distance, that their Chapmen may come up: Then the Blacks draw near the Mats, and having view'd the Heaps, leave the Quantity of Gold they think fit by those they like, and then retire in their Turn. If the Heap of Salt does not please them, however, they lay down their Gold by it, and by a Sign understood among them, the Arab who owns it, comes up to add or diminish. When they are agreed, the Arab takes up a Handful of Salt, and lays it by the Gold: Then they make a Signal to the Alcair's Officers to come and measure the Salt, who take the twelfth Part of it for the Alcair, and an ounce out of every Pound of Gold. This Barter is carry'd on without speaking a Word, or the least Disorder committed on either Side. If it happens that the Blacks are guilty of giving any Offence, the Alcair causes them to be punish'd immediately, hanging them by the Chin on very sharp tall Poles, where they remain as an Example to others, till their Limbs drop off. The Arabs are adjudg'd to lose their Salt and Beasts of Burthen, which are forfeited to the Alcair, besides the 500 Bastinadoes the Checque orders them to receive on their Buttocks, after the manner of their Country. These Arabs returning home sell their Gold Dust to Moorish or Jewish Merchants, who send it with other Goods to Morocco and Tarudant, and these convey it on to Santa Cruz, Saphya and Sale.

Besides these Commodities of Gold Dust, Ostrich feathers, Dates and Indigo, they send down to the Sea Ports abundance of tann'd and raw Hides, of Raisins of the Sun, of Copper made in Pigs like Bricks, of Wax, of Tin and Wool, as also Goat Skins to make Morocco Leather. Trading for Corn, Horses, or other Cattle is forbid in these Kingdoms, unless there be Arms, Powder, or other Warlike Stores given in Exchange. These are the Commodities that come from Tetuan, Alcassar, Arzila, Sale, Azamor, Saphya and Santa Cruz; in return for which our Merchants carry out of Europe, Spanish Plate, fine Silks, as Brocades, Velvets, strip'd and plain Taffeties, Silk Scarves, fine English and Spanish Woollen Cloths, Dutch and French Linnen, Muslins to make Turbants, fine red and black Caps, such as the Moors and Jews wear; raw Silk, all sorts of Spice and Drugs, Cotton, Brazil Tobacco, Sugar, Logwood, Tartar, Allum, Brimstone, all sorts of Paper, Steel, Iron, Lead, Iron Work; Pedlars Ware, as Knives, Scizars, Pins, Needles, Padlocks, Looking Glasses, and small Tooth Box and Ivory Combs: There are several other Sorts of small wares, too tedious to mention; all of which, except Plate, the Duty whereof is but two in the Hundred, pay 10 per cent, either imported or exported, to the King, and 2 per cent to the Consul. I shall not speak of the Arms offensive and defensive, and other Martial Stores fit to arm and equip the Pirates, which are daily imported, notwithstanding the Censures of the Church, and the Prohibitions of Princes: For at this time not only Merchants, but almost all Mankind, has regard for nothing but Interest, and care little how ill their Wealth is gotten, provided they may keep up some Shew of Reputation in the World.

An American scholar gives a modern account of the traditional trade of charcoal-burning.

From Henry Munson, *The House of Si Abd Allah . . .*, 1984, pp. 191–2.

My cousin Si Muhammad is a *talib*. He memorized the Holy Qur'an in the mosque of the village of the two springs, which is right next to the village of the streams. He is a good Muslim who prays every prayer at its time. He does not go with women other than his wife. And he does not smoke *kif* or even cigarettes. He makes a little money chanting the Holy Book on the seventh day after births and at circumcisions, weddings and funerals.

Si Muhammad has six goats and about a dozen chickens. Sometimes, he works for the government public works programme for 750 francs ($1.67) a day. And he has a little mint garden. But mostly he depends on charcoal. He was caught by the ranger for a second time in 1977. And the judge in Tetuan made him pay 10,000 francs ($22.22). That is a fortune in the hills where many Jbala do not see that much money in a month. Al-Hajj T only pays thirty-five or forty francs a kilo for the charcoal that he buys in Dar Shawi though he sells it for 120 francs a kilo in Tangier in the winter, when people use a lot of charcoal to heat their homes as well as to cook their food. Tangier is cold and damp during the winter rains and a brazier full of glowing charcoal burns away the cold and the dampness.

When you make charcoal, you pile up roots and sometimes branches and then you cover them with leafy branches, which you then cover with dirt, leaving a hole at the top of the mound. You set fire to the leafy branches under the dirt so that gradually the fire will burn the roots and big branches into charcoal. But when the roots, the leafy branches and the dirt are all wet, it is hard to light a fire. If the rains *do* hold off long enough for you to make a mound of charcoal, you still have to bring it down to Dar Shawi by mule. And the paths are all muddy and slippery when they are not in fact fast-flowing streams. So a mule has a hard time making it down to the valley without breaking a leg. God preserve us. Moreover, you have to bring your charcoal down early in the morning or at dusk after the sunset prayer so that the forest rangers won't see you and confiscate that charcoal you spent ten days making and which will feed your family until you make some more, God willing. Usually Jbala bring their charcoal down about the time of the evening prayer. Every evening mules come down from the hills loaded with charcoal. Just as in the morning they come down loaded with freshly cut mint for the 8.30 bus to Tangier. Mint and charcoal – that's all that's keeping people in the high hill villages, where only one man in fifty has any plough land in the valley.

The water carrier has long been a striking figure in a Moroccan market.
From Eleanor Elsner, *The Present State of Morocco*, 1928, pp. 94–6.

The negro slaves of the great chieftains interested me very much. They were always passing through, elbowing their way among the dense crowd, going on errands to the native city, busy with the affairs of their master. They wear the usual native robes but have a huge silver ring in the left ear, which is the sign of the slave.

The water carriers were even more curious. These are half-naked natives, carrying their dripping goat-skins slung across their shoulders, holding the leg of the goat-skin to which is affixed a brass tube with a cork in it, in one hand; and the burnished brass cup in the other. They glide in and out among the people, uttering their strange guttural cry, and they do a roaring trade. The smallest coin in Morocco is paid for a cup of water, and the skins are very quickly emptied on a hot day. I loved to watch a group of water-carriers at a fountain, filling their goat-skins, chattering and laughing and often splashing the water from the fountain over each other. The preparation of these skins for water carrying is very peculiar. They are the natural skins of the goats, from which the whole body is removed in some clever fashion, through the neck, and I was told that the skin, when all the flesh and bones had been taken out, was turned inside out and thoroughly cleansed. It is then turned back so that the hair is at the outside. The hoofs are cut off, three of the legs are tied up with goat gut and the fourth has a brass tube with a cork fitted securely into it. A strap from one fore and one hind leg slings it across the carrier's shoulders and he wears on his back a long cuirass of leather to protect his body from the wet skin.

When it is empty it hangs limp and shapeless, and its carrier takes it to the nearest fountain, undoes the neck aperture and refills it by tying it to one of the taps, of which there are always several in the wall fountains. It is a weird sight to see three or four of these empty skins being filled together, from limp looking bags of leather they assume almost the appearance of a living animal; as the water fills so the legs fill out, the skin heaves and moves almost as though the animal was breathing. When it is quite full its owner takes it from the tap, quickly ties up the neck securely and is off again with the wet, dripping skin wobbling about his back. On a really hot day the water-carrier refills his goat-skin twice in an hour, so although he receives something rather less than half a farthing for each cup of water, he makes quite a decent living.

Snake-charming is another feature of a Moroccan market. James Riley gave a vivid description of the art.

From James Riley, *Loss of the American Brig Commerce . . .*, 1817, pp. 551–2.

The two serpent-eaters were dressed in haicks only, and those very small ones. After they had gone through with their religious ceremonies most devoutly, they appeared to take an eternal farewell of each other: this done, one of them retired from the room, and shut the door tight after him. The Arab within seemed to be in dreadful distress – I could observe his heart throb and his bosom heave most violently; and he cried out very loudly, 'Allah houakibar!' three times, which is, as I understand it, 'God, have mercy on me!' The Arab was at the farthest end of the room: at that instant the cage was opened, and a serpent crept out slowly; he was about four feet long, and eight inches in circumference; his colours were the most beautiful in nature – being bright, and variegated with a deep yellow, a purple, a cream colour, black and brown spotted, &c. As soon as he saw the Arab in the room, his eyes, which were small, and green, kindled as with fire: he erected himself in a second, his head two feet high, and, darting on the defenceless Arab, seized him between the folds of his haick, just above his right hip bone, hissing most horribly: the Arab gave a horrid shriek, when another serpent came out of the cage. This last, was black, very shining, and appeared to be seven or eight feet long, but not more than two inches in diameter: as soon as he had cleared the cage, he cast his red fiery eyes on his intended victim, thrust out his forked tongue, threw himself into a round coil, erected his head, which was in the centre of the coil, three feet from the floor, flattening out the skin above his head and eyes in the form and nearly of the size of a human heart; and, springing like lightning on the Arab, struck its fangs into his neck, near the jugular vein, while his tail and body flew round his neck and arms in two or three folds. The Arab set up the most hideous and piteous yelling, foamed and frothed at the mouth, grasping the folds of the serpent, which were round his arms, with his right hand, and seemed to be in the greatest agony – striving to tear the reptile from around his neck, while with his left he seized hold of it near its head, but could not break its hold: by this time, the other had twined itself around his legs, and kept biting all around the other parts of his body, making apparently deep incisions: the blood issuing from every wound, both in his neck and body, streamed all over his haick and skin. My blood was chilled in my veins with horror at this sight, and it was with difficulty my legs would support my frame. Notwithstanding the Arab's greatest exertions to tear away the serpents with his hands, they twined themselves still tighter; stopped his breath, and he fell to the floor, where he continued for a moment, as if in the most inconceivable agony, rolling over, and covering every part of his body with his own blood and froth, until he ceased to move, and appeared to have expired.

Many travellers to Morocco come back with a pair of locally-made slippers, although the local people increasingly wear plastic 'flip-flops'. The ancient craft was described by R. Guyot in an article in *Hespéris*, 1936, which has been translated and abridged by the editors.

The guild of shoemakers in Fez has 957 master-craftsmen who employ at least a similar number of workmen so there are some two thousand people directly engaged in this trade. The shoemakers are and have always been one of the largest guilds and, with the tanners and the butchers, one of the most turbulent. They are divided into three sections, corresponding with the three areas of the city and these sections maintain teams for sporting events and organise group picnics. They used also, although they lacked any official character, to be a sort of militia for defending Fez against attack by the neighbouring tribes. The shoemakers have their own patron saint and hold an annual festival in his honour and at least another forty saints are said to have followed the same trade.

They work in three sorts of premises: firstly, in little shops in the old city opening directly on to the street; secondly in a room in a *fondouk*, and thirdly, also in a *fondouk*, a large workshop shared with other master-craftsmen. Most of these premises are owned by the mosques, although some belong to rich families and very few, apart from the shoemaker to the royal family, own their own workshops. The rent of the smallest is about 10 francs* a month. Some are decorated with verses from the Qur'an, some with drawings by patrons or apprentices and some with pin-ups torn from French magazines. Very few have artificial lighting and they maintain the old tradition of starting work when it is light and finishing when it becomes dark.

Leather for the traditional slipper, the *babouche*, is sold by public cryers in the Foundouk es-Sbitriyine. Usually the shoemaker does not know who has tanned it. Goatskin is used for the upper part of the slipper and sometimes for the inner sole, sheepskin to line the upper part and cowskin for the outer sole. With one goatskin, costing between 12 and 35 francs according to its quality, and a sheepskin costing 8 to 15 francs, the craftsman can make between three and six pairs of slippers which cost 80 francs each. Half the skin of a cow, costing 40 to 50 francs will provide soles for 14 or 15 pairs. Ladies' slippers are usually made of the same materials of those of men but embroidered with patterns in cotton or silk.

The makers do not sell directly to the public unless the shoes have been ordered but usually their wares go to merchants who may take the whole production of one craftsman: some Fassi craftsmen have links with establishments in Casablanca or Meknes. Most slippers, however, are sold by a public cryer – a *dallal*. These men, about a hundred of them, provide one of the most colourful spectacles of Fez and may be found every day except Friday between the afternoon prayer and sunset in the Suq Sabbat, a little narrow street, sixty metres long, full of shouting, gesticulating salesmen. Along this street are the shops of the merchants, usually about 2 metres 50 high, 1.50 wide and 2 metres deep; they sit impassively, often immersed in a book, although they might beckon over the *dallal* if a price interests them. When a craftsman has finished some shoes, perhaps only two or three pairs, he sends an apprentice with them to Suq Sabbat. There he confers with a *dallal* who walks along the street telling the merchants the price that he hopes to get. When he gets a serious offer, either from a merchant or an ordinary customer, he goes back to the shoemaker and if agreement is reached, he receives his commission, usually 3%. Often a *dallal* has a regular agreement with a particular maker and may hope to earn, on a good day if the suq is busy, about 12 francs; on a bad day he may get nothing.

The Inspector of the Market will publicly shame a shoemaker whose product is faulty. Anyone dissatisfied with the workmanship of a pair of slippers can take them back to the merchant from whom he bought them, where there will be no difficulty in identifying the mark of the maker. He will then inform the Inspector who will fine the delinquent and nail up the offending shoes in the Suq Sabbat with the name of the maker for all to see.

This traditional pattern is, however, in the process of change. Muslims still buy the *babouche* to wear on religious occasions but shoes imported from Europe or Japan are now to be found in the market and are being bought increasingly for everyday wear.

* *At the time this article was written there were about 80 francs to the pound sterling and 16 to the dollar.*

A description of different methods of looking into the future at the time of his travels.
From Leo Africanus, *Description of Africa*, 1550 (1896 edn), vol. II, pp. 457–8.

Now let us speake of the fortune-tellers and diviners, of whom there is a great number, and three kindes. For one sort useth certaine Geometricall figures. Others powring a drop of oile into a viall or glasse of water, make the saide water to be transparent and bright, wherein, as it were in a mirror, they affirme that they see huge swarmes of divels that resemble an whole armie, some whereof are travelling, some are passing over a river, and others fighting a land-battell, whom when the diviner seeth at quiet, he demandeth such questions of them as he is desirous to be resolved of: and the divels give them answers with the beckning, or with some gestures of their hands and eies: so inconsiderate and damnable is their creduilitie in this behalfe. The foresaid glasse-viall they will deliver into childrens hands scarce of eight yeeres old, of whom thy will aske whether they see this or that divel. Many of the citie are so besotted with these vanities, that they spend great summes upon them. The third kinde of diviners are women-witches, which are affirmed to have familiaritie with divels: some divels they call red, some white and some black divels: and when they will tell any mans fortune they perfume themselves with certaine odours, saying, that then they possesse themselves with that divell which they called for: afterwards changing their voice, they faine the divell to speake within them: and then they which come to enquire, ought with great feare and trembling aske those vile and abominable witches such questions as they meane to propound, and lastly offering some fee unto the divell, they depart.

An encounter with one of the many Moroccan cotton traders who had been abroad.

From Jim Ingram, *Land of Mud Castles*, 1952, pp. 37–8.

Walking one day along a street in Fez I found the way blocked by a burly, white-robed Moor who was ambling sedately along, and dodge as I might from one side of the narrow street to the other, I could not pass him.

'By gum, owd lad, I wish you'd let me pass', quoth I to myself, aloud. 'Hey, shift thisen, gormless!'

Judge my surprise when the Moor turned about, thrust a brown bearded face close to mine and growled: 'Keep a civil tongue in thi head, thi cheeky young devil, or happen I'll clout thi ear-oil for thi'.

'Eeh, mister, I'm right sorry', said I, taken aback. 'But where did you learn to speak Lancashire?'

'In Manchester, same as yourself,' replied the Moor promptly.

'What? Are you from Manchester? You'll be saying you are in the cotton-trade next'.

'I am an' all', replied the Moor with a grin. 'But come along with me. I know who you are, and I want to talk with you'.

He led the way through an arched gateway into a cobbled courtyard surrounded by stone buildings. The place was a *fondouk*, with stables on the ground floor and room above for travellers to lodge and store their goods in. Camels, donkeys and mules were tethered in the courtyard, while their owners squatted on the carved wooden galleries which projected from the upper storeys of the buildings. Behind were lock-up shops where travelling merchants could display their goods.

My companion ascended some stairs and led the way into a large room which appeared to be an office-cum-warehouse, for it was full of boxes and bales, and at the far end was a table with a battered typewriter on it and various cabinets with books and papers lying about.

He clapped his hands and a boy served us with cups of thick black Turkish coffee. While I sat on a cushion sipping it Ben Slimane described commercial relations between Fez and my native city of Manchester. A number of Moors from Fez, it seemed, lived in Manchester, dealing in cottons for the Moroccan market. Ben Slimane had been sent there as a young man to learn the shipping trade, and with the Moor's ready facility for learning languages had not only learned standard English but had acquired a knowledge of Lancashire dialect as well. Now he was back in Fez selling cotton goods to his countrymen. To many Moors, he said, the name of Manchester was far more familiar than was London.

His business, I discovered, was not only extensive but extended into some curious byways. Caravans distributed the cotton goods to the various agents and traders located around Fez, often making payment in figs and dates, grain or hides, so that perhaps several transactions took place before a deal was completed.

A piece deploring the degeneration of craftsmanship.
From Joseph Thomson, *Travels in the Atlas and Southern Morocco . . .*, 1889, pp. 311–13, and 375–8.

The author, travelling in the Atlas, was hospitably received by Kaid Taiyib Gundafi, although put into 'a miserable windowless room in an outhouse, reeking with dirt, and evidently swarming with bugs and fleas'. His companion was stung by a scorpion which was in his pyjamas but rendered 'quite talkative and jocular' as a result of treatment with a bottle of brandy. Taiyib had been educated by a school teacher who had been kidnapped by his father and held until the old Kaid considered that his son had learned all that was necessary.

The Kaid sent for our inspection some of the most beautifully worked daggers with gold and silver sheaths that we ever saw in Morocco. Afterwards he came himself with quite a bundle of large coarsely made women's jewellery in gold and silver. The gold and silver were the proceeds of the spoliation of the valley.

To ensure that his daggers and jewellery should not cost anything, the Kaid's father had employed a Jew of Amsmiz to work on them for over two years, and then paid him the stipulated amount and sent him away rejoicing, immediately after, by order of his employer, to be murdered and robbed as he passed through the gorge of Nyfis. For our inspection Taiyib also sent his horse trappings, which undoubtedly were extremely valuable and gorgeous. There were three sets of bridles and saddles one mass of gold and silk. We calculated that each would have cost from £150 to £200 – that is to say, if they had been paid for, but the gold was the hard-won money of the poor mountaineers. As for the workmanship, which was of the best, it had not cost much either; for an Algerian Moor famed for his kill in this class of work was beguiled into the mountains, and there forcibly kept for twenty years, with no better remuneration than his food and clothes. That at least was the man's own story . . .

A gorgeously coloured carpet, one or two mattresses, and several cushions form almost the sole appointments of a Moorish house. There may be a rude box for small articles and letters, one or two candlesticks or more elaborate candelabra for use at night placed on the floor, and among the very well-to-do, a European clock more ornamental than useful; but these are usually the sum of the requirements of the Moor. Throughout Morocco there is nothing more disappointing to the traveller than this absence of things beautiful, whether for the adornment of the person or the house. One naturally expects to find all sorts of beautiful and quaint objects, to see picturesque houses, and even get peeps into the most delightfully fanciful interiors. That such things existed in earlier days is made every now and then apparent as we wander through Marrakesh and assiduously attend auction-sales. But to know that an object is beautiful, that it shows careful and loving workmanship, and reflects the graceful fancy we associate with things Moorish, is also to know that it is old. In everything we see there is evidenced a frightful degeneracy in genuine workmanship and artistic taste. To the painter, the enduring colours of other times are as much unknown as is his ancestor's skill in blending them into effective scroll-work. The stucco arabesque is equally becoming a thing of the past, simply because there is no demand for it, and consequently the workmen are dying out, with no others educated to replace them. The rugs and carpets reflect the same degeneracy. Aniline dyes of gorgeous hue have almost entirely replaced the enduring vegetable colours formerly employed, and with the colours the skill in effective and harmonious arrangement is also disappearing. The beautiful glazed tiles are now not made, except to a small extent in Tetuan; Fez still keeps a certain reputation for coarse though bold and effective pottery and beautifully worked cloth waistbands for women; Rabat for carpets and embroidery; Mogador for brass trays and silver ornaments, and Marrakesh for various kinds of leather-work. At each of these places the tourist may pick up a few objects worth taking away, but even then he will find that the best things are old, whether carpets, daggers or guns.

There is no difficulty in detecting the cause of this degeneracy. It is the notorious misgovernment which is at the root of this, as of all the other evils which are ruining the Empire. What temptation is there for anyone to set up for himself a handsome well-built house, when the chances are that he will not be allowed to die in it, and that sooner or later it will pass into the hands of the Sultan or of strangers? To show any signs of luxurious tastes, and of wealth to gratify them, would only serve to apprise the government of the fact with the inevitable result of entailing on the owner a ruinous contribution, or imprisonment till such time as the authorities were satisfied that there was nothing more to be squeezed out of him. Wealth of any kind will never remain two generations together in the same family before the Sultan has swallowed everything in his omnivorous maw.

An even worse influence than this system of wholesale plunder tends to the rapid deterioration of Moorish art and the disappearance of skilled workmen. These latter are now becoming so rare, that the moment one is discovered to have greater capabilities than his companions, he is immediately pressed into the service of the Sultan or the governor. Not however to be petted and honoured and made much of, as was the good old fashion, but to be compelled to work for little more than his bare livelihood. I have mentioned two instances of this in connection with the Kaid of Gundafi. Hundreds similar could easily be adduced. It is the ruin of a workman to get a reputation for genius or cleverness in any branch. His only way of escape – and it is one not infrequently adopted – is to botch his work and subject himself to a flogging, and eventually to dismissal if he persists in his deliberate error. That is how the descendants of the people who built the Alhambra and made their reign in Spain glorious by their marvellous buildings encourage and foster art in these days.

Details of the different regional types of embroidery. From G. E. Holt, *Morocco the Piquant*, 1914, pp. 172–4.

Moorish embroidery is very wonderful – too wonderful for a mere man to write about to any extent. Each town has its own distinctive style, and it is difficult to tell which is the most attractive. The Fez work is the finest, and yet the Meknes has in it a certain attractive opalescent effect, which to me is more charming than the cameo-like fineness of the Fassi needlework. The Fez embroidery frequently runs four hundred stitches to the square inch – and the number of stitches is always the same in the same design, no matter how often it may be repeated. Moorish embroidery is the same on both sides, and varies from the complex designs of Fez and Meknes to the comparatively simple Rabati and Slawi where the stitches vary from half an inch to an inch in length. The Rabati embroiderers use more than one colour on a design while the Slawis usually confine themselves to one striking colour. I may compare the Rabati embroidery to the colour scheme of a kaleidoscope – dashes of different colours at all sorts of angles, while the Meknes embroidery is in splashes of colour much like an impressionistic oil painting.

The embroideries of Tetuan greatly resemble Slawi and Rabati work, but it is almost invariably done upon silk instead of cotton or linen. It is interesting to note that Tangier embroidery has degenerated to such an extent through foreign influences, that what little there is of it consists of the least artistic designs, worked with a coarse yarn in long stitches on a cheap scrim. It is absolutely valueless.

The Rif embroidery is most interesting because it differs so greatly from that of all the rest of the country, and is so much like the ornamentation of the American Navajos. The running cross design, like a series of connected X's – XXXXXXX – is in large use, and varied in many ways. The 'lightning streak' is distinguishable, and a figure which approximates the swastika design. The checkerboard figure is also used in the Rif work, in a simple form, and in the Meknes embroidery in a more elaborate one.

The finished effect of Fez embroidery is very much like fine massed bead-work, the raised design standing out in clear, sharp outlines. The thread used by the needlewomen is the very best hand-spun silk procurable, coloured with vegetable dyes. The colours are marvellous to those of us accustomed to the sharp mineral dyes of the Occident; striking Oriental blues, vivid crimson, royal purple, and black are the most commonly used. Although the work is exquisite – as nearly perfect as hand-work can be – the materials and colouring the finest made, there is, to the artistic eye of Western nations, one distressing drawback to the finished work. The workers use for the background of all this excellence a cheap, coarse, flimsy white cotton cloth about the same grade as that used in the flour-sacks of the Western mills of America. In fact on some of the more modern work one can distinguish the half-obliterated green or red or blue lettering of some popular brand of flour.

The Fassi workers use a great deal of black on white, and the finished pieces are very effective, the black silk thread being very glossy, and, of course, the best quality. Among these workers the colours are never mixed. The commonest design is a conventionalized tree, very stiff and very straight. The needlewoman uses her cloth in the shape in which she procures it, be it long or short, oblong or square. Then, squatting upon a cushion, with no pattern but one in her own mind – one memorized by her ancestors for generations – she proceeds to border the cloth with the time-honoured designs of the Fassi.

The hard life of a letter carrier.
From S. L. Bensusan, *Morocco*, 1904, pp. 61–2.

Very often, at morning, noon and sunset, we would meet the *r'kass* or native letter-carrier, a wiry man from the Sus country, more often than not, with naked legs and arms. In his hand he would carry the long pole that served as an aid to his tired limbs when he passed it behind his shoulders, and at other times helped him to ford rivers or defend himself against thieves. An eager, hurrying fellow was the *r'kass*, with rarely enough breath to respond to a salutation as he passed along, his letters tied in a parcel on his back, a lamp at his girdle to guide him through the night, and in his wallet a little bread or parched flour, a tiny pipe, and some kief. Only if travelling in our direction would he talk, repaying himself for the expenditure of breath by holding the stirrup of mule or horse. Resting for three to five hours in the twenty-four, sustaining himself more with kief than with bread, hardened to a point of endurance we cannot recognise, the *r'kass* is to be met with on every Moorish road that leads to a big city – a solitary, brave, industrious man, who runs many risks for little pay. His letters delivered, he goes to the nearest house of public service, there to sleep, to eat sparingly and smoke incessantly, until he is summoned to the road again. No matter if the tribes are out on the warpath – no matter if the powder 'speaks' from every hill – the *r'kass* slips through with his precious charge, passing lightly as a cloud over a summer meadow, often within a few yards of angry tribesmen who would shoot him at sight for the mere pleasure of killing. If the luck is against him he must pay the heaviest penalty, but this seldom happens unless the whole countryside is aflame. At other times, when there is peace in the land, and the wet season has made the unbridged rivers impassable, whole companies of travellers camp on either side of some river – a silver thread in the dry season, a rushing torrent now. But the *r'kass* knows every ford, and, his long pole aiding him, manages to reach his destination. It is his business to defy Nature if necessary, just as he defies man in the pursuit of his task. He is a living proof of the capacity and dogged endurance still surviving in a race Europeans affect to despise.

A visit to the shop of a perfume seller and herbalist. From Eleanor Elsner, *The Present State of Morocco*, 1928, pp. 244–8.

The perfume seller was an old, old man, with a very wrinkled face. He smiled at us with a humorous twinkle in his eye, saying that he knew ladies always loved perfumes, and as he himself spoke better French than the Mokhaznis we got on very well indeed. He lived in the queerest old house, with the very smallest courtyard I ever saw. His room, which was also his shop, gave on to this courtyard, and a verandah, covered with jasmine and roses, made the room seem even darker and smaller than it really was. All round it were wooden boxes, almost like pigeon-holes, full of bottles and paper packets. There were no seats, only cushions on the floor, and a huge bowl of flowers stood at one side of the old man's low wooden table. As we entered a young Moor was just leaving; he carried in his hand a tight little posy of flowers all bound very closely together, long and narrow, in the shape of a small carrot. It swung from a tiny ribbon, and he carried it on the end of his finger very carefully. Had he not gone I do not know how we could possibly have got into the tiny room; as it was the Mokhaznis had to sit outside on the balcony. The old perfume seller called his servant, who brought us two leather cushions and placed them on either side of him, and down we sat on the floor, the three of us completely filling the little room.

The old man had the usual low, round, wooden table before him. It had a very thick top with what looked like ivory buttons round it. He pressed one suddenly, and a tiny drawer opened, showing a long glass phial within, and we saw that the table was full of little secret drawers in which the most precious scents were kept.

Oh, those scents! I shall never forget them! He made us try one after another, putting one drop on the backs of our hands, rubbing it and then asking us to guess what the perfume was. Every flower was represented. The pure, distilled essence, and the smallest drop was enough to perfume the whole courtyard.

When we found he could talk French we plied him with innumerable questions, and directly he saw that we were really interested he became interested himself, and in the usual polite Moorish fashion he told us all about his fascinating trade. He was a great herbalist as well as a perfumer, in fact I think he was more interested in his herbs than his perfumes. All the little wooden boxes in his wall were filled with special herbs, gathered and dried under unique conditions.

There was thyme, picked under a waning moon; asphodel, gathered before dawn; orris and musk dried when the planet Mercury was at its zenith; agrimony, picked while Venus was an evening star; garlic taken from the ground while she was a morning star. He told us that clover, cut and dried during the month of Ramadan, had most special virtues, and that the roots of certain herbs gathered during the time of the new moon, dried in the mid-day sun and powdered at dusk on the same day were a sovereign remedy for melancholia. There was no end to the strange things he told us. Charms, potions, special doses for mental as well as physical ailments – in fact he could cure anything! Immediately we asked him about love charms – yes, he had several, but what sort of love charm did we want? Something to bring back an erring husband? Something to retain a straying lover? Something to enhance a love already begun? Something, perhaps to make our children obedient, or merely something to sweeten friendship?' We decided on the latter and he said, 'I have just made such a one – the young man who left me as you arrived took it with him – I will make one for each of you. Only you must tell me, is the friend a man or a woman?' We watched him prepare these charms with the greatest interest. He took two sticks of wood something like orange sticks, and laid them on the table before him together with some long threads of green silk. He took from his bowl of flowers a small rosebud, fixing it on the end of the orange stick and perfumed it with one drop from one of his secret phials. He arranged round it a little ring of mimosa blossom and then some small leaves of orange flower. Next came a ring of blue forget-me-nots, very broad this, measuring almost an inch, and then another inch of pale pink night-scented stock. He finished it off at the bottom with soft green moss, leaving a long loop of silk at the end, and laid it aside for a moment whil he made the second. This was fashioned almost the same way, except that the leaves stripped from a clove carnation and tiny, star-like jasmine flowers replaced the forget-me-nots and the stock in the first. The second one was secured to the wooden stick with rose-coloured silk, and when they were finished we realised that the posy the man had been carrying away, whom we met on our arrival, was one of the same charms. The old perfume seller said, 'you must wait for five minutes while they dry, and in the meantime I will give you' – pointing to my young friend – 'a recipe for something which will take your freckles away. Do not be afraid of it. It may not sound very convenable, but I assure you it is efficacious. You must take the ground powder of mimosa flowers, the liver of a still-born kid and the entrails of a porcupine. Dry them for one hour in the sun, pound them together in a mortar and soften them with orange flower water. Use this on your face each night for a week and you will have no freckles. Will you use it?' 'If you can tell me where I can procure the entrails of a porcupine I will attempt to make it and will certainly use it.' The old man shook his head. 'I am a perfume seller,' he said, 'but I think any butcher will procure for you the entrails of a porcupine. Will the other lady have a recipe?' The other lady decided she would like a recipe, and he gave me one to make the eyes bright. It was not so difficult as that for removing freckles, but as I was never able to procure one of the ingredients I never had it made up. The juice of foxglove stalks to the extent of four grammes was to be mixed with honey, aconite and the whiskers of a white cat, which he assured me would dissolve in this concoction! It was to be used only every third night, beginning on the first of the month – 'and if you use it regularly, you will conform to the Moorish idea of beauty in a very short time.' When we asked what this idea was he gave it us as a poetical translation of the Arab saying – '*Belle comme la lune dans sa quatorzième nuit*' – 'as beautiful as the moon in her fourteenth night.'

Slavery existed in Morocco until quite recently. Jackson and Mauran show that although their lives were not always as bad as thought, nevertheless slaves were often acquired in the degrading circumstances narrated by Cowan and Johnston.
From G. A. Jackson, *Algiers . . .*, 1817, p. 95; from Dr Mauran, *La Société marocaine*, 1912, pp. 129–31; and from George Cowan and R. L. N. Johnston, *Moorish Lotos Leaves*, 1883, pp. 123–6.

Negroes are to be found as governors of cities, commanders of the bodyguard, eunuchs to the harem, and filling other offices of the state. The same man, who, kidnapped at his parents' door, and brought westward, would handle the hoe, if sold in a northerly direction, wields the baton of command; and by his talents, steadiness, and bravery, is considered the pillar of the state. The same female, who, if exported across the Atlantic, should daily be lacerated by the stripes of the cow-skin, be the daily victim of the brutality of one sex, and the malignity of the other, now sits upon a throne, because chance pointed her captivity hither.

The first luxury acquired by any Moroccan who makes money is to buy a slave. In the coastal towns, female slaves are much more numerous than those of the male sex who are to be found only in the palaces of high officials. The townsfolk prefer females who can do domestic work.

Some old gentlemen and widowers who have a female slave to look after the house become so attached to them that they set them free or even marry them.

These slaves can come from almost anywhere in the Sahara. Treated almost like animals they are the sad flotsam of tribal raids or internal disputes. They arrive at the great Moroccan cities after cruel marches along secret tracks, led by sinister merchants who have often succeeded in finding protection from one of the great European powers.

In most cities there is still a slave market but it is usually held in the inns where Europeans never go except by chance or in disguise. But it is not there that the best specimens can be found for the really valuable slave girls are sold secretly and never put on public display.

It is very bad form to sell a slave and the action brings a house into discredit. They must be treated gently, well fed and well dressed. They can be beaten for serious offences but the worst punishment is to be thrown out of the house or even sold. In the event of systematic ill treatment a slave has the right to summon her master before the Qadi who can compel him to sell her. But there are many slaves, who, having arrived in the household as children, grow and eventually die there, regarded with affection by all. They have guarded the babies, helped them to make their first steps, watched over their sleep. Later they became the confidantes of the young girls or young men of the family, confidantes discreet and devoted.

I have known young women who have forced their husbands, almost as a condition of marriage, to allow them to keep the faithful negress that they have come to regard as their second mother.

The slaves often get their own back for there are no men who are worse looked after than the Moroccans. Many times I have had to hide a smile as the master of the house, with impressive dignity, claps his hands to call a servant. The slave girls take at least a quarter of an hour to do the simplest thing.

A slave market is held in Marrakesh twice a week, in a square court, some thirty paces across, on each side of which is a row of mud-walled booths, mostly in a decayed condition. Down the centre is a kind of arcade, between whose crumbling columns runs a double row of stone benches. Taking our places on one of these seats, we observed that the booths were gradually filling with grave and reverend signiors in spotlessly clean haiks, with town loafers in coarse, hooded cloaks, mountaineers determined to see all the sights of the city, and, taking up their position in a secluded corner of the market, a score or so of veiled Moorish ladies.

'Three hundred and twenty ducats', cries a jaunty auctioneer, stepping briskly on to the scene, followed by a couple of boys, of perhaps twelve and eight years old. Girding his cloak around him with a business-like air, and repeating at intervals the latest bid offered, he leads them from booth to booth, where they undergo a close and skilful scrutiny by intending purchasers. They are questioned to see if they know Arabic; their teeth, hands and joints critically examined. (As many of the slaves now domesticated in Morocco were originally obtained by the kidnapping which is still practiced in the neighbourhood of the Soudan, a knowledge of Arabic in the younger slaves is an accomplishment to be considered in their price). By this time upwards of two hundred people have been assembled. Other auctioneers appear, introducing to the public their chattels, male and female, of whom some are bashful, some sulky, and others remarkable for the meretricious finery distributed about their otherwise scanty garments, and for a leer intended to captivate some indulgent (and rich) purchaser. One little girl, half draped in a shift of gaily striped print, paced with naked feet that dreary enclosure until her price rose to 450 ducats – at the present exchange, about ten pounds – and was then bought in. A young negro giant followed, whose repulsive physiognomy and shuffling gait seemed the index to a whole volume of rascality; he was knocked down at two pounds, and we found by a calculation based upon his apparent weight, that his market value was about threepence per pound – just half the present price of beef.

12

Education and Rites of Passage

Many of the customs and practices described in this chapter could have been found in other parts of the Muslim world and some, indeed, on the other side of the Mediterranean. Unique, however, to Morocco was the Feast of the Tolba, described by Loti. Many of the rituals have now been greatly changed by westernization and also by the facts of economic life and there can be few weddings or funerals today as elaborate as those described by the Sharifa of Wazan. The system of education described by Michaux-Bellaire has, of course, also changed but only a few years ago in remote villages one could see Koranic schools of the type that he mentions. The extracts show the importance of religion in all the principal episodes of Moroccan everyday life.

Popular beliefs surrounding childbirth.
From Dr Françoise Legey, *The Folklore of Morocco*, 1935, pp. 106–9, and 132–5.

RITES FOR CURING STERILITY

A barren woman is under a reproach for the whole of her life. Hence a widow whose marriage was childless finds it very difficult to marry again. It is said of her that she is a mule and that if she remarries she will bring neither milk nor butter with her.

The struggle against barrenness is therefore only natural.

Men eat the testicles of a sheep when it is they who are in fault.

Women swallow the testicles of a cock; among the Jews the women eat the foreskin of the newly circumcised infant, in order to become fertile and to have boys.

Moroccan women make *tagines*, or stews, with the placenta of sheep and goats and with the foetus of sheep and of dogs. They hope to thus obtain the prolific virtue of these animals and practise opotherapy unawares.

When a barren woman assists at a birth in the mountains of the Glaoui, she catches hold of the after-birth which has just been expulsed, takes it between her teeth, and runs away and spits it out on the ground, and sits on it for about an hour. When the ministering midwife has finished looking after the mother and child, she goes up to the barren woman, makes her place herself as if she were in labour, and exhorts her to expel her child, and makes her go through the pretence of giving birth. The evil spell which made her barren is thus conjured and she becomes fertile.

In order to combat the evil spell cast upon her, the barren woman also draws water in dead silence from seven Semmaoui wells, which are never covered. She washes herself in this water on Friday and then pours it out at the threshold of the mosque at the hour of the Great Prayer. With the water she has cast away the evil spell which will no longer be able to work; for the faithful, charged with holy blessing, will destroy its evil strength when they walk over the water. To complete the rite she fumigates herself with sulphur and assafoetida under her clothes. Instead of water from the seven wells, she sometimes uses the urine of her mother, which will transmit to her the fruitfulness of a woman who has had a child.

On the coast a barren woman washes away the bad luck in the sea. She takes a comb and a handful of *alfa* and goes to the shore with a relation or friend who she can trust. She seeks out a deserted spot and undresses herself and offers her body seven times to the waves, which thus wash away all the evil, the *bass*, which she has been carrying, and bear it away as they roll back. Then she combs her hair and scrubs herself with the *alfa*, which serves as a brush, and then she throws away the comb and her hair combings, and the *alfa*, into the sea, and says:

> *Hana kesst fikoum et tabâ*
> *Li tâbani fi korchi,*
> *Bach t'helli hazami.*'
> 'I cast in you (O Waves) the evil fate
> Which cast a spell on my belly,
> That you should unfasten my girdle.'

If pregnancy does not take place in due time after this the barren woman is tattooed in order to combat her evil fate. A cross is pricked in between her shoulder-blades and another is tattooed on her ankles. This has great magic power, for it keeps off the evil eye of the genii of the earth as well as that of human beings.

To complete the rite, the woman throws into the sea the chemise that she was wearing when it was performed and seven pebbles upon which a *taleb* has written:

> '*Tleq straha had el oulia.*'
> 'Release this woman from her evil fate.'

Plants which produce an abundance of seed, and vegetables with quantities of leaves, are also used to combat sterility. A handful of *harmel*, for instance, is taken and washed seven times and is then passed seven times over the fumes of incense. It is kneaded with dates, and a paste is made of it and eaten night and day. As the *harmel* and date palm have a great many leaves and yield abundant fruit, it is thought that they impart their powers of reproduction to the sterile woman.

A very complicated preparation called *khemira*, or leaven, is also taken to cure barrenness. The woman who takes it is supposed to acquire the remarkable power of reproduction exercised by heaven. This mixture is generally prepared by a sorceress, or by a *mokaddema* or servant of a sanctuary. She takes some chervil, fennel, cress, and harmel, all of which plants yield seed in abundance, and adds some amber. She sacrifices a new-born puppy (the dog being a prolific animal), cuts it up into small pieces, and lets everything soak together for seven days in a vessel containing water, and then at the end of seven days she sends it all to the childless woman, who mixes it up with ordinary broth and partakes of it for three days. She also has the pieces of puppy cooked and eats them up. The third day she goes to the bath and resumes conjugal relations with her husband.

The visit of a woman [to a new mother and baby] who has not purified herself after sexual relations with her husband is equally forbidden, as well as that of one who is strongly perfumed, for the odour of perfumes is supposed to be fatal for the baby. A woman in love is also tabooed, on account of the magic odour of the talismans with which she is covered.

Live cinders for a fire must not be given to a neighbour until the mother is up on foot again; it would cause the child to get virulent ophthalmia, which would make it lose its sight. Neither must salt nor yeast be lent, for that would bring impetigo upon it.

For that same reason dried peas and beans should not be cooked in the house during the first seven days after childbirth. Dried beans are used in funeral rites, and to prepare them for food would entail the death of the mother or of the child.

If a doubtful friend, or a stranger, penetrates into the room of the young mother, the perfume-burner is at once made ready, and a mixture of alum and harmel is burnt during the whole of the visit. If the visitor, contrary to custom, takes the child in her arms, she is not allowed to lay it back in bed; the person who is burning the perfumes takes it and passes it three times through the fumes emanating from the incense-burner, in order to purify it from the contact and to destroy all evil results.

As the blood of the mother in childbirth might be used for spells against her, it is hidden from every eye. Only the midwife may touch it, and for this reason it is she who washes all the linen of her patient, as well as the baby's clothes, which she washes and dries behind closed doors, where no eye can fall upon them. She must in addition be careful to spread them out over articles made of copper, such as mortars and trays; for copper keeps away the devils who might be tempted to pollute the linen, and thus contaminate them with mortal illness for the baby.

The *n'fissa*, or lying-in woman, only takes her meals with the midwife during the seven days following upon the confinement. Even if other persons should eat in the same room, she must have special meals prepared for her, which only the midwife may share.

If two women give birth to their child at the same moment, and in the same room, which is sometimes the case in consequences of polygamy, they must offer each other an egg directly they have been delivered, and eat it up so that neither of them should do the other any harm. They exchange infants when they put them for the first time to the breast, they forgive each other for any past offences, and speak words of amity together, so that their children should in no way suffer from their rivalry.

Mother and child are never left alone during the first seven days for fear of the child being changed by devils before it has received its name. The infant is never changed by devils before birth; but it is constantly exposed to this danger afterwards, and it is anxiously guarded by means of magic until it has grown up. Directly after birth a velvet bag containing harmel, alum, salt, and an open knife is placed by its side, and must never leave it. If the baby is moved to another part of the room, the bag must go with it.

When she first gives suck to her babe, the mother smears vermilion over her breasts to hide the dark colour of her skin, so that the lips of the babe should always be red.

In order to make the father love the child, a little of the meconium is rubbed on the soles of his shoes. This is supposed to strengthen the tie between him and his offspring. The third day after the confinement the face of the young mother is painted with saffron, or vermilion, so as to efface the mask of pregnancy.

To prevent her from having hemorrhage, an amulet written out by a *taleb* is attached to her right thigh. Tiny ligatures are bound round the first finger of each hand and round her arms and thighs, and compresses of cold water are applied to her abdomen with the object of cooling her blood. Cold compresses and ligatures are also supposed to stop the flow of blood.

Against any uterine complications which might arise after the confinement the midwife takes a little sugar, dips it in the blood of the confinement, and rubs some three times on her patient's right heel.

Jewesses also give honey and melted butter to the mother to relieve her after-pains.

If the woman sleeps heavily and does not easily wake up to put her baby to the breast, she is made to swallow some earth taken from an ants' nest, as ants are supposed to sleep very lightly. Among the Jews she is made to drink out of the pail which serves to water a thoroughbred horse, which is also noted for sleeping lightly. If on the other hand the mother is too fussy over her baby, and cannot get to sleep, she makes an offering to Sidi Sacy and tells him:

> 'Oh, holy Sidi Sacy, son of Sacy,
> Give me my meed of sleep.'

When a newly delivered woman has no milk, she is given a species of very liquid porridge made of pounded lucerne seeds, for lucerne is supposed to give milk to cows. At Marrakech an offering is made in her name to the holy Moulksour, who is the *Moul l'halib*, The Master of Milk. A little water from his shrine is then given to her to drink, and this suffices to give her an abundance of milk.

The great Sidi Bel Abbes Elli Iqdo koul Hadja, He who Furnishes Everything, also furnishes milk in abundance for nursing mothers. It suffices to fill a jug with water from his sanctuary, and to leave it on his tomb for a whole night, and if the young mother then drinks of it she will have a plentiful flow of milk.

The Jewesses of Marrakech send for water drawn from a *Khottara* of Bab el Khemis called *tireret*, and make the nursing mother drink it, so that her milk should flow freely. In point of fact, water from the shrines of the patron saint of each town, or of each tribe, is supposed to give the same result.

When the umbilical cord drops off on the third or fourth day, a little dust is taken from under the mother's bed and is put with the dried-up cord into a little bag, which is fastened to the clothes of the new-born infant. This sachet is left in contact with the babe for three days and is then sewn into his pillow, and is supposed to be a watchful guardian against devils.

The ceremony for naming a new-born child.
From Rev. Lancelot Addison, *An Account of West Barbary* . . ., 1671, printed in Pinkerton, vol. XV, pp. 433–4.

When the child is seven days old, the Moors give it a name, and the father of it makes a feast. But the imposition of the name is done in public assembly; for the father at the evening-sallah (prayer) carries to the church several dishes of cuscussow, of which he sets one apart for the priest, and the rest to be eaten up by the people. And when prayers are ended, the congregation demand of the father what he will call his child, and if the name he gives it be not satisfactory to the people, they will decide by lots what he shall be called, for every man here has a vote in the naming of his neighbour's child. And when they have agreed the point, all pray that the child may live, prove rich and valiant, and understand the Alcoran; then they eat up the cuscussow and depart. It is observable that the priest, neither at the naming nor circumcision of the child, has any appropriate office, of which I could find no other reason, unless the Moors estimate of these ceremonies, which they never reckon among the essentials of religion.

The feast of the Prophet's birthday.
From Ali Bey, *Travels*, 1816, pp. 24–9.

The festival of *El-Mouloud*, or the birth-day of the Prophet lasts eight days. At this period infants are circumcised, and every day, both morning and evening, a sort of concert is executed before the door of the kaid's house. This music is composed of a large rude drum, and two bag-pipes ruder still, and very discordant.

During this festival, we went to perform our devotions at an hermitage or sacred place, two hundred fathoms from the town, and in which the mortal remains of a saint are revered. It serves at the same time as an habitation for another living saint, a brother of the deceased, and who receives the offerings for both. The sepulchre of the dead saint was covered with different pieces of silk, cotton and silver stuff, and in a corner were some Moors singing in chorus verses out of the Koran.

Circumcision is publicly performed at this chapel and is a feast for the family of the Neophyte. When they proceed to the sacrifice, a certain number of boys are assembled who carry handkerchiefs, sashes, and even miserable rags, which they fasten like flags to long sticks, or reeds; this group is followed by music, consisting of two bag-pipes which are played in unison, but not therefore less discordant, and two or more drums of a very hoarse sound, a band sufficiently disagreeable to an ear accustomed to European music. The father, or nearest relations, follow with the persons invited, who surround the child mounted on a horse, of which the saddle is covered with red cloth.

If the child be too young, he is carried in the arms of a man on horseback. All the rest are on foot. The Neophyte is generally covered with a sort of cloak made of white linen, and over this cloak he wears a red one adorned with various ribands, and a fillet or band of silk is tied round his head. A man walks on each side of the horse with a silk handkerchief in his hands, with which he drives away the flies from the child and from his horse. Some women, wrapt up in their enormous Haiks or burnous, close the procession.

At ten in the morning I left my house, and pressing through the crowd, I went to the chapel. I found on my way groups of three or four or more children, who were going to endure the ceremony. The country was covered with horses, soldiers, inhabitants, Arabs, and collections of women, entirely enveloped in their concealing garments, and sitting in hollows of the ground or under the shade of trees. These women, as the children passed by, uttered cries exceedingly shrill, which are always considered from them as signs of mirth and of encouragement.

After having reached the hermitage, I crossed a yard crowded with people, and entered the chapel, where I found what may be called a real butchery.

On one side of the saint's sepulchre were placed five men dressed only in shirts and drawers, with their sleeves turned up to their shoulders. Four of these men were sitting in front of the door of the chapel, and the fifth was standing at the side of the door, in order to receive the little victims. Two of those, who were sitting, held the instruments of the sacrifice, the other two had each a purse or little bag, filled with an astringent powder.

Behind these four ministers was a group of about twenty children of all ages and colours, who had also their part to play, as we shall see presently; and at the distance of some yards an orchestra of the same kind as I have described before, was executing its discordant tunes.

Every time that a Neophyte arrived, his father, or the person who was there to represent him, walked before him, and, entering the chapel, kissed the head of the operating minister, and made him some compliments. The child was then brought forward, and, immediately seized by the strong-armed man who was appointed to receive the victims; and he having lifted up the gown of the child, presented him to the operator. At this moment the music began to sound with its loudest noise; and the children, who were seated behind the ministers, started suddenly up, and shouted with great vociferation, to attract the attention of the victim, and, by the motions of their fingers, directed his eyes to the roof of the chapel. Stunned with all this noise, the child lifted up his head; and that very moment the officiating priest laid hold of the prepuce, and pulling it with force, clipped it off with one motion of his scissors. Another immediately threw a little astringent powder on the wound, and a third covered it with lint, which he tied on by a bandage; and the child was carried away.

The whole operation did not last half a minute, though it was executed in a very clumsy manner. The noise made by the children and the music prevented me from hearing the cries of the victim, though I was close to them. However, their gestures proved sufficiently what they suffered. Every child was afterwards put on the back of a woman, who took him home, covered with her Haik or burnous; and followed by the same train with which he had arrived.

Edouard Michaux-Bellaire described traditional education in an article in the *Revue du Monde Musulmane* of October 1911 which has been translated and abridged by the editors.

The system has not changed over the centuries and to learn what it was like hundreds of years ago we need do no more than look at it as it is now. There is no government support for the schools which are maintained entirely by the local inhabitants. In some towns, however, there are some teachers of the Qur'an who receive small salaries out of mosque funds.

Primary education consists of learning the Qur'an by heart and the procedure is always the same in towns or in tribal encampments. Each child carries a wooden board of irregular shape, about 40 centimetres long and up to 24 wide, covered with a layer of clay on which he writes with a reed. The ink is made out of burnt wool, or better still out of a burnt ram's horn. When the child has learned to write the letters and then to join them, the teacher, the F'qih, starts to dictate the first Surah of the Qur'an which begins 'In the name of God, the Merciful, the Compassionate'. The teacher does not need a book: he knows the Qur'an by heart. As the board is covered with writing, the pupil memorises it. His memory is stimulated by fear of the F'qih's rod on the soles of his feet; for this punishment he is held by two of his comrades who hold up his feet for the teacher to strike. No explanation of the text is given and the teacher himself would probably be embarrassed by a request for any. The teacher himself knows the Qur'an with every detail of spelling, intonation and accents but he does not understand it, or try to understand it, any more than his pupils do.

In the towns the school is usually a single, ground floor room, without windows, with light coming only through the door. There is no furniture except for mats and a sort of bench on which the teacher squats with his legs folded underneath him. The children sit on the floor in the same fashion. In the Arab villages of the plains, the school is usually a tent, or a reed hut or a roughly built brick shed. The teacher is supported by the villagers who either give him a share of their produce or a piece of land for which they provide the seed and do the cultivation. At shearing time they give him a proportion of the wool and when various stages of the Qur'an have been reached, the villages give a feast for the teacher and the children. A new teacher is welcomed into the village in procession with pipes and drums, greeted almost as a bride. In the mountains horseman gallop around him firing shots in the air. He very often leads the prayers in the mosque, cuts the throat of the first sheep of the 'Id and organises the recitation of the entire Qur'an on the night of the 27th Ramadan which is performed by the Tolba, those who know it by heart.

Children go to school as soon as it is light and stay there until noon. They then go home for lunch and return to school where they sleep until 1.30. The F'qih then awakes them and classes continue until sunset when the students go out while the teacher prays. They return until the Asha prayer, an hour and a half after sunset. At this time the school is lit by a glass jar with olive oil and a wick made from a twist of cotton, hanging by a chain from the ceiling.

The pupils who go on to secondary education start with grammar and syntax. Grammar is learned from a book in verse written by a scholar who died in 1324 which is so concise that it needs considerable explanation. Syntax is learned from a poem of 1000 verses written a century earlier on which there are various commentaries. They then progress to 'The Profitable guide to what it is indispensible to know in science and religion' which was written in Fez early in the seventeenth century. As previously with the Qur'an secondary education usually consists of learning by heart with minimal comprehension. Nothing is done to develop the faculties of the youngsters or to open their minds to new ideas – on the contrary the more they learn the more rigid their ideas become and the more they apply themselves to externals without reaching understanding.

The life of these secondary students follows very much the same pattern as before with the difference that they spend much time alone memorizing their texts. When they have finished, they are qualified to act as Adoul, notaries in the law courts, or even as Qadis in rural areas although those in cities require higher education. Those students who have the Qur'an by heart form a sort of fraternity which holds picnics for which they prepare months in advance. People dare not refuse, for fear that Divine wrath might be invoked by the scholars and provide food, perhaps even sheep or a cow for which they are rewarded by a blessing. Tents, carpets, mattresses are borrowed and they eat and drink and dance with young men made up as girls. These parties, one in Larache in 1903 was attended by 500 Tolba from local tribes, last until the food runs out.

Higher education is available only in Fez where there are ten Medrasas. These are not colleges as there is no teaching there, only lodgings. Most were founded by Sultans and are maintained by funds from properties given by them and by subsequent benefactors. The students pay no rent and receive two loaves a day. The students used to take a form of examination after three years and those who failed were rejected but the rest could keep their rooms for another seven years. After ten years, they were no longer fed and were considered to have finished their education. Now there is no longer an examination and students can stay as long as they wish: some have been there for more than thirty years.

Lectures start at six o'clock in the morning and continue until the afternoon prayer. Each Professor has his own place beside one of the pillars of the Qaraouyin mosque where he places his mat which he has carried rolled up under his arm. The students sit in a semi-circle around him. He never carries the book that he is expounding but one of the brighter students holds it and reads out a sentence which the professor explains. The most distinguished professors may occupy one of the twelve chairs – a platform with three steps on which he sits cross-legged. History has never been taught and geography and lexicography stopped some years ago. On Thursdays and Fridays there is no teaching and there is a three-week break at the two main religious festivals. If a professor dies there is a holiday for three days, ten days if he was particularly distinguished. There is also a month's holiday, usually in April, for the feast of the Tolba.

The feast of the Tolba, just mentioned, is described in this extract.

From Pierre Loti, *Morocco*, 1889 (1929 edn), pp. 199–202.

Rumour has it that the Sultan of the Tolba is in flight since last night.

He was an ephemeral king, a little outside the walls, in his improvised, white canvas town. At the door of his tent he had a counterfeit battery of large cannons, made of pieces of wood and reeds. He was, though with more dignity, something like the 'Pope of Fools' of our Middle Ages.

In the university of Fez, which has remained unchanged since the epoch of Arab splendour, it is an ancient custom, each year, in the spring vacation, for the students to spend ten days in high festival; to choose a king (who buys his election, at auction, by force of gold); to encamp with him in the fields on the river bank; then to levy a tax upon the population of the town, in order to be able at night to make merry with song and music, couscous and cups of tea. And the people of the town lend themselves to these amusements with a smiling submission; they come, all – viziers, merchants, craftsmen, by corporations and with banners at their head – to visit the camp of the Tolba and bring presents. And, finally, the Sultan himself, the true Sultan, comes also to pay homage to the Sultan of the Students, who receives him on horseback, under a parasol like a caliph, and treats him as an equal, calling him 'my brother'.

The Sultan of the Tolba is always a member of one of the distant tribes, who has some special favour to ask for himself or for his people, and he profits by this unique interview with the sovereign to obtain it. Very soon afterwards, for fear lest it might be taken from him, for fear also of reprisals on the part of those whom he has had to punish in the case of good government, one fine night, clandestinely, he disappears – an easy thing to do in Morocco; across the deserted campaign he seeks refuge in his own country.

At the end of these days of mirth the students re-enter Fez. Those of them who have not completed their studies return to their little work-cells, in those kinds of cloisters that are called medrasahs and are places almost holy, forbidden to unbelievers. The Sultan sends daily to each of them a loaf of bread which constitutes almost the whole of their usual fare. During the day they live in the mosques, especially in the immense Karaouin, squatted down to listen to the lectures of the learned professors, or kneeling in the act of prayer. Those who, after seven or eight years of study, have obtained their degree of doctor return to their own country surrounded with a high prestige. As I have said, they have come sometimes from very distant parts, these tolba of Karaouin; they have been gathered from the four winds of Islam, attracted by the renown of this holy mosque, which contains, it seems, in its libraries, ageless and priceless volumes, accumulated there in the days of Arab greatness, brought from Alexandria or carried off from the convents of Spain.

The sciences taught at Karaouin include astrology, alchemy and divination. The 'mystic numbers' are studied there, and the influence of the stars and of demons, and other tenebrous things which for the moment have disappeared from the rest of the world – until the day perhaps when, in another form, shorn of the marvellous, they will reappear triumphant as the beyond of our positive sciences. The Koran and all its commentators are paraphrased at great length, as also Aristotle and other ancient philosophers. And side by side with so many grave and arid things, extraordinary affectations of style, of diction, of grammar, subtleties of the Middle Ages which we are no longer able to understand; they are like the designs, so elaborate, so delicate, wrought here and there on the grim bastions and the high walls.

Further details of the Feast of the Tolba are given in an article by Pierre de Cenival in Hespéris *in April 1925. The public cryer of the book market went round the students shouting the highest bid so far for the office of sultan: in 1923 it had been nearly £500. Someone known for his wit was chosen to impersonate the Inspector of the Market and raise money. The Jews provided a 'state' seal and the real sultan loaned a horse, clothes and regalia. Many rich citizens put up their own tents nearby to enjoy the music and the parties. On the third or fourth day a member of the royal family brought the sultan's tribute of sheep, flour, butter, sugar, tea, money etc. On another day it was announced that the Jews would bring tribute of oxen and sheep: this invariably turned out to be cats and rats in cages and this traditional joke was always greatly enjoyed. When the real sultan arrived, the student sultan, identically dressed and attended, would demand to know how a mere Emperor of Morocco dared to visit the mightiest emperor in the world – the ruler of fleas, lice and other creatures. The pseudo-Inspector of Markets would make a speech full of jokes and the farce was maintained until the real sultan, having asked permission to leave, started to withdraw, whereupon the student sultan would jump from his horse and present his petition which could be for something like a government post, the liberation of a prisoner or the lifting of taxes on his village.*

Few of the people of the Souss could earn their living locally so many of the men went north to work in shops, usually belonging to a member of the family who had already established himself. After living an extremely frugal and hard-working life, many of them bought their own shops in which, in turn, they were joined by their younger brothers, children or nephews. The women remained behind but the men, when they were able to afford to marry, returned to the Souss to find a bride.

From John Waterbury, *North for the Trade*, 1972, pp. 33–4.

It was my mother who found me my wife. That was in 1940. My father had already died ten years earlier. I had already been in the north fifteen years. The way I found my wife was not the way it usually happened. Usually it was the father who would suggest a suitable wife to his son, sometimes following the advice of his wife. But the father never made the suggestion directly to his son. An uncle or cousin would do it, telling the son about the merits of such and such a girl. The son would know what was up. He would then try to get a glimpse of the girl. There were little arrangements that could be made. The son would hide in the palm trees near the girl's house, and she might come out to grind the argan nuts while the brothers would pretend not to notice she was being watched. If the son didn't like what he saw, he could make a counter proposition to his father, but always through his uncle or his cousin. Father and son would then bargain indirectly until they agreed on a choice.

With me it was my mother who had to play my father's role. As it turned out the girl was from Ait Talib. My mother had a woman friend in Ait Talib who was originally also from Tahala, and she told my mother what a wonderful, strong girl my future wife was. The girl had no brothers. It was one of my older cousins who was an intermediary between the two families and between my mother and myself. I agreed to the marriage. I came down to the valley from Larache and on April 20 1940 we were married, and in October I left to go to Tangier. A year later I came back with 60,000 francs and built our house. She is my only wife. She's not weak like these younger girls. She's worked in the fields. She's literate too; my eldest daughter taught her how to read and write. Best of all she's a good saver and doesn't waste money like most women do.

A detailed account of a marriage ceremony lasting nearly a week.
From Emily, Shareefa of Wazan, *My Life Story*, 1911, pp. 125–38.

The wedding ceremonies now commenced by the bride going to the Hamman, or steam-bath. . . . A strong negress enters the bride-elect's chamber and approaches the bed, where she is hidden behind a curtain and wrapped in a large white sheet. The negress bends her back, and the bride is hoisted on, amid 'zahrits,' benedictions, native music, and the free sprinkling of orange and rose water and burning of incense. . . . The negress deposits her burden at the bathroom door, and the bathwomen take the precious burden in charge. From one and a half to two hours the purifying process goes on, and in the meantime the assembled guests are entertained with music and tea-drinking. When the bath is terminated, the procession is reformed and the bride deposited on a bed, generally in another room on the ground floor, if there is a room suitable. After an hour or two of repose, and in the early hours of the morning, say, between 1 A.M. and 3 A.M., the guests again reassembled in the bride's chamber to see her anointed with henna . . .

Sometimes a professional stainer will be summoned, and patterns will be designed with henna paste, which must be dried over a charcoal fire. This takes a very long time, and one can but admire the effect produced afterwards, especially when the design is interwoven with the delicate tracing of 'El Harkos.' I have on one or two occasions had my hands decorated with 'Harkos,' and at a distance Europeans thought I was wearing black silk mittens . . .

Male friends and acquaintances of both families have been invited on the morning of the second day to witness the sacrifice of a bullock at the bride's house, in front of the principal entrance. After the sacrifice they are invited into the house, the women folk being conspicuous by their absence, unless they are slaves or others accustomed to assist on such occasions. To the strains of violins, guitars, and other native instruments combined, tea, cakes, and biscuits of native manufacture are served, though to-day European biscuits are much in vogue. Then follow three or four courses consisting of meat, chickens, and the couscous. . . . In the evening the ladies come in their second-best gowns, and until the early hours of the morning dancing, singing, and feasting are kept up. Early in the afternoon young girls arrive arrayed in gorgeous attire and bedight with jewellery . . . Each child-guest has brought sugar, tea, and candles, sometimes only the former, which are the perquisites of the musicians, who are in attendance practically the whole five days of the wedding festivities. Tea, with a meal to follow, is served to the children before leaving, and the feast is terminated when the mistress of the ceremonies, standing in front of the musicians seated in the patio or hall, names the donors of so much sugar, tea, and candles. Each name is pronounced separately with this formula: 'The daughter of so-and-so presents so much; may God bless and thank her, and may we soon all be assembled to assist at her wedding.' After that they each present a piece of silver or a silk handkerchief, which latter goes to the bride's trousseau, and the mistress of the ceremonies receives her *douceur* for proclaiming the several donors . . .

As a rule the bride is invisible, except at midnight of the third day, when henna is freely applied to her hands and feet before the assembled guests, who hold lighted candles round the bed. This is done to the strains of native music and 'zahrits.' It is not etiquette for her to look at or speak to an outsider, and she must be abnormally shy, even if she does not feel so . . .

The afternoon of the fourth day is for the reception of the married ladies. Relatives, friends, and acquaintances don their best, and load themselves with jewellery, pearls having the predominance. This occasion is seized by young brides to make the first appearance after marriage, which generally takes place just within a year. These young wives are painted in a most grotesque manner . . .

Once the party is seated, all eyes are turned upon the bride, and the guests offer congratulations on the effect of her dress. But first the usual compliments as to health have been made, the mistress of the ceremonies has proclaimed who each guest is, and the musicians have been gratified with a substantial 'tip.' . . .

When the evening is nearly spent, comes the ceremony of presenting the wedding gifts. The mistress of the ceremonies takes her stand in front of the musicians. Near her sits the mistress of the house, or a friend, holding certain little packets containing sums of money, which are counted before the assemblage. These silver coins the mistress of the ceremonies throws piece by piece into a handkerchief spread for the purpose. One example will serve. The mother will hand perhaps ten dollars – it may be more or less according to the circumstances; the mistress of the ceremonies will then proclaim the giver much in this manner: 'God be with (here the name of the donor), wife of —, mother of the bride (or whatever relation the donor may be).' Then, as each piece is thrown on to the outspreading handkerchief, the mistress of the ceremonies repeats the formula, 'Thanks be to God and to her,' meaning the donor. Therewith numerous blessings and such good wishes are invoked for the future prosperity of her household. . . . Then follow the bride's presents from relatives and friends. These gifts consist of brocaded silks, cloth, gauze, muslin, silk handkerchiefs and, very rarely, some jewellery in the shape of earrings and bracelets. Each gift is proclaimed in the same manner as the monetary offerings, and when all have been given, a general inspection is held. The parcel is now remade, and taken away by the mother for the bride's future use, amid 'zahrits.' Tea and supper with a little more music end the day, and the guests return to their homes.

The fifth day is passed in comparative quietness until late in the afternoon, when the arrival of the bride's decorated litter in which she is to be conveyed to her future husband reminds one that it is time to begin the bride's toilette . . .

A professional dresser arrives, and she with intimates of the family passes to the bride-elect's chamber. On the bed behind the curtains the bride, attended by two or three friends, begins her change of raiment. The other guests are seated round the room, and the musicians are stationed in the hall, or patio, singing or playing as the case may be. . . . To-day coloured dresses are worn, the head-dress is supplemented by additional handkerchief and scarves, and a tiara, if possible; then, too, powder and rouge are fully used, and El Harkos dots, smaller than beauty patches, are not forgotten. The eyebrows are manipulated with El Harkos, or khol, and lengthened, and khol is not forgotten for the eyes. Khol is powdered antimony, as fine as flour, and not unknown to my European sisters. No belt is put on; only a handkerchief is loosely knotted round the waist to keep the garments in their place. The dressing being completed, a transparent veil is fixed at the top of the head and falls over the face.

The bride sits in the centre of the bed, supported by pillows, and a friend on each side of her. The professional dresser remains, so that when the curtains are drawn aside she lifts the veil for the bride to be admired by the assemblage. One sees in the bride an inanimate figure, eyes shut, hands folded in her lap. The dresser is congratulated on her work of art, and down goes the veil, to be again lifted when another group of people comes to inspect the bride, whom they criticise audibly. While this visiting is taking place, the drums and fife are making themselves heard at the door, for the musicians have come with the mule to take the litter with its precious burden to the bride's new home. Male guests are assembling in the streets with lanterns of all shapes, big and little and multi-coloured, accommodated with chairs borrowed from all quarters. The drums and fife peal out their third and last summons for the bride, and all is hurry and skurry in the house. The litter is dragged to the door of the bedchamber, the stout negress sitting on the extreme edge of the bed bends down, and the bride, enveloped in laces and muslins, is hoisted on to her back. She then passes with her load to the entrance of the litter, the coverings of which have been previously lifted in front, and, on the floor inside, a large blanket has been folded for the bride to sit on. The bearer goes on to her knees, inclines her head forward, and the bride goes into the litter head first almost, and is soon seated cobbler-fashion with the help of the negress and a friend. A little arrangement of dress is necessary, but nevertheless it is all most cleverly done . . .

The male guests rally round the litter, and then march round the town in a perfect blaze of candlelight. The male musicians march in the rear. On arriving in front of a mosque or sanctuary, the procession stops, the music ceases, and a short prayer is offered up. Drums announce the conclusion of this rite, and off they go again until they reach the bridal home. Here the mistress of ceremonies, who has walked behind the litter with a huge green or red wax candle blazing in her hand, enters the house, and announces the arrival of the bride. The women folk disperse for the time being, the 'zahrits' is prolonged, and the musicians in the house play their hardest.

The litter is now carried by the men into the house to the door of the bridal chamber. Immediately on depositing their burden the bearers discreetly retire. The mistress of the ceremonies is already there. Sitting on a chair a muffled-up figure is observed. This is the bridegroom, who at a sign from the mistress of the ceremonies stands up, extending his arm across the doorway. The bride on being taken from the litter passes underneath. The mistress of the ceremonies kneels with her back to the entrance, and two other women assist the bride to get on to the back of the mistress of ceremonies. A bride would be unlucky to put her foot to earth at this period. The mistress of the ceremonies thus deposits her on the nuptial bed, which is hung with silk and lace curtains, depending from a canopy, or simulated one.

On the night before, the bridegroom-elect entertains his bachelor friends in almost a similar way to that followed in the bride's house, with this difference, that he is the central figure, so to speak. He sits muffled up on a chair, face covered, and speaks to no one. He may or may not take the proffered cup of tea, and has a master of ceremonies, who entertains his guests far into the small hours of the morning. Whatever presents of money or kind are offered are taken charge of by the master of ceremonies for the time being. The sixth day is one of repose, and enables the bride to make the acquaintance of the husband's family. The seventh day, after noon, the bridegroom's family holds a reception, for which the bride is dressed very gaily, painted and rouged almost to a point of eccentricity. She sits on the bed, her face covered with a veil, which is raised by the professional dresser when guests approach to offer their congratulations. . . . The bride stops at the doorway of each room, and on arriving at the kitchen door a fish is produced, and a pretence is made of scraping it on her foot – a symbol of plenty in the culinary department.

A return is made in the same order to the bride's chamber. This time she is seated on a raised daïs in the centre of the room, facing the doorway, and one and all go forward to congratulate her before departing for their several homes in peace.

A much less grand wedding, in the countryside, was witnessed by this writer.
From Edmundo de Amicis, *Morocco*, 1897, vol. I, pp. 210–12.

The relatives and friends of the bride conduct her, with much shouting and many discharges of fire-arms, to the *duar* of the groom seated upon the back of a camel and entirely enveloped in a white or light-blue cloak. She is perfumed, her nails are stained with henna, her eyebrows blacked with burned cork, and she is usually fattened up for the occasion with a certain herb called *ebba*, much used by young girls. The groom's *duar*, for its part, invites all the neighbouring *duars* to attend the festivity, as many as from one to two hundred men, mounted and armed with guns, often responding to the invitation. The bride dismounts before the house of her future husband, and, seated upon a saddle padded and decked with flowers, witnesses the fete. While the men go through a 'powder play' the women and girls form a circle in front of her, and dance to the music of a pipe and drum all around a *haik* spread on the ground, into which every guest throws a piece of money in passing for the use of the young couple, while a crier announces the amount of the gift in stentorian tones and invokes a blessing on the giver. Towards evening the dancing and firing cease, the guests all seat themselves on the ground, and enormous dishes of kuskussu, roast chicken, mutton cooked on a spit, sweetmeats and fruit are handed around, the supper lasting until midnight. The next day the bride, dressed all in white, her hood drawn down and a red scarf wrapped around her head so as to cover the mouth, makes a tour among the neighbouring *duars* to collect more money, accompanied by her friends and relatives. After this the groom goes back to his toil in the fields, the bride betakes herself to the millstone, and love flies away.

From Emily, Shareefa of Wazan, *My Life Story*, 1911, pp. 150–51 and 153–7.

Lalla Heba, the stepdaughter of Emily, died a week after giving birth to a stillborn child.

The screaming, screeching of women came from all parts of the town, and then the Arab death-dirge suddenly struck my ear. Miss – and I were clutched and dragged, I don't know if by men or women, or both, and away we went to Lalla Heba's house. The sight in the hall was indescribable. Women were in hysterical convulsions, their bodies contorted, their faces in some instances covered with blood, caused by deep scratches mostly by their finger-nails, or possibly by those of others. Their chests were bare, and they thumped themselves until the chest was a mass of bruises, for in their frenzied grief they had lost all control over themselves. One woman clung to a door; her eyes were almost starting from her head, and yet she sang the Arab dirge, swaying herself to and fro as the door moved one way or the other. I managed to get through this grovelling mass of humanity, hoping I had not stepped upon anyone, for they nearly pulled me into their midst by clinging to my skirts. I managed to get up the stairs to Lalla Heba's room, which was crowded with Shareefas and others round the doorway. They also were swaying with their bodies, but none of the trying scenes of the hall, though every now and then the Arab dirge started outside the room. The Arab dirge resembles at the first few bars an uncanny laugh, then follow a few more in a pathetic strain in the minor key, then back again into the first motif, with a kind of heart-rending shriek at the end . . .

Burial takes place a few hours after death. If the house has a basement, the body is generally carried to a lower apartment, if the deceased should have died upstairs. A professional is hired to prepare the body for burial. Preparation consists in its being washed three times from head to foot with warm water and soap. The water must be brought from outside, as no fire is lighted in a house for three days after a death has taken place therein. Orange and rose water are freely used, attar of roses and incense, and other scents of native production. The water from Zemzem, the holy well of Mecca, is sprinkled over all. The nostrils and ears are plugged with camphor wrapped in cotton wool, and the same is placed under the armpits. About twelve yards of calico would be required to make a shroud, which is fashioned into garments just basted together. These consist of a shirt, drawers, two handkerchiefs for the head, on which also a turban is folded. The body, once dressed, is then rolled in a long piece of calico, and knotted at the head and foot. Tolba sit around after the body is placed on the bier, but not if the ceremony takes place in the mosque, and recite portions of the Qur'an; lighted candles are also placed near.

The bier is now brought in, and the coffin placed upon it, and covered with a haik. If a coffin is not used, the body is enveloped in the haik, which is removed at the grave side. The two big toes are tied together immediately after death, and if the approach of death is apparent in a sick person, the sufferer is always turned to face to the East. In case of sudden death this is the first office performed. During ablutions the body is kept in that direction.

I did not return to the house, for I had not sufficient pluck to encounter the writhing mass of humanity a second time, and I knew that when the coffin was removed from there a repetition of the early-morning scenes would take place. Every male in Wazan attended the funeral, robed in white; walls were covered with women also in white; even the trees swarmed with boys and girls watching what proved to be a magnificent procession. The first intimation was like hearing the surging of the sea in the far distance. Very slowly it became more distinct, then all at once a patch of white appeared among the trees on the side of Bou Hellal. I distinguished men, and then the cortege was in view, and the chanting from some two thousand throats became quite audible. The Arab women's dirge was intermingled with the men's sonorous voices, a heart-rending shriek now and again arose from somewhere . . .

At last the bier came in sight, borne on the shoulders of men. The rough coffin in which the body had been placed was invisible. The bier is an elongated cage, which is covered much in the same manner as the bridal litter. In this case there were flags worked in gold and silver spread on brocaded silks of many hues. The death-chant is really beautiful: harmonious, true, impressive music. Imagine some two thousand male voices chanting in unison while with measured steps – broken by short halts now and again when the bier-carriers change hands – the company swept on.

A few prayers from the Qur'an were recited as the body was laid in the already prepared grave. Bread, figs and money were freely distributed to the poor, and one and all returned to his house, leaving the grave-digger to cover up all that was mortal of the young bride. People who go to the grave seldom, if ever, neglect to recite a prayer. Daily pilgrimages are made to the new grave, and tolba recite at different intervals. For three days relations, friends, and acquaintances supply the meals at the house of mourning. On the third day dishes of couscous and bread and figs are distributed to the tolba and others, sitting round the last resting-place. This ceremony is repeated by most families on the fortieth day.

A woman on becoming a widow is at once rolled up in haik until new white garments, generally calico, are procured. She must wear no coloured garment for the period of four months eleven and a half days. Her laundry must also be done on Saturdays only, unmixed with that of her household. The hammam in solitude is also another restriction for the newly made widow, and if she bathes at a public bath, she must return home before the afternoon prayer. In Wazan she must not go out of her room after that time. Permission is accorded to visit friends after four months, but on no account may she attend festivities. She mut be very careful not to go about barefooted. The clothes worn at death are usually given to the poor, and little heed is paid to the question if death has taken place through contagious disease or not.

In the case of virgins, or women who have passed away in childbirth, or infants, the 'zahrits', or joy-cry, accompanies the body to the door of the house. If the deceased is well-to-do, or possesses slaves, it is customary to free one or two of them. These follow the bier, holding their certificates of freedom aloft at the end of a long cane, and a slave is often purchased for the purpose by the heirs. Many a one who has taken refuge in the *Zawia* owes her freedom to such circumstances.

13
Doctoring

Morocco has today hospitals as good as any in the world but in the past, as elsewhere, people had to rely upon quacks and medicine-men. This chapter shows the obedience accorded to these 'healers' and suggests that the most gruesome cures seemed to bring the most blessed relief. Visiting western doctors, with less fearsome medicines, were greatly welcome but they had their problems – particularly when doctoring in the royal harem as the extract from Lempriere shows. Many of them were missionaries – one of whom would insist upon his patients learning the Lord's Prayer by heart before he administered medicine and refused to give half a dose to a man who wished to learn only half the prayer.

The practice of blood-letting seen at a country fair.
From Captain G. D. Trotter, *Our Mission to the Court of Morocco*, 1881, pp. 14–15.

A large 'sok' or fair was being held in the neighbourhood, the chief object of interest to strangers being a professional bleeder, who sat outside his ragged little tent with a semi-circle of patients in front of him waiting their turn to be operated upon in the following manner: A small incision having been made somewhat behind the ear, a cupping-glass, or rather tin, was applied, filled and emptied three or four times, and the contents poured into a rapidly filling pool by the doctor's side. The patient then deposited a small coin with the operator and his place was taken by another. This practice of blood-letting is almost universal among the country people, who believe that the removal of an ounce or two of extra blood before the hot season commences will render them less liable to be affected by the heat of the sun; as most of them go about not only bare-headed, but with their crowns closely shaven, no doubt some cooling process of this sort is necessary. The little scars caused by the above process, and which many of our servants bear on the back of the neck, had always been a puzzle to me; for though the Moor's head is generally a mass of cicatrices, there is a certain form and regularity about these others which attracts one's attention, and I am glad to have discovered the cause.

This piece tells of how Thornton tried one of the quacks for himself.

From Philip Thornton, *The Voice of Atlas*, 1936, pp. 155–60.

I mentioned earlier a storyteller from Sous country. He was, amongst other things, a doctor, and I met him originally in Marrakesh, when I went at the suggestion of a friend to ask him if he could prescribe a cure for some poisonous flea bites that I had on my ankle. I had been to two French doctors and neither had done me the slightest good. Each day my ankle became more and more swollen, and I began to wonder what was going to happen when one morning my groin started to swell. So screwing up my courage I went into the Djmaa l'Fna to look for this curious man who was said to be able to cure almost any disease.

At last I found him sitting underneath a bright green umbrella patched with pieces of aeroplane fabric. Arranged in front of him were an enormous number of peculiar-looking bottles and odds-and-ends of animals. He himself was jet black, and had upon his head the biggest turban I have ever seen. I was introduced to him by an Arab friend, who explained what the trouble was. He invited me to sit down and show the bites that were causing the trouble, and after a moment's reflection, said that he had a cure which, although extremely painful, could be guaranteed to be effective. If I would come back in half an hour's time he would have everything prepared.

So I wandered off, vainly trying to believe that I was not frightened, and that I might as well try this man's medicine after the efforts of Europeans had failed. When I returned again, there was a small screen erected, so that the inquisitive crowd could not see what he was going to do. On a small chafing dish a black thing about the size of a walnut was being slowly fried in a clear red oil. You have doubtless heard of the filth of the East – in fact it seems to be the thing that most travellers talk about – but I must say, in justice to this jet black physician, that his garments and equipment, though extremely crude, were spotlessly clean.

I sat down opposite and exposed my leg. He ran gentle fingers up and down the calf and felt the tension of the swollen flesh around the ankle. Taking a big instrument rather like a knitting needle with a pea on the end, he probed the sore, first dipping the nob into the hot oil. As I did not twitch or complain of the pain, he squeezed the flesh as hard as I could bear, making the blood circulate towards the poisoned area. Deftly and suddenly he stuck a red-hot spatula into the wound and held me down on the ground as the cauterization took place. The pain, you may imagine, was exquisitely unpleasant. The little black ball was cut in half, and a chunk of it stuffed into the wound. On top of it, with a length of fibre he strapped two wads of pounded dates to the leg.

The whole of this treatment cost me a little over one-and-sixpence. In Fez I had been charged 35s for an ineffective injection that had only made me feel very ill. He instructed me to go home and sit still until sunset, when I was to return to have the dressing changed. I went back to the hotel and slept until the evening; and when I got up I found that the swelling had gone down, though the wound hurt very much still.

The physician was pleased to see me walking so well and when he took off the dressing, to my astonishment and delight I found the inflammation had almost disappeared. The other half of the little black ball that had been prepared in the morning was applied to the wound, but this time no dates were used, simply a length of banana leaf. I asked what it was that had had such a remarkable effect on the poisoning, and when I promised not to try the cure by myself, he told me that it was a mixture of the venom of three scorpions and the gall of a fox had been used. This was pounded up and fried in oil from the scorpions' bodies, making an extremely powerful antidote, I suppose, to the poison the fleas had injected.

I had a long talk with the old man about the use of his strange medicines, and he told me of some incredible cures; locusts, for instance, could be used medicinally in no less than 360 different ways. The very appearance of these creatures indicated their supernatural powers. Picking a dried locust out of a small bag, he showed me how its neck and eyes were like an elephant, its legs were those of a camel, and its head resembled that of a bull. Hanging above him was a coil of dried jackals' intestines and in a bag nearby were a dried liver and a bunch of a dozen jackals' tongues. I wonder if you know that a jackal has a sevenfold liver, and that is one of the reasons why he is able to go about at night and not sleep like other animals? In fact, night watchmen sometimes eat pieces of jackal's liver to keep awake.

The fat of the jackal is used as a chest embrocation in cases of severe pneumonia. Its intestines are used for purposes of magical fumigation. When I told him that I was in Marrakesh for the purpose of studying music and dancing, he said that I ought certainly to eat a jackal's tongue, as it would greatly help my voice to acquire the Arab timbre. Oddly enough, jackal's flesh is forbidden as being 'abominable' in the Qur'an. There lay in front of him, in little piles, a quantity of teeth of different animals: foxes' and bears' teeth in particular. If you have acute toothache you can procure a fox's tooth taken from the same part of the mouth as the tooth that aches, and can often effect an immediate cure by hanging it in the sun for three days. Love potions are made with the saliva of foxes, and naturally are very expensive, on account of the difficulty of catching a fox for the purpose.

There was also a great pot of bear's grease. This is used as a 'base' in very much the same way as petroleum is used by the European chemist to make up his ointments. There are a number of magical ointments that can be made simply by distilling the water in which portions of the Qur'an have been boiled and mixing the residue with the powdered essence of some magical animal. The cat, for instance, has great medicinal powers, and a cat's tail sewn in the set of your trousers is an excellent guard against sea-sickness or sudden death; the connection between the nine lives of the cat and sharing in this power by annexing its tail is obvious.

The next morning I came back before the sun got up and showed my bites to the 'doctor', who said that I was making satisfactory progress. There was no doubt that his treatment had reduced both the swelling and the inflammation; he recommended that I should wear a pigeon's foot on a string round my left wrist, in order to hasten up the process of healing. This treatment cost fourpence extra and proved to be quite effective.

Curtis was asked, as many western travellers were, to deal with a common complaint.

From Dr James Curtis, *A Journal of Travels in Barbary . . .*, 1803, pp. 39–41.

Nothing can surpass the ignorant and barbarous state of the inhabitants; they have no mode of computing the time, or of ascertaining the precise era of any particular event. On my asking the Governor of Alcazar his age, I was greatly surprised to learn that he could not answer with exactness; and indeed there was not a Moor in the country who could tell his age with precision. The only reply to be obtained from them was, that they were born before some particular event, such as a great action of the Emperor or their Princes, a battle in such a place, or a rebellion. The Governor insisted that he was ill, and requested me to feel his pulse, and when by my desire he stated the nature of his complaint, it appeared that before the plague he had had many wives who expressed themselves perfectly satisfied with him, but since that event he had had but one, and yet he found his vigour and strength getting impaired; he was no longer satisfied with himself, and therefore requested me to prescribe something to recruit him. Another Moor preferred a similar complaint, and desired me to send him some cantharides. Both these persons appeared to be about seventy years old but had no conception that old age made any difference to the human constitution.

A more recent account of local medicine.
From Rom Landau, *Invitation to Morocco*, 1950, p. 100.

The great ingenuity of medicine-men is illustrated by the way that they make use of large red ants for closing skin wounds. Though they know how to sew up wounds, they neglect modern means of disinfection, and in consequence their stitches easily fester and burst open. So instead of more orthodox methods of sewing up a wound, they often apply the following treatment. They place a living red ant on the wound after holding the two edges of the skin together in such a way as to leave part of both edges protruding. The ant, which has very powerful mandibles, instantly closes these on the skin, and is then cut off with a pair of scissors. But its mandibles remain closed in the skin over the wound, and, like clips, keep the two edges together. It depends on the length of the wound how many ants are applied. During one such operation which I watched, half a dozen were used. As soon as they had been cut off, the wound closed.

This extract illustrates the difficulties in treating ladies in the emperor's harem.
From William Lempriere, *Travels from Gibraltar to Tangier, Sallee* . . ., 1791, printed in Pinkerton, vol. XV, p. 723.

One of my new patients being ready to receive me, I was desired to walk into her room; where to my great surprise, I saw nothing but a curtain drawn quite across the apartment, similar to that in a theatre, which separates the stage from the audience. A female domestic brought a very low stool, placed it near the curtain, and told me that I was to sit down there, and feel her mistress's pulse.

The lady, who had by this time summoned up courage to speak, introduced her hand from the bottom of the curtain, and desired me to inform her of all her complaints, which she conceived I might perfectly perceive by merely feeling the pulse. It was in vain to ask her where her pain was seated, whether in her stomach, head or back; the only answer I could procure, was a request to feel the pulse of the other hand, and then point out the seat of the disease, and the nature of the pain.

Having neither satisfied my curiosity by exhibiting her face, nor made me acquainted with the nature of her complaint, I was under the necessity of informing her in positive terms, that to understand the disease it was absolutely necessary to see the tongue, as well as feel the pulse: and without it I could do nothing for her. My eloquence, or rather that of my Jewish interpreter, was, however, for a long time exerted in vain; and I am persuaded she would have dismissed me without any further enquiry, had not her invention supplied her with a happy expedient to remove her embarrassment. She contrived at last to cut a hole through the curtain, through which she extruded her tongue, and thus complied with my injunction as far as was necessary for a medical view, but most effectively disappointed my curiosity.

14

Religion

Morocco has been a Muslim country for well over a thousand years but in the rural areas many pre-Islamic practices continue. In the great *Madrasahs* of Fez scholars have taught and commented upon the Sacred texts and have exercised influence throughout the Muslim world but in the mountains there is still a belief in the powers of local saints to act as intercessors with God. These local saints, the *marabouts*, played an essential role in preventing inter-tribal fighting, settling disputes and providing security for trade-routes. Many miracles are attributed to them and their shrines are still places of pilgrimage. The most important saints are more than purely local figures – the Sharifs, descendants of the Prophet of whom the king is one, are respected throughout the country. In this chapter we can see accounts of both orthodox Islam and of its regional variations. These are some of the moral and physical aspects of humankind which have been from time immemorial changeless. Some of the pieces have a great deal of humour which adds to rather than detracts from the seriousness of the subject. This is particularly so of the pieces on saints by Dermenghem and a saint by Doutté.

An explanation of the concepts of purity and impurity.
From Louis Brunot, *Au seuil de la vie marocaine*, 1950, pp. 60–62.

The knowledge of what is pure and what impure is essential to the understanding of Islam and dominates every religious act. This is a concept totally alien to Christianity at least in the importance which Muslims attach to it, and has no parallel in, for example the Catholic doctrine of a state of grace. There is no middle ground between pure and impure: it follows that one is either in a state of purity or one is not and that is a matter that has to be put right.

Purity is a physical thing, a meticulous bodily cleanliness, which in the eyes of a believer has little to do with western preoccupations of hygiene. It is a ceremonial washing of the hands, the feet, the head and at certain times the entire body. Purity demands the pulling out of the hair of the armpits and the private parts. Indeed it is a sort of baptism which is renewed each time that the worshipper goes to perform a religious act. There is one condition, however, that is necessary every time that this ritual is performed: the Muslim must state that the act is deliberate and carried out to obey divine precepts. Without that the purification is valueless.

The proof that this is a religious matter, rather than a matter of hygiene or cleanliness is that ablutions can be carried out with sand or by rubbing with a pebble if no water is available. Some nomadic tribes always carry with them a pebble for their ablutions, some preferring it to water. In comparison we Christians are clean but never pure.

One must be in a state of purity before praying or touching a copy of the Holy Qur'an, the Word of God, before sacrificing an animal, before carrying out any action that has religious significance. Impurity can be minor or major, and has to be dealt with by either minor ablutions (washing the head and the extremities) or major (washing the entire body).

The notion of impurity concerns not only the body but also animals, objects and particularly food. Thus the pig and his cousin the wild boar are impure. If you have to speak of them you say *Hashak* – begging pardon for mentioning such a thing. Soiled clothes are impure and so are the excretions themselves. Eating impure meat is forbidden and this includes any non-acquatic animal that has not been ritually killed by a male Muslim. There are foods which horrify all Muslims and one can get an idea of them from Leviticus Chapter xi. A Muslim can feast on locusts but would not for the world eat frogs' legs. They try to avoid invitations to eat with us for they cannot be sure that the food might not have been fried in pork fat or that a pigeon might not have had its throat cut or that a chicken might have been killed by a woman or without the proper ritual.

The position of Sharifs in the country.
From Gerhard Rohlfs, *Adventures in Morocco . . .*, 1874, pp. 50 and 108.

There is no aristocracy in Morocco in our sense of the word, the highest class consisting of Sharifs or descendants of the Prophet. They have multiplied exceedingly; and there are districts or cantons composed entirely of Sharifs, who are distinguished by having as a handle to their name the word Sidi or Mulai (Lord). The present dynasty is a family of Sharifs. This dignity is not continued on the female side: that is, if a Moor marries the daughter of a Sharif, the children are not Sharifs. On the other hand, whomever a Sharif may marry, the children are always Sharifs. He may marry a Christian or Jewess without their being converted; the children are Sharifs. He may marry a negress also without prejudice to his children, but she must be converted to the faith: even his children born in concubinage have the same rights as those born in wedlock. The Sharifs form a privileged class, having the right to insult people by cursing their ancestors without fear of receiving similar compliments in return. It would be an offence against religion to curse the family of the Prophet. The Sharifs are more honoured than the Marabouts, who are saints or the descendants of saints – more honoured even than the chiefs of great tribes . . .

During my stay at Wazan I enjoyed the hospitality of the Grand Sharif and spent almost the whole day with him. Sometimes I was present when pilgrims brought him gifts, and kneeling down before him earnestly implored his blessing. He would give it, and then often turn his back on them, and say to me 'What fools these people are to bring me money'.

The place of religion in the daily life of the people.
From John Windus, *A Journey to Mequinez*, 1725, printed in Pinkerton, vol. XV, pp. 455 and 458.

In their houses they are always sitting on matts or lying. They daily spend five or six hours sitting on their hams before their doors, thinking it most ridiculous to walk up and down a room, against which they argue, saying, Why should a man move from one end of the room to the other, without apparent cause? can he not as well stay in the place he is in, as go to the other end purely in order to come back again?

They seem not (as we do) to observe the day for business, and the night for sleep, but sleep and wake often in the four-and-twenty hours, going to church by night as well as day, for which purpose their talbs call from the top of the mosques, having no bells, every three hours throughout the city. In going to the church they observe no gravity, nor mind their dress, but as soon as the talb begins to bellow from the steeple, the carpenter throws down his ax, the shoe-maker his awl, the taylor his shears, and away they all run like so many fellows at football. When they come into the church, they repeat the first chapter of the Alcoran standing; after which they look up, and lift up their hands as much above their heads as they can; and as their hands are leisurely coming down again, drop on their knees with their faces towards the Kebla; then touching the ground with their foreheads twice, sit a little while on their heels muttering a few words and rise up again; this they repeat two or three times. When there are many at prayer together, you would think they were so many galley slaves a rowing by the motion they make on their knees . . .

They have another extravagant fancy, which is that God will grant their requests by being importuned; and in the time of great rains, the children will be all day running through the streets, calling for fair weather, and in drought for rain; this they do with an hideous noise, sometimes for eight days together: if God does not give the children rain, the saints and learned men go into the fields and call for rain; and if that does not do, then they all go together bare-footed and meanly clothed to the tombs of their saints and there they ask rain; the Emperor sometimes performs this piece of devotion himself. But if all these fail, they turn all the Jews out of town, and bid them not return without rain; for they say, though God would not give them rain for their prayers, he will give the Jews rain, to be rid of their importunity, their stinking breath and feet. This was done some time ago in Tangier.

Celebration in Tangier of a religious feast.
From James Richardson, *Travels in Morocco*, 1860, pp. 27–9.

The Ayd Kebir (great feast) was celebrated today, being the first of the new year. It was ushered in yesterday by prayer in the mosques. About 9 a.m. the governor, the commandant of the troops, and other Tangier authorities, proceeded to the open space of the market, attended with flags and music, and some hundred individuals all dressed in their holiday clothes. The white flag, typical of the sanctity of religion, floated over others of scarlet and green; the music was of squeaking bagpipes, and rude tumtums, struck like minute drums. The greater part were on horseback, the governor being most conspicuous. This troop of individuals ascended a small hill of the market place, where they remained half an hour in solemn prayer.

No Jew or Christian was allowed to approach the magic or sacred circle which enclosed them. This being concluded, down ran a butcher with a sheep on his back, just slaughtered and bleeding profusely. A troop of boys followed quickly at his heels pelting him with stones. The butcher ran through the town to the sea shore, and thence to the house of the Kady – the boys still in hot and breathless pursuit, hard after him, pelting him and the bleeding sheep. The Moors believe, that if the man can arrive at the house of the judge before the sheep dies, that the people of Tangier will have good luck; but, if the sheep should be quite dead, and not moving a muscle, then it will bring them bad luck, and the Christians are likely to come and take away their country from them. The drollest part of the ceremony is, that the boys should scamper after the butcher, pelting the sheep, and trying to kill it outright, thus endeavouring to bring ill luck upon their city and themselves.

The next few extracts concern saints.
The first is from Emile Dermenghem, *Le Culte des saints . . .*, 1954, p. 12.

Popular legends tell many stories of competition amongst saints. Once Sidi Mhammed ben Aouda went to visit Sidi Abderrahman, proudly riding upon a lion, confident that this would establish his superiority over his rival.

'Where shall I put my lion for the night?', he asked his host.

'In the stable with my cow'.

Going into the house Ben Aouda found in it many beautiful young girls and expressed his astonishment.

'The divine presence', said Sidi Abderrahman, 'can manifest itself between beautiful earrings and long tresses as well as between the peaks of mountains'.

The next morning, Ben Aouda, ready to leave, went to the stable to retrieve his lion. It was not there: the cow had eaten it.

The next author writers here of saints and their blessings.
From Edward Westermarck, *Ritual and Belief in Morocco*, 1926, vol. I, pp. 197–8, 41, 49, 73, 76–7, 80–81, 89–92, 233.

There are various ways in which a person may be filled with the *baraka* of a saint. The latter may transfer *baraka* to his follower simply by spitting into his mouth. Or the saint may eat some food in the presence of his follower on the last day they spend together and then tell him to eat of what is left; when the *khadim* has finished his meal, the saint says to him, 'You have taken the loaf of bread', meaning that the servant has now partaken of his *baraka* . . .

It is characteristic of all *baraka* that it produces wonderful effects by physical contact. A person derives supernatural benefit from kissing the hand, foot, shoulder or garments of a saint. The water in which a saint has washed his hands is wholesome to drink and in Fez people like to wash their hands in the same vessel as has been previously used by a shereef. It is also believed that if a schoolboy drinks the water in which scribes have cleansed their hands after a meal, or the water with which he has cleaned his writing board, he will more easily learn the Qur'an. A holy man may make a schoolboy apt to learn his lessons, and an apprentice learn his trade, by spitting in his mouth. If a shereef or scribe is offered tea or milk to drink, he ought to leave some of it to be drunk by those whose guest he is. Sexual intercourse with a saintly person is considered beneficial. Chenier speaks of a saint in Tetuan who seized a young woman and had commerce with her in the midst of the street; 'her companions who surrounded her, uttered exclamations of joy, felicitated her on her good fortune, and the husband himself received complimentary visits on this occasion'. Supernatural benefits are expected even from homosexual intercourse with a person possessed of *baraka*. I know of an instance in which a young man, who was regarded as a saint on account of the miracles he performed, traced his holiness to the fact that he had been the favourite of a shereef; and it is a common belief among the Arabic-speaking mountaineers of Northern Morocco that a boy cannot learn the Qur'an well unless a scribe commits pederasty with him. So also an apprentice is expected to learn his trade by having intercourse with his master . . .

The saints of Morocco comprise not only real men and women, living or dead, but also a large number of individuals who never existed. The country is full of holy places said to be connected with departed saints who have either been buried there after their death or have sat and prayed there while alive. In many cases these statements are founded on actual facts; in others the saintly person has undoubtedly existed, whereas his connection with the place in question is purely imaginary; but very frequently the saint is only a personage invented to explain the holiness attributed to some place or object of nature on account of its unusual appearance or some other mysterious quality. It is not always possible to decide whether a saint associated with a holy spot has existed or not, but very commonly the nature of the place, together with the fact that the saint has left no descendants, suggests his mythical origin; and the same is often the case with the name given to him. Sidi Mimun, that is 'Good Luck', and Sidi Boqnadel, or 'The Master of Oil-Lamps', are common names for dead saints, some of whom are represented as human saints and others as saints of the *jinun*. Among the Ait Warain there is the sanctuary of Sidi Madqi Haja, or 'Finished Business', much visited by petitioners; and on a small island in a lake in the district of the Mnasara the root of a fig tree which was blown down some time ago, indicated the place where Sidi Qada Haja, or 'He who attends to Business' has rested, and is in consequence an object of worship . . .

There are also holy mountains in Morocco. The Jebel al-Akhdar got its *baraka* in the following manner. When Adam was ploughing in Abda, to the south-west of Dukkala, (some people believe that Adam and his wife Eve (Hawwa) were actually born in Dukkala but those who have read the literature are aware that they were born in Paradise and only subsequently went to Dukkala), Eve went to the east to fetch food for him. On her way back she met in Dukkala a huge serpent which did not allow her to proceed. Adam then called out to all the mountains that the mountain which came first and placed itself on the serpent would become as holy as Arafat, and this was done by the Jebel al-Akhdar. It is so holy that those who take part in a feast there are considered to acquire thereby a merit equal to that which is conferred on a Muslim by the Pilgrimage to Mecca. In the district of Igliwa in the Great Atlas there is a certain mountain with a boulder on the top. Three times in the hottest part of the summer the people of the neighbourhood take butter there as an offering to the saint of the mountain; should they omit doing so, the animals grazing on the slopes of it would become ill or die, or their owners would themselves become ill or suffer some other misfortune. Sacrifices are also made at the boulder, or money is put into a hole in it by persons who are anxious to get the assistance of the saint. The butter and the meat may be eaten by the people on the spot, but nothing of it must be carried away from there; once when a man took back with him some butter for the feast with which he was going to celebrate the occasion when his son had learned the whole of the Qur'an by heart, the son soon afterwards fell from the animal which he was riding and broke his arm. The saint of the mountain is not buried there; he is a living saint, whose footsteps can be seen at a certain spring, and he has the same name as the mountain itself . . .

Great efficacy is ascribed to sea-water. In Dukkala a woman who has been the victim of another woman's black art bathes in the sea and lets seven waves go over her, and drinks of the water. In the same province a person who suffers from typhoid bathes in the sea so early that he can be back home by sunrise – should he see the sun he would become most dangerously ill – and puts some seaweed on his head, leaving it there until the evening. In the sea there are forty saints, or the sea itself is a saint: it prays day and night: the waves are its prayers. People from the Rif who are on the sea in a gale offer a silver coin, invoking Sidi Muhammad Labkhar. More frequently silver coins are, in similar circumstances, thrown into the sea as offerings to Sidi Bel Abbes; and we are told of a French steamer which was once saved by a Moor's throwing his dagger overboard in the name of that saint, with the result that the sea grew calm and the dagger was discovered in the alms-box of the saint at Marrakesh. The Sultan must not travel on the sea; the people say that one sultan should not ride on another sultan. The antipathy of the sea to the Sultan is so great that once when Mulai Hassan visited Tangier, the sea on his arrival rolled back beyond the ordinary borders of the ebb-tide. Sexual intercourse on the sea may wreck the boat.

Whitewashed domes, the tombs of local saints, are a prominent feature of the countryside. The practices associated with them are also described.

From Edward Westermarck, *Ritual and Belief*, 1926, vol. I, pp. 61–4, 188–94.

The word *mqam* is in Dukkala applied to a place where a saint has prayed or rested during his lifetime and is often indicated by a ring of stones. The word *siyid* is applied to a place where a saint is buried and the grave of an important saint is in many cases marked by a cenotaph, like a large chest which is covered with coloured cloth; there are commonly several coverings, one over the other. At each corner of the cenotaph there may be a short rod, supporting a brass ball and in the centre a rising in the shape of two converging flights of steps, with a covering on which professions of faith or passages of the Qur'an are embroidered with gold. Close to the cenotaph there is a money box into which visitors put their cash contributions. Many saintly places in Northern Morocco contain one or more cannon-balls, with which visitors, especially sick people, touch their heads or bodies. To explain their presence it is said that when the Sultan wanted to shoot some friend or *protégé* of the saint, the latter attracted the bullet so that it fell down in his sanctuary . . .

The sanctity of a saint is communicated not only to the building in which he is buried and the objects contained in it, but to everything inside his *horm*, that is the sacred domain of the saint. The *horm* may be restricted to the building over his grave, but it may also extend far beyond it. Whilst Sidi Ben Nor has no *horm* outside his *kubba*, the *horm* of another great Dukkala saint, Mulai Abdallah consists of the whole space inside the cairns made on spots from which his shrine becomes visible to travellers; and anybody who can see the tower of his mosque is in his *horm* and consequently protected by him against persecutors. The limits of the *horm* of Sidi Bel Abbes in Marrakesh are marked by a chain while that of Mulai Idris in Fez, which contains streets with houses, shops and a hot bath, has for its borders three wooden fences; neither the inhabitants of the houses in the *horm* nor anyone who has entered it can be touched by the government, and the shops there pay no public taxes. Very frequently the *horm* of a *siyid* has natural borders; if it is situated in a grove, for instance, the whole grove is commonly its *horm*. Sidi Heddi's *horm* in the Bni Aros includes the little river near his shrine, the fish in it being inside the *horm* and therefore sacred . . .

The dead saints generally live on amicable terms with each other, and form a society by themselves. All the great saints of Morocco assemble on the day of Arafa at Mulai Abdsslam's shrine at Wazzan, and go from there to Mount Arafat near Mecca to join the pilgrims. But not even saints are perfect, and discipline has to be maintained, if need be, by punishment or threats. Sidi Hedi once broke his right leg at the place where he now has his grave as a punishment inflicted on him by the other saints for having injured boys who had teased him on account of his queer behaviour and curious dress; this happened, of course, while he was alive, but he was already looked upon as a member of the society of saints. If a dead saint takes no notice of a petition, although *ar* has been put upon him, the petitioner may go and complain of him to some greater saint, who is then supposed to impress upon him the necessity of listening to the request and to threaten him with God and the Prophet if he refuses to do so.

The assistance of saints is secured not only by humble supplications and offerings but by means of a very different character: in numerous cases the petitioner puts pressure upon the saint by putting *ar* upon him. The word *ar* is used to denote an act which intrinsically implies the transference of a conditional curse for the purpose of compelling somebody to grant a request; and *ar* is frequently cast on dead saints, as well as on living men and *jnun*. There are various methods of putting *ar* upon saints, such as the throwing of stones upon a cairn connected with the saint, the tying of rags or clothing or hair to some object belonging to the *siyid*, the knotting of palmetto leaves or a white broom growing in its vicinity or the killing of an animal.

I have sometimes asked how it is that a saint, although invoked with *ar*, does not always grant the request addressed to him. The answer has been that he no doubt does what he can, but he is not all-powerful, and God may refuse to listen to his prayer. Occasionally he appears in a dream to the person who put *ar* on him, tells him that he is unable to help him, and advises him to go and slaughter an animal at the shrine of another saint, Sidi So-and-so; and in such a case the *ar* is no longer considered to rest on the saint. In any case the casting of *ar* on a saint is held to be a very efficient method of securing his assistance. But the saint does not like it. I was told that it makes him frown and shake his head in the grave.

The influence exercised by dead saints is not always of a friendly character. While bountiful to those who deal with them in the right manner, they are dangerous to those who provoke their anger. A saint would severely punish the appropriation of, or interference with, a thing which is in his *horm*. Of a certain Rif saint I was told that when a man went to his grave to steal corn he fired off a shot which killed the robber, though no bullet was found in the dead body. Another Rif saint is said to make stones fall down from the sky and kill anyone who is guilty of theft, homicide, or any other offence inside his *horm*; and should anyone attempt to take away earth from the mountain on which Sidi Bukhayr has his grave, the saint would make him blind. The saints of Masst, in Sus, even require a person who goes to another tribe to clean his slippers before he crosses the border, so as not to carry away with him any earth from their country. A mounted policeman who spent a night at a *siyid* in the neighbourhood of Fez killed and ate a cock which he found there, regardless of the protests of the people; but he did not do it unpunished. For the next day, when the *muezzin* made his cry, he suddenly crowed like a cock, and the same thing happened at every call to prayer, until he removed the curse by making a sacrifice to the saint and giving some money to his descendants. No animal or bird must be shot in the vicinity of a *siyid*. A British ambassador who shot two pigeons on the hill Giliz outside Marrakesh where there is a cave in which Sidi Bel Abbes used to meditate, died on the following morning.

A frequent punishment for theft committed at a *siyid* is that the thief is unable to leave the place. A man stole at night a bucket from Sidi

Abella u Muhammad's shrine at Aglu and then, as he thought, went away. But when it was dawning, he found to his astonishment that he was still at the *siyid*, and that the bucket had stuck to his calf: and it could only be removed after an operation, which made him lame. A tribe in Dukkala have twenty subterranean granaries in the *horm* of their patron saint; and once when two men went there at night to steal corn, the saint deprived them of their memory, so that they could not find their way back but were caught in the morning not far from the *siyid*. Elsewhere, also, people protect their property from robbers by placing it near a shrine; thus an enclosure of stones near Sidi Hbib's shrine, at a place where the mule which took his body up the mountain rested, is a depot for wood and other things. In Dukkala it is the custom for women who are losing hair to take it to a shrine and leave it there, in order to prevent other women from getting hold of it for the purpose of practising witchcraft.

Some saints not only resent theft committed at their sanctuaries but also punish robbers who merely pass by, either preventing them from proceeding further until they are caught, or making it impossible for them to sell the stolen object, so that they are found out at last. So if a thief passes Mulai Abdsslam's sanctuary, the saint either sends someone to take away from him the thing he has stolen, or makes him fall down and break his leg so that he can walk no further. The reason for their hostility to an offence which does not directly concern them seems to be that they have been so often appealed to in oaths taken by persons suspected of theft that they have at last come to be looked upon as permanent enemies of thieves and guardians of property, quite independently of any invocation.

The story of the saint Lalla Aziza and the celebrations each year at her tomb.
From Abel Brives, *Voyages au Maroc*, 1909, pp. 256–8.

The tomb of Lalla Aziza in the Seqsawa valley is in a large village surrounded by Barbary figs. Below the village are irrigated gardens with olive trees, figs and different types of nuts. Fields of barley extend along the bank of the Wadi. In the centre of the village is a large square, in a corner of which stands the tomb of the Saint, a building ten or twelve metres square, neat and pretty, roofed with green tiles.

Lalla Aziza had been born on this very spot and from early childhood had been sent to watch the goats on the mountain. Instead of staying with the other children along the riverside where there was abundant pasture, Lalla Aziza used to go to the top of the mountain where there was nothing but rocks. But her goats were just as fat as those of the other shepherd children. This showed that God had taken particular notice of this little girl. This annoyed her father who, disregarding the flourishing state of her flock, nevertheless demanded that she should stay in the valley and several times he beat her when she disregarded his orders.

One day when Lalla Aziza had taken her flock to the very peak of the mountain where never a single blade of grass had grown, her father, accompanied by some of the village folk went to find her and started to rebuke her for disobedience. 'Father', she replied 'Just look what your goats are eating' and he saw that their mouths were full of corn.

From that moment, it was clear that God had taken a special interest in the child. As she grew up, her piety was obvious. She loved to be alone and seemed to be ever in prayer but her tasks were always done.

As she was one of the prettiest girls in the village many young men wanted to marry her but she refused them all. One day as she was walking by the river one of her rejected suitors started to chase her: the road ended in the mountain-side; there was no way out but the rocks opened and she vanished before the astonished eyes of her pursuer.

Now her reputation for holiness spread far and wide and the Sultan himself wished to see her. At his command she went to Marrakesh and in the city everyone was amazed at her sanctity. She was greatly admired and her influence grew so that the Sultan himself became jealous and threw her into prison. On several occasions he sent her plates of food that had been poisoned but she never touched them.

One day, however, it was her faithful servant who offered her the poison. She said, 'By God, I shall eat it and for God I shall die' but before she took it she ordered that her body should be put on a mule and that it should be buried where it stopped.

She swallowed the food and died; her body was put on a mule that raced away so quickly that no one could follow it. That same day it arrived in Seqsawa, where her corpse was recognised and buried with great honour.

The citizens of Marrakesh built a fine *Koubbah* in her honour and the Sultan granted their request that she should be buried there. This was done but at the same time her body remained in Seqsawa where the Sultan ordered that an identical *Koubbah* should be erected.

This was the story that we were told and every year great celebrations, attended by huge crowds, take place at the tomb of Lalla Aziza.

A cow of the purest unspotted white is led to the stream near the *Koubbah* and there, in profound silence, everyone awaits the reaction of the Saint. A shrill cry suddenly comes from the tomb and this is the signal hoped for: the women reply with excited *youyous* and the men fire their rifles in the air. The cow is then killed and its skin shared amongst the crowd. No matter how many people are present there is always enough for all of them and the same holds true for the meat. This miracle of the multiplication of the skin and the meat happens every year, to the great joy of the mountain folk who hold Lalla Aziza in the highest reverence.

A story of an incident near a saint's tomb.
From Edmond Doutté, *En Tribu*, 1914, p. 29.

Sidi Mohammed ben Sadoun, of Armat near Marrakesh, is known for the following miracle: if anyone who quoted the Holy Qu'ran near his tomb omitted or mispronounced a word, a stern voice from the grave would correct them. Two men from the Sous had wagered with the local people that such a thing was impossible. They approached the tomb and one of them started reciting a verse but, deliberately or otherwise, said that he could not remember its end. Immediately they heard the voice coming from the depth of the tomb finishing the lines. One of the Sousis shouted back 'if you are alive, come and join us: if you are dead, stay there and shut up'. The offended saint was never heard to speak again.

This account of miracles attributed to local saints has been translated and abridged by the editors.
From Edouard Montet, *Le Culte des saints . . .*, 1909, pp. 51–63.

Leaving Larache by the coastal route after about a day's march one comes across the great salt lagoon of Ez-Zerga, separated from the Atlantic by a narrow spit of land. Between Ez-Zerga and the Atlantic is the *kubba* of the famous marabout Sidi Bou-Selham, the hero of many tales. When I asked if the sea came into Ez-Zerga I was told that it had once but Sidi Bou-Selham was walking along the shore when he came to a canal linking the lake and the ocean. Not wishing to wet his feet, he took off his cloak and threw it into the sea which drew back and was replaced by a bar of sand. It is for this miracle that he is known as Sidi Bou-Selham, (My Lord, the Man with the Mantle).

In another version Sidi Bou-Selham is said to have been an Egyptian who walked from the banks of the Nile all the way along the Mediterranean which he did not really like. It was only when he came to the Atlantic that he decided to stay. He had hardly arrived and was washing in the sea when he was brusquely addressed by the local Saint. 'Hey Fellow!', sneered the resident 'I don't think much of you. When I wish to perform my ablutions, the sea comes to me to wash my feet'.

Stung, Sidi Bou-Selham retorted 'If you speak to my like that, I swear that the sea, through the power of Allah, will go as far as Fez and the girls of the city will be able to bathe in it'.

Clambering up the dune, Sidi Bou-Selham set off for the interior, trailing his stick behind him and followed, step by step by the sea. Soon the water covered the whole of Ez-Zerga.

He would have gone on but suddenly a lady saint of Fez appeared, agitatedly waving her hands. Two beautiful Fassi girls materialized and plunged into the new lake. 'Stop', begged the lady saint 'your prophecy has been fulfilled. The girls of Fez have bathed in the sea'. Sidi Bou-Selham halted and the sea advanced no further . . .

Sidi Bel-Abbes arrived one morning outside the gates of the great city of Marrakesh, very poor but preceded by a reputation for extraordinary sanctity. Before going in he asked the local saints for permission to reside there: they were enjoying a monopoly of the alms of the faithful and did not want to share them with a newcomer but found it difficult to refuse outright. One of them had an idea. They sent Sidi Bel-Abbes a bowl overflowing with water: the symbolism was clear, the bowl represented Marrakesh and the water already filling it showed that there was no room for another saint. 'If you can get anything in there', said the cunning conspirators, 'you are welcome to join us'. Sidi Bel-Abbes took a rose and let it wither in the sun: then he plunged it into the bowl where it absorbed the water that it touched but did not cause any to overflow. The rose bloomed again and the selfish saints got the message. Sidi Bel-Abbes was free to live in Marrakesh amongst them . . .

Mulai Bou Shaib is the patron saint of Azemur and the story of an incident in which he was involved shows that in Islam, as in Christianity, great sinners can sometimes become great saints. Before they became saints Sidi Ben Daoud and Mulai Bou Azza had been bandits with their own cunning method of operation. When they saw only one or two wayfarers, Ben Daoud would lie on the ground covered with a cloth and Bou Azza would say to the innocent passer-by 'This man has just died, help me to carry him to a house nearby'. When the 'corpse' had been carried into an isolated spot, Ben Daoud would come to life and join his accomplice in robbing and even killing their victim. One day they saw Mulai Bou Shaib walking alone along the road and Bou Azza asked his assistance to move the body. 'Let us see that he really is dead', said Bou Shaib and as Bou Azza lifted the cloth, he fell back in horror – the body was already being eaten by worms. From that moment Bou Azza became the disciple of Bou Shaib who one day took him beside a pond and told him to wait. Bou Azza waited for an entire year, although moss grew on his shoulders and he had for food only the blades of grass that grew by his feet. At the end of the year Bou Shaib returned, and satisfied with the obedience of his follower, took him back to Azemur where they lived together. Sidi Ben Daoud became a saint because he had been struck down by Mulai Bou Shaib, Bou Azza because he became his faithful servant.

This account of the customs and legends of the coast near Mogador has been translated and abridged by the editors.
From an article by Robert Montagne in *Hespéris*, 1924, pp. 101–104, 112–16.

If you go along the coast ignoring the main roads, about two hours from Mogador you come across the *Koubba* of a saint of so long ago that no one knows anything about him but Moulay bou Zergtoun is regarded as a patron of sailors. His tomb is built very close to the sea, on a little cliff of a grey so gentle that it merges into the Ocean. Behind it is a plain dotted here and there by great lumps of chalky rock that resemble the abandoned shells of gigantic tortoises. Along the coast are dunes, dotted with coarse grass and juniper bushes.

The festival of Moulay bou Zergtoun is held on a Friday around the middle of October. Into the area flood pilgrims from Chiadma, Mogador and the tribes of the north. Each family builds itself a little hut of branches, covered with grass and surrounded by a low wall of stones and there they spend two days under the protection of the saint whose blessings are especially potent on the Friday. Indeed, it is believed that on that day he grants all prayers and so one must never refuse to lend a friend, or even a stranger, an animal that he may ride to the festival even if it means that one cannot go oneself.

A husband may not prevent his wife going if she wishes. Last year a jealous man decided to go on his own but the saint exacted a horrible penalty. He was found drowned upon the rocks but his donkey returned home to pick up his wife and take her to the fair.

At the festival women are free to walk around as they wish and their husbands have no right to object. They usually remain veiled but can mingle with strange men. Decorous flirting is allowed and all through the Friday youths wander through the crowds in groups of seven or eight, their guns in their hands. When they find a fair lady who will accept their homage, they dance around her and then, all together, fire their guns in the air: the lady thanks them with a trilling of *you-you-you*.

The Saint himself exerts a rigid discipline over the proceedings and is implacable towards any man who has evil thoughts: the women need not therefore show their usual modesty because there will be no danger to their virtue. Indeed women of the Oulad-al-Hajj who normally remain in strict seclusion from the eyes of strangers, may be found bathing naked among the rocks: if they withstand the shock of seven large waves in succession they may hope to become mothers within a year. Nearby groups of men and youths enjoy the sight and are not shy in their comments: the Saint permits this provided they do not harbour improper thoughts.

The young girls, more timid, go and bathe further away in the hope that they may soon obtain a husband. Even mares have their chance on this holy day for they are led to stand in the foam among the rocks so that they, too, may bring forth fine offspring.

During the day tribal horsemen show their skill in fantasias while the children enjoy themselves on wooden horses. In the evening the story-tellers and the jugglers take over until around midnight when each family goes to its little hut and stays there singing until daybreak, accompanying themselves on tambourines, flutes and fiddles.

Love-making is forbidden, I am told, even amongst married couples. Any advance by a man towards a woman is punished inexorably by the Saint and every year there is a crop of sudden deaths by drowning or other accidents that cannot otherwise be explained . . .

Moroccan men used to group together in religious brotherhoods, each with their own distinctive rites. Two are described here. The first deals with the Aissawiyah, and the second describes the dance of the Hamadshas.

From Hugh Stutfield, *El Maghreb*, 1886, pp. 36–8; and from Edith Wharton, *In Morocco*, 1927, pp. 55–7.

The Aissawiyah profess to be able to swallow broken glass and sharp stones, to touch venomous snakes, and to bruise and gash themselves. They resemble somewhat the dancing dervishes of Turkey, and may be described as the Salvation Army of Morocco, their antics bearing about the same relation to the civilisation existent there as do those of our dervishes to the contemporary enlightenment in England.

They began quite close to the hotel; half a dozen lunatics with shaven crowns and black wavy hair streaming down their shoulders, formed a circle, and commenced a sort of dance, bobbing up and down, and wagging their heads in unison with monotonous howlings, till they worked themselves up into a frenzy. Behind came the invariable tomtoms and three large banners. So they went slowly forwards, throwing themselves about in grotesque contortions, but always keeping up the regular beat of the dance, and emitting convulsive gulps and groans and sobs, which in the aggregate swelled into a hoarse murmur. One or two, apparently finding it warm work, stopped and took off every stitch of clothing, except a thin pair of linen drawers, and in this airy costume went to work on the orgie with a will. In the Soko a live sheep was brought them. The whole mob of devotees rushed upon it like a pack of ravening hounds, and tearing the beast limb from limb, tossed the fragments in the air, smearing themselves with blood, and swallowing gobbets of the warm and quivering flesh. A second and a third sheep were thus served, and no doubt a Christian or Jew would have been still more welcome prey. At the gate of the town I climbed up on a wall, and from this safe coign of vantage looked down upon the throng as it passed a few feet below. By this time there was a perfect mob of fanatics, all worked up into transports of delirium. Some grovelled on the ground, imitating the cries and actions of wild beasts, foaming at the mouth, and rolling about in contortions, calling loudly upon Allah the while. One fellow had gashed his arm with a knife, and was covered with blood: at another performance I witnessed, a huge negro was to be seen literally gnawing at a woman's arm, from which a stream of blood flowed, she suffering it quietly, and looking as though she rather enjoyed it. Two or three had their hands tied behind their backs, to prevent them from doing mischiefs, for the *mokaddems*, or high priests, have complete power over them, and seem able to soothe them, even in their greatest fury. The actions of the women were particularly loathsome as they jumped about and yelled with excitement. Now and again one would embrace another or sink into the arms of a friend from sheer exhaustion. Altogether it was a most beastly spectacle but the whole thing is perfectly *bona fide*; there is no suggestion of sending round the hat at the close of the performance, which takes place in a mosque unseen by Christian eyes.

In its centre an inspired-looking creature whirled about on his axis, the black ringlets standing out in snaky spirals from his haggard head, his cheek-muscles convulsively twitching. Around him, but a long way off, the dancers rocked and circled with long raucous cries dominated by the sobbing booming music; and in the sunlit space between dancers and holy man, two or three impish children bobbed about with fixed eyes and a grimace of comic frenzy, solemnly parodying his contortions.

Meanwhile a tall grave personage in a doge-like cap, the only calm figure in the tumult, moved gravely here and there, regulating the dance, stimulating the frenzy, or calming some devotee who had broken ranks and lay tossing and foaming on the stones. There was something far more sinister in this passionless figure, holding his hand on the key that let loose such crazy forces, than in the poor central whirligig who merely set the rhythm for the convulsions.

The dancers were all dressed in white caftans or in the blue shirts of the lowest classes. In the sunlight something that looked like fresh red paint glistened on their shaved black or yellow skulls and made dark blotches on their garments. At first these stripes and stains suggested only a gaudy ritual ornament like the pattern on the drums; then one saw that the paint, or whatever it was, kept dripping down from the whirling caftans and forming fresh pools among the stones; that as one of the pools dried up another formed, redder and more glistening, and that these pools were fed from great gashes which the dancers hacked in their own skulls and breasts with hatchets and sharpened stones. The dance was a blood-rite, a great sacrificial symbol, in which blood flowed so freely that all the rocking feet were splashed with it.

Gradually, however, it became evident that many of the dancers simply rocked and howled, without hacking themselves, and that most of the bleeding skulls and breasts belonged to negroes. Every now and then the circle widened to let in another figure, black or dark yellow, the figure of some humble blue-shirted spectator suddenly 'getting religion' and rushing forward to snatch a weapon and baptise himself with his own blood; and as each new recruit joined the dancers the music shrieked louder and the devotees howled more wolfishly. And still, in the centre, the mad *marabout* spun, and the children bobbed and mimicked him and rolled their diamond eyes. Such is the dance of the Hamadshas.

15

Music, Dancing, Storytelling, Sport

This chapter shows how the people of Morocco amused themselves before the television age and the visitor will see how these traditions have been retained. Nothing is more redolent of the past than the sight of fascinated crowds grouped around the story-teller as they were in the Baghdad of Harun al-Rashid or the Fez of Mulai Idris. The reader may wonder what sort of stories are being told so we enclose a translation of one of them.

Three commonly used musical instruments.
From Philip Thornton, *The Voice of Atlas*, 1936, pp. 80–84.

The three chief stringed instruments of the Arabic orchestra are the rebab, oudh and kamanjah. Of these the first and last are played with a bow, and the oudh – a lute of eight or ten strings – is played with a plectrum made of a goose's or a raven's quill. The tuning of the rebab, which has two strings, one of thick gut, and one of twisted camel or goat hair, is a major fifth, the lower note being the keystone of the maqam (key) selected for the performance of the melody. It has a curious boat-shaped construction. The two eyes on either side of the peg at the top to which the strings are attached represent the eyes of an owl. This is to make the instrument watchful and careful in its 'singing', and to guard the musician against Jnun taking possession of him while he is playing. Sidi Ahmad, my instructor, told me that his grandfather, whilst once playing the rebab, found that the bridge persistently dislodged itself from underneath the strings, and he was unable to think of any explanation of this phenomenon, until it occurred to him that he was playing the maqam hijaz without taking the precaution of facing Mecca. This maqam is the particular musical property of a powerful Jinn, who once upon a time was a famous professor of music at Fez. But owing to his lax morals and appalling blasphemy he turned into a pig-headed cat. He is very rarely seen except on the first Tuesday of the month, but can manifest his power whenever the maqam hijaz is played at the wrong hour of day.

The rebab form is found in all primitive countries and there is no doubt that it was taken by the Arabs into Spain and by the troubadours over the Pyrenees into Europe. Its tone is like a deep viola and its compass an octave and four notes. The lower string is often played as a drone for the accompaniment of singing. The rebab is played by the leader of an orchestra, and is regarded as the most ancient and honourable of the instruments. I have heard it described as the 'Boat of Fatima' for there is a tradition that the Prophet's daughter Fatima sailed down the Red Sea on a rebab.

The kamanjah is the Arabic name for the fiddle. Originally it was a rectangular instrument with two, occasionally three, strings. But today the importation of European violins has made the kamanjah in its primitive form rare and the modern Arab prefers the four-stringed instrument. But he does not play it in the orthodox way under his chin. He sits cross-legged on the ground, and rests the instrument on his left knee with the bridge and strings facing outwards. The left hand very often rocks the instrument against the bow in order to produce a more piercing and strident tone.

The oudh is the most spectacular of the instruments in the orchestra. The Egyptian form has ten strings, these are tuned in pairs, as also are those of the Moroccan oudh. This instrument has a deep quality of tone and is extremely beautiful to listen to. The variety of technique in playing it is astonishing. At times it sounds like the guitar, a mandolin, a harp or even a zither. The plectrum is held not between the thumb and first finger, but between the tips of the third and fourth fingers. The fingers themselves do not appear to be much used in the technique, most of it being pure wrist work.

Harris witnessed tribal dancing in the mountains near Tangier. From Walter Harris, *Morocco that Was*, 1921, pp. 248–51.

In the Anjera tribe in the early years of this century there were two great families, the Deilans and the Duas. Both were amongst my intimate friends. I had been – always dressed as a native and always received as a welcome guest – at the weddings of several of the Sheikh

Deilan's sons in their village on the mountain-tops, where hundreds of the tribesmen would be collected spending the moonlight nights in feasting and singing, for the time of full moon, and generally late spring, summer, or early autumn were chosen for these festivities. What wonderful nights they were! On the most level spot that could be found in the neighbourhood of the village the mountaineers would congregate, leaving an open circular space in their centre, with vacant 'aisles' in the closely-gathered throng radiating into the crowd. To the music of shrill pipes and drums – wild exhilarating music to those who have learned to appreciate it – the dancers, trained boys, would take up their stand in the centre and slowly at first, then faster, begin to dance. These mountain dances have nothing in common with the ordinary oriental dance that is witnessed in the towns and in the plains. There is none of the inartistic and suggestive wriggling that to the European point of view is so ungraceful. Dressed in long loose white garments, almost reaching to their feet, with flowing sleeves held back by cords of coloured silk, and with a small scarf thrown over the head so as to half veil the face, the youths moved gracefully in and out, each dancing alone, and yet fitting his dance into a plan of concerted movement.

The mountain dancing begins by the performers standing motionless for a few moments, the head thrown back, and the arms loosely falling to the side. Then, to the time of the music, there is a sudden quick movement of the feet – a little soft stamping – but without the least motion of the body. As the musicians increase their energy the dancer's body takes life. The movement of the feet is accentuated, and suddenly he glides forward toward his audience, with outstretched arms, raising the scarf from the face for a moment, and then once more the body becomes motionless. But, as if against his will, the music conquers him. The movements become more general. The feet are raised higher from the ground, and the dancer gyrates and falls on one knee, rises again and glides, holding the body almost motionless, up the empty aisles that lie open between the sections of the crowd. Never is the graceful posing abandoned; the veil, now half raised, now drawn down again, the little tremble of the shoulders and the gliding movement of the feet – all has a charm and artistic merit. Every now and again, with a quick turning movement of the body, which sends the loose folds of the long white garment floating round him, the dancer falls on one knee before one of the guests, and, removing the veil, awaits the pressing of a silver coin upon his forehead, and to receive the exaggerated and poetical compliments of the donor.

There is one movement in these dances which is admirable, though there are few who can accomplish it, for it means a complete subjection and training of the muscles. The dancer suddenly stands erect with outstretched arms, the head thrown back. Then from his feet up a little trembling – a little shudder, as it were – passes up the body, to die away in the tips of the fingers of the outstretched hands. In its upward movement each portion of the limbs and body trembles alone; the rest is motionless, and even the trembling is so delicate that it might pass almost unperceived. The rigidity of the body is undisturbed, and one feels rather than sees this ascending 'nervous thrill' which illumines the figure, as though giving life to a statue.

Describing the performances of story-tellers.
From H. M. P. de la Martinière, *Morocco*, 1889, pp. 13–14.

The Arab story-tellers have always appeared to me to be incomparable actors, whether they seek to fan into flame the smouldering passions of their audience by religious and warlike poems, charm by marvellous accounts the dreamy imagination of their hearers, or strive by means of an apologue to impress upon them some philosophical truths. They bring into play all the resources of ingenious pantomimic action – simple, though highly expressive and picturesque. The play of their features attracts the eyes, whilst their speeches charm the ears and stir the soul. Their gestures, now grave, now comical, now violent, but in constant and perfect harmony with the thoughts or images which they seek to convey, the noble gracefulness of their movements, the long snowy drapery flowing from their heads, with its many folds gathered under the arm or thrown back over the shoulder, form an *ensemble* which gives the orator an appearance of power and antique grandeur.

Occasionally, an orchestra consisting of tambourines and fifes will aid in heightening the emotions and rapture of the audience. The melody begins with deep bass notes, which support the recital and make it more forcible; then follows a short, rapid, violent beating of tom-toms, and finally a rolling succession of raps as an accompaniment to the feelings of the orator when he sums up his improvisation in poetical and passionate accents. At this point the fifes, tambourines and tom-toms burst out together into a frightful discord. The musicians throw their instruments up in the air, and with comical skill catch them again as they descend, without much interruption to their performance. Finally, they all rise to solicit some small reward from the audience.

This story of the rich merchant's child has been translated and abridged by the editors.
From A. Benachenou, *Contes et récits*, 1960.

Once upon a time there lived in Mogador a merchant whose riches were only equalled by his kindness and generosity. Every Friday he gave food and money to the poor; and Hous, for that was his name, was held in such esteem that he did not have an enemy in the world. He seemed happy in his great palace with fountains of white marble specially imported from Italy and gorgeous tiles brought from Fez but he had one great sorrow – he had no child. He would have exchanged his entire fortune for an heir and prayed constantly that God would grant him one.

One day his wife died and he felt more miserable than ever. He spent long years alone, wrapped up in his grief. However, one morning he was riding on his mule to inspect his country estate, deep in thought when he was startled to find himself addressed by a man of great age, with a long white beard, leaning on a stick, and holding a sheepskin.

'Peace be on you Hous, God has heard your prayers and will grant you a son'.

'Peace be on you, excellent old man. You must have come from far for you bear the marks of a long journey. Take this purse to help you on your way'. The old man took the gift and said:

'Your time of sorrow will soon be over and happiness will come to your house. Take in marriage Halima, the young shepherd girl on your estate. If God wills, she will bear you a son whom you must call Ali'. With that the old man covered himself with his sheepskin and vanished as if by magic. Hous was perplexed and rather frightened by this unexpected encounter. Was he suffering from hallucinations, he asked himself. Was he dreaming? How could this stranger know the most secret desire of his heart. Then he started to rejoice – the stranger must have been a friendly *jinni* who had taken human shape.

He went on to his farm, gave orders to his servants and returned home. That night after he had retired to bed he saw again in a dream the old man whom he had met on the road.

'I command you, Hous, to take in marriage the young shepherd girl Halima. If you do not obey me not only will you never have a child but a great misfortune will fall upon you'.

This grave warning startled Hous from his sleep. Although it was the middle of the night he ordered his servants to saddle his mule and he went at once to his farm. Immediately upon his arrival he begged his tenant Ahmad to grant him the hnd of his daughter Halima. Ahmad, a simple honest fellow who worked the land with the aid of his children – Halima, the youngest and prettiest was in charge of the sheep – thought that his master had lost his wits. Impatiently Hous repeated 'Yes, I wish to marry your daughter. You know that I have been a widower these many years but my most earnest desire is to have a child. In a dream a visitor from another world ordered me to marry your daughter'. Ahmad argued that his daughter had hardly expected to marry the richest merchant in the city but Hous would brook no argument, the ceremony soon took place and the little shepherd girl became mistress of the finest palace in Mogador.

In due time she gave birth to a fine boy which of course they called Ali. You can imagine the joy of the family and nothing could exceed to happiness of Hous. He did not, however, know that at the very same moment that Ali was born, a family of *jinni* had also given birth to a son that they also had called Ali. The *jinni* family were jealous of the human child and vowed to destroy him. The opportunity soon came. One day Halima was washing out the tea things and poured the boiling water down the lavabo. At that moment she heard the most frightful screams coming from her little boy and rushed to his side. He was twisting on the bed, crying and gesticulating as if he were possessed by a demon. The distraught mother picked him up and tried in vain to comfort him but he only cried the louder. Hous also came running but neither prayers or burning of herbs could comfort the child. Hous sent for doctors, quacks, wise men, and magicians but none of them could help. The child refused all food and cried night and day. Hous was in despair and his huge fortune seemed worthless if it could not help his son.

On the seventh day, a Friday, the child was still suffering and after mid-day prayers, Hous saddled his mule and went into the countryside to think and pray alone. Suddenly, going round a corner, he found himself face to face with a horseman dressed all in white.

'Peace be with you Hous. May God come to your aid. I see that you are sad. Perhaps I can help?'

'Welcome stranger, whoever you are, but what can you do against the incurable illness afflicting my little boy. Numerous doctors, magicians and wise men have failed to find out what is wrong with him. How could you help?'

'I would gladly accept your hospitality', said the stranger, 'if I did not have to carry out a delicate mission in furthest Sous on the edge of the desert. I offer you my services, perhaps they can be of help'.

'I do not want to take you away from your duty. I have resigned myself to accepting the will of Allah and His unalterable decision. If my son must die I will have to bow before the blow that has struck me'. Hous then described the sufferings of his child to the stranger.

'If you agree to accompany me', said the stranger, 'to my master in furthest Sous, he will know about the sickness of your boy and even how to cure it. Would you like to consult him? It will be a long journey, but you will not regret it. I will take you on my enchanted horse, and in a day and a night we will be there, if God wills'.

Hous accepted, mounted behind him and in a flash the city of Mogador looked in the distance the size of a child's toy. They flew over dunes and olive groves, then the palm trees of Marrakesh with the Kutoubia sticking up in the middle. They went over the snows of the Atlas, over deep valleys, and, twenty-four hours to the minute after they had left Mogador they landed in the middle of a sandy desert. The stranger tapped the earth with his toe and it opened to show a great staircase of coloured marble.

His companion took Hous by the hand and down they went to an immense courtyard, showing a huge shining house, with walls of crystal as beautiful as fairyland. A fountain seemed to make music of unworldly beauty while forests of fruit trees gave off enchanting scents. Hous, who had had no opportunity all day to say his prayers, began his ritual ablutions. As he prayed, looking over his left and right shoulders, a multitude of creatures in human shape appeared and cried in a single voice,

'Peace be upon you, Hous, true believer of true believers. Our master wishes to see you'.

Hous obeyed and was led into a great room with colonnades finely carved and encrusted with gold precious stones. In the middle a shining throne was occupied by a giant with a golden crown and shining white wings sprouting from his shoulders.

'Welcome, Hous, our palace is open to all human beings but you are the first ever to have come. Your misery has aroused our compassion. We know all about the sufferings as well as the happiness of humankind'.

Hous, with great emotion, could only mutter a few incomprehensible words but their meaning did not escape the giant.

'Your child is ill. God will end his sufferings if you do as I tell you. Return home at once. Go to Marrakesh, enter the mosque of Sidi Bel Abbes and stand by the middle pillar. When the faithful have left you will be approached by a big bony man dressed in a white robe. His eyes will flash with anger because you will have offended him. He will draw a sword but do not be frightened. Say "Peace be upon you" and he will calm down and ask you why you have lingered in the sanctuary. You will tell him and he will give you orders which you must follow to the letter. My peace go with you'.

Hous lost consciousness and when he came to, he found himself outside his house in Mogador. As soon as he entered he heard the screams of his little boy. His wife was at the bedside – more dead than alive for she had not eaten for ten days. An air of death hung around the house. Hous related his adventures and, despite his exhaustion, at the urging of his wife, set off on his mule for Marrakesh.

The following day he arrived at the hour of the evening prayer and went at once to the mosque of Sidi Bel Abbes. After finishing his devotions he stood against the central pillar. Suddenly he saw an enormous devil, black, boiling with anger, with flames emerging from his mouth and eyes that seemed in danger of burning down the sanctuary. He was terrifying as he loomed over the merchant. Hous was terrified and would have loved to run away but suddenly he seemed to hear a voice which said 'Remember, it is the life of your child that is at stake'. He plucked up courage, approached the giant and said 'Peace be upon you'. The giant immediately softened and asked how he could help.

'I would like you to help to cure my son. I have come here on the instructions of the Great *Jinni* of Furthest Sous, in the land of Hamran'.

'The health of your son does not depend on me, but you have only to follow me and I will lead you to the *jinni* who will be able to cure him'.

No sooner said than done. Hous and his companion arrived at the edge of a large pool.

'Stay here, human being! During the night a group of *jinnis* will emerge from this pool. Demand to speak to their leader, a *jinni* with long ears, two golden horns and an eye in the middle of his forehead. Do not be frightened by his appearance. Recite the *Fatiha* (the opening verses of the Holy Qur'an) and this will save you from his wrath. He will ask what you are doing there. You will ask him to intervene to cure your son. He will cure him, if God wills'.

Hous waited long, so long that he was overcome by sleep, propped up by a wall near the pool. He was woken by a loud noise and heard himself being questioned.

'How dare you put yourself in our path. When I have dealt with your son, your turn will come and then that of your wife. I shall wipe out your entire family'. Hous then heard another voice say:

'Why have you harmed this man who has done nothing to you?'

'He is my mortal enemy', replied the unknown. 'His wife burned my son with boiling water.* I have already avenged myself upon his son but that is not enough for me'.

Hous felt a super-human courage and energy and was ready to give his life for his child: he seized the demon by the throat, squeezing him so hard that a flame shot from his eye. 'Brigand', he cried 'you are the cause of my misery. I shall not let you go'. The *jinni* chief, he with the golden horns, intervened, asked Hous to release his adversary and promised to cure his son. He threatened the other demon that if ever again he harmed Hous or his family, his life would be forfeit. At that moment came the call for morning prayer and the demons vanished.

Hous said his prayers and then set out for Mogador which he reached the next day. He found his son cured, sleeping peacefully. His wife said that the miracle had happened at the time of morning prayer the previous day.

* *It is widely believed that* jinnis *lurk down the lavabo where they are liable to fall asleep. If unpleasantly disturbed they may react in the way that the one in this story did. It is therefore considered prudent to warn them before using the toilet with a formula such as* Rukhsa, ya Mubariqin *(With your permission, O Blessed Ones).*

The performance of the laib al-baroud *in front of official visitors to the sultan was a duty laid upon the tribes along the route. The other was the provision of* Muna *which Trotter also describes. For Sir John Hay's party and their escorts a village handed over eight sheep, about a hundred eggs, candles, sugar etc. When one French mission did not receive as much as they thought their due, the minister had the local chief tied to the flagpole which bore the Tricolor and flogged. According to one of the mission the victim then thanked them for drawing his attention to the dignity of France.*

Other travellers, such as Moroccan officials and even tourists with a passport, expected to be fed by the villages through which they passed.

From Captain Trotter, *Our Mission to the Court of Morocco*, 1881, pp. 22–3.

We rode on till the ground in front opened out into a valley with smooth turf at the bottom and low hills on either side. Here the 'powder play' began; the spectators, consisting of ourselves and part of the escorts, rode slowly along one side of the slope; while the remainder, together with a number of villagers who had come out to see the fun, move parallel with us on the opposite side. Over the flat ground between us thunder the five or six horsemen who take part in the performance; in perfect line they move, twirling their long guns in graceful movements round their heads, often throwing them high in the air and catching them again as they come down. Usually the rider in the centre holds his up horizontally, as if for the others, to use a military term, 'to dress by'. At a given signal the guns are all discharged, or ought to be, as the riders dash past the individual they specially wish to honour. On this occasion, for some reason or other, most of them missed fire, so to those of us to whom the performance was new it was less effective than it might have been. The most striking part of the 'laib al-baroud', however, is the utter recklessness and *abandon* which the riders display. With their loose and graceful robes flowing far behind them in the breeze, they tear along at the fullest speed they can extract from their unfortunate horses, whose gory sides betoken the means taken to urge them to it. Allowing the reins to lie perfectly loose upon the animals' necks, they pick them up when the charge is over, and wheel round to join their comrades again. There is often some delay in the start, and the final signal is never given till the starter has got them away well together. A single horseman is sometimes left behind, but this, it seems, is not the result of accident, but because his horse is either too fast or too slow for his comrades, and would consequently spoil the order of advance; this cavalier, however, makes up for his tardy start by following at full speed, and going through the wildest contortions as he tears along in rear of the others; now he is aiming his long gun at a foe in front; how he turns right round in his saddle and points it at one behind; lastly, with a loud yell of 'Allah', he discharges it into the ground, and reining up his panting steed, rejoins the others, while another set take their place, and the sport is continued.

Sir Charles Payton wrote about all types of field sports in Morocco. This time he was fishing for mackerel.
From Sir Charles Payton, *Moss from a Rolling Stone*, 1879, pp. 66–72.

Sidi Mohammed, the fisherman, was waiting so, picking up my sea-rod, tackle, a loaf of bread, an orange and a bottle of water, I hastened down to the beach. . . . From a shed at a corner of the wall came lame Ben Asher, the 'reis' or captain of the fishing boat, limping over the shingle with some short bamboos in his hand. The *reis* had had his leg broken some years ago, and, with the characteristic *insouciance* of the Moorish fatalists, he had not had it set, but simply left Dame Nature to make the best job she could of it; and it was not a brilliant success, but, decidedly crooked, though still of some use for purposes of locomotion.

Then came 'Black Sam', a tall, muscular, good-looking negro, well known to the captains of steamers trading on the Morocco coast – in fact, he had once saved the life of an English captain, capsized from a small boat in a nasty sea. Cassem, a merry-looking young Moor, came next, and then, with Sidi Mohammed, our crew was complete. The boat was rocking on a slight ground-swell, at some little distance from shore. A little brown Moorish boy divested himself of his scanty white clothing, swam out to her, and brought her in.

Soon we were clear of the rocks, and the boat was bounding merrily over the waves leaving behind the pretty panorama of Casablanca, with its frowning battlements, its white houses, the towers of its mosques, the big nests of storks, and the quaint forms of the birds themselves clearly defined against the sky, now rapidly assuming its almost unvarying cerulean hue, while outside the walls trains of camels approaching the gates with loads of wool, beans, and other country produce, and a palm-tree here and there on the horizon, made me thoroughly realize that I really was in Morocco. So much the more did it seem marvellously queer that I should be going mackerel fishing – a sport principally associated in my mind with certain sweet nooks on the Cornish coast. But mackerel we were certainly going to catch; and Mohammed, who acted as interpreter on the occasion – for my knowledge of Arabic was *exceedingly* limited – grinned most encouragingly as he said 'By and by plenty fish! Pick 'um up very quick!' . . .

Soon the sport grew fast and furious; mackerel of all sizes swarmed in the clear blue waters, from a fathom to two fathoms down. Fish would often rush at the bait directly it got below the surface, and though many of them would turn away from it, there was never long to wait before the bait would disappear in the jaws of a voracious 'striped-back'. Then I would strike smartly, and haul the fish straight into the boat before he recovered from his first astonishment.

But oftentimes the mackerel were too big to be treated in this unceremonious fashion, and would pull vigorously, making the line 'swish' through the water, bending the tough little rod, and often pulling it right under water. My shipmates, who were all busily engaged in the sport, often lost hooks by the extreme vigour with which they struck and pulled in the fish, and seemed quite amused at the time I would take to overcome the resistance of a fat mackerel of about a pound . . .

Hearing an exclamation from Reis Ben Asher, who stood next to me, I looked down into the water and saw that a shark seven or eight feet long had taken his bait. The brute was hooked, but did not seem aware that anything was the matter with him, for he only swam lazily along close to the surface, giving us a good view of his ugly lead-coloured form, his great forked tail, and his vicious-looking eyes. I looked round in vain for gaff or boat-hook – none to be had.

The Moor just held on, gazing at the shark, ejaculating occasionally, for my benefit the words 'Perra de la Mar!' – 'dog of the sea'. He also uttered strange words in Arabic, which I took to be uncomplimentary to the parents and grand-parents of the shark. Ben Asher held on, the bamboo bent, crack went the gut, and the brute went quite unconcernedly away . . .

A little before noon we reached the beach, where a number of Europeans in light clothing, and many Moors and Jews in picturesque garb, were waiting to see our catch. The fish were soon thrown out on to the shingle, a grand and glittering heap. The Moors did not count them – they are not fond of counting – some of them saying that they should 'take what Allah sends them and be satisfied' but I should estimate the total catch, in about three hours and a half of fishing, at a little over five hundred mackerel and scad (very few of the latter). I had, as usual, kept a careful account of every fish I caught, and my individual catch (single rod and single hook) consisted of 157 mackerel, 4 scad, 1 shad – a morning's work with which I felt pretty well satisfied.

16

Food and Entertaining

It is very difficult to find a Moroccan restaurant in England but the food of that country is just as delicious and as firmly based on traditional cookery as that of China or India. There is no need in Morocco itself to go to the grandest restaurants since for a few pennies one can get a sizzling *Kebab* and wash it down with *Gris de Boulouane*. The most famous dishes, couscous, tajina and bastilla are made from ingredients available in the local suqs and from travellers' descriptions, have not changed for centuries. It is of course impossible to omit the subject of *Nahnah* – the mint tea which it seems possible to drink twenty or thirty times a day – and this is well covered by the Sharifas of Wazan who also describes entertaining. We include a picture of a grand dinner with a local governor and the rather more earthy meals of the slaves of Mulai Ismail. We have included some actual recipes although we are unable to find one for the fricassee of ostrich and heroic omelettes of its eggs mentioned by Cowan and Johnston.

To begin with some recipes.
From Irene F. Day, *Kitchen in the Kasbah*, 1975, pp. 76–7, 64–5.

CHICKEN WITH EGGS AND ALMONDS
Sjdeda Bilbeid Bilooz

STEP 1 Clean and cut up one or more chickens and bathe the portions in a mixture of:
2 tablespoons hot water
½ teaspoon saffron
½ teaspoon salt

STEP 2 Put in a deep pot, one after the other:
the chicken

1 cup onion, diced fine
1 teaspoon black pepper
1 heaped tablespoon cinnamon
½ teaspoon ground cumin seed
¼ teaspoon ginger
¼ teaspoon curry
¼ teaspoon grated nutmeg
½ cup parsley, chopped fine
1 scant tablespoon salt
⅓ cup olive oil (poured over all)
1 tablespoon butter

Cook over high fire, stirring contents frequently for 10 minutes. (Moroccans, holding lid on firmly with both hands, simply shake or toss the whole pot in the air.) Then add:

4 cups hot water (if a very large chicken or 2 chickens, add an extra cup water)

Cover and continue cooking until chicken is done (approx. 1 hour).

STEP 3 Apart, blanch and toast:

1 cup almonds

Apart also, hardboil:

1 egg per person

SERVE Chicken on individual plates, thus:

1 portion chicken (without sauce)
2 tablespoons almonds, as garnish
1 hardboiled egg, whole or quartered

Dress with:

1 tablespoon chicken stock

Note The sauce remaining from this and other similarly prepared chicken dishes makes a wonderful soup stock base for later use.

CHICKEN WITH ALMONDS AND CHEESE
Sjdeda Bi Looz Bi Shjbn

STEP 1 Put in deep pot or casserole:

1 chicken, cut in portions
1 cup onion, diced coarsely
½ cup parsley, minced
1 teaspoon black pepper
¼ teaspoon saffron
1 tablespoon cinnamon
1 tablespoon salt

¼ teaspoon nutmeg
¼ teaspoon curry
¼ teaspoon ginger
1 tablespoon butter
4 cups warm water

Cover and cook over medium-high fire. When chicken is tender, remove from broth. Save broth for soup stock.

STEP 2 Add together in saucepan:
7 tablespoons butter
¾ cup grated Parmesan
1 tablespoon minced parsley
½ cup blanched, peeled, very lightly toasted almonds, chopped fine

Heat above almost to a boil, then add:
1½ cups water (or chicken stock)

Mix well, then over a low flame bathe chicken in sauce until it is golden and has absorbed much of liquid.

SERVE Hot, with any remaining sauce as dressing.

FISH AND CARROTS

L'Hootz Bijada

(Serves 6)

This is an excellent way to dress up any inexpensive grade of fish. Ingredients here suffice to prepare 3 lbs – allowing ½ lb per person.

STEP 1 Boil together in salted water:
2 cups carrots, cubed coarsely
2 cups potatoes, cubed coarsely

When cooked, drain and set aside, but keep 1 cup of the liquid.

STEP 2 Pound into a paste in mortar:
1 tablespoon garlic, diced fine
½ cup parsley, chopped fine
½ teaspoon salt
1 teaspoon ground cumin seed
½ teaspoon hot red chili peppers

STEP 3 Put, in layers one atop the other in wide shallow saucepan or frying pan:
1 large onion, sliced
several stalks of parsley
the fish, cut in crosswise portions
1 teaspoon black pepper

1 tablespoon salt

Cover fish with cold water and parboil for 10 minutes.

STEP 4 Melt in saucepan:

¼ cup butter

Add into butter over fire, mixing well:

spice paste (Step 2)
potatoes and carrots (Step 1)
1 cup water (from potatoes and carrots)

When liquid boils, remove the potatoes and carrots; lay fish in the liquid. Leave on medium fire 10 minutes.

SERVE On large serving platter, fish garnished with potatoes and carrots. Squeeze drops of lemon juice over all.

SWORDFISH STEW
L'Hootz F'Tadjeen
(Serves 4)

Other similar dry, meaty fish may be used to make excellent stew. Put one atop the other in layers in casserole:

1 lb fish, cut in chunks
1 cup onion, sliced thin lengthwise
1 teaspoon *lacama* (equal proportions: cinnamon, black pepper, curry, ginger, nutmeg)
1 cup potatoes and carrots, diced
1 cup tomatoes, crushed or cubed fine
1 tablespoon salt
1 teaspoon sweet red pepper
½ teaspoon saffron

Lastly, over all, pour:

½ cup heated olive oil

If available, place on top:

1 sweet red pimento

Simmer slowly for about ¾ hour. Do not mix.

SERVE Hot, with drops of lemon juice.

Pellow was employed as a slave at the palace.
From Thomas Pellow, *The Adventures* . . ., 1742 (1890 edn), pp. 57–8.

This cuscassoo of the Emperor's [Mulai Ismail], as being to feed about nine hundred men, was brought out into the court in a cart upon wheels; when dividing ourselves into several companies of seventy or eighty in a company, we had all our messes served out from the cart in large bowls, and set in the middle of us on the floor, sitting as close around it as possible we could. Though I cannot say we had fowls, yet we did not want, in lieu thereof, for a good store of beef and mutton, and which, instead of decently cutting, we with our hands hauled to pieces, two pulling one against another; and anyone first taking hold on a piece of meat, and another, his next neighbour, not taking speedy hold also on the same piece, it was accounted brutish. For as they are allowed at their meals only the use of their right hands, therefore if a man is not so assisted by his neighbour, whereby he may the easier separate it, it is reckoned the greatest injury that can be offered them; and it is really a very dangerous way of eating, especially when people are very hungry, therefore they are generally attended, during that time, by several persons with clubs in their hands, in case any should by chance swallow a piece too large for their gullets, and it should stick therein – which through their greediness often happened – and then one of those attendants gave the party a very hearty blow with his cudgel in the neck, by which means it was generally discharged either up or down, and in case it was not, then they repeated the blow till it was. This did I often see, and have been as often diverted by it.

A description of the wide variety of produce eaten in the country.
From George Cowan and R. L. N. Johnston, *Moorish Lotos Leaves*, 1883, pp. 251–9, 269–70, 274–5, 276–7.

Goat's flesh is extensively consumed, and 'the country Moors' – says Chenier – 'eat camels flesh with a good appetite; but the taste of this meat is insipid, and the broth has a white tincture unpleasing to the eye'. My own experiments on elderly camels' flesh lead me to prefer gutta-percha as an edible 'by a large majority'. Moorish fowls, capons excepted, are generally as scraggy as they are cheap; which is saying a good deal. The natives are very partial to squabs, infant pigeons, which, when artistically spatchcocked, make a capital *entrée*. Ducks and geese are very rare birds except in Mazagan. The facts that turkeys are common only in Marrakesh, and that rabbits are unknown south of Rabat, I leave zoologists to explain.

The inhabitants of the sea-ports are large consumers of fish, of which the first in the scale of merit ranks the *shebbel* – christened the Barbary salmon – a species of shad to which it is infinitely superior. Next come sardines, which, when fresh from the sea, fried in olive-oil with a dash of lemon, may vie with the Greenwich whitebait. Red mullet –

'the woodcock of submarine plantations' – (though outraged by native cooks, who, miserable heathens! reject its sublime liver, and never dream of an envelope of oiled paper) and the delicate silvery 'Father of Abraham' – in size a herring, in savour a poem – claim honourable mention. Huge thunnies, ponderous rock-cod, light-pink 'snapppers' scaling up to a dozen pounds, weightier and rosier 'stump-noses', sapphirine gurnards, bass, gray and black bream, gray mullet, herrings, pilchards, mackerel, anchovies, turbots, plaice and soles, abound at certain seasons in various fishing grounds all along the coast, together with a score of other kinds – some brilliantly striped or spotted and unknown in Billingsgate Fish Market. Such for instance are the *tasargelt* and *irgal* – caught in large quantities in the bay of Agadir – which, baked, dried, or salted, are in great demand among the Moors of the interior and the palm-people of the Sahara who account kippered fish a sovereign specific for a surfeit of fruit. Turtle are also plentiful, it is said, at Agadir, where the natives have not discovered the galoptiousness of calipash and calipee. The lobster, the crab, the prawn, the shrimp – even the oyster – serve almost as often to bait the lines of Moorish fishermen as to grace native gastronomy while to the native Jew such luxuries are utterly tabooed. But the Moors eat slimy octopods and the greasy conger is by no means despised by the natives who cut the eels into fillets, which are soaked in a sort of pickle (composed of pounded cinnamon, nutmegs, garlic, parsley-seed and chilies) then fried in oil. Skates, sting-rays, dog-fish, gar-fish, barnacles and sea urchins are also eaten by the poorest Moors . . .

Many native dishes – such as *tinjeea*, *tajin* and *hassoua* seem mere exaggerations of the French *chiffonade*, the Spanish *olla*, or the Scotch hotch-potch and cock-a-leekie in their infinite confusion and undescribable variety of odds and ends. European guests are not infrequently appalled by the mysterious medleys of fish, flesh and fowl, with spices, herbs, vegetables, seeds, fruit, and sugar or honey; as, for instance, a fowl and a hare stewed with raisins, apricots, red peppers, lentils and butter; or beef baked with slices of melon; or the far-famed couscasoo.

The foundation of the dish is flour (wheat, millet, or maize), deftly granulated with water (or milk) by the fingers, till the globules be fine enough to pass through a medium-sized sheep-skin colander; after which they are strained for a couple of hours, or more, according to quantity, in the perforated upper compartment of a kind of double stew-pan, whereof the lower half contains sufficient water to boil either the meat, poultry, or (rarely) fish or game, together with onions, garlic, slices of pumpkin, beans, dried peas, raisins, and sometimes dates or preserved apricots with capsicums. Soaked in the broth, to which oil or butter is added, the granules are served up in large stoneware or wooden bowls or platters, crowned with the meat and vegetables sometimes garnished with eggs painted several colours. First dipping his fingers into water – on great occasions rose or orange scented – the Moor plunges the fingers of the right hand into the smoking mess, after the fashion of Little Jack Horner. M. Chenier, who must have been afflicted with exceptionally vulgar Moorish friends, states that 'the meal ended, they lick their fingers and wipe them on their clothes. Those who keep negro slaves call them and rub their hands in their hair; or, if any Jew happens to be present, they make a napkin of his garments'. Couscasoo usually makes its appearance at the principal daily meal, about 3 p.m. . . .

Fruit is, in favourable years, remarkable for its abundance, variety, and (with the exception of apples, pears, peaches, apricots and plums) general excellence. In addition to the citrons, lemons, limes (sweet and sour), shaddocks, prickly-pears, mulberries, walnuts and chestnuts, common in many parts of Morocco, there are various localities famed for fruits of exceptional size or savour, such as the oranges of Tetuan, the quinces of Mequinez, the pomegranates of Marrakesh, the figs of Fez, the dates of Tafilet and Akka, the almonds of Soos, the melons of Duquella (Jackson mentions water-melons 'four of which were a camel-load'), the grapes of Tagodast, large as hen's eggs and the olives of Terudant.

Butter is not bad when fresh, except when composed of the milk of camels, cows and goats indiscriminately mixed. The Moorish connoisseur, however, prefers his butter old and crusted, and often buries it in earthen jars until it has acquired the proper bouquet. Desert-travellers allege that this old butter, melted, has a peculiar virtue of assuaging thirst. In some parts, the intestinal fat of cows, sheep, and goats is made into great rolls, and sold to the poor instead of butter.

The repulsive Moorish snail, *el babbus*, stewed or fried in rancid oil, is a dose from which my experimental audacity recoils. Neither can I fancy locust – boiled in salt water or vinegar and fried in oil with pepper – which are relished as greatly by the natives as the shrimp by the cockney. In some parts of the country there are certain gigantic stag-beetles which are often eaten by Moorish urchins and I am assured that there is in the neighbourhood of Azamor a slug about three inches in length which is eagerly sought after as an article of food – to be either boiled, baked or stewed . . .

In South-Western Algeria, on the borders of Marocco, wherever mutton is scarce, well-fed dogs, skinned, cleaned and skewered, are prominent on the butchers' stalls. Jackal is esteemed a delicacy; and the flesh of the hyaena is eaten, though rarely, because it is supposed to cause stupefaction. The mountainteers, says Chenier, eat lion's flesh despite its strong scent and toughness. Moulai Ismail's favourite dish is reported to have been roasted fox. I have seen a couple of Moors discussing the same delicacy with obvious relish, and Lempriere assures us that the tent-dwellers not only eat foxes, but cats also. Braithwaite speaks of an imperial rat-warren near Mequinez where 'the rats burrow like rabbits and are said to be as good meat'. Stewed hedgehog is highly popular; I rather like it in couscasoo although the meat is curiously glutinous. It is also baked, I am told, gypsy fashion, in a shroud of clay and aromatic leaves, entombed in red-hot cinders. The palm-people have a weakness for fricasseed ostrich and heroic omelets of its eggs. Thousands of starlings are snared during the date harvest, and eaten with as keen gusto as if they were ortolans. Roast cuckoo is considered a *bonne bouche*; and there are on Mogador Island edible hawks so highly prized as to be sent as presents to the Sultan.

Hay was entertained by the Grand Wazir.
From John Drummond Hay, *A Memoir*, 1896, pp. 272–3.

The party rode to the house of Sid Musa through the deserted streets in bright moonlight, which enabled them to avoid the holes and pitfalls abounding in this decaying town [Marrakesh]. Well-dressed dependants waited at Sid Musa's door to take their horses, and, following a man with a lantern, they soon found themselves in a small but beautiful court, with a fountain playing in a marble basin in the centre. Near this stood five tea-kettles on little charcoal stoves, and as many diminutive tables, each bearing a tray covered with a silk kerchief – suggestive of tea. Sid Musa welcomed them and led the way into a room furnished with two gorgeous beds, chairs, sofas and divans covered with brocade and satin. Handsome mirrors, draped with embroidered silken scarves, hung round the walls, which were covered with velvet arras embroidered in gold. These hangings, which cover the lower portion of the walls of every respectable Moorish dwelling, and vary in richness of material according to the wealth of the owner, appear to be a remnant of their ancient life as nomad

Arabs. The hanging resembles the side of the tent still in use among the Moors. The design is invariably a succession of horse-shoe arches in different coloured materials and more or less richly embroidered. In mosques and holy places, and in them alone, mats, often very fine, are used for the same purpose.

The menu was as follows:–

Roast pigeons, stuffed chickens, stewed lamb, turkey with almonds, and highly flavoured siksu (like an Italian pasta but round and very small); olives in oil; oranges cut in sections and spiced, served as a vegetable; salad of olives and mint; eggs poached with olives and oil; chicken fricassee, with a rich egg sauce; chickens with red butter – a piquante sauce; stewed mutton with fried eggs; chickens stewed with almonds and sweetened.

Dry siksu; rice made up in a sort of porridge; bowls of new milk; almond tart, flavoured with musk; pastry dipped in honey.

Dessert: oranges, almonds, raisins, nuts and fourteen dishes of confectionary, including 'kab ghazal' or gazelle hoofs, little cakes of that form, from which they take their name, made of pastry thickly iced and filled with a concoction of almonds.

A pleasant preparation of unripe figs, much resembling chutney, was served with the stewed lamb.

The only beverage was water, slightly flavoured with musk and essence of citron flowers.

Of this menu the turkey, the fricassees of chicken and the dry siksu were pronounced excellent, but some of the other dishes were horrible concoctions.

After dinner the ladies were invited to visit the harem, whither Sid Musa proceeded to conduct them. Through the horseshoe arch of the entrance showed a large court planted with orange-trees, illuminated by the full moon and by numerous lanterns held by black slave girls. Here, picturesquely grouped, the gorgeously apparelled ladies of the harem awaited them. A stream of dazzling light from a room on one side of the court played on the glittering jewels with which they were loaded, producing altogether quite a theatrical effect.

Lunch with one of the local representatives of the Glaoui. From Rom Landau, *Invitation to Morocco*, 1950, pp. 127–8.

As soon as he had sat down opposite me on one of the large, silk-covered pouffes, a servant brought a silk table-cloth and spread it over the carpet at our feet. Another man placed upon it a low round table; a third appeared with a copper basin, and a fourth with the jug from which he poured water over our hands. A fifth stood ready with an embroidered towel. We had hardly finished drying our hands, when yet another man appeared with an enormous china dish measuring some three feet across and covered with a coloured wicker cover narrowing at its top to a point like a Chinese coolie hat.

Our first course consisted of an entire roast lamb. I waited for my host to show me by example how to tackle the beast in front of us but did not have to wait long. He put his thumb and index finger into what looked the most succulent part of the flesh, and tore off a piece. I followed his example, and after we had each had about half a dozen morsels, the khalifa beckoned the servant to take the dish away. Instantly another dish of equal dimensions was set before us. This time it contained rice swimming in butter, and a servant handed us long, wooden spoons. The rice was followed by four crisp chickens with a pimento gravy. After we had had a few morsels, another dish was brought in, one of the best I have ever tasted. The top consisted of the lightest imaginable *mille feuilles* pastry, and underneath it were pigeons stuffed with tomatoes and hard-boiled eggs. I felt sorry when the khalifa ordered a servant to take it away. But we had to tackle yet another three meat courses, each done with a different vegetable. The last course consisted of the traditional kus-kus, made however in a non-traditional way with courgettes and raisins. The desert consisted of oranges, and was followed by coffee. Finally water and soap were brought for our hands.

I have not mentioned that half-way through the meal a servant placed in front of each of us a glass of what looked like milk. Since cow's milk was rare, and there were plenty of goats about, I feared that it was goat's milk, one of the very few things that I am unable to swallow. Determined, however, not to commit a *faux pas*, I decided to do what was expected of my, only hoping that I should not bring the stuff up again. When the khalifa raised his glass to his lips, I followed his example and, closing my eyes, took a sip. But the Olympians' ambrosia was as nothing compared to the smooth liquid that delighted the palate: it was cool, of a fragrance unlike any I had ever enjoyed, and though at first indefinable, tasted of almonds. Only later did I find out that this drink, called orgeat, quite as expensive as champagne, was considered one of the chief delicacies of Moorish *gourmandise*. It consists of the juice of crushed almonds to which is added the essence of orange blossoms, a few drops of rose-water, and a little sugar.

We were but two for lunch yet there had been enough food for at least a dozen hungry men. But, in spite of apparent feudal extravagance, nothing is wasted in a Moorish household. The Caid Brahim's wife and daughters lived at Telout, and possibly as soon as a dish left our table it was carried into the women's quarters to serve as their lunch. And then there were the more distant relations, the retainers and the servants. Quite obviously it was more economical to cook one big meal for the entire household than several separate ones. By the time that the salukis and whippets in the courtyard were given the remnants of our feast, nothing but the bones would be left.

Entertaining Moroccan women.
From Emily, Shareefa of Wazan, *My Life*, 1911, pp. 92–5.

Moorish ladies in general are very observant, and their criticisms of visitors are most remarkable, be they sisters or of another nationality. To accommodate my Moorish lady visitors, the room was arranged *à la Mauresque*, viz. with mattresses covered with sheets and coloured muslin, and plenty of multi-coloured silk cushions were strewn about. I had my own negress to bring in the tea, which is served first, after the musicians have duly sung and played. Dinner follows about an hour or less after. Fatimah, dressed in gala costume, brings in a low table, and her second follows her when she returns with a tray laden with tiny cups and saucers, in the centre of which are two teapots, to be used for black and green tea respectively. On another small table is a tray containing two tea receptacles, or caddies. These may be of glass, silver, or ordinary tin canisters. A large glass bowl or dish containing about two pounds or more of sugar, a glass containing mint, lemon, verbena, wild thyme, or some other herb, a glass or any fancy box containing slips of scented wood, a plated or brass incense-burner, two plated scent-sprinklers, containing rose and orange flower water, and a tumbler with a long-handled silver spoon in it, and also used as slop-basin, complete the equipment. This tray is on a line with the one containing the cups and saucers. Next, Fatimah arrives with a hissing samovar, and her second enters with a brass tray, which she places on the floor to receive the samovar. To the right of the tea-maker is yet another tray with native cakes and a basket with native biscuits, and later, I introduced European biscuits as I had introduced the black tea. This last, though much objected to at first, is more used in Tangier, and to a great extent in Fez, than green, and as for European biscuits, no function is complete without them to-day.

The process of tea-making is this: A handful of green tea is thrown into the pot and well rinsed with boiling water; then the herb chosen is put in, and sugar in lumps fills the pot. Boiling water is now added, and the concoction is allowed to stand for a few seconds. The scum is now removed, and the tea stirred; then the tea-maker, washing her hands previously, pours a little into a cup to taste as to sweetness. Being satisfied, she fills each tiny cup, and Fatimah, with her second, proceeds to distribute the same, the recipient placing it in front of her on the ground, having taken the precaution to spread a muslin handkerchief over her lap beforehand; then the cakes and biscuits are presented. Black tea prepared in the same way is in general use. When all are served, tea-sipping commences, often in a most audible manner. Tea-drinking is accompanied with scent-sprinkling and incense-burning to perfume the clothes. The women eat and drink slowly, and chatter all the time. Three cups and no more are taken. A little rest comes before the passing round of the pretty brass jug and basin for each guest to wash her right hand before dinner is served.

For dinner, large low wooden tables are set before every six or eight guests, and the dishes placed one after the other in the centre. Bread is taken from a basket, broken up, and distributed over the table. With 'Bismillah' (in the name of God) a sippet is taken, and some one will part a chicken in suitable pieces in such a dexterous manner that the hand used is only soiled at the finger-tips. Sometimes two persons engage in the operation of dissection, with the same happy result. To refuse a choice bit from a fellow-guest is a great breach of etiquette. Fish is usually served last, otherwise it would give a fishy flavour to succeeding dishes if served first. Soup is a breakfast dish, and is never omitted during Ramadan, the fasting month, the fast being broken by this appetising concoction, excellent of its kind when well prepared, to say nothing of being most nourishing. The Moors call this soup 'hurra.'

This brings me to another dainty named 'cous-cous,' the staple dish of Morocco, made of semolina and fine flour, worked up into pellets of various sizes on flat-edged trays with the palm of the hand, salt and water being added as required with a large wooden spoon. It can be manipulated into granular particles as fine as the finest sago, or as large as a pea. Generally four sizes are used, the finest to eat with young pigeons, or to be served with sugar and milk after butter has been rubbed in. Another size is used to make a dish of chicken or mutton, or to be mixed with sour milk, another to be used in a dish of preserved meat (koleah) and the coarsest is for the soup. When used fresh, it is steamed twice over; butter is rubbed in while the material is steaming hot. The couscous is heaped in a conical form on the dish, on which it has been placed lightly. If for meat or chicken, the cone is depressed, and the meat put in the depression covered with browned onions or vegetables, or both; if for pigeons, they are buried in the dish; if as a sweet, the cone remains. A design is carried out in powdered cinnamon over the couscous, and plenty of powdered sugar is distributed over the whole. Powdered sugar accompanies this dish in small saucers and glasses of milk fresh or sour.

17

Superstitions and Spells

Morocco has always been famous for its magicians – people who have seen the pantomime *Aladdin* will remember that the wicked Abenazer who tricked Widow Twankey into handing over the magic lamp came from that country. Clearly many of the charms, spells and superstitions are pre-Islamic some, like the hand of Fatima, mentioned by Colville, given subsequent Muslim respectability. In this chapter we have relied heavily upon the two stalwarts of Moroccan folklore, Legey and Westermarck. We cannot, of course, omit Agnes, Lady Grove, who, the reader will have realized, is quite one of our favourite authors.

Methods used to seek protection from the evil eye.
From Captain Colville, *A Ride in Petticoats and Slippers*, 1880, p. 147.

One notices a rude representation of a hand, painted in red, on many of the door-posts. This is intended to protect the inmates from the influence of the evil eye. The Moors have a great belief in this influence, and think that Christians possess it in a marked degree. So far is this belief carried that many tradesmen will hide their more valuable goods if they see a Christian approaching their shop; not as a precaution against any shop-lifting tricks, for such civilised habits have not yet reached Fez, but for fear that their wares should be spoilt, perhaps spirited away altogether, by a glance from the evil-dealing optic of the Nazarene.

Beliefs about pregnancy which she declared to be widespread.
From Lady Grove, *Seventy-one Days Camping*, 1902, pp. 54–5.

The superstitious ignorance of the Moors is illustrated by one curiously prevalent belief. I heard of one woman, who was anxious to exhibit her sister's baby to a visitor, exclaiming 'By God, Senora, it's the biggest baby that ever was seen, owing to its having been three and a half years asleep in its mother's womb'. The lady in question had been married three years and a half before the appearance of the baby, hence the belief that that was its period of incubation. One particularly lazy Jewess accounted for every stupidity she committed by reminding her exasperated employer that she had slept for seven years in her mother's womb, and had never quite got over it. A widow, too, will go on patiently awaiting the advent of a baby many years after her husband's death, and if by any chance one appears, there is not necessarily any scandal: if she has been discreet, no one but the defunct husband need ever be suspected.

An eighteenth-century minister and chronicler reported that the last of the 528 sons of Mulai Ismal was born 18 months after his death, regarding this as yet one more sign of his tremendous baraka.

Two she-demons, much feared by the superstitious.
From Vincent Crapanzano, *Hamdusha*, pp. 143–4 and 147.

Aisha Qandisha is always libidinous and quick-tempered. She never laughs, and is always ready to strangle, scratch, or whip anyone who insults her or does not obey her commands. She may appear to believers either as a beauty or as a hag with long pendant breasts. Usually, even in her beautiful manifestations, she has the feet of a camel, a donkey or an ass. Sometimes she appears with the legs of a woman and the body of a goat with pendant breasts. Throughout northern Morocco there are places sacred to her. These are usually pits, grottos, springs, and fountains, as well as other spots where someone is said to have seen her or where something uncanny has taken place. However, she is capable of appearing in many places at the same time.

When Aisha Qandisha presents herself to a man as a beautiful woman, a seductress, that man will have no defence against her power unless he immediately plunges a steel knife into the earth. He is then privileged to reject her entirely or to make a 'marriage contract' with her that is to his own advantage. (This is infrequent for Lalla Aisha invariably hides her camel's feet under a flowing caftan.) If a man has been unfortunate enough to sleep with her before discovering her identity, he becomes her slave forever and must follow her commands explicitly. Otherwise, she is sure to strangle him . . .

Lalla Malika is very beautiful and dresses, they say, with a lot of chic. She demands the same elegance of her followers. She is a flirt and quite promiscuous, and she especially enjoys relationships with married men.

When Lalla Malika sees someone she likes, she goes up to him and passes her hands in front of his eyes. The person then sees only clouds. He sees nothing but Lalla Malika. He cannot remember his house. She calls him by name and tells him that she is next to him and asks him to accept her wishes. The man agrees. "I want you to marry me", she says. "I want you to sleep with me". The man agrees, say, on condition that he has the liberty to have intercourse with other women. Lalla Malika agrees. Once they have come to an agreement, the man asks to see her. (He has not seen her up to this time.) She appears in front of him with clothes embroidered in gold, sometimes with long hair and sometimes with short. The man can then marry her or sleep with her. It is all the same. She tells him to wear perfumes, to shave often, and to wear new clothes. "Then you'll have your liberty", she tells him. "I'll even help you escape prison".

Lalla Malika is always gay, and she does not attack her followers. She likes to laugh and tickle them, and she is responsible when a group of women suddenly begin giggling.

The next four extracts all come from Legey.
The first piece is from Dr Françoise Legey, *The Folklore of Morocco*, 1935, pp. 199, 201, 203.

To cure warts, one should look at the moon at the moment when it appears on the first day of the month, and at the same time apply apple flour on the wart, and brush them with a new broom; or else, on the first Thursday in the month seven bits of straw should be stolen from the matting in a mosque and set on fire, and the warts should be touched with the burning ends. They are also supposed to be cured by being lightly burned with a blue paper on which the *taleb* has written a spell and which he has set on fire . . .

A cure for syphilis of the throat and mouth is to swallow the ashes of a crow which has been cremated in a new cooking pot, after being knocked down and stunned. Pills are made of the ashes mixed with honey and given to the patient, who is supposed thus to absorb all the strength of the bird, which is renowned for its long life. Syphilis is such a widespread disease in Morocco that there is a saying that he who does not have it in this world will suffer from it in the next . . .

In cases of irritation of the bladder wild mint is put on a brick, on which the patient is then made to pass water, after which it is taken to the nearest thoroughfare and left on the ground. The pain attending the miction is supposed to have passed into the brick, and will be absorbed by the first person who sets foot on it.

From *The Folklore of Morocco*, pp. 272–3.

In Morocco, as in every country in the world, interpretations are put upon dreams. If a serpent, for instance, is seen in a dream, it is thought to have been sent by the *moualin al-ard*, the masters of the earth, as a herald of good fortune.

To dream of dogs is a sign of enemies; the bite of a dog shows that an enemy will hurt one.

If one dreams of a man riding on a camel, it means that he is going to die; but if he is riding a mule he will grow very rich. If one sees him get off his mule, it is presage of coming ruin for him.

If one dreams that a dead person is calling and asking something, it is supposed to indicate a speedy death in the family; but if the dead person makes one a present, it is supposed to be a promise of prosperity, for it means that he is watching over one. To dream of a cat or of a child; of barley, of maize, or of rain is a sign of good fortune. To dream of a thief means good fortune and safety. But dreams of corn, of grapes, or of beans are omens of death.

From *The Folklore of Morocco*, pp. 31–5.

The earth is the abode of the jinni, but they are specially fond of desert places, of drains, of lavatories, and ruins and cemeteries. They come up to the surface of the ground at night, and from the moment of the Prayer of Asr, between three and four o'clock in the afternoon, one should be very careful not to offend them. So that if water-closets are being built, or if one is digging a well or the foundations of a wall, work should be stopped at that moment for fear of hurting a jinni. They are very capricious, and it is well known that if the ground is being dug up and they don't like it, they will destroy all the works in the night . . .

They are thought to have been created at the same time as human beings. And every human being has his double among them, who is born and who dies with him, and whose subterranean life is exactly the same as that of his human counterpart . . .

It is thought that the devils or jinni have fluid bodies which can take any shape. Seventy-seven transformations are attributed to them. But when they come among human beings they more generally take the form of some domestic animal, like a cat or a dog; and one can never be certain whether one is dealing with a real animal or with its double from the subterranean world. Cats and dogs should therefore never be killed, for there would be danger of hurting a jinni who had taken their shape, and of incurring his vengeance.

The most dangerous time of the night is between half-past eleven and half-past two in the morning. During this portion of the night one should never go out in the street, one should never go to a lavatory, to the kitchen, to the Moorish baths, to a fountain or to a well: for all these places are haunted then by startling and horrible apparitions. It is then that the *Maezt Dar L'Oudou*, the Goat of the Lavatories, is in possession. She bleats ferociously, and terrorizes those who are imprudent and disturb her. She appears in any lavatory, but is most dangerous in the public ones outside mosques . . .

The *Baghlet El Qebour*, the Mule of the Graves, also haunts the entire *Houz* of Marrakesh at this hour. She was once a widow, who during her lifetime either prostituted herself or remarried before the prescribed time of her widowhood was expired. When she died God punished her by making her take the shape of a mule every night except Wednesday. She is very wicked and buries alive those who are thoughtless and who try to climb on her back to get home quicker, when they see her standing saddled in front of some house.

From *The Folklore of Morocco*, p. 89.

Fleas should never be put to death. If one catches a flea one must take it between two fingers and throw it away as far as possible; for the flea is under the protection of the Prophet. One day when he was sleeping soundly a flea bit him and woke him just in time for the hour of prayer. He was so glad of the bite that he promised the flea that it should never be killed or burned. He said to it:

> 'He who kills thee shall be killed
> He who crushes thee shall be crushed
> And may God send thee into the hands of an old woman, for she will not have the strength to hurt thee'

And he let the flea go.

The last piece in this book is a selection of proverbs. From Edward Westermarck, *Wit and Wisdom in Morocco*, 1930.

What the devil does in a year, an old woman does in an hour.

He who marries a woman with reddish hair will lose his property and also the cow.

An unjust government is better than corrupt subjects.

There is no blessing in a woman who travels, and there is no blessing in a man who does not travel.

He who has intercourse with a she-camel, may God give him a lot of bugs and an ant.

He who goes into the sea is gone, and he who comes out of it is like a new-born.

He had never crawled, and as soon as he crawled he fell into a well.

Eat according to your own taste, and dress according to the taste of others.

The owner of an umbrella goes, as it pleases him, in the sun or in the shade.

The wealthy man's speech is pure silver, and the poor one's is coated with dung.

If a wealthy man breaks wind, they consider him like a canary bird when it sings; if a poor man breaks wind, they insult him and in addition give him a drubbing.

None but a dog bites in his own house.

He stayed the night in the marshes; in the morning he was one of the frogs.

One fish makes the pannier stink.

He whom you hate in the street will show you his bottom in the hot bath.

You will have to wait till the donkey climbs a ladder and the salt blossoms.

The clouds are not hurt by the barking of dogs.

A gentleman without reading is like a dog without training.

The sight of books removes sorrow from the heart.

To make friends with a wild beast is better than to make friends with an inquisitive person.

A pool with stagnant water is just the one that swallows people.

Slowness comes from God and haste from the Devil.

Eating worms is better than accepting the hospitality of the niggardly.

If your friend is honey, don't eat it all.

The dumb one is only understood by his mother.

He who has been bitten by a snake is frightened by a rope.

The snake does not bite itself.

Glossary

Abd	a slave. In the plural *Abid* is used for members of the black regiments raised by Mulai Ismail
Alim	a scholar of *Shariah* law
Amin	a government official, usually with financial responsibilities
Ashur	literally 'a tenth' – a Muslim tax
Askar	(regular) soldier
Barakah	a grace or blessing that comes from God and can be transmitted by favoured individuals
Baya	formal recognition of a ruler by the Muslim community
Bayt al-Mal	the treasury of the Mulim community
Blad	the country
Caid	a military rank and/or a local official, often a tribal chief. European travellers tended to use the word for any important Moroccan that they met
Dhahir	a decree
Fatwah	an opinion on a point of Islamic law issued by a qualified scholar
Fqih	a scholar, often used for a teacher
Habus	property bequeathed for (usually) religious purposes
Hadiyah	literally 'a gift' but used to denote a tax paid to the Sultan on formal occasions
Hajib	a high court official usually rendered 'Chamberlain'
Jamaa	a gathering of notables to discuss tribal matters or render justice
Jaysh	the army
Jihad	literally 'striving' but used to mean warfare with religious objectives
Khalifa	literally 'a successor'. Used in Morocco for either the viceroy of a sultan or the deputy of a local official

Laib al-baroud	'powder play', the Moroccan sport of firing from the saddle of a galloping horse
Mahallah	a military expedition
Mahdi	the man expected by Muslims to return and lead the community to righteousness
Majlis	literally 'a sitting down', used for a council or audiences held by an important person
Makhzan	literally 'a store' (from which the French *magasin*), used to mean the Government of Morocco
Marabout	a religious leader or his successors, usually of local significance. Recognition of a marabout was essentially by local acclaim: the British writer who defined the word as 'the Moroccan equivalent of the title of Doctor of Divinity conferred by the Emperor' was wrong!
Mashwar	the great court-yard of a royal palace
Mawlud	a birthday, normally that of the Prophet Muhammad
Mokhazni	an employee of the Makhzan, usually a policeman
Muhtassib	an official responsible for enforcing good behaviour in a city
Mulai	literally 'My Lord', a title of respect paid to the Sultan, his family and important religious leaders
Muna	literally 'a gift' but normally means the obligation of a community to provide food for travellers
Naib	a deputy
Pasha	originally a Turkish military title but used by Europeans to mean the governor of a town
Qadi	the judge of the *Shariah*
Ramadan	the month of fasting during which warfare was banned
Shariah	the corpus of Islamic law based on the Qur'an and the doings and saying of the Prophet
Sharif	a direct descendant of the Prophet
Sidi	literally 'My Lord', a title of respect
Talib	a student of religious law
Tariqah	a religious brotherhood
Ulama	plural of *Alim*, the religious notables
Zawiah	a religious centre, usually based on the tomb of a marabout and housing a mosque and a school

The transcription of Arabic words can vary according to the

nationality of a writer or the system used. For example the word for a river bed is written *Wadi* in English, *Oued* in French and *Guadi* in Italian. Some of the transcriptions in this anthology will therefore be different from one text to another but it is hoped that this glossary will help the reader to identify them.

Authors and Editions Quoted

ADDISON, Rev. Lancelot (1632–1703). As an undergraduate at Oxford he attacked Puritanism so ferociously that he was summoned before the University authorities to retract upon his knees. He was ordained after the Restoration and appointed Chaplain to Lord Teviot, the Governor of Dunkirk. When that city was sold to the French in 1661 Teviot was sent as Governor of Tangier and took Addison with him. Addison appears to have remained in the city for about eight years before returning to a living in Wiltshire. He ended his career as Dean of Lichfield. He wrote several other works on Islam to which, for his time, he was not wildly hostile.
An Account of West Barbary, Oxford, 1671 (the edition used is that printed in Pinkerton, John, *A general collection of the best and most interesting Voyages and Travels in all parts of the World*, London, 1808–1814).

ALI BEY EL ABASSI (pseudonym of Domingo Badia y Leblich, c1766–1818) was a Catalan who, after studying Arabic and science at Valencia, in 1802 visited London and appears to have discussed with the African Association the possibility of his exploring the continent by going south over the Atlas. In June 1803 he landed at Tangier in apparently perfect disguise as a descendant of the Abbasid Caliphs from Aleppo with unlimited wealth. According to his account he was accepted almost as a brother by Mulai Sulaiman who sent him wives, possibly to spy upon him. Despite the stories that he tells of the stir made by his visit, Moroccan scholars have found no reference to him in contemporary chronicles. It is likely that he was the agent of either the Spanish government or of the French, although it is difficult to see what his employers got for the huge sums that he must have cost them. It appears from his own account that the Moroccan government was by no means sorry to see him leave but he may have been ordered by Napoleon to perform similar tasks in Arabia. His account of Mecca was the first scientific and accurate report by a European. He returned to Europe, had numerous meetings with Napoleon and settled in Paris as General Badia. In 1818, commissioned by the French government to explore the area of Timbuktu, he set out again for Mecca, intending to join a caravan of returning pilgrims. He died, however, in Damascus, according to some French sources, poisoned by British agents.
The Travels of Ali Bey el Abassi, American edition, Philadelphia, 1816.

AMICIS, Edmundo de (1846–1908), fought against the Austrians in 1867 and was always interested in military matters. He was also a travel writer with works on Holland, Constantinople and so on. His account of Morocco, based on a visit in 1875, using information from well-established Italian merchants, is one of the most useful of the period. Written in Italian, it was translated into French and English. The edition quoted, *Morocco: Its People and Places*, a translation by Maria Hornor Lansdale, was published in two volumes in Philadelphia in 1897. His best known work is the three-volume *Romance of a Schoolmaster*.

ANDREWS, Clarence Edward (born 1883), was Professor of English at Ohio State University. He wrote a study of Richard Brown and a book on the writing and reading of verse. He was also joint editor of collections of Romantic and Victorian poetry. During and after the First World War he was involved in relief work in France and in the Balkans.
Old Morocco and the Forbidden Atlas, New York, 1922.

AUBIN, Eugène, was the pseudonym of Descos (born 1863). A member of the French foreign service, he had already travelled in most of the Muslim countries when in September 1902 he was appointed First Secretary of the French Legation in Tangier. In 1903 he spent six months on an official mission in Fez. His book which was crowned by the Académie Française, is generally regarded as the best account of pre-Protectorate Morocco and originally appeared in the form of letters written for journals. He also wrote books on the British in India and Egypt, Persia, and Haiti.
Morocco of To-Day, London. 1904.

BASSET, Henri, (1892–1936), was the Director of the Institut des Hautes Etudes Marocaines.
'Les Troglodytes de Taza', *Hespéris*, 1925.

BEAUCLERK, Captain G. An officer of the Royal Welch Fusiliers, he was serving at Gibraltar in 1826 when Mulai Abdel Rahman asked the Lieutenant-Governor to send a doctor. Beauclerk went with him. His account is lively and intelligent and soon after publication was translated into Polish.
A Journey to Morocco, London, 1828.

BEL, Alfred, was Professor of Arabic at the University of Algiers.
La Réligion musulmane en Berberie, Paris, 1938.

BENACHENOU, A., a Moroccan scholar, has written numerous books in Arabic and French on history, dialects, law etc. *Contes et récits du Maroc*, Rabat, 1960.

BENSUSAN, Samuel Levy (1872–1958), was Literary Adviser to the Theosophical Publishing House and Editor of the *Theosophical Review*. He was also Musical Critic of the *Illustrated London News* and wrote plays, dialect comedies and poetry – his last book was published at the age of 83. He worked as a special correspondent in Morocco. His *Morocco*, London, 1904, has charming coloured illustrations by A. S. Forrest (1869–1963).

BORELY, Jacques (1874–1947). Born in Provence he was never able to decide between painting and poetry, being a friend of both Cézanne and Mistral. He was appointed a magistrate in Fez in 1919 and was then posted to Rabat where he caused surprise by choosing to live in the native quarter. Marshal Lyautey made him Director of the Service des Beaux-Arts et des Monuments Historiques. He was responsible for many new buildings and for careful restoration of old ones such as the Koutoubia. He did much to encourage artists such as Dufy to visit the country. He was retired in 1936, taught at Cairo University and published several books.
Le Maroc au pinceau, Paris, 1950.

BORROW, George (1803–81), was a remarkable linguist who travelled on foot through much of Europe from Russia to Spain acting for the British and Foreign Bible Society. He was particularly interested in gypsies. His books mingle fact and fiction. During his travels in Spain he briefly visited Tangiers in 1836.
The Bible in Spain, London, 1893 edition.

BRAITHWAITE, John, was a captain in the service of the Royal African Company who saw active service by land and sea. He claimed to have been the first British soldier to enter Gibraltar when it was captured in 1704. He accompanied a kinsman on a diplomatic mission to Venice and campaigned in the West Indies. In 1729 he accompanied Consul John Russell on a mission to Fez. Although he had no previous knowledge of the country, Braithwaite was an excellent observer and left a particularly interesting account of court life.
History of the Revolutions in the Empire of Morocco upon the Death of the late Emperor Muley Ishmael, London, 1729.

BRIVES, Abel (born about 1865), studied geology in Algiers and obtained a doctorate for his research there. He prepared a geological map of Algeria. He travelled widely in Morocco between 1901 and 1907. Later he did much geological work in the Sahara, finding and developing sources of water. He ended his career as Professor of Mineralogy in Algiers. His book shows that in addition to his profession he was deeply interested in anthropology, folklore etc.
Voyages au Maroc, Algiers, 1909.

BRUNOT, Louis, was a distinguished linguistic scholar who collected Arabic and Hebrew texts. He also published a reference grammar of Moroccan Arabic.
Au seuil de la vie marocaine, Casablanca, 1950.

BUFFA, John, was a physician who was sent by the Governor of Gibraltar in 1806 to treat the Governor of Larache, whose secretary advised him to flee for

his life if he failed to cure his patient. He later went on to Meknes and Fez to treat the sultan. His book is useful when he speaks of what he himself saw but is not always reliable in other ways.
Travels through the Empire of Morocco, London, 1810.

BUTLER, Alban (1711–73), was a Catholic priest who spent much of his life travelling around Northern Europe investigating stories of saints and their miracles. At a time when priests were forbidden to work in England, he was given special permission to do so by the Duke of Cumberland because of his work on behalf of the English wounded at the Battle of Fontenoy.
Butler's Lives of the Saints, has been through numerous editions, the one used being published in London in 1956.

CAILLIE, René (1799–1838), was a poor orphan who left France at the age of 17 to earn his living in Senegal. He travelled widely in West Africa, passing for an Egyptian Muslim. In 1828 he crossed from the Ivory Coast to Tangier, returning to France to give the first European account of Timbuktu. He was awarded the Gold Medal of the French Geographical Society but many Englishmen regarded him as an impostor. He was a good observer although he did not have sufficient background knowledge always to get things right. He died in obscurity.
Travels through Central Africa to Timbuctoo and across the Great Desert to Morocco, performed in the years 1824–28, London, 1830 (reprinted 1968).

de CASTRIES, Colonel Count Henry (c1845–1927). After the Franco-Prussian War, he served for ten years in Algeria, mainly in the desert and on the Moroccan frontier. He then left the army and formed a team of collaborators who searched all the major European archives for unpublished documents about relations with Morocco between 1530 and 1845. His *Sources de l'histoire du Maroc*, runs to 26 volumes of which the first was published in Paris in 1905.

COLVILLE, Captain Henry E. of the Grenadier Guards (1852–1907). In the winter of 1879–80 Colville, accompanied by his wife, both in Moroccan dress, rode from Fez to Oudjda, covering an area then little known to Europeans. Later he was engaged on intelligence duties in the Sudan and in Burma. From 1893 to 1895 he was Acting Commissioner in Uganda where he put down a local rising. Colville commanded a division in the Boer War and was knighted. His account of Morocco is well observed but rather marred by scorn for backward natives.
A Ride in Petticoats and Slippers, London, 1880.

COWAN, George D. and Johnston, R. L. N. Cowan was a merchant who lived for more than 25 years in Mogador. Johnston (1854–1918), who arrived in Mogador in 1879, was also a merchant and at the same time vice-consul there from 1885 to 1900. He was also the correspondent of several newspapers. They both knew the country very well.
Moorish Lotos Leaves: Glimpses of Southern Marocco, London, 1883.

CRAPANZANO, Vincent (born 1939), took a doctorate at Columbia and has taught at various universities. His particular interest is in psychiatric anthropology and he has written several books on Morocco.
Hamdusha, Berkeley, 1973.

CUNNINGHAME GRAHAM, Robert Bontine (1852–1936), was a Scotsman who spent much of his early career in the Argentine as a cowboy. From 1886 until 1892 he was Liberal MP for North Lanarkshire. He was later a friend of Keir Hardie with whom he founded the Scottish Labour Party, for which he contested several elections. He was also a friend of Joseph Conrad, W. H. Hudson and Bernard Shaw who is said to have modelled *Captain Brassbound* upon him. In 1897 he decided to see Tarudant where only Lempriere had been before him. His experiences made him urge that Europeans should cease interfering in the country. He was regarded by Wilfred Scawen Blunt as one of the finest of all British travel writers, the equal of Doughty and the superior of Sir Richard Burton.
Mogreb-el-Acksa, London, 1898.

CURTIS, James, was an army surgeon who was sent by the Governor of Gibraltar to accompany an embassy to Fez. On recrossing the Straits he was captured by the French and held a prisoner of war for some time.
A Journal of Travels in Barbary in the year 1801, with observations on the gum trade of Senegal, London, 1803.

DAWSON, Alec John, was an artist who became well-known for his wartime drawings of British and French soldiers. He wrote several books on dogs, including one for the young.
Things Seen in Morocco, London, 1904.

DAY, Irene F.
Kitchen in the Kasbah: Moroccan Cooking, London, 1975.

DEFOE, Daniel (1660–1731), first became known as a pamphleteer but is best remembered for his novels, particularly *The Life and Strange Surprising Adventures of Robinson Crusoe, of York, Mariner* which was based on the real-life story of Alexander Selkirk and first appeared in 1719. The edition used is that of 1869.

DELACROIX, Eugène (1798–1863). The famous painter was greatly inspired by North Africa. He managed to attach himself to a military mission to Fez in 1832. *Selected Letters 1813–1863*, selected and translated by Jean Stewart, London, 1971.

DERMENGHEM, Emile, was a famous Arabist who translated folk tales from Fez and wrote a life of Muhammad. He was also interested in free-masonry.
Le Culte des saints dans l'Islam maghrebin, Paris, 1954.

DOUTTE, Edmond, (1867–1926), was compelled by ill health to live in North Africa where he became a professor at the University of Algiers. A sociologist and orientalist, he wrote authoritatively on Islam, magic and tribal life.
En Tribu, Paris, 1914.

EICKELMAN, Dale (born 1942), is a distinguished American scholar who has published much valuable work, particularly on Morocco and on Oman.
Moroccan Islam, Austin, Texas, 1976.

ELSNER, Eleanor, wrote travel books on Spain, France and other Mediterranean countries. She took considerable trouble to read up about these countries before going there and was a good observer.
The Present State of Morocco, London, 1928.

EPTON, Nina Consuelo, had a Scottish father and a Spanish mother with possible Moorish blood and was educated in France, taking a degree at the Sorbonne. From 1943 to 1956 she was in charge of French Canadian programmes on the BBC World Service. During her visits to North Africa she had trouble with the French authorities owing to her sympathies with the nationalist leaders. She has written a large number of travel books, some biographies and *Love and the English, the French and the Spanish*.
Saints and Sorcerers: A Moroccan Journey, London, 1958.

FOGG, Walter, taught in the Department of Geography and Anthropology of the University College of Wales at Aberystwyth.
'A Moroccan tribal shrine and its relation to a nearby tribal market', *Man*, July 1940.
'Changes in the lay-out, characteristics, and function of a Moroccan tribal market, consequent upon European control', *Man*, September 1941.

FOUCAULD, Vicomte Charles de (1858–1916), born into an aristocratic family, he became a cavalry officer. Stationed in Algiers he was mainly noted for his dissolute life until hs resigned his commission and set himself to study Arabic, Hebrew and Berber. Then, disguised as a poor Jew, he made the most famous and daring of all explorations of Morocco, visiting parts south of the Atlas never before seen by a European and suffering great hardships. He then spent some time in southern Algeria before in 1890 becoming a Trappist monk in a monastery in Palestine. He was ordained priest and then returned to the Sahara, where with some companions he hoped to convert the Tuareg. He also assisted French penetration of the area. He was greatly respected by the Tuareg as a marabout but in 1916 he was murdered by a Sanussi raiding party. The slow process of his canonization began in 1926.
Reconnaissance au Maroc en 1883–1884, Paris, 1888.

GLEICHEN, Major-General Lord Edward (1863–1937), was the son of Admiral Prince Victor of Hohenlohe-Langenberg and his mother was the daughter of an Admiral of the Fleet. He entered the Grenadier Guards in 1881 and in 1884 and 1885 served with the Guards Camel Regiment. He was then

transferred to intelligence duties, including making assessments of Morocco, until 1899. In 1893 he was attached to the staff of Sir West Ridgeway in Tangier for four months. In 1896 he performed special duties in the Sudan and in 1897 was attached to a mission to Addis Ababa. Gleichen was wounded in the Boer War and then was appointed Director of Intelligence of the Egyptian Army and Agent for the Sudan in Cairo. From 1903 to 1906 he was Military Attaché in Berlin, before taking the same post in Washington. In 1909 he went as Military Attaché on another mission to Fez. In the Great War he fought in France before being appointed Chief of the Intelligence Bureau. He wrote several books on his experiences and one on the statues of London.
A Guardsman's Memories, London, 1932.

GROVE, Lady (Agnes; 1864–1926), was the daughter of Major-General Pitt-Rivers, the founder of scientific anthropology. Her first publication was in the *Oxford High School Magazine* and she wrote a series of books such as *On Fads*, *The Human Woman* and *The Social Fetich*. She was extremely active in public life being a member of the Executive Committee of the Women's Liberal Federation, the Anti-Vivisection Society and President of the Forward Suffrage Union and a local councillor. At times her book on Morocco reads like a parody of such literature but it also contains some interesting material.
Seventy-One Days Camping in Morocco, London, 1902.

GUYOT, R., was a Captain-Interpreter with the Service des Affairs Indigènes. He was assisted in the article that we have used by the well-known academics Robert Le Tourneau and Lucien Paye.
'Les Cordonniers de Fez', *Hespéris*, 1936.

HALIBURTON, Robert George, QC, FRGS
pamphlet, *The Dwarfs of Mount Atlas*, London, 1891.

HALL, Luella Jemima (1890–1973), took a doctorate at Stanford University and taught social sciences for more than forty years. She also wrote on the formation of counties in North Dakota.
The United States and Morocco 1776–1956, Metuchen, NJ, 1971.

HARRIS, Walter B. (1866–1933). A man of large private means, he settled in Tangier where he acted as correspondent for *The Times* for forty years. He spoke Arabic well and travelled on donkey-back or foot, disguised as a poor native. In 1903 he was captured by the famous bandit Raysuli and appears to have quite enjoyed the experience. He was extremely knowledgeable about the country but often was not inclined to let facts spoil a good story. He was often, also, deliberately mischievous. In addition to his works on Morocco, he wrote a very good account of travel in Yemen.
The Land of an African Sultan, London, 1889 (?)
Tafilet, Edinburgh, 1895
Morocco that Was, London, 1921.

HAY, Sir John Drummond (1816–93). He was born in France and at the age of 16 he went to live with his father, who had been political agent and consul-general in Tangier since 1829. In 1840 he was posted to the Embassy in Constantinople where he remained until 1844 when he succeeded his father in Tangier. He held the post until his retirement in 1886 so that the two Drummond Hays have the unique record of representing Great Britain in a single post for nearly sixty years. Sir John had an exceptional knowledge of Morocco and was the trusted adviser of a succession of sultans, one of whom invited him to be his Foreign Minister.
Western Barbary: Its Wild Tribes and its Savage Animals (the editions of 1844 and 1861 contain some differences)
A Memoir of Sir John Drummond Hay, London, 1896.

HOLT, George Edmund, was an official of the American Consulate in Tangier from 1907 to 1910 and served on various international bodies there.
Morocco the Piquant, London, 1914.

HOOKER, Sir Joseph Dalton, and BALL, John. Hooker (1817–1911) was the son of the first Director of Kew Gardens, a post in which he succeeded his father in 1855, and was the most distinguished botanist of his time. He headed several notable expeditions, to the Himalayas (1846–9) from which he brought back many rhododendrons and to Morocco in 1871. He was President of the Royal Society and later a holder of the Order of Merit. Ball was also a botanist who accompanied Hooker and also travelled widely collecting plants. Their book is very Victorian with its honesty and liberalism, tempered by their assumptions of innate superiority.
Journal of a Tour in Marocco and the Great Atlas, London, 1878.

HORNE, John
Many Days in Morocco, London, 1925.

al-IDRISI, Abu Abdullah Muhammad, was asked by King Roger II of Sicily to make a large silver map of the known world and to write a geography book as an explanation of it. The work, *Géographie*, was completed in 1154 and was still regarded in Morocco as authoritative at the beginning of the twentieth century when a scholar in Fez refused to believe in the existence of America because it was not to be found on Idrisi's map. The edition used is a translation by Jaubert, Paris, 1840.

INGRAM, Jim, was born in Manchester but taken to Canada as a child. He wrote several travel books, the most interesting of which described a journey in Russia and a tramp across Lapland.
Land of Mud Castles, London, 1952.

JACKSON, G. A., set out to write a complete history of the pirates of the African Continent. Despite its title, *Algiers* has almost as much about Morocco and sections on Tripoli and Tunis. It appears to have been compiled from the accounts of captives and other travellers and there is no evidence that the author himself went to North Africa.
Algiers: A Picture of the Barbary Coast, London, 1817.

JACKSON, James Grey, was a merchant who spent many years in Mogador and Agadir. He was particularly interested in animals, natural history and geography.
An Account of the Empire of Marocco and the District of Suse compiled from Miscellaneous Observations made during a long Residence in, and various journies through, these countries. To which is added an accurate and interesting Account of Timbuctoo, the great Emporium of Central Africa, London, 1809.

KERR, Dr Robert. He arrived in Rabat in 1886 as 'agent of the Presbyterian Church of England', and although he obviously knew the country well, his bigotry and intolerance make his books appear almost a caricature of works by a missionary. He deserves to be remembered for the observation that 'as far as ignorance and superstition are concerned, there is little to choose between the Mohamedans and the Roman Catholics, except where the latter have come into contact with enlightened Evangelical Protestantism'.
Pioneering in Morocco, London. 1894
Morocco after Twenty-Five Years, London, 1912.

La MARTINIERE, H. M. P. He went to Morocco in 1882 as an archaeologist, took part in a diplomatic mission in 1885 and served in the French Legation from 1887 to 1891 when he was posted to Algiers to deal with Arab affairs. He returned to the Legation in Tangier in 1899, remaining until 1902 when he became Consul-General in Rome. He had an expert knowledge of the country.
Morocco, London, 1889
Souvenirs, Paris, 1919.

LANDAU, Rom (1899–1974), gave in *Who's Who* his professions as 'author and sculptor' and his recreation as 'talking to dogs'. He made numerous visits to Morocco, his first in 1924. Before the war he wrote an international best-seller *God Is my Adventure* and was co-founder of the World Congress of Faiths. During the war he was an air-gunner from 1939 to 1941 and then worked in political intelligence. From 1952 to 1967 he was a professor at the University of the Pacific. After the war, while not alienating the French, he established cordial relations with Sultan Muhammad V and his son, the future Hassan II. Altogether he wrote over forty books on philosophy, religion, world affairs, biography etc. many of them translated into the principal European languages.
Invitation to Morocco, London, 1950
The Beauty of Morocco, London, 1951.

LANE-POOLE, Stanley Edward (1854–1931), was the son of the scholar who compiled the most famous of Arabic-English Dictionaries and a great-nephew of Edward Lane who translated *The Arabian Nights* and wrote one of the best surveys of a people in *The Manners and Customs of the Modern Egyptians*. He himself began his career in the coin department of the British Museum but then wrote a series of books which became standard works. He was later Professor of Arabic at Trinity College, Dublin.
The Barbary Corsairs, London, 1890.

LEARED, Arthur, was a doctor who published works on the digestive system, flatulence, blood and infant mortality. He had no background knowledge of Morocco, could speak no Arabic and did not travel beyond the coastal towns and Fez, but was a good observer and wrote pleasantly.
A Visit to the Court of Morocco, London, 1879.
Marocco and the Moors, London, 1891

LEBLANC, Vincent, is generally regarded as perhaps the most untrustworthy of all travel writers. He says that he spent his life on the move to avoid his wife 'one of the most terrible women in the world'. In Mecca he claims to have seen bulls in the Great Mosque being used to draw water from Zemzem and also recounts how a prince was turned by his wicked stepmother into 'an exceeding pretty and tractable ape'. He states that he accompanied a French mission to Morocco and his section on that country is fairly accurate, allowing for some Provençal exaggeration. His account, first published in France in 1608, translated by F. Brooke, was published in London in 1660 as *The World Surveyed or the famous voyages and travailes of Vincent Le Blanc or White of Marseilles who from the Age of Fourteen years to Threescore and Eighteen, Travelled through most parts of the World. The whole work enriched with Many Authentick Histories*.

LEGEY, Françoise, spent fifteen years as a doctor in Morocco, coming into contact with every class of society. Her book is unequalled as a source for the way of life and beliefs of Moroccans in the early part of the twentieth century.
The Folklore of Morocco, translated by Lucy Hotz, London, 1935.

LEMPRIERE, William (died 1834). He was born in Jersey and joined the Army Medical Service. He was serving in Gibraltar in September 1789 when Sultan Muhammad III asked the Commandant, General O'Hara to send a doctor to Tarudant to treat his son Mulai Abdsulam who was suffering from a cataract. Lempriere's treatment was a success but the only reward he received was 'a gold watch, an indifferent horse, and a few hard dollars'. He was then summoned to Marrakesh by the sultan where he was asked to treat ladies of the harem. He thus obtained unprecedented access to the domestic life of the royal family. Very much against his will he was detained in Morocco until February 1790. He was then appointed surgeon to the troops in Jamaica where he remained for five years. He wrote *Practical Observations on the Diseases of the Army in Jamaica* and retired as Inspector-General of Army Hospitals.
A Tour from Gibraltar to Tangier, Sallee, Mogadore, Sant Cruz, Tarudant, and thence over Mount Atlas to Morocco, including a particular account of the Royal

Harem, London, 1791. The edition used is from Pinkerton (reference given under Addison).

LEO AFRICANUS (Hassan al-Wazzazi al-Fasi) was born in Granada but was taken to Fez at an early age. He was trained at the Karaouiyin University and held various judicial offices as well as fighting against the Portuguese. He also visited Timbuktu. In about 1520 he was captured by Italian pirates off Jerba and taken to Rome. He attracted the attention of Pope Leo X who baptised him, gave him his own name and encouraged him to write a description of his homeland. Leo wrote it in Arabic and himself translated it into Italian. First published in 1526, it is a book of enormous importance, the first comprehensive account of Morocco and the main source of information on the country until the late nineteenth century. It shows, in its descriptions of Fez, how little the old city has changed. Budgett Meakin (q.v.) writing in 1899 said that he had been able to use it as a guide book in remote areas. It is believed that after the death of his patron Leo reverted to Islam and settled in Tunis. There are numerous translations and editions of his *Description of Africa*, the one used being that in the Hakluyt Series, published in London in 1896.

LEWIS, Percy Wyndham (1882–1957), was born in a yacht off the coast of Maine but brought up in England. Mainly known as an artist, he was trained at the Slade and in Paris and became the pioneer of a new kind of art called Vorticism which he publicized in a journal called *Blast*. He was a close friend of Ezra Pound, whose Fascist sympathies he shared. He was also noted for his belligerence, enjoying major quarrels with James Joyce, Virginia Woolf, Hemingway and Proust. He wrote novels and philosophical and critical works. He travelled widely, and he and his wife did a journey by donkey in the Souss.
Filibusters in Barbary, London, 1932.

LILIUS, Aleko, also wrote a book on Chinese pirates.
Turbulent Tangier, London, 1956.

LITHGOW, William. A Scot, he was generally known as 'Cut-lugged' or 'Lugless Will' after his ears had been cut off by the brothers of a girl that he had seduced. He spent some months in Morocco in 1609. He may well have been the first tourist to go there – all previous visitors and subsequent ones until the mid-nineteenth century had some official reason to go there. He took a particular interest in the vices of Fez. On his way home he was caught and tortured by the Inquisition and concluded that the Moors were more civilized than the Spaniards. He became very popular showing his scars in London and was awarded a pension by James I.
Totale Discourse of the rare adventures and painful peregrinations of long nineteenth years Travayles from Scotland . . ., London, 1614.

LOTI, Pierre, pseudonym of Louis Marie Julien Viaud (1850–1923). He was a French naval officer who wrote several novels, mostly about the sea. He also wrote romantic accounts of exotic places. He spent only thirteen days in Fez in

April 1889, accompanying a French diplomatic mission. The translation of his *Au Maroc* used here is by W. P. Baine, third edition, London, 1929.

LYAUTEY, Hubert, Marshal of France (1859–1934), was called by Lloyd George 'one of the finest sons ever born to France'. A cavalryman during the 1880s he spent much time in Algeria riding round the country on horseback and learning Arabic. He then served in Indo-China and Madagascar before he was posted in 1903 to command the district of Western Algeria along the Moroccan frontier. He remained there for seven years winning friends across the border by showing respect for the local people and offering them economic advantages. In 1911, while he was commanding an army corps in Rennes, he was ordered to Morocco. The extract chosen illustrates the principles on which he worked. Arab nationalists regarded him as the most dangerous of all imperialists because the respect that he showed towards the people that he ruled and his conception that it was his duty to bring them peace and prosperity made them acquiesce in foreign rule.
Paroles d'action, Paris, 1927.

MACKENZIE, Donald, worked for the British and Foreign Anti-Slavery Society in Morocco and later in the Red Sea and East Africa. He deplored the vices that Europeans had introduced into Morocco but at the same time he was involved in an attempt to establish a trading post at Cape Juby which, he claimed, was beyond the jurisdiction of the sultan. This was seen as a first step towards flooding a depression in the Western Sahara enabling steamers to reach Timbuktu. Although they were supposed to constitute an outpost of Christianity, the traders at Port Juby were deeply involved in smuggling and gun-running. The British Government admitted that the settlement was illegal but, when it was put out of business by Moroccan troops, forced the sultan to compensate Mackenzie. Cape Juby is now known as Tarfaya.
The Khalifate of the West, London, 1911.

MacNAB, Frances. She was the sister of a missionary, resident in Mogador and travelled in Morocco in 1901 and 1902. She was very disapproving of much that she saw, particularly the Europeans, but came to the conclusion that 'considering their history, the Moors are very good natives'. She also wrote *British Columbia for Settlers*, *On Veldt and Farm* and *Relics: Fragments of a Life*.
A Ride in Morocco, among Believers and Traders, London, 1902.

MARMOL Y CARVAJAL, Luis de (born about 1520). He was a native of Granada who at the age of fifteen joined Charles V in his expedition against Tunis. He was taken prisoner and spent about eight years as a captive during which he seems to have travelled widely. It is always difficult to tell when his information is first-hand, when it has been copied from Leo and when, quite simply, it is pure invention. His *Descripcion general de Áffrica, con todos los sucesos hasta el año 1571, de guerras que a avido entre los infideles y el pueblo christiano* was published in Granada in three volumes in 1573. The edition used is a French translation by D'Ablancourt published in 1667.

MAURAN, was a doctor sent by the French government to Rabat in 1905 and he remained there for many years. He had a good knowledge of the country and wrote books on native medicine published in Rabat and one on public hygiene to which Marshal Lyautey wrote a preface.
La Société marocaine, Paris, 1912.

MAXWELL, Gavin (1914–69), after Stowe and Oxford, worked in Special Operations during the war before being invalided out as a major. He then bought the Island of Soay in the Hebrides, establishing the Soay Shark Fisheries. Maxwell was an early member of the Wildfowl Trust and wrote numerous books, probably the best-known being *Ring of Bright Water* about an otter that he had brought back from the Tigris Marshes, about which he also wrote. He wrote about his childhood in *House of Elrig*. Much of his book on Morocco is derived from Walter Harris but there is some good personal observation.
Lords of the Atlas: The Rise and Fall of the House of Glaoua 1893–1956, London, 1966.

MEAKIN, Budgett (1866–1906). At the age of eighteen he was appointed Assistant Editor of *The Times of Morocco*, published in Tangier which had just been started by his father, a former tea-planter in India. He won many enemies by exposing corruption on the part of the Moroccan government and dirty dealings by Europeans, in particular the close relations between the British Consulate-General and a notorious scoundrel and brothel-keeper in Marrakesh. He showed an unusual sympathy for the local people. He often travelled in local dress, adopted the name of Tahir ben Mikki and mastered the local dialect on which he wrote a book in 1891. In 1890 he returned to the UK hoping to interest a publisher in a book modelled on Lane's famous *Modern Egyptians* and trying to get the Scottish Geographical Society to sponsor an expedition to the Central Atlas. Meakin ceased running the paper in 1893 and thereafter travelled widely in Europe and visited all the main Muslim areas in Asia and Africa. He briefly returned to Morocco in 1897. In 1902 he was decorated by the Ottoman Sultan for his works on Islam. His four books on Morocco constitute a veritable encyclopaedia and contain an enormous amount of information. The two used in this selection are:
Land of the Moors, London, 1905
Life in Morocco, London, 1905.

MICHAUX-BELLAIRE, Edouard (1857–1930), went to Morocco in 1885 to work in a bank and remained there for the rest of his life. He became French Agent in El Ksar and in 1908 was appointed Director of the French Scientific Mission in Tangier and was responsible for training generations of officials. Later he was in charge of the Sociological Section of the Protectorate Government. He had a very great academic and practical knowledge of the country.
'Au palais du Sultan marocain', *Revue du Monde Musulman*, Paris, August 1908

'L'enseignement indigène au Maroc', *Revue du Monde Musulman*, October, 1911.

MIEGE, Jean-Louis, was born in Rabat in 1923, the son of the Director of Agricultural Research. He taught in a school in Rabat before becoming a professor at the University of Aix-Marseille. He has also been Director of the Centre for Mediterranean Research and President of the Institute of Mediterranean Studies. His four-volume *Le Maroc et l'Europe* is a model of scholarship.
Morocco, Paris, 1952.

MONTBARD, Georges Loyes, was an artist, born in Burgundy. In 1894 he spent two months in Morocco, travelling with Walter Harris to Fez. He had an artist's eye for interesting detail. He made a similar tour in Egypt.
Among the Moors, London, 1894.

MONTAGNE, Robert, was a naval officer picked out by Marshal Lyautey to study social-anthropological questions. He was also much involved with the training of French officials for service in Morocco and later, having founded CHEAM in Paris, for duties also in other parts of the Islamic world. He had an enormous knowledge of the Arab countries and published much upon them. In his later years he was a strong opponent of relaxation of French control over Morocco.
'Coutumes et légendes de la côte berbère', *Hespéris*, Paris, 1924.

MONTET, Edouard, was Professor of Theology at the University of Geneva for over thirty years. He was primarily an Old Testament scholar, writing on the origins of the Pharisees and Saducees and the Jewish views of the after life. However, he also translated the Qur'an.
Le Culte des saints musulmans dans l'Afrique du Nord et plus spécialement au Maroc, Geneva, 1909.

MOUETTE, Sieur (1652–91), was captured by pirates in 1669 and spent twelve years in captivity. He gives picturesque accounts of the lives of the prisoners.
Entertaining Travels in Fez and Morocco, London, 1710.

MUHAMMAD V, was born about 1909 and was chosen by the French to succeed his father as sultan in 1927. For many years he remained quietly in the background but after the war he took the lead in calling for the end of the French Protectorate. In 1953 the French sent him and his son the future King Hassan II into exile but two years later they were forced to bow to overwhelming demands for his return and grant Morocco independence. Muhammad assumed the title of king, brought about a national reconciliation and announced his intentions of ruling as a constitutional monarch but political quarrels eventually forced him to assume the office of prime minister himself. In February 1961 he unexpectedly died on the operating table during minor surgery. The extract chosen shows his objectives as a monarch.
Le Maroc à l'heure de l'indépendence, Rabat, 1957.

MUNSON, Henry J. (born 1946), is an American scholar who has also written on Islam and Revolution.
The House of Si Abd Allah: The Oral History of a Moroccan Family, Yale, 1984.

MURRAY, Mrs Elizabeth, spent some time in Tangier in 1844 and was there while it was bombarded by the French. Some statements in her book so offended Spanish officers that several of them challenged her husband, who held a consular position, to a duel.
Sixteen Years of an Artist's Life in Morocco, Spain, and the Canary Islands, London, 1859.

OCKLEY, Simon, (1678–1720), went to Cambridge University at the age of fifteen and, because he needed money, was appointed Lecturer in Hebrew two years later. He then became Curate at Swavesey but was never promoted in the church because of rumours of a drunken indiscretion at the table of the prime minister. He was, however, also Professor of Arabic at Cambridge, the best scholar of his day, responsible for introducing many classical Arab authors to the West and he wrote a *History of the Saracens*. Somehow a fragment of a manuscript by an unknown writer came into his hands and he published it under the title of *An Account of South-West Barbary: containing what is most remarkable in the Territories of the King of Fez and Morocco. Written by a Person who had been a Slave there a considerable time, and published from his Authentick Manuscript*, London, 1713. It is a fairly accurate account of the country and has interesting details of Mulai Ismail and the sufferings of captives and natives at his hands.

OGILBY, John (1600–76). He was a Scotsman who began life as a dancing-master and then built a theatre in Dublin which was blown up in the Civil War. Returning to England he was shipwrecked, losing everything but he ended up in Cambridge where some kindly scholars taught him Greek. In 1661 he had an important part in organizing the Coronation of Charles II who later appointed him as 'Their Majesties Master of the Revels in the Kingdom of Ireland'. Ogilby built a large and valuable library which was burned in the Great Fire of 1666 and as a consolation he was given the post of King's Cosmographer and Geographic Printer. He was allowed to hold lotteries in which his books were the only prizes, amongst them a sort of early encyclopaedia of Africa – a huge book of nearly 800 pages with beautiful plates and maps.
Africa: being an accurate description of the regions of Egypt, Barbary, Lybia, and the Billedulgerid &c, London, 1670.

ORWELL, George (1903–50), went to Morocco in September 1938 and remained, mostly at Marrakesh, until the end of March 1939. While there he kept a diary, wrote numerous letters and contributed to various journals. The extracts were published in *New Writing*, Christmas, 1939.
Collected Essays, Journalism and Letters, London, 1968.

PADDOCK, Judah, wrote a very genuine and honest account of his sufferings after being shipwrecked in 1800.
Narrative of the Shipwreck of the Oswego *on the Coast of South Barbary, and of the sufferings of the Master and Crew while in bondage among the Arabs; interspersed with numerous remarks upon the country and its inhabitants and of the peculiar perils of that coast*, London, 1818.

PAYTON, Sir Charles (1843–1926), spent his life in the Consular Service. He was in Mogador from 1880 until 1893, when he was posted to Genoa; he finished his career in 1911 as Consul-General in Calais. From 1867 until 1914 he was Angling Correspondent of *The Field*. Listed by titles alone, he appears to have written more on Morocco than any other author but nearly all his output was about fishing and field sports. He wrote two volumes of autobiography including:
Moss from a Rolling Stone, London, 1879.

PELLOW, Thomas (born *c*1704). A Cornish boy, he went to sea at the age of eleven and on his first voyage was captured by the Sallee Rovers. Mulai Ismail took 10 per cent of the pirates' booty and Pellow was part of his share and was employed as a slave in the palace. Later he was transferred to the army and took part in several campaigns from the Riff to the Sahara. He lived as a Moor and married a Moorish wife. After 23 years he managed to escape. He was therefore able to give a unique insider's account and his general accuracy has never been doubted.
The edition used is *The Adventures of Thomas Pellow of Penryn, Mariner: Three and Twenty Years in Captivity among the Moors – Written by himself and edited with an introduction and notes by Dr Robert Brown*, London, 1890.

PEPYS, Samuel (1633–1703). He kept one of the most famous of all diaries from 1660 until failing eye-sight caused him to stop in 1669. From 1660 until 1679 when he was dismissed and imprisoned on suspicion of being involved in the Popish Plot, he was Secretary to the Commissioners of the Admiralty, proving himself an exemplary civil servant. In 1683 when Charles II determined to abandon Tangier which had been part of the dowry of Catherine of Braganza, Pepys was recalled to government service as an adviser to Lord Dartmouth who was sent to effect the decision. Pepys' notes on the Tangier expedition, like his diary, were kept in a shorthand of his own invention. Like his diary, too, they contained passages which shocked later editors and were omitted in the volume available to the present writers.
The Tangier Papers of Samuel Pepys, published by the Naval Records Society, London, 1935.

RANKIN, Reginald (1871–1931). The eldest son of a baronet, he stood for Parliament as a Conservative while still at Oxford and, having failed, went off to serve in the Boer War. He then qualified as a barrister. In 1903 and 1904 he was Private Secretary to the Secretary of State for the Colonies. In 1908 he was War Correspondent for *The Times* in Morocco and in 1912 in Bulgaria. He served in the army during the First World War. Rankin was Governor of the

Royal Agricultural Society. His collected works, published in ten volumes, include a translation of Wagner, a book on gardens and one on Tunisia.
In Morocco with General D'Amade, London, 1908.

RICHARDSON, James (1806–59). Educated for the evangelical ministry, he worked for the spread of legitimate commerce which, he hoped, would lead to the abolition of the slave trade and the spread of Christianity. He went to Morocco in the hope of persuading the sultan to ban slavery throughout his dominions but was unable to proceed beyond Tangier and Mogador, of which his accounts, put together after his death, are very good although he only spent a few weeks there. He travelled widely in Algeria, Tunisia, Libya and Central Africa on which he wrote travel books. In 1850 he set out for Lake Chad, leaving his newly married wife in Tripoli, but died at Bornu.
Travels in Morocco by the late James Richardson, edited by his widow, London, 2 vols, 1860.

RILEY, James. Much of the material in his book, although it was quickly translated into French, German and Dutch, is second hand but his own experiences, differing little from those of other shipwrecked sailors, are of interest.
Loss of the American brig Commerce, wrecked on the Western coast of Africa in the month of August 1815, with an account of Tombuctoo and of the hitherto undiscovered great city of Wassanah, Hartford, CT, 1817.

ROHLFS, Gerhard (1831–96). A German, he trained as a doctor and served with the French army in Algeria from 1855 to 1860. He then made a long journey, alone, in the guise of a penniless renegade. At first he was ignorant of the language but he penetrated into places, such as Tafilet and Tuat, where no European had previously been. He was more an adventurer than a scientific explorer and the unfortunate loss of his notes detracts from the value of his work, which does, however, contain much lively and interesting information. He was awarded the Gold Medal of the Royal Geographical Society. Later he travelled in Abyssinia and became Consul-General in Zanzibar. His account, published in German in 1867 was translated into English as *Adventures in Morocco and Journeys through the Oases of Draa and Tafilet*, London, 1874.

ROUTH, Enid M. G., wrote biographies of Tudor figures.
Tangier: England's Lost Atlantic Outpost 1661–1684, London, 1912.

SAVORY, Isabel, had already written *A Sportswoman in India* when she spent a few months in Morocco in the winter of 1901/2. At times her book is more interested in the animals than in the people and she condemns arbitrary rule because it was prejudicial to breeding good horses – officials were liable to steal any that looked promising. She was a good observer and a lively writer.
In the Tail of the Peacock, London, 1903.

SITWELL, Sacheverell (1897–1988), was the younger brother of Osbert and Edith Sitwell and shared their eccentric childhood. His main ambition was to

be taken seriously as a poet but he never reached the top flight. His early works were on the neglected subject of Southern Baroque architecture. Later he wrote biographies of musicians and travel books. He appeared rather self-indulgently sensitive and highly-strung.
Mauretania, London, 1940.

SMITH, John (1580–1631). In his teens he served as a mercenary with the French army fighting the Spaniards and when that war ended he joined the Netherlands army which was still fighting against Spain. When peace was made he entered the service of the Habsburgs fighting the Turks and was subsequently granted a coat of arms by the Prince of Transylvania. Smith was enslaved after being captured by the Turks but was befriended by a Turkish noblewoman, killed his master in Bulgaria and made his way to Morocco which he reached in 1606. The following year he was one of the 105 emigrants who founded the Colony of Virginia, searching for Eldorado. He was taken prisoner by the Indians but released by the famous Princess Pocahontas. Smith became president of the colony and founded Jamestown. There is much dispute amongst scholars as to the veracity of his memoirs. The edition used has been: *The Adventures and Discourses of Captain Iohn Smith, sometime President of Virginia and Admiral of New England*, London, 1883.

STUTFIELD, Hugh E. M. (1858–1929), was a barrister who climbed in the Rockies as well as travelling in Morocco. He was much interested in mysticism and wrote an extraordinary book, *The Brethren of Mount Atlas. Being the First Part of an African Theosophical Story*, about a fictitious community of Gurus, one of which was called Singmeasongo. He also attacked priestcraft and the Church of Rome in several works. His book on Morocco is lightened by his sense of humour although he felt acutely the wrongs which its people suffered.
El Maghreb, London, 1886.

SURDON, Georges, was President of the Court of Appeal in Algiers. In addition to most comprehensive legal works he also translated Ibn Khaldun, the famous North African fourteenth-century sociologist and historian.
Institutions et coutumes des Berbères du Maghred, Tangier, 1938.

THARAUD, Jerôme (1874–1953) and Jean (1877–1952). Before the First World War the brothers were associates of Charles Peguy, who combined a devout and mystical Catholicism with anti-clericalism and socialism, while Jean was the secretary of Maurice Barres, another Catholic mystic. They published their first book together in 1898 and in 1906 won the Prix Goncourt. They were very learned, enthusiasts for exoticism, writing novels and travels which were superior journalism in exceptionally fine French. They were firmly convinced that it was the mission of France to bring its culture to other peoples without destroying what they found there. One of their main interests was Eastern European Jewry. They both became members of the Académie Française.
Fes, ou le bourgeois de l'Islam, Paris, 1930
La Chaîne d'or, Paris, 1950.

THOMSON, Joseph (1858–95), was one of the major African explorers. The son of a Scottish stonemason, at Edinburgh University he studied geography, botany and geology. At the age of 20 he led a caravan towards Lake Tanganyika and he spent ten of the next sixteen years in Africa, walking an estimated 15,000 miles. He was the first to climb several mountains and swim in several lakes, writing such books as *Through Masai-land*. He appears to have been a typical Victorian explorer, totally out of sympathy with the people; he whipped his servants and bullied local chiefs and was obviously very proud of this. He knew nothing of the language, history or culture of the people but he gave an account of parts of the Atlas never before described. Thomson had to give up his travels in Morocco to lead a projected expedition to rescue Amin Pasha which ultimately was cancelled. Later he was employed by Cecil Rhodes in an unsuccessful attempt to get possession of Katanga.
Travels in the Atlas and Southern Morocco: A Narrative of Exploration, London, 1889.

THORNTON, Philip, wrote other books on music and travel, including one on the Balkans.
The Voice of Atlas: In Search of Music in Morocco, London, 1936.

TRANCHANT DE LUNEL greatly impressed Lyautey, who made him responsible for seeing that modernization of cities did not destroy anything good and beautiful from the past.
Au pays du paradoxe – Maroc, Paris, 1924.

TROTTER, Captain Philip Durham of the 93rd Highlanders (1844–1918), accompanied the mission to Fez of Sir John Drummond Hay in 1880. Later he was engaged in the Nile campaign. He ended his career as a colonel and was knighted.
Our Mission to the Court of Morocco, Edinburgh, 1881.

TURNBULL, Patrick Edward Xenophon, was born in the Transvaal in 1908. After Sandhurst, he served in the army from 1928 to 1931. Then he spent some time with the Foreign Legion in Morocco. His first novel was published in 1938. He returned to the army in 1939, campaigning in France and Burma and also serving in Lebanon, Cyprus and Greece before retiring as a colonel in 1956.
Black Barbary, London, 1938/9
The Hotter Winds, London, 1960.

TWAIN, Mark (Samuel L. Clemens 1835–1910). After a tour of Europe, including a visit to Tangier, he established his reputation as a humourist with *The Innocents Abroad*. The edition used is that of Collins Pocket Classics.

USBORNE, Admiral Cecil Vivian (1880–1951), joined the Royal Navy at the age of fourteen. During the First World War he invented an anti-mine device,

was Senior Naval Officer in Corfu and Salonica and commanded the Naval Brigade on the Danube. Later he invented a quick-firing anti-aircraft gun and a gunnery indicator. After two years as Director of Naval Intelligence, he retired in 1933. He then visited Morocco where he was very well received by the French military authorities who spoke very freely to him. He rejoined the Royal Navy in 1939 and spent the war on Special Duties.
First Moroccan Journey, London, 1938.

VAIDON, Lawdom, is the pseudonym of David S. Woolman (born 1916) who wrote a history of the Riff Republic of Abdel Karim. He served in the American Air Force in India and the Caribbean before, in 1952, settling in Tangier as a freelance journalist. He claims to have been the table tennis champion of northern Morocco for seven consecutive years.
Tangier: A Different Way, Metuchen, NJ, 1977.

WATERBURY, John, is one of the leading American experts on Morocco and on Egypt and has written on the Hydropolitics of the Nile Valley.
North for the Trade, Berkeley, 1972.

WATSON, Robert Spence (1837–1911), was a solicitor on Tyneside and a leading Liberal politician, being appointed to the Privy Council in 1906. He was also President of the Society of Friends of Russian Freedom. He wrote numerous books on legal and philosophical matters. He visited Morocco in 1879 and was received with enormous respect and hospitality because his interpreter (Watson knew no Arabic) gave out that he was the brother of the English Shareefa of Wazan.
A Visit to Wazan, the Sacred City of Morocco, London, 1880.

WAZAN, Emily, Shareefa of (1850–1944). In 1872 Emily Keene, the daughter of the Governor of Surrey Prison, went out to Tangier as governess to an English family. There she fascinated the Shareef of Wazan, who despite being a notorious rake, was, after the sultan the most venerated religious figure in Morocco. They were married and she bore him two sons. The Shareef lived like a mediaeval prince, sending out 600 meals a day to pilgrims who had come to make their devotions and he had great influence over numerous tribes. After fourteen years of marriage he divorced her by telegram but seven years later when he was dying, he called her to his bedside. Emily's book is one of great charm and full of insights into Moorish life.
My Life Story, London, 1911.

WEST, Gordon, also wrote *Jogging Around Majorca*.
By Bus to the Sahara, London, n.d.

WESTERMARCK, Edward (1862–1939), was a Swedish/Finnish anthropologist/sociologist who made his reputation with a three-volume *History of Human Marriage* which was translated into several European languages and into Japanese. He paid frequent and prolonged visits to Morocco. He lectured

in numerous universities before holding simultaneously the Chairs of Practical Psychology at Helsingfors and Sociology in London. His books are full of fascinating material, available nowhere else.
Ritual and Belief in Morocco, 2 vols, London, 1926
Wit and Wisdom in Morocco, London, 1930.

WHARTON, Edith (1862–1937). The well-known American writer was greatly influenced by her friendship with Henry James and wrote several psychological novels including *The House of Mirth*. Her works, a novel or a collection of short stories almost every year, were praised for her clear style and well-chosen vocabulary. She was the first woman to receive an honorary doctorate of literature from Yale University. She spent a month in Morocco in 1917 and was entirely dependent upon the French military administration for transport and so on, so her book, though it contains some fine descriptions of places, is otherwise hardly well-informed.
In Morocco, the edition used is that of 1927 in The Traveller's Library.

WILLAN, Thomas Stuart (born 1910), was Professor of Economic History at Manchester University. His main works were on Elizabethan trade and navigation on English canals and rivers.
Studies in Elizabethan Foreign Trade, Manchester, 1959.

WIND(H)US, John, accompanied a mission led by Captain Charles Stewart which set out for Meknes in July 1720 after several attempts to obtain the release of British captives had failed. After lavish expenditure upon rich gifts for Mulai Ismail himself and most of his court officials, Stewart succeeded in signing a treaty in January 1721 which brought about the release of 293 English captives. Windhus was a shrewd observer and his book was the first by an Englishman since that of Addison.
A Journey to Mequinez, London, 1725. The edition quoted here is printed in Pinkerton (details under Addison).